POSTEXILIC PROPHETS

A Christian Interpretation

James E. Smith, Ph.D.

Postexilic Prophets

Copyright James E. Smith © 2007

Dedicated to
Professor John R. (Jack) Lup
Former Student
Colleague
Friend

Unless otherwise indicated, the translation that appears in this volume is that of the author.

ISBN 978-1-4357-0127-4

PREFACE

Biblical history in the Persian Period centers on the ministries of Zerubbabel, Ezra, and Nehemiah. Their ministries were enhanced by the preaching of three great prophets, Haggai, Zechariah and Malachi. The surviving writings of these men of God are the last three books of our Old Testament. Found within these books are blunt sermons, fascinating visions, enigmatic action parables, and numerous predictions with messianic implications. In this commentary we will permit their voices to speak to us across the centuries. We will come to understand their concerns, their passion, their disappointments and hopes. The Holy Spirit will use their words as goads to prod us into to re-evaluating our priorities, our fears, and our appreciation for the magnificent kingdom of heaven of which we are citizens.

In general commentators attempt to determine how the people who first listened to a prophet understood his words. It is not, of course, possible to conduct a survey of the postexilic community to ascertain how they understood the messages of Haggai, Zechariah or Malachi. Even if such a survey were possible, that would not mean that the audience understood correctly the divine intent behind the prophet's words. Even if one could interview a prophet personally there is no assurance that he completely understood the implications of the words he spoke.

Clearly the prophets anticipated the coming of a great Prophet, Priest and King who would establish a new covenant with Israel. They understood that Israel would undergo a metamorphosis. For them the Israel of the future could not be contained within the old boundaries of the Promised Land. The kingdom of Messiah would be world-wide in scope. The Israel of the future would include Gentiles on an equal footing with Jews.

A Christian brings to the work of exegesis a set of presuppositions that often results in a new understanding of the words of prophetic scripture. A Christian assumes that Christ is the Master Teacher, the final word on understanding the Old Testament. Following the lead of their Teacher the Apostles elucidate hundreds of passages and themes of the Old Testament. Guided as they were by the Holy Spirit their teaching becomes the final word on the true meaning of any text.

A Christian recognizes the church as the kingdom anticipated in Old Testament prophecy. Words spoken to or about Israel, Judah, Ephraim, Jerusalem and Zion are applied by the Apostles to the church. Christians are the true sons of Abraham because they share Abraham's faith in Christ. The church is the Israel of God, the modern equivalent of the Twelve Tribes of the Old Testament. I have brought these perspectives to the study of the postexilic prophets.

I have taught the postexilic prophets for forty years in Bible college classrooms. This material fascinates me. In pursuing the meaning of each text I have perused a wide-range of commentaries. I have found the commentaries of Laetsch, Leupold and Deane most helpful in understanding the text from a Christian perspective. My own position on numerous exegetical issues has shifted over the years as new light became available. I claim no originality, unless it is in the expository outlines of the text which are found herein.

James E. Smith
Florida Christian College

CONTENTS

Preface   3

Haggai:

   Introduction
   Commentary
      Ministry of Motivation (1:1-15)   17
      Ministry of Encouragement (2:1-23)   39

Zechariah:

   Introduction   63
   Commentary
      Messages during Temple Construction
         (1:1-6:8)   71
      Symbolic Coronation (6:9-15)   135
      Messages after Temple Construction
         (7:1-14:21)   143

Malachi:

   Introduction   261
   Heading and Prologue (1:1-5)   269
   Priests Sin against Love (1:6-2:9)   277
   People Sin against Love (2:10-4:3)   303
   Concluding Words (4:4-5)   347

Bibliography   353

ABBREVIATIONS

A. Bibliographical

ANEP James R. Pritchard (ed.), *The Ancient Near East in Pictures Relating to the Old Testament* (2d ed., Princeton: Princeton University Press, 1969).

ANET James R. Pritchard (ed.), *Ancient Near Eastern Texts relating to the Old Testament* (3d ed., Princeton: Princeton University Press, 1969).

BDB Francis Brown, Samuel Driver, and Charles Briggs, *A Hebrew and English Lexicon of the Old Testament* (Oxford: Clarendon, 1907).

BHS Karl Elliger and Wilhelm Rudolph (eds.), *Biblia Hebraica Stuttgartensia* (Stuttgart: Deutsche Bibelgesellschaft, 1977).

EBP J. Barton Payne, *Encyclopedia of Biblical Prophecy* (New York: Harper & Row, 1973).

GKC Emil Kautzsch (ed.), *Gesenius' Hebrew Grammar* (trans. A.E. Crowley, 2d ed.; Oxford: Clarendon, 1910).

IDB Arthur Buttrick (ed.), *Interpreter's Dictionary of the Bible* (New York: Abingdon, 1962).

ISBE James Orr (ed.), *The International Standard Bible Encyclopedia* (Grand Rapids: Eerdmans, 1947).

LSOT David Dorsey, *The Literary Structure of the Old Testament* (Grand Rapids: Baker, 1999).

MPEEC Thomas McComiskey (ed.), *The Minor Prophets; an Exegetical & Expository Commentary* (Grand Rapids: Baker, 1998).

NIDOTTE William VanGemeren (ed.), *New International Dictionary of Theology & Exegesis* (Grand Rapids: Zondervan, 1997).

TWOT R. Laird Harris, Gleason Archer, and Bruce Waltke (eds.), *Theological Wordbook of the Old Testament* (2 vols.; Chicago: Moody, 1980).

B. Bible Versions

ASV	American Standard Version
BV	Berkeley Version
JB	Jerusalem Bible
KJV	King James Version
NASB	New American Standard Bible
NEB	New English Bible
NIV	New International Version
NJPS	New Jewish Publishing Society Translation
NKJV	New King James Version
NRSV	New Revised Standard Version
RSV	Revised Standard Version
TEV	Today's English Version

C. Periodicals

EQ	*Evangelical Quarterly*
ET	*Expository Times*
GJ	*Grace Journal*
JETS	*Journal of the Evangelical Theological Society*
SCJ	*Stone-Campbell Journal*

D. Commentary Series

AB	Anchor Bible
CB	Century Bible
EBC	Expositor's Bible Commentary
ICC	International Critical Commentary
OTL	Old Testament Library
PC	Pulpit Commentary
SBB	Soncino Books of the Bible
TOTC	Tyndale Old Testament Commentaries
WBC	Word Biblical Commentary

E. General

LXX	Septuagint

Mss   Manuscripts
MT   Masoretic Text

HAGGAI
Prophet of Temple Building

INTRODUCTION

Haggai has been called "the prophet of divine shaking," "the matter-of-fact prophet" (Box); "the master builder" (Ward); and "the prophet of relative values" (Morgan). Perhaps the most picturesque title which has been bestowed upon him is found in the Harper Study Bible: "the goad of God." The sharp-pointed messages of this man were used of God to provoke his people to frenzied action in rebuilding the temple of the Lord.

Background

During the latter years of his long reign of forty-three years Nebuchadnezzar devoted his attention to building projects around Babylon. He was succeeded by his son Amel-Marduk in 562 BC. In the Bible this king is called Evil-Merodach. He was responsible for releasing the Judean king Jehoiachin who had been taken captive to Babylon in 597 BC. Amel-Marduk was followed on the throne by Neriglissar (560-556 BC), Labashi-Marduk (556 BC) and Nabonidus (556-539 BC).

A. Fall of Babylon

Nabonidus was more interested in archaeology than in governing the Babylonian Empire. He spent a great deal of time out of the capital. He neglected the sacred rites by which his kingship was received annually from the god Marduk. Belshazzar his son was de facto king in his father's absence. The Book of Daniel calls Belshazzar "king" although the Babylonian sources found to date suggest that he occupied a secondary position under his father Nabonidus. The biblical writer refers to Nebuchadnezzar as the "father" of Belshazzar because he was the greatest predecessor on the throne.

In 550 BC Cyrus revolted against his overlord Astyages the Mede. He conquered Ecbatana, capital of the Median Empire, the same year. By 546 BC Cyrus had pushed his conquests to Lydia in Asia Minor. In 539 BC he determined to challenge Babylon for the rule of the world.

According to Daniel 5, Belshazzar was engaged in a desperate attempt to regain the favor of Babylon's gods as Cyrus approached his capital. Exactly how Cyrus gained access to the city is not clear. Accounts by the Greek historians Herodotus and Xenophon suggest that his troops diverted the Euphrates River which ran through the city.[1] The Persian troops then waded through the river gates to surprise the defenders within. The cuneiform sources, however, declare that the Babylonians opened the gates of the city to welcome Cyrus as a liberator from the hated Nabonidus and his son Belshazzar.[2]

So that he might press on to other conquests in the east, Cyrus appointed a certain Gubaru as king over the now fallen Babylonian empire. This Gubaru may be the ruler known as Darius the Mede in the Book of Daniel (Dan 6).[3] Daniel held a position of great honor in this Medo-Persian administration.

B. Edict of Cyrus

During his reign of ten years Cyrus (539-530 BC) established a reputation as the great liberator. He permitted all peoples who had been deported to Mesopotamia by the Assyrians and Babylonians to return to their native lands. The Jews benefited from this policy. The edict allowing them to return to Judea is contained in Scripture in two versions, the official Aramaic form (Ezra 6:3-5) and the popularized Hebrew version (Ezra 1:2-4).

Under the leadership of Zerubbabel (Sheshbazzar)[4] a group of some fifty thousand Jews returned to the Promised Land in 538 or 537 BC. Many chose to remain in Babylon because during the exile there they had become prosperous

---

[1] Herodotus, *Persian Wars*, 1:190-91; Xenophon, *Cyropaedia* 7:5.
[2] The cuneiform accounts which allude to Babylon's fall are 1) the Nabonidus Chronicle (ANET, 306); 2) the Persian Verse Account of Nabonidus (ANET, 312f); and 3) the Cyrus Cylinder (ANET, 316).
[3] It is equally possible that Cyrus had two throne names, Darius the Mede being the title conferred upon him by the Median component of his empire.
[4] Scholars are not in agreement as to whether Zerubbabel and Sheshbazzar were two names for the same person, or two different persons.

Haggai: Introduction

merchants. Only the most spiritually committed desired to return to the ruins of Palestine to rebuild their nation and their temple.

The first order of business upon their return was the rebuilding of the altar on the site of the ruined temple in Jerusalem. To these devout Jews worship was central. As soon as they had settled in their homes, the foundations of the temple were prepared. Materials were gathered for the immediate reconstruction of the house of the Lord. At that point, however, difficulties set in. Opposition arose from the peoples of the land. The builders became discouraged. The temple work ceased. Not one stone was set on that foundation for over fifteen years.

C. Darius the Great

Cambyses succeeded his father Cyrus as ruler of the Persian Empire. This king is not mentioned in the Bible. Nothing of significance happened as far as the Jews were concerned during his reign. Cambyses died under mysterious circumstances while on a campaign to Egypt in 522 BC. One of his generals, Darius, claimed the throne.

From 522-520 BC Darius had to crush rebellions against his rule in various parts of the empire. The famous Behistun inscription records his successful efforts to assert his rule throughout the empire.

In 520 BC God raised up two prophets, Haggai and Zechariah. In August of 520 BC Haggai preached a blistering sermon in which he challenged the people of Judea to build God's temple. The work resumed immediately. Three other messages of Haggai are recorded. All were delivered before the end of the year 520 BC. Just before Haggai delivered his last oracle, Zechariah was called to deliver his first message. He too focused on the work of temple building.

In spite of opposition, the temple work concluded by March 515 BC. The hands of Zerubbabel which had commenced the work back in 538 BC also completed the work.

Haggai: the Man

A. Name

The name Haggai means "festive" or "festival." The name suggests that Haggai may have been born on one of the great OT holy days. Though no other person in the Bible has this name, it has turned up in a fifth century BC tablet at Nippur. The name also appears frequently in the Elephantine papyri from the same period.

B. Biography

Not much is known about Haggai, not even the name of his father. From 2:3 students have inferred that he had seen the first temple. This would mean that in 520 BC he was about eighty. Jewish tradition states that he spent most of his life in Babylon. Scripture contains no clue as to when he returned to Judea.

C. Ministry

Haggai's ministry lasted only four months, from late August to mid-December of 520 BC. He had a single-track mind. His focus was on the building of the temple of God. For some fifteen years no work had been done on the temple. The community leaders, Zerubbabel and Joshua the high priest, were discouraged. Under the preaching of Haggai and his younger contemporary Zechariah (Ezra 5:1; 6:14) Yahweh stirred up the hearts of the postexilic community. In six months Haggai accomplished more than any other OT prophet. He was "a steam-engine in trousers" (Pfeiffer). By the time he retired or died, the work of reconstructing the house of God was well under way.

D. Tradition

Early Christian tradition considered Haggai to be from a priestly family. In the light of 2:10-14 it can be said that this prophet knew the finer points of the ceremonial law. He also was knowledgeable about political events and agricultural practices.

Haggai: Introduction

Tradition connected Haggai's name with the Book of Psalms. He is mentioned in the headings of several psalms in the ancient versions.[5] Haggai may have arranged these psalms for temple worship. Later tradition also regards Haggai as one of the founders of the Great Synagogue, a deliberative body which was the fountainhead of Pharisaic oral law. Along with his fellow postexilic prophets, Haggai is also said to have introduced into the Hebrew alphabet the five terminal letter forms.

Haggai: the Book

A. Special Features

1. Precise dating. The Book of Haggai contains only thirty-eight verses. It is second only to Obadiah in the brevity of its contents. These oracles are precisely dated in terms of the year, month and day of the reign of Darius the Great. Since the chronology of this period is on solid ground, these dates can be converted to the modern calendar rather easily.

2. Authority formulas. Besides precise dating, the book also articulates most forcefully the prophet's claim to be inspired of God. The formula *the word of Yahweh came* appears 5x, as does also the messenger formula (*thus says Yahweh*). The oracular formula (*oracle of Yahweh*)[6] is used 11x. The strongest claim to inspiration is found in 1:3: *Then spoke Haggai, Yahweh's messenger in Yahweh's message unto the people.*

B. Key Exhortations

The key exhortation in the book is *set your heart upon your ways*. This challenge appears twice in the complete form (1:5, 7) and three additional times in an abbreviated form

---

[5]Haggai's name is found in the headings of the following psalms: In the Latin Vulgate alone: Ps 111 (112); in the Syriac Peshitta alone: Pss 125, 126; in the Greek Septuagint alone: Ps 137; in the Septuagint and Peshitta: Pss 146-148; in the Septuagint, Peshitta and Vulgate: Ps 145.

[6]The Hebrew noun *ne'um* is invariably translated by the English versions as a verb: "says" or "declares."

Postexilic Prophets

(2:15, 18). The use of the imperative *be strong* 3x in 2:4 also should be noted.

C. Style

Haggai is certainly less poetical than his prophetic predecessors; but parallelism is not altogether lacking in the book. This book contains what might be called "elevated prose," "unadorned, but hard-hitting."[7] The use of the rhetorical question is a favorite device of this prophet. He uses it 5x in the book. Haggai "is not wanting in pathos when he reproves, or in force when he exhorts."[8]

D. Structure

The book consists of four oracles delivered on three different occasions. The first oracle is designed to motivate the people to get busy on the temple project. The last three were oracles of encouragement to the workers. The structure of the book is displayed in the following chart.

STRUCTURE OF HAGGAI			
A Call to ACTION	A Call to COURAGE	A Call to PATIENCE	A Call to HOPE
Reproof	Encouragement	Blessing	Promises
Ch. 1	2:1-9	2:10-19	2:20-23

E. Predictive Element

Payne regards fifteen of the thirty-eight verses (39%) in the book as predictive. The main predictions are the shaking of the present order so that the kingdom of Christ might be ushered in (2:6-7; 21-22); the coming of the Desire of Nations (2:7); the greater glory of the temple in the messianic age (2:9); and the elevation of Zerubbabel (i.e., one of his descendants) to authority in the messianic age (2:23). Only the first of these predictions is cited and explained in the NT (Heb 12:26, 27).

---

[7]Richard Wolff, *The Book of Haggai* in "Shield Bible Study Outlines" (Grand Rapids: Baker, 1967), 17f.
[8]George L. Robinson, "Haggai," *ISBE*, 2:1318f.

COMMENTARY

PART ONE:
MINISTRY OF MOTIVATION
Haggai 1:1-15

The postexilic community in Jerusalem had become complacent. The temple foundations had been laid back in 537 BC. No further work, however, had been done. In 520 BC God addressed the complacency by a prophetic word through an old man named Haggai. This first oracle was Haggai's call to action.

Introduction
Haggai 1:1

The opening v has the function of dating the oracle, credentialing the speaker, and naming the recipients.

Date of the Oracle
Haggai 1:1a, b

Like several of the prophetic books, Haggai's book has no formal title. He begins with a date. Chronology was very important to this prophet.

A. **Year** (1:1a):
In the second year of King Darius... Haggai began to speak to his countrymen in *the second year of King Darius*, i.e., Darius Hystaspes (522-486 BC), also known as Darius the Great. The king had spent his first year and part of the second putting down rebellions all over the Persian Empire.

B. Month and Day (1:1b):

On the first day of the sixth month... Haggai numbered rather than named the month in which his ministry began. His younger contemporary Zechariah used the Babylonian month names as did Nehemiah and Esther. Perhaps Haggai, being older and more conservative, could not bear to use the month names which were associated with Babylonian religion. In any case, the message of the Lord came to him in the sixth month of the year.

The *first day* of that sixth month was the fateful day when the God of the covenant spoke to Haggai. On a lunar calendar the first day of the month was a new moon. At least every quarter, perhaps every month, the new moon was celebrated as a religious holiday.[9] He whose name means "festival" first received divine revelation on a festival day!

Converting the chronological data supplied by Haggai, scholars have computed that this prophet's ministry began on August 29, 520 BC. By this date Darius was master of the empire. So Haggai began to preach in a time of peace following eighteen months or so of international uncertainty.

Credentials of the Speaker
Haggai 1:1c, d

A. Inspiration (1:1c):

The word of Yahweh came... Came (*hāyāh*) is the verb "to be." In this formula it does not describe motion, but active presence. This clause is used about 122x in OT to describe the prophetic experience. It affirms that the message delivered by the prophets originated in heaven, but it veils the process in which that word was delivered over to a chosen vessel. God's word was, in fact, a divine gift to the prophet. Haggai was not bashful about claiming that he was the recipient of divine revelation. *The word of Yahweh* came to him,

---

[9]Ps 81:3; Isa 1:13, 14; 66:23; Hos 2:11; Amos 8:5. It was also a time of trumpet sounding, symbolically calling Yahweh to aid his people (Nm 10:10).

Haggai: 1:1-15

and by him to the people. "For the first time in the postexilic era, the authentic voice of prophecy was heard."[10]

B. Instrumentality (1:1d):
In the hand of Haggai the prophet... The divine word came into Haggai's care, his stewardship. This terminology is unusual in prophetic books, but frequent in Pentateuch (of Moses) and in the historical books. The word of Yahweh originates in heaven, but it is entrusted to hand-picked messengers. God watches over the reception of his word by the prophet. He also guides in the dissemination of his word through the prophet. This guarantees the accuracy of the words that are used to convey the message. Haggai's right to speak came not because of his family status. His father's name is omitted. That did not matter. What was really important is that he had received the divine word.

The term *prophet* refers to one who receives God's word from heaven and reveals it to men. Haggai, like Habakkuk, refers to himself as *the prophet*. He was the spokesman for Yahweh, the instrument by whom the divine word was to be presented to the postexilic community. More than any other biblical prophet—5x—Haggai refers to himself as *the prophet*. This man was very conscious of his responsibility to proclaim what God had placed in his hand. This simple description of the man suggests that at the time this book was published, Haggai was so well-known that no further designation was necessary.

Recipients of the Oracle
Haggai 1:1e-j

The first oracle is addressed to two leaders of the postexilic community.

A. First Addressee (1:1e-g):
1. Name (1:1e): **to Zerubbabel...** First, Haggai names Zerubbabel. His name means "seed of Babylon." Others sug-

---
[10]Joyce Baldwin, *TOTC*, 37.

19

gest the meaning is "begotten in Babylon" or "dispersed to Babylon."

2. *Ancestry (1:1f)*: **son of Shealtiel...** Zerubbabel was the grandson of King Jehoiachin. The young king had been deported to Babylon in 597 BC. He subsequently was released from prison by Amel-Marduk the son of Nebuchadnezzar about 560 BC. Though he was descended from the royal family, no evidence exists that the Persians, much less Zerubbabel himself, ever expected that he would sit on the throne of his ancestors as king.

A problem arises regarding the father of Zerubbabel. Whereas the text here says he was the son of Shealtiel, 1 Chr 3:19 lists him as the son of Pedaiah, the brother of Shealtiel. Probably he was the son of Pedaiah by birth. His father died while Zerubbabel was young. His uncle Shealtiel adopted him as his own son. Both Matthew (1:12) and Luke (3:27) regard Shealtiel as the father of Zerubbabel.

Baldwin calls Zerubbabel "heir apparent to the throne of David." This statement is probably, but not certainly, true.

3. *Office (1:1g)*: **governor of Judea...** Governor *(pachah)* was an Assyrian title that passed into Hebrew usage. Zerubbabel was the governor of Judea. No doubt he was appointed to that office by the Persians; but the circumstances of that appointment are not narrated. In the structure of the Persian Empire, the governor of Judea reported to the governor of the Trans-Euphrates Province, who in turn reported to the satraps of the Persian Empire (cf. Ezra 5:3). There was at this time also a governor in Samaria.

Some question exists as to the precise relationship between Zerubbabel and Sheshbazzar (Ezra 1:8, 11; 5:14, 16). While some think that these are two separate individuals, the best view is that these are two names for the same person.

B. **Second Addressee** (1:1h-j):

1. *Name (1:1h)*: **and to Joshua...** The second addressee is Joshua, also spelled Jehoshua and Jeshua. Translated into the Greek version the name became *Jesus*.

2. *Ancestry (1:1i)*: **son of Jehozadak...** Joshua's grandfather Seraiah had been slain by Nebuchadnezzar in the af-

termath of the fall of Jerusalem in 586 BC (2 Kgs 25:18ff). His father Jehozadak had been carried into captivity by the same king (1 Chr 6:15).

3. *Office (1:1j):* **the high priest.** In the Persian period the high priesthood was an office of considerable prestige. The Persians granted subject people religious freedom.[11]

Reproof for Neglecting God's House
Haggai 1:2-6

Haggai's first oracle begins with a rebuke for neglecting the house of God. He first speaks of the reason for the neglect (1:2-4); then he spells out the results of that neglect (1:5-6).

Reason for the Neglect
Haggai 1:2-4

A. Messenger Formula (1:2a):

Thus says Yahweh of Hosts... The oracle begins with a messenger formula. This formula is used 5x in the book. Royal ambassadors who delivered written documents in the name of their king first recited the message orally before handing over the written word. They introduced their oral word with this messenger formula. *Thus* (*kōh*) directs attention to the content of the prophetic message which follows. *Says* (r. *'āmar*) is perfect tense which functions here not so much to indicate a past action as to indicate decisiveness.

The title *Yahweh of Hosts* first appears in the Bible in 1 Sam 1:3. The title is used some 300x in the OT, 247x in the prophetic books. The title is especially popular in the exilic and postexilic period. It is used 14x in Haggai, 54x in Zechariah, and 24x in Malachi. *Hosts* is used of the angelic armies, the armies of Israel and the stars in the sky. The title emphasizes the invincible might behind Yahweh's commands. He is

---

[11]For the typological significance of Joshua, see *ET* 23 (1921-23) 217f; *EQ* 21 (1949) 161 ff; A.H. Curtis, *The Vision and Mission of Jesus,* 131ff.

Lord of all powers seen and unseen in the universe and in heaven.[12]

The use of the title "Yahweh, God [of] Hosts" in Ps 80:4 may be a clue to the true meaning of this title. The word *God* (*ᵉlōhîm*) is in its absolute, not its construct form. This grammar takes "hosts" to be in apposition with God and Yahweh. Thus the title means "Yahweh God [who is] Hosts." The title means more than the fact that Yahweh is in charge of hosts; it means that he is every potentiality and power. *Hosts* is an intensive plural denoting in the most comprehensive way the power of God.

B. Excuse of the People (1:2b, c):

1. Wrong time (1:2b): **This people says, The time has not yet come...**[13] The postexilic community was claiming it was not time to begin temple construction. Haggai seems to be placing in opposition his *thus says Yahweh* with *this people say*. They were speaking when they should have been listening. The language *this* people rather than "my" people suggests contempt for the indifference and lack of action in the community.[14] Although he was speaking to the leaders, Haggai may have gestured toward the assembled people as he said these words. Essentially the sin of the postexilic community was that they had their priorities all wrong. *Says* (r. *'mr*) is perfect tense connoting completed action. The people had made up their minds. They were resolute in the conviction they express.

2. Wrong priority (1:2c): **for Yahweh's house to be built.** The term *house* is used 8x in reference to the temple in Haggai. Twice the prophet uses the term *hêchāl*, meaning "palace" or "temple." The temple was not just a good luck charm (Jer 7:4). There is no evidence that the temple must be

---

[12]Cf. NIV "the LORD Almighty."

[13]*bō'* as it stands is a defective infinitive. Others read perfect "The time has not come." This reading has the support of all the ancient versions. But an infinitive not preceded by a finite verb can be used absolutely as equivalent to a finite verb. Thus no emendation of the text is necessary.

[14]The expression *this people* appears 85x over fifty of which are favorable. So the phrase itself is neutral. Context, however, seems to point to the negative connotation in this case.

Haggai: 1:1-15

present to validate the offerings presented to the Lord. The temple was viewed by Israelites as Yahweh's earthly dwelling, the palace of the Great King. To refuse to build the temple was tantamount to saying that it did not matter whether or not Yahweh was in their midst.

The people were not denying their responsibility to rebuild God's house. They simply did not view this as the right time to commence the project. For fifteen years or so they had been procrastinating. The decree of Cyrus in 538 BC had authorized them to rebuild the house of Yahweh (Ezra 1:2-4). Yahweh had stirred up the Persian emperor to issue this decree (Ezra 1:1). So in effect the Jews had a divine as well as a royal mandate to build. When they faced opposition and legal barriers the Jews gave up on the project. With each passing day it became easier to find reasons not to begin the work. Uncommitted people never find the times auspicious to engage in the difficult and expensive.

Why did the community feel that the time was not right to renew the construction of the temple? The times were tough. Resources were few. One or more of the following objections were probably being voiced: We need to wait until we can do the job right. The Persians might not approve. Neighboring peoples might resent the work. We have our outdoor altar, that's more than our fathers had in Babylon. Jeremiah's seventy years are not yet up. Attendance has been down lately. Ezekiel saw a vision of a new temple, yet he said nothing about us building one. God miraculously will provide a temple for us when he is ready.

People can always find some plausible reason for failing to build up the house of God.

Why was the prophet so concerned about the rebuilding of the temple? The temple was the center of religious life for the Jews. It was a type of the spiritual temple of the future age. The rituals of the temple were designed to portray the need for redemption and the penalty of sin. The temple would be the mechanism to hold together as a people the covenant nation until the coming of Christ. Building the temple would demonstrate that their priorities were straight; that they realized their national mission. The temple would meet the outward conditions of having God dwell in their midst. The absence of the temple would mean the extinction of national religion (Kirkpatrick; G.A. Smith). The temple was a visible sign of the restored relationship between the covenant nation and their God. The outward temple glory was a reminder of the real glory that attends God's presence. The temple was a significant bond linking together the Jewish community around Jerusalem and the multitudes in exile.

Haggai's concern for the building of God's temple in his day is properly applied to the building of God's spiritual temple today. The rebuilding of the physical temple in the sixth century BC was a necessary preparation for the first coming of Christ; the completion of the spiritual temple is a necessary preparation for the Second Coming (Rom 11:25). Cf. also Mt 16:18; 1 Pet 2:5; Eph 2:20-21. Christians then must get busy hewing out of the quarry of this world stones that by God's Spirit can be added to the spiritual temple.

C. Question of the Prophet (1:3-4):

1. Authoritative question (1:3): **Then the word of Yahweh came by the hand of Haggai the prophet, saying...** The formula repeated from v 1 strengthens Haggai's claim for the divine origin of his message. The addition of *saying* (*lē'mōr*) introduces a direct quote which in this case comes in the form of a rhetorical question to unmask the hypocrites of the postexilic community.

2. Pointed question (1:4a): **Is it time for you, you I say...** The second person pronoun in this line is emphatic. Haggai addresses the conventional wisdom and convenient excuse of the people expressed in v 2. The language implies that the Judeans were in denial about the true state of affairs within their land. Haggai rips the mask from the face of the play actors.

3. Embarrassing question (1:4b): **to dwell in your houses—paneled ones—...**[15] The question Haggai asked was

---

[15] *Sᵉphūnîm* (*paneled*) without the article is in apposition with the noun, not strictly an adjective as in NIV. The literal meaning of the word is "covering." This raises the possibility that the complaint is that they had a roof over their head, while the Lord's house remained unfinished. See Herbert

Haggai: 1:1-15

embarrassing for three reasons. First, it was embarrassing when compared to the attitude of David in 2 Sam 7:2. The attitude of this community is in stark contrast to the attitude of David. He could not bear the thought of his God dwelling in a tent while he lived in a palace. At least in David's day Yahweh had a tent!

Second, it was embarrassing when compared to their excuse: If they could build comfortable houses[16] for themselves, their conditions could not be too bad. The truth was that their personal comfort ranked higher on the list of priorities than reconstructing the house of God.

Third, the question was embarrassing because of the ostentation implied. The term *paneled* (*s^{e}phūnîm*) comes from a root meaning "to cover in, panel." The root is used of Solomon's buildings (1 Kgs 6:9; 7:3, 7) and Jehoiakim's palace (Jer 22:14). Nothing was too good for their personal dwellings. The paneling was probably of cedar wood, perhaps the same wood which had been gathered earlier (Ezra 3:7) for use on the temple. The construction delay may have tempted the people to use that cedar for their personal dwellings rather than let it go to waste.

4. *Accusatory question (1:4c):* **while this house is in ruins?** While the postexilic community enjoyed their paneled homes, at the temple site people were content to make-do with an open-air altar. No temple construction work had been done since 537 BC when Zerubbabel had led in laying the foundations of the house. In Haggai's day the temple site was in *ruins* (*chārēbh*). This is the very adjective used to describe the condition of the temple after it was sacked and destroyed by the Babylonians in 586 BC (Jer 33:10; Ezek 36:35, 38; Neh 2:3, 17).

Wolf, *Haggai and Malachi; Rededication and Renewal* (Chicago: Moody, 1976), 17.
[16]Baldwin suggests the reference may be specifically to the governor's residence, hence the point of addressing Zerubbabel and Joshua. The plural "houses" weighs against this view.

Result of the Neglect
Haggai 1:5-6

A. **Authoritative Word** (1:5a):
And now this is what Yahweh of Hosts says… And now (v^e '*attāh*) expresses logical consequence. In view of the ruined condition of God's house and the indifference of the people with respect to rebuilding it, Haggai calls upon his audience to take stock of their situation. On *Yahweh of Hosts*, see on v 2.

B. **Intellectual Challenge** (1:5b):
Set your heart upon your ways. In Hebrew psychology *the heart* is the center of thoughtful consideration as well as volition and aspiration. *Set your heart upon* means to give thoughtful consideration (cf. Job 1:8). *Your way* (*derekh*) refers to their lifestyle, they habitual behavior. Honest evaluation compelled these people to admit that their lives were not being blessed.[17] The Giver of every good and perfect gift cannot smile on spiritual indifference, convoluted priorities, laziness, and fear. The challenge expressed in this imperative becomes for Haggai a rallying cry, a slogan which encapsulates his message to the people. The challenge appears 4x in the book. In respect to this challenge Moore has this cogent comment: "The events of life are the hieroglyphics in which God records his feelings towards us."[18]

C. **Indisputable Fact** (1:6):
Conditions in Judea had been bad. Haggai calls attention to three disturbing conditions that prevailed in the restoration community.[19]

---

[17]Less likely, the challenge could be taken to mean, "consider where your behavior is leading."

[18]T.V. Moore, *Prophets of the Restoration* (Banner of Truth Trust, 1979), 66.

[19]Motyer departs from the usual interpretation of scarcity to emphasize lack of satisfaction (cf. Dt 28:38). In his view, nobody was starving or naked or penniless. People were deriving no satisfaction from the material things of life because they were neglecting their religious obligations.

Haggai: 1:1-15

1. Inadequate harvests (1:6a): **You have sown much, but are bringing in little.** First, they were experiencing inadequate harvests. Their labors were not being rewarded. The Hebrew uses a particularly vivid construction: a finite verb (*you have sown*) followed by the first of four absolute infinitives. This construction stresses the on-going nature of the condition described.

2. Inadequate food supplies (1:6b): **You eat, but never have enough.** Lit., "eating, but not for satisfaction."[20] They did not have enough food. Apparently the people were afraid to use what they needed for fear of exhausting their supplies.

3. Inadequate drink (1:6c): **You drink, but never have your fill.** Lit., "drinking, but not for stimulation." They did not have enough drink to satisfy their needs. *Stimulation* (*šokhrāh*) comes from a root that means "to get drunk." Perhaps the idea is that they did not have enough wine to drown out their misfortunes. The root, however, also is used of social drinking or drinking with enjoyment (Gn 43:34). So the meaning is probably that there was not enough fruit of the vine even to have a satisfying taste.

4. Inadequate clothing (1:6d): **putting on clothes, but it is not possible[21] to get warm.** Lit., "clothing, but nonexistence of warmth to him." The preposition plus object interrupts the second person pattern of the passage. Perhaps Haggai intends to individualize the previous generalities. The point is that the individual citizen did not have clothing that was adequate to keep him warm.

5. Inadequate wages (1:6e): **the wage earner earns wages unto a punctured bag.** The idea is that their wages disappeared so fast that it was like they had lost it through holes in their money pouch. The cost of living was such that it seemed they were losing most of their money before they even spent it. In modern terms, the restoration community was experiencing runaway inflation.

---

[20]Infinitive absolutes add force to v 6 and imply frequentive action. The infinitive absolute is used in place of the finite verb and is determined by it (Keil).
[21] 'ēn + infinitive.

Exhortation to Build God's House
Haggai 1:7-11

Haggai was not merely a social critic. He was not content to merely gripe about what was wrong in his society. He had a plan. He now begins to motivate the restoration community to get busy.

Appeal Presented
Haggai 1:7-8b

A. Urges Further Introspection (1:7):
Thus says Yahweh of Hosts: Set your heart upon your ways. The appeal for action is reinforced by the messenger formula. It is Yahweh, the God whose house has been neglected, who is appealing to this people through Haggai. For the second time he urged self-examination (cf. 1:5).

B. Urges Necessary Preparation (1:8a):
Go up into the mountains and bring down timber... Haggai urged his people to gather materials for the temple project. The hill country around Jerusalem was well wooded at this time (cf. Neh 2:8; 8:15). The emphasis in this v is on using what is immediately available Olive, myrtle and palm trees were available locally. This wood could be used for scaffolding. Heavier support beams would have to be imported from Lebanon.[22] Ancient builders set wooden layers in rock walls to minimize earthquake damage.

The emphasis is here on the wood rather than the stone for two reasons. First, the stone foundations of the new temple had already been laid. Second, additional stone was readily available right on the site from the ruins of the first temple.

---

[22]Support beams had been imported back in 537 BC when preparations for temple re-construction were first made. Whether any of those beams were still usable or even still available is unknown.

C. Urges Immediate Action (1:8b):

And build the house. Haggai urged the work to commence immediately. Solomon used conscription to build the first temple. This prophet expected voluntary labor. What was important to Haggai was not the magnificence of the project but the existence of it. Their building efforts would indicate that they really wanted the Lord to dwell among them.

Appeal Reinforced Positively
Haggai 1:8c, d

A twofold glorious promise was offered to reinforce the appeal to get busy on the temple work.

A. God Pleased (1:8c):

That I may take pleasure in it. The first motive for temple building is *that I [Yahweh] may take pleasure in it.*[23] The highest motivation for the believer is to please the Lord. To know that Yahweh would delight in that "house" would spur on a people discouraged by the realization that they would not be able to build a temple anything like as magnificent as the one built earlier by Solomon. *Take pleasure* (r. *rtsch*) is related to the noun used in Lv 1:3 to express satisfaction with a properly presented sacrifice. So the rebuilt temple, regardless of magnificence, will be regarded by Yahweh as an acceptable offering.

Why will the Lord take pleasure in a rebuilt temple? Of course he always delights in the fruit of labor done in love for him. More than that, however, is involved here. In that rebuilt house the sacred rites of Mosaic faith will be performed. The temple furnishings and the rituals associated with them were designed by God to set forth continually the greater glories of the Church Age. Thus the rebuilt temple was a preparation for the coming of Christ.

---

[23] ASV and BV render 1:8 as a promise rather than an incentive: "and I will take pleasure in it and I will be glorified."

B. God Glorified (1:8d):

That I may be glorified, says Yahweh. The second motive for temple building is *that I [Yahweh] may be glorified* (r. *kbd* in Niphal).[24] At the very least these words mean that God will accept the work as done for his glory. Perhaps the idea is that by constructing the temple the Jews will be declaring to the world that their God was worthy of a dwelling place where he could be worshiped.

When the first temple was dedicated "the glory of Yahweh" filled the house. The priests were not able for a time to carry on their temple duties because of that glory (1 Kgs 8:11). Something even more wonderful will happen in that second temple. The Lord himself, incarnate in the flesh, will bring glory to the place by teaching in its courts.

Rabbinic exegesis is often curious and even humorous to western students of the OT. The rabbis noticed that a letter—the letter *hey*—was missing from the verb *be glorified*. Letters in Hebrew also serve as numbers. The letter *hey* is the number five. Operating on the assumption that nothing is omitted from the text without significance, the rabbis thought the absence of *hey* indicated the five articles missing from the second temple: the ark, Urim, heavenly fire, Shekinah, and the Holy Spirit of prophecy (*Yoma* 21b).

Appeal Reinforced Negatively
Haggai 1:9-11

The prophet offers some negative reinforcement to his appeal for temple building by further allusion to the plight of the restoration community.

A. Description of the Present Plight (1:9a, b):

1. Disappointing harvests (1:9a): **looking for much, and behold (it came) to little.** First, they were experiencing

---

[24]The written text (*Kethibh*) has simple imperfect. The recommended reading (*Qere*) has a cohortative ("and I will bring glory to myself"). Laetsch renders as a reflexive: *that I may appear in my glory*, i.e., prove I can keep my covenant promises.

Haggai: 1:1-15

disappointing harvests. The yield was certainly less than expected, perhaps even less than was sown. *Looking* (r. *pnh*) is an infinitive indicating timelessness. Every time they looked for a great harvest they were shocked (*behold!*) to discover that it was meager. *To little* places a preposition (*lamed*) on the noun for emphasis, i.e., "how very little."

2. *Devastating blight (1:9b):* **for you brought it to the house, and I blew upon it.** Second, they were experiencing devastating blight. *For* (*vav*) introduces explanation.[25] *House* likely refers to a barn. Whenever they brought their meager harvest to the barn, Yahweh *blew* upon it. The Hebrew construction suggests customary or repeated action. The reference is probably to some sort of blight or decay which attacked the crop after it was housed.[26]

B. Explanation of the Present Plight (1:9c-11):

1. *Immediate cause (1:9c):* **Why? (oracle of Yahweh of Hosts). Because of my house that is ruins while you run each man for his own house.** Why was the postexilic community experiencing such agricultural disasters? Haggai anticipates the question on the minds of the Judeans. He answers it by citing two facts. *Oracle of Yahweh* (*n^e'um Yahweh*) is the strongest assertion of revelation/inspiration found in OT. This formula affirms that the message that originated in heaven is voiced by the prophet on earth as though God himself were speaking in own person.

Haggai cites two related reasons as the immediate cause of the present plight of the postexilic community. First, he calls attention to the condition of God's *house*. Unfinished building projects are ugly. They bear testimony to fear, lack of resolve, bad planning, or change of purpose. The community's indifference to the things of God tainted and contaminated everything else they attempted to do. "The ruined skeleton of the Temple was like a dead body decaying in Jerusalem and making everything contaminated" (Baldwin).

---

[25] GKC §154a.
[26] Others understand the text to be saying that God blew away the harvest as if it were mere stubble. In effect the winnowed crop is brought in to be winnowed again.

Postexilic Prophets

Second, Haggai cites the inordinate concern of the postexilic citizens for their own houses. While the temple project had been abandoned over fifteen years earlier, the citizens of the postexilic community *run each man to his own house*. *Run* (r. *rūts*) is a participle indicating continuous action. The verb connotes being zealously concerned about something. See Ps 119:32; Prov 1:16. *His house* contrasts with *my house*. The reference could be to *the house* (barn) in the opening line, or to a dwelling place (cf. v 3). If the latter, then three "houses" are mentioned in the v. In either case the center of their interest was their own affairs, not the house of God. These convoluted priorities rendered useless all their hard work in the fields.

2. *Instrumental cause (1:10):* **Therefore on account of you**[27] **the heavens kept back some dew and the earth withheld its produce.** *Therefore* (*'al-kēn*) introduces the consequences of their cavalier attitude towards God's house. *On account of you* (*'alêkhem*) is emphatic.[28] Because they cared more for their own houses than for God's house, *the heavens keep back some dew*. In the rainless summers of Palestine survival of vegetation depended upon the dew. Diminution of this moisture meant that the earth failed to produce. Judea's economic woes were not due to poor farming methods or market forces or even "natural" disaster. Yahweh was directly involved in disciplining the community that professed faith in him.

3. *Ultimate cause (1:11):* **And I summoned a drought on the land and the mountains, on the grain, the new wine, the oil and whatever the ground produces, on men and cattle, and on all the labor of your hands.** Their agricultural failures did not result from some natural change in weather patterns. Yahweh reveals that he personally had intervened in the world of nature to turn off the supply of moisture. The current drought was a *musar* judgment—a disciplinary disaster—designed to force God's people to reassess their priorities. The forces of nature are but tools used by God to accom-

---

[27]Or, *over you*.
[28]The prepositional phrase is doubly emphasized by being placed before the verb and by its assonance with the preceding word.

Haggai: 1:1-15

plish his purposes on earth. *Drought* (*chōrebh*) is related to the word for ruins (*chārēbh*) in 1:9.

The drought brought a chain-like devastation upon the entire nation. First to feel its effects were *the land* and *the mountains* where the crops were grown.

Second, the crops—*grain, new wine, and oil*—were affected. These were the most important agricultural products of Palestine.[29] The grain grew in the valleys. The grapes which produced the wine and the olives which produced the oil grew on the mountains. In fact all that the ground produced was affected.

Third, *men and cattle* which depend upon vegetation for survival felt the effects of the drought. Animals suffer as a result of man's indifference to God. Animal husbandry is not profitable in a drought.

Fourth, *all the labor* of their hands was ultimately affected.[30] Craftsmen, for example, could not concentrate on their labors because of the gnawing hunger pangs due to food shortages.

Response in Building God's House
Haggai 1:12-15

The last paragraph of Haggai 1 relates the response to the prophet's call to action. The work was resumed with the right spirit (1:12), with divine blessing (1:13-14), and with haste (1:15).

Work Resumed in the Right Spirit
Haggai 1:12

A. **Spirit of Unity** (1:12a):
Then Zerubbabel son of Shealtiel, Joshua son of Jehozadak, the high priest, and the whole remnant of the peo-

---

[29]Pieter Verhoef, *The Books of Haggai and Malachi* in NICOT (Grand Rapids: Eerdmans, 1987), 76.
[30]There is no reason to follow Motyer and restrict the expression to agricultural efforts. *The labor of your hands* is climatic rather than explanatory.

ple... The temple work resumed with the spirit of unity. Zerubbabel the governor and Joshua the high priest were joined by *all the remnant of the people*. What a gratifying sight it is when spiritual leaders have the wholehearted support of the congregation. This is the first use of the term *remnant* in the book. Only when the restoration community began to obey the Lord were they worthy to be called *the remnant of the people*. Haggai regarded the small group of returnees as the fulfillment of Isaiah's remnant theme.

B. Spirit of Obedience (1:12b-d):

1. Ultimate authority (1:12b): **obeyed the voice of Yahweh their God...** *Obeyed* (r. šmʻ) means "hear;" but when used with an indirect object it means "listen" with the connotation of "give heed" or "obey." The *voice* of Yahweh is heard when his word is proclaimed. The civil authority (Zerubbabel), the head of religion (Joshua) and the citizens of Judea found common ground in obedience to God. It is obedience that converts theology into personal relationship with the deity.

2. Instrumental authority (1:12c): **even the words of Haggai the prophet...** The voice of Yahweh and the words of Haggai are identical. Such passages as this are foundational to the biblical doctrine of verbal inspiration. The words, not just the thoughts, of the prophet came from God. The people accepted Haggai's first oracle as the very word of God himself. Thus in this situation to obey the voice of Yahweh meant to obey *the words of Haggai the prophet*. A prophet was the mediator of God's word to man.

3. Recognized authority (1:12d): **recognizing that Yahweh their God had sent him.** *Recognizing that* (kaʼašer) is lit., "like which; in accordance with." The people recognized Haggai as having the prophetic office. Their pre-exilic ancestors for the most part had rejected all those whom God raised up to deliver his word. The restoration community recognized that *Yahweh their God had sent* Haggai unto them. The grounds upon which they accorded him this recognition are not known. *Their God* recognizes that Yahweh has returned to them because they have returned to him.

Haggai: 1:1-15

C. Spirit of Reverence (1:12e):
And the people were afraid of Yahweh. Afraid of Yahweh is lit., they "feared from before Yahweh." The idiom is stronger than had *Yahweh* served as a direct object of the verb, i.e., "they feared Yahweh." The point is that the work resumed with the spirit of reverence.

This v points to genuine conversion, for the fear of God is the spirit of true faith. "They had been startled wide awake by the voice of God" (Baldwin). Theirs was not the unwilling obedience of terror, but the hearty service of godly fear. The voice of God through his prophetic messenger had awakened them from their indifference. The explanation of their present difficulties made them realize that worse awaited them if they failed to renew the temple work. The paralyzing fear of hostile neighbors was displaced by the energizing fear of the Lord. Obedience is the demonstration of one's fear or reverence for God.

Work Resumed with Blessing
Haggai 1:13

A. Authority of the Message (1:13a):
The previous v showed the remnant responding to God's word; this v shows them encouraged by that same word.

1. First claim of authority (1:13a): **Then Haggai, Yahweh's messenger...** The temple work was resumed with divine blessing. When the people got busy on the project the Lord sent them a message of consolation through his prophet. Haggai is called here *Yahweh's messenger*. This title usually refers to the special messenger—a manifestation of God himself—who visited Israel at different times (e.g., Gn 16:7). Haggai is the only prophet to use this title.[31]

2. Second claim of authority (1:13b): **in Yahweh's messengership to the people...** The word which Haggai was about to deliver was so important that Haggai emphasizes his

---

[31]The title "messenger" (*mal'āch*) is used by Malachi to refer 1) to the priest (2:7); 2) the one who would prepare the way for God (3:1); and 3) the Messiah (3:1). The name Malachi itself means "my messenger."

credentials in yet another way. He referred to the office in which he functioned as *Yahweh's messengership*. He had been commissioned by Yahweh as his messenger.

B. Message of Consolation (1:13c):

I am with you (oracle of Yahweh). After this double emphasis upon the authority of his word, Haggai delivered the message. In the Hebrew it is but two words: *I am with you.* This is the shortest oracle in the Bible. This is then followed by the oracular formula, *oracle of Yahweh*. Thus a two-word oracle is surrounded by assertions of the authority of the utterance. Nonetheless the power of those two blessed words is not lost in the verbiage but rather is enhanced by it even as a beautiful frame enhances the beauty of a picture. Now that the remnant had resumed the work on the temple their God was with them, empowering, sustaining, blessing, observing. This is a word of commendation which was designed to uplift those who had so recently committed themselves to a tremendous task.[32]

It is worth noting that God's presence was secured prior to the completion of the temple. Submissive hearts, not ornate buildings, make possible his presence. We can discern here that it was not the house per se that interested the Lord; the temple was but an outward symbol that the people wanted the Lord to dwell among them. When hearts long for God, he will not long remain distant.

Work Resumed Because of Stirring
Haggai 1:14a, b

As the people responded to God's word (v 12) they were quickened by it. Not only was Yahweh with his people in some passive or supportive sense; he was actively involved in the work.

---

[32]Several others heard a similar assurance of God's presence: Jacob (Gn 28:15); Moses (Ex 3:12); Joshua (Josh 1:15); and Jeremiah (Jer 1:8). The theme reached a new level of significance in the words of Jesus: "I am with you always" (Mt 28:20). Ultimately believers will find that "the tabernacle of God is among men" throughout eternity (Rev 21:3).

Haggai: 1:1-15

A. Stirring of Leaders (1:14a):
So Yahweh stirred up the spirit of Zerubbabel son of Shealtiel, governor of Judah, and the spirit of Joshua son of Jehozadak, the high priest... So renders the connective *vav*. Evidently the leaders had themselves succumbed to indifference. The verb *stirred up* (r. *'ūr*) often is used in the sense of rousing from sleep. The recognition that God was speaking through Haggai awakened the people after about fifteen years of indifference. This stirring is the work of the Holy Spirit according to 2:5. The Spirit working through the word is a pattern with which Christians are familiar from the NT. That the governor and the high priest are first named suggests that the spiritual stirring began with them.

B. Stirring of Remnant (1:14b):
And the spirit of the whole remnant of the people... Yahweh stirred spirit of *the people* as well as the leaders. The threefold use of the word *spirit* emphasizes God's work on the inner man—the rational, volitional aspect of humankind. The same language is used to explain why so many decided to return to Judah in 538 BC. For the most part, those who were being stirred by God now were the same people who had felt a similar stirring some eighteen years earlier (Ezra 1:5). The text emphasizes that *all* the remnant were stirred by the Lord. Such as had no building skills doubtless were supportive of the effort in other ways.

Yahweh stirred up the spirit of the temple builders primarily through the messages of Haggai. His call to action got the attention of the remnant. The oracle of assurance in the preceding v supplied additional motivation when the enormity of the task was confronted. To know that the Lord is with his people in any enterprise is motivation enough to make them want to do the work. If God used other means to stir these hearts those means are not indicated in the text.

Work Resumed with Haste
Haggai 1:14c-15

A. Nature of the Work (1:14c):
They came and began to work on the house of Yahweh of Hosts, their God... As a result of the mighty stirring by the Lord, the restoration community *came* (r. *bō'*), thus ironically reversing the excuse that the time had not *come* in 1:2. *Work* ($m^e lā'khāh$) is used in Exodus to refer to tabernacle work. Perhaps that is the reason Haggai wrote *they...began to work* rather than simply "they worked." Their *work* was *on the house of Yahweh of Hosts*. The reference is probably to that unglamorous site preparation which must precede any building effort. Materials had to be gathered and moved to the site. Debris had to be removed. No doubt spade, wood and rock work was available for even the most unskilled laborers.

B. Urgency of the Work (1:15):
On the twenty-fourth day of the sixth month in the second year of King Darius. The reconstruction efforts began on the twenty-fourth day of the sixth month. Only twenty-three days had passed since Haggai began to preach (cf. 1:1). After about fifteen years of indifference the mighty word of this mighty preacher stirred this community to resume this most important work.

There is some dispute over whether the phrase *in the second year of King Darius* should be regarded as the concluding words of ch 1 or the opening words of ch 2. The latter is probably correct, although nothing momentous hinges on the placement of this phrase.

PART TWO:
MINISTRY OF ENCOURAGEMENT
Haggai 2:1-23

The second ch of Haggai contains three oracles delivered on two different dates. In these oracles Haggai issued a call to courage (vv 1-9), a call to patience (vv 10-19), and a call to hope (vv 20-23). The prophet's purpose was to bolster the temple builders. While it took the prophet only one message to restart the temple work, it took three oracles to encourage the builders to stay with on the job.

Call To Courage
Haggai 2:1-9

Introduction
Haggai 2:1-2

A. Date (2:1):

On the twenty-first day of the seventh month, the word of Yahweh came by the hand of the prophet Haggai... Haggai's call to courage was delivered almost a month after the temple work had begun, and about seven weeks after Haggai's first message. The twenty-first day of the seventh month on the modern calendar is October 17, 520 BC. This was the last day of the Feast of Tabernacles which memorialized the Exodus from Egypt (Lv 23:43; cf. Hag 2:5). During this feast Israelites were required to leave their homes and "camp out" in make-shift huts. A *hut* or *booth* (*sukkāh*) is also used in Scripture to portray the shelter provided by Yahweh in the messianic day (Isa 4:6). So Tabernacles, like the Lord's Supper, looked forward as well as backward.

Perhaps during the week-long holidays the workers had time to reflect on what they had accomplished, and the amount of work yet remaining. Even more important, Solomon's temple had been dedicated in the seventh month. Perhaps that anniversary led to some unfavorable comparisons with the present effort. In any case, discouragement had set in. Haggai received from the Lord a revelation designed to lift the spirits of the workers. On the clause *the word of Yahweh came by the hand of Haggai* see on 1:1.

B. Directive (2:2):
Say please to Zerubbabel son of Shealtiel, governor of Judah, to Joshua son of Jehozadak, the high priest, and to the remnant of the people. Ask them... The particle *nā'* (*please*) tends to soften the imperative *say* (r. *'mr*) a bit. Haggai was directed to deliver a message to Zerubbabel, Joshua and the remnant. The purpose of this oracle was to boost the morale of the builders and strengthen them in their resolve to complete the task. On the term *remnant* see on 1:12.

Haggai accomplished his goal by assuring the builders of divine blessing (2:3-5); and by sharing with them revelations of future glory (2:6-9).

Assurances of Present Favor
Haggai 2:3-5

A. Present Discouragement (2:3):
Haggai's message begins with three questions that set the stage for the encouragement to follow.

1. First question (2:3a): **Who of you is left who saw this house in its former glory?** The first question identifies a particular segment of the remnant to which Haggai is speaking. The question presupposes that some were still living who had seen the first temple. At the laying of the foundations in the first year of their return people were present who had seen Solomon's temple (Ezra 3:12). The temple had been destroyed some sixty-six years earlier in 586 BC. Haggai may have been among those who had seen the first temple.

By referring to the temple as *this house* Haggai was identifying the building under construction with Solomon's temple. Scholars refer to the period from 520 BC to AD 70 as the period of the second temple. To the Jews, however, there was only one temple. "There is a unity to the temple throughout history, whatever the outward form."[33]

The former glory of the temple refers to the way that structure appeared just before the destruction of Jerusalem. The temple had been refurbished several times. In the course of the centuries it had been sacked and stripped of much of its precious metals even before 586 BC. Even so that building and its surrounding courts were an architectural masterpiece.

2. Second question (2:3b): **How do you regard it now?** The second question is the setup for the third. It calls upon those who had seen the temple in its former glory to make a comparison. Placing *now* (*'attāh*) at the end of the question highlights it. Perhaps some who had come in from outlying areas to the feast were registering disappointment over what they saw taking shape on temple mount.

3. Third question (2:3c): **Is not such a one as nothing in your eyes?** Lit., "is not the like of it like nothing?" Haggai articulates (and perhaps endorses) the sentiment that many were expressing privately. The paraphrase of NIV is "Does it not seem to you like nothing?" The people must have been discouraged with the work which was now taking place. Foundations generally do not inspire a great deal of enthusiasm. Back in 537 BC some of the community wept when they saw the foundations of the second temple (Ezra 3:12). Apparently some were thinking that the present effort was inferior to the previous temple. Achievements of the past often cast pale light on present accomplishments.

B. **Encouragement to Steadfastness** (2:4):

Haggai's encouragement to steadfastness is emphasized by five techniques in the text.

1. Threefold directive (2:4a): **But now be strong, O Zerubbabel (oracle of Yahweh). Be strong, O Joshua son of Jehozadak, the high priest. Be strong, all you people of the land (oracle of Yahweh)...** The direct address makes the encouragement emphatic. The political leader (Zerubbabel), the religious leader (Joshua) and *the people of the land* are ad-

---

[33]Herbert Wolf, *op. cit.*, 30.

dressed. Some think that the *people of the land* were the national assembly. It is better to take these words as reference to the common people as over against the leaders. Cf. the use of the phrase in Ezra for adversaries of the Judeans.

Second, the encouragement to steadfastness is emphasized also by the threefold repetition of the imperative *be strong* (r. *chzq*). This imperative is connected with new beginnings that have intimidating implications (cf. Josh 1:6). These are the same words spoken by David to Solomon before the building of the first temple (1 Chr 28:10).

2. *General imperative (2:4b):* **and work.** Third, encouragement is emphasized by the use of an explanatory imperative: *Work!* Positive action is the best antidote for timidity.

3. *Powerful incentive (2:4c):* **For I am with you (oracle of Yahweh of hosts).** Fourth, the encouragement is emphasized by a promise: *for I am with you!* The personal presence of the Lord always gives courage, determination and the conviction that he will not permit his cause to fail.[34] Cf. Mk 6:50. Finally, the threefold use of the oracle formula baptizes the encouragement from start to finish in divine authority. On *oracle of Yahweh* see on 1:1. Discouragement arises when we listen to naysayers, or to ourselves. Faith and courage grow when we listen to the Lord.

C. **Encouragement to Fearlessness** (2:5):

Yahweh gives two reasons why the temple builders should not fear. Then he issues a command to banish fear.

1. First encouragement (2:5a): **with the word[35] which I covenanted with you when you came out of Egypt.** God stands behind the covenant word. The concept of Yahweh's presence with his people was as old as Sinai. Reference to the exodus ties Haggai's message to the occasion—the Feast of

---

[34] Baldwin, *TOTC*, 47.
[35] The first two words in v 5 (*'et hadābhār*) have been taken to be 1) a direct object and 2) the object of the preposition. Of those who take the former position the phrase is taken as the direct object of 1) the verb "work" in the previous v (the intervening words being regarded as parenthetical); or 2) a supplied verb, e.g., "I have (or will) confirm (or establish)" the word (Cashdan). It is best, however, to take *'et* as a preposition. God was standing behind his covenant word.

Tabernacles. Perhaps the festival reminded the Judeans of Yahweh's mighty deeds on their behalf in the past. By comparison the present circumstances seemed discouraging and intimidating.

2. *Second encouragement (2:5b):* **and my Spirit is standing firm in your midst** (cf. KJV; RSV). Yahweh is not with his people merely as a passive observer. *My Spirit* refers to the active power of the Lord (Zech 4:6). The same Spirit who was so active in the exodus period (Isa 63:10-14)[36] was still at his post among God's people.

The Judeans viewed their situation as hopeless, their work as fruitless. Over against their glum assessment is this positive and invigorating word of Yahweh. In late Hebrew the verb *'āmād* means "to stand fast." Here the form is a participle. It indicates continuous action. God the Spirit will protect them from their adversaries. He will energize them in their work. Such promises are meant as shock therapy for the despondent and a prod for the lethargic.

The role of the Holy Spirit in the OT dispensation was more extensive than generally is recognized. The Holy Spirit 1) strove with men against sin (Gn 6:3; Neh 9:30; Acts 7:51); 2) gave leadership for special purposes (Judg 6:34-36); 3) gave physical strength for special exploits (Judg 14:5f.; 15:14-20); 4) gave ability for special services (Ex 31:2-5; 28:3); 5) gave inspiration in expression for special tasks (2 Sam 23:1f.); 6) gave moral and spiritual courage for special needs (2 Chr 24:20-22). The OT prophets foresaw the day when the Spirit was going to have a ministry for all of God's people (Joel 2:28; Isa 59:21; Ezek 36:26f; 37:14).

3. *Third encouragement (2:5c):* **Fear not!** The words are in the imperative, reminding believers that fearlessness is not a desirable option but rather a divine mandate. According to 1:12-14, the people feared Yahweh. That is proper fear—a fear that is incompatible with any other fear. Yet the child of God must battle to keep lesser fears from encroaching upon godly fear and paralyzing godly service.

---

[36] The Spirit endowed the tabernacle craftsmen (Ex 31:3; 35:31), rested upon Moses and the elders (Nm 11:17, 25-29), commandeered Balaam's tongue (Nm 24:2), and filled Joshua (Dt 34:9).

Revelation of Imminent Shakings
Haggai 2:6-7a

A major portion of Haggai's second oracle is devoted to revelations of future glory. The passage has messianic implications. This is the most difficult, yet most significant section of the book. God is about to shake things up in a big time way as he prepares to bring the Messiah into the world. Haggai speaks of the imminent shaking as both physical (v 6) and national (v 7a).

A. Physical Shaking (2:6):
Haggai sets forth five great truths about the coming divine shaking.

1. Renewed shaking (2:6a): **For thus says Yahweh of Hosts: Yet...** Haggai appreciated the staggering implications of what he was saying and thus undergirded his words with this claim to inspiration. *For* (*kî*) introduces the reason the remnant can continue with the temple project with full confidence that their work will not be in vain. God is about to act. A great shaking will prepare the way for the messianic age.

The preparatory shaking will be a repetition of what had taken place previously. The word *yet* (*'ôd*) retains its primary sense of repetition or return, especially when connected (as here) with a temporal term or phrase. So the idea is "yet again." The previous shaking was what took place at Sinai (Heb 12:26). Haggai envisioned a new era ushered in with great commotion.

2. Final shaking (2:6b): **once more...** The shaking will occur but *once more* (*'achat*). Only one more time will God reveal himself in history in the manner and significance of Sinai. The Septuagint and the Book of Hebrews render "once for all time." (*eti hapax*) The gospel dispensation will endure unto the end of time.

3. Imminent shaking (2:6b): **it is a little while...** The shaking will begin in a very short time ($m^eat\ hî'$). Some think that the vicissitudes of the Persian Empire are intended (Keil). Others think the shaking was to begin with the coming of Messiah (Pusey; Deane). The *little while* is measured in reference to God's plan not man's experience.

4. *On-going shaking (2:6d):* ***I will shake...*** The Hiphil participle conveys "that the Lord will cause a series of shakings" (Baldwin). Earthquake is a symbol for God's supernatural intervention.[37] The term is not indicating so much physical convulsions as it is "the reaction of the created to the Creator" (Motyer).

5. *Universal shaking (2:6e):* ***the heavens and the earth, the sea and the dry land.*** Haggai uses the untranslatable sign of the direct object (*'et*) 4x to introduce *heavens, earth, sea* and *dry land*, i.e., the entire world, perhaps even the universe. By way of contrast, at Sinai there was a local, literal shaking.[38] Disturbances of greater magnitude accompanied the advent and ministry of Christ: the star, the angels, darkness at noon when he died on the cross; the earthquake at his resurrection, and the ascension; Pentecost. The introduction of Christianity also produced a moral and spiritual shaking.

B. **Shaking of the Nations** (2:7a):

And I will shake all the nations... Great political upheavals took place before the first coming of Christ. The Persian Empire fell to Alexander the Great. The Greek empire divided after Alexander's death, and the fragments of that empire warred among themselves until the Romans conquered the world. Cf. Dan 2:36-45. The conversion of the nations was a result of the political shaking. As the gospel was carried out into the Roman Empire the critics of Christianity exclaimed that the disciples had "upset the world" (Acts 17:6).

Revelation of Coming Messiah
Haggai 2:7b

And the Desire of all nations will come. This translation follows the rendering of KJV. Other translations: "They will come with the wealth of all nations" (NASB); "the desired of

---

[37] Amos 8:8; 9:15; Isa 2:13-21; 13:13; 29:6; Joel 3:16; Ezek 38:20.
[38] Judg 5:4-5; Ps 68:8-9; 77:15f; Ex 19:16-18. The plagues also may have been considered part of the shaking which introduced the Old Covenant.

all nations shall come" (NIV); "the treasure of all nations shall come" (NRSV). More recent English translations translate the noun as a plural: "the precious things of the nations shall come." The idea is that converted Gentiles will bring their wealth to the temple of God. Certainly this is a biblical concept (cf. Isa 60:5; 61:6), but that does not settle the translation issue here. In defense of the older rendering of this prediction it will be necessary to discuss the subject, the verb and the title used by Haggai.

A. Subject

Desire (*chemdāh*) is singular in the received text, though the same consonants could also be vocalized as a plural. The term certainly can have a personal reference. It was earlier used of Saul (1 Sam 9:20). All the desire of Israel—the hope for a successful monarchy—was fixed on Saul. The term may be used of the Messiah in Daniel 11:37. In the plural the word is used of Daniel (Dan 9:23; 10:11, 19) and of Esau (Gn 27:15). On the other hand, the term in both the singular and plural can also refer to wealth, especially silver and gold (e.g., 2 Chr 32:27; 20:25).

B. Verb

Come (r. *bō'*) in the Hebrew is plural. Most commentators think that the plural verb prohibits a personal messianic interpretation of the phrase "Desire of nations."[39] It is true that normally in Hebrew when a plural noun specifies one person, a singular verb is used. The singular noun, however, could have a collective sense and thus govern a plural verb.[40] The multi-faceted character of the Messiah might call for the plural verb in this passage.[41]

---

[39] A disagreement in number between subject and verb is not that uncommon. In Haggai 1:2, for example, "this people" is singular, and the verb "says" is plural. Cf. also Amos 6:1.

[40] Herbert Wolf, "'The Desire of All Nations' in Haggai 2:7: Messianic or Not?" *JETS* 19 (Spring 1976): 97-102.).

[41] Messiah may be regarded as collective being both God and man, being prophet, priest, and king (Wordsworth); or the object of desire contains in itself many objects of desire (Pusey).

Haggai: 2:1-23

C. Title

How is Messiah the Desire of all nations? He embodies the noble attributes to which even Gentiles aspire. He brings with him the gifts that make life purposeful and death tolerable. He promises what all men strive for, viz. eternal life.

Revelation of Future Glory
Haggai 2:7c-9

Three promises are attached to the coming of the Desire of all nations: 1) the filling of the house, 2) the greater glory of the house, and 3) heavenly peace.

A. House Filled (2:7c-8):

1. Declaration (2:7c): **and I will fill this house with glory, says Yahweh of Hosts.** The term *glory* (*kābhōd*) can refer to material splendor (Gn 31:1; 1 Chr 29:12) or to the personal presence of God (Ps 26:8). God filled the tabernacle (Ex 40:34f; Nm 14:21) and the first temple with glory (1 Kgs 8:11; 2 Chr 5:14; 7:1-3; cf. Hag 2:3). Ezekiel predicted that a future temple was to be filled with glory (Ezek 43:4f; 44:4). The temple which was under construction as Haggai spoke was financed largely out of the Persian royal treasury (Ezra 6:8-12). Later that same temple was enlarged and beautified by the extravagances of Herod the Great (Lk 21:5; Jn 2:20).

Material splendor alone, however, cannot fill God's house with *glory*. The glory associated with the temple was the result of the Lord's personal presence, the Shekinah glory as it was called in Jewish tradition (cf. Ex 40:34-35; 1 Kgs 8:10-11). Yet Jewish tradition recognized that the Shekinah glory was absent from the second temple (*Yoma* 21b). Thus the promise that Yahweh will fill that house with *glory* is best taken as a reference to the presence of Christ in the temple. He filled that place with a glory which it never before had experienced (cf. Mal 3:1). When baby Jesus was brought to the temple by Joseph and Mary, the aged Simeon praised God

47

that his eyes had been permitted to see "the glory of your people Israel" (Lk 2:32).[42]

2. *Confirmation (2:8): **The silver is mine and the gold is mine (oracle of Yahweh of Hosts)**.* The promise of glory for the temple is reinforced by means of this declaration. Some were discouraged because what they were building was not as ornate as the temple their forefathers had known. They should not, however, worry about the poor offerings which were being brought for the temple project. Earth's riches already belonged to the Lord. More important to him than silver and gold is the faithful, obedient and loving service of his people.

B. Greater Glory (2:9a):

Greater shall be the latter glory of this house than the glory of the former [house], says Yahweh of hosts. The second temple never physically surpassed the first temple, all the efforts of Herod the Great notwithstanding. This promise, therefore, must be interpreted spiritually of the messianic temple, the church of Christ. The temple which was under construction in 520 BC was but a type or shadow of the spiritual temple of the NT dispensation, a temple built up of living stones—the precious souls that obey the gospel (1 Pet 2:5). The messianic temple is superior to the material temple in its worship, its builder, its dimensions, its materials, its influence, and its duration.

C. Heavenly Peace (2:9b):

And in this place I will give peace (oracle of Yahweh of Hosts). The thought now moves from what the latter day temple is (a place of glory) to what that temple provides. Messianic prophecy is full of promises of an ideal peace (e.g., Ezek 34:25; Mic 4:3f; Zech 8:12). The history of the material temple is filled with strife. Again the promise must relate to Christ's kingdom, the latter day Jerusalem and spiritual temple (Heb 12:22).

---

[42] Other passages referring to the glory of the messianic age: Isa 35:2; 40:5; 60:2, 7; 66:18; Zech 2:5.

To summarize: Haggai foresees a shaking that results in the appearance of Messiah who fills God's house with glory and gives real peace to his people. One thinks of the rending of heaven (Mk 1:10) and the shaking of earth (Mt 27:51; 28:2) that were associated with the coming of Messiah. Even the old temple itself was shaken (Mk 15:38), signaling the removing of the old to make way for the new. One thinks of the risen Lord who proclaimed peace to his disciples (Jn 20:19-21; Eph 2:14-17). Yet all of this only sets the stage for the final shaking of heaven and earth (2 Pet 3:10) and the gathering of the saints around the throne (Rev 7:9-14) in that heavenly city that is illuminated by the glory of God and the Lamb (Rev 21:22-23).

Call to Patience
Haggai 2:10-19

Introduction
Haggai 2:10-11

A. **Date** (2:10a):
On the twenty-fourth day of the ninth month, in the second year of Darius... Haggai received his third oracle from the Lord just over two months after his second oracle, and about three months after the work on the temple had resumed. Converted to the modern calendar, the date of the third oracle is December 18, 520 BC. Early rains come in mid-October. The ground softens; planting and plowing begin. By mid-December this work had been completed. By this date also Zechariah already had started his ministry.

B. **Revelation** (2:10b):
The word of Yahweh came to the prophet Haggai. The word *came to* (*'el*) is a slightly different formula than used previously in 1:1, 3, 2:1. It may imply that Haggai had been seeking a special word from the Lord at this time.

Postexilic Prophets

C. Addressees (2:11):
Thus says Yahweh of Hosts: Ask the priests what the law says… Haggai was directed to ask the priests a question concerning a principle of law. The priests were the teachers of the law. The question was not designed to test them on their knowledge of the laws of purity (as in Jewish interpretation). He knew that they were able to answer the simple question he posed. Haggai's purpose was to elicit an answer which explained why the circumstances of the people had not changed markedly even though they were now busy building the temple. The question was asked to make the lesson sink into the minds of his hearers.

Principles of Law
Haggai 2:12-14

A. First Hypothetical (2:12):
1. Posed (2:12a): ***Suppose a person carries consecrated meat in the wing of his garment and that wing touches some bread or stew, some wine, oil or any food, will it become consecrated?*** *Suppose* (*hēn*) introduces a hypothetical situation. A priest who had been offering sacrifice accidentally gets some consecrated meat caught in *the wing of his garment*, i.e., in the border corner or fold of the breast. This portion of the garment then accidentally brushed against some non-consecrated food—bread, stew, wine, oil or any food. The question then which the priests are asked to answer: Would the holy meat impart holiness to the object accidentally touched? *Consecrated meat* (*bᵉsar qōdeš*) appears elsewhere only in Jer 11:15.

2. Answered (2:12b): ***The priests answered, No.*** The priests answered the prophet's question with an emphatic "No!" According to Lv 6:27 their answer was correct. The *wing* or cuff of the garment—what was directly touched by the holy meat—was holy, but not what the cuff touched.

B. Second Hypothetical (2:13):
1. Posed (2:13a): ***Then Haggai said, If a person defiled by contact with a dead body touches one of these***

things, does it become defiled? A second question was directed to the priests. It aims to make the case that defilement is much easier to transfer than holiness.

2. *Answered (2:13b):* **Yes, the priests replied, it becomes defiled.** Again the priests gave a correct answer. An unclean person communicated his uncleanness to everything he touched (Nm 19:22). Such uncleanness lasted seven days. It could only be removed after elaborate ritual (Nm 19:11).

C. Legal Principle Applied (2:14):

1. Nation defiled (2:14a): **Then Haggai responded and said, So it is with this people and so it is with this nation in my sight (oracle of Yahweh).** Haggai made an application of the legal principle regarding defilement. *This people* refers to those ethnically related who share a common history of relationship with Yahweh. *This nation* refers to the same group as a political entity—a nation among nations. The language *this nation* is language often used of heathen nations. It may be a sign of contempt (but cf. Zeph 2:9).

Israel had been set apart to the Lord, and was therefore holy (Ex 19:6). Just what had defiled the nation? Perhaps they were defiled by the wicked among them (Cashdan), or by their foreign contacts (Bloomhart). More likely, however, it was their fifteen years or so of indifference regarding the work of the temple which had caused the defilement (Baldwin).

2. Work defiled (2:14b): **and so it is with all the work of their hands.** Just as in the case which Haggai posed to the priests, everything the defiled people touch was defiled. Therefore, their temple work was unclean. Because the work of God had been neglected, every other work of the people was defiled.

3. Worship defiled (2:14c): **and whatever they offer there is defiled.** *Offer* is lit., "bring near," a regular idiom for sacrifice. Even the sacrifices placed on the altar were defiled by the defiled people. These words probably were spoken by the prophet as he pointed to the provisional altar erected many years earlier (Ezra 3:2). "The faint aroma of sanctity coming from their altar and sacrifices was too feeble to pervade the secular atmosphere of their life."[43] Failure to build the temple proclaimed that Yahweh did not matter. Attempting to offer sacrifices without the house was attempting to secure the blessings of heaven without personal connection with the Lord of heaven.

Review of Past Calamities
Haggai 2:15-17

A. Challenge (2:15a):
Now please set your heart from this day and forward. Set your heart is the same expression used in 1:5 and 1:7. The phrase means "to consider." *This day* is probably referring to the twenty-fourth day of the sixth month when the work on the temple resumed. *Forward* (*māʿlāh*)[44] challenges the listeners to observe the change that is about to take place in their circumstances. Before taking up that thought, however, Haggai inserts a parenthetical note recalling past circumstances.

B. Decisive Date (2:15b):
From before stone was laid on stone in Yahweh's temple. These words introduce a parenthesis that extends through v 17, the main thought again being taken up in v 18. Haggai invites his audience to look back over the months and years before the temple project was renewed. What was their condition like before they resumed the temple work?

C. Disappointing Harvests (2:16):
1. Regarding grain (2:16a): **through all that time**[45] **when anyone came to a heap of twenty, there were only ten.**

---

[43] A.B. Davidson, quoted by George L. Robinson, "Haggai" in *ISBE*, 2:1318.
[44] *Backward* is supported by LXX, Targum, Rashi and most commentators; *forward* is supported by Cashdan and Motyer. There is no clear example where the word refers to past time.
[45] The first word in v 16 (*mihyōthām*) has been left untranslated by NIV. NASB has "from that time." NRSV = "how did you fare?" BV and ASV = "through all that time." NKJV = "since those days." Idea: during the period when you were neglecting temple building, here is what happened. The

Through all that time is lit., "at the time of their being." Prior to the resumption of the temple work the situation of the remnant was desperate. During that time one would come to *a heap* of sheaves[46] which should have yielded twenty measures of grain. That heap when it was threshed, however, only yielded about half what would normally be expected.

    2. Regarding wine (2:16b): **When anyone went to a press to draw fifty measures, there were only twenty in respect to the vat.** The vintage was as disappointing as the harvest. Haggai uses two technical terms relating to viticulture. *Press* (*yeqebh*) can refer either to the storage vat (Isa 5:2) or to the vat where the grapes were pressed (Job 24:11). *Vat* (*pūrāh*) elsewhere is used only in Isa 63:3 where it is used of the upper treading vat. Here, however, it seems to refer to the receptacle into which the juice flowed after the grapes were crushed by the treading. Perhaps the two terms together referred to both the upper treading vat and the lower storage vat (Motyer). In any case the point is clear. They expected to find fifty measures of juice, but found only twenty.

D. Devastating Judgment (2:17):

    1. Divine action (2:17a): **I struck all the work of your hands...** The indifference of God's people did not go unnoticed or unpunished. Haggai amplifies what he said in 1:10-11. The disappointing harvests were not an accident of nature but an act of divine intervention. These divine judgments affected *all the work of your hands,* i.e., God was frustrating everything they tried to do. Nothing goes right in the life of a believer who does not give priority to God.

    2. Divine agents (2:17b): **with scorching, mildew and hail...** Yahweh used a triad of *musar* (corrective) disasters to shake up and wake up his people. *Scorching* (*šiddāphôn*) is the blight caused by the blasting of the east wind coming in from the hot desert. In a dream Pharaoh saw the grain of Egypt blasted by this wind (Gn 41:6). *Mildew* (*yērāqōn*) re-

---

term *pūrāh* in Isa 63:3 refers to the vat itself. Here the LXX is correct in understanding a liquid measure. The word is only used 2x in OT.

[46]NIV inserts *measures* following the LXX. The insertion is unnecessary. Actually the *heap* is a collective of sheaves awaiting threshing.

fers to fungus caused by too much moisture. These opposites indicate that Yahweh had employed the entire range of weapons in his arsenal against the complacent remnant. *Hail (bārād)* was especially devastating to vines (Ps 105:32-33).

3. *Remnant's reaction (2:17c)*: **yet you did not turn to me (oracle of Yahweh).** The Hebrew is brutally blunt and terse: "but nothingness of—with you—to me." *To me* in this construction is idiomatic for "giving allegiance to" or "siding with." The Judeans showed no inclination to want Yahweh in their midst in spite of the disciplinary disasters. In temporal judgment the object is to get the attention of people, to call them back to God. Crop failures and agricultural disasters prior to the rebuilding effort did not bring the remnant to repentance. On *oracle of Yahweh* see on 1:1.

Promises of Renewed Prosperity
Haggai 2:18-19

A. Dismal Prospects (2:18-19b):

In the three months since the temple work had resumed, no improvement in the circumstances of the remnant had been experienced.

1. Challenge (2:18): **Set please your heart from this day and backward, from this twenty-fourth day of the ninth month, to[47] the day when Yahweh's temple was founded. Set your heart.** Haggai presents a double challenge to the builders to *set your heart*, i.e., "consider." See on 1:5. *This day* refers to *the twenty-fourth day of the ninth month*, the day on which Haggai was delivering this third oracle (2:10).

The people should reflect on the period from the day Haggai was speaking back to the day *when Yahweh's temple was founded* (r. *ysd* in Pual). The word is used both of initial construction, and of the act of commencing a restoration project. Haggai probably is not referring to the time when the foundation of the temple was originally laid back in 537 BC; he probably refers to the more recent renewal of the work on

---

[47]Hebrew is *lᵉmin*. The *lamedh* indicates the time from which the *min* is to be reckoned: "to the time from which..." Most take the word to mean "to" or "unto" not "from."

Haggai: 2:1-23

the twenty-fourth day of the sixth month. In the ancient world more than one foundation ritual was common in building temples.[48]

2. *Question (2:19a):* **Is there yet any seed in the barn?** *Seed* refers either 1) the product of the harvest, i.e., the grain; or 2) that which would be required to plant the next crop. *Barn* ($m^e g\bar{u}r\bar{a}h$) is found only here. Its meaning is deduced from context.

Whether Haggai anticipated a positive or a negative answer to his question is not clear. If negative, the seed already had been used for sowing or consumed and used up. Thus even while they were building the temple the builders had to worry about the adequacy of the food supplies. If the situation was desperate back in August, it was even worse in December.

If he anticipated a positive answer to his question, then Haggai is calling attention to the fact that even though the seed is still in the barn, he is predicting a good harvest. In view of past harvests there were little prospects for improvement.

3. *Observation (2:19b):* **Until now, the vine and the fig tree, the pomegranate and the olive tree have not produced fruit.** *Until now* (*'ad*) is lit., "up to, as far as." The word is used as a particle of emphasis. The vines and fruit trees had not produced. There was no sign of leaf or fruit on the trees—nothing by which one could judge the future produce; yet the prophet predicts in the following v an abundant crop, dating from the people's obedience.

The vine (*haggephen*) and *the olive* (*hazzayit*) are fruits characteristic of the Promised Land (Dt 8:8). Abundant production of these fruits signaled good times ahead.

B. Future Blessing (2:19c):
From this day on I will bless you. Yahweh promises that the blessing will begin immediately. *This day* refers to December 18, 520 BC, the date of this third oracle. Thus the workers needed to be patient.

---

[48]Donald Wiseman, "Haggai," in *The New Bible Commentary*, 784.

HAGGAI 2:15-19				
Before stone was laid to stone (2:15)	Work Resumed 6/24	From day temple foundation was laid (2:18)		Haggai's 3d Message 9/24
Conditions Bad		Conditions Still Bad, But shortly will improve		
About 15 Years		3 Months in 520 BC		

Why did blessings not begin three months earlier when the work commenced? Had they been negligent or half-hearted in their work? There is no evidence for this. Up to this point they were experiencing the effects of the last crop failure. But things were about to change. Divine blessing was in the pipeline, headed their way.

Call to Hope
Haggai 2:20-23

Haggai delivered his fourth oracle on the same day he delivered his third oracle. See on 2:10. The people's temple devotion will pave the way for a wonderful new era. The Davidic kingdom will be restored, achieving at long last the world-wide influence anticipated in biblical literature for half a millennium.

Two points are made in this final call for hope: the kingdoms of the world will be shaken (vv 21-22); and the kingdom of God will be unshaken (v 23).

Introduction
Haggai 2:20-21a

A. **Authority** (2:20a):
  1. *Source of message (2:20a):* **The word of Yahweh...** Haggai undergirded every message with assurances that what he spoke to the postexilic community came ultimately from Yahweh.
  2. *Agent of message (2:20b):* **came to Haggai...** Elsewhere Haggai claimed that the divine word came in his hand,

i.e., by him as the instrumental agent. Here the word came to him

3. *Time of message (2:20c):* ***a second time on the twenty-fourth day of the month...*** The date is the same as that of the third message. The previous message stressed temporal blessing; this one focus of messianic blessing.

B. Addressee (2:21a):
Tell Zerubbabel governor of Judah that... Zerubbabel was head of the nation and representative of the house of David. Temporal and messianic blessings have been announced to the people generally. Now spiritual blessings are announced to Zerubbabel. In the opening message of this book Zerubbabel was called upon to be the prime mover in rebuilding God's house. By so doing he secures for himself the promise that God will build a "house" for him.

Worldly Kingdoms Shaken
Haggai 2:21b-22

A. Extent of the Shaking (2:21b-22c):
1. *In general terms (2:21b):* ***I will shake the heavens and the earth...*** By means of a participle + a pronoun Haggai stresses the immediacy of the promise which initially appeared in 2:6. The phrase *the heavens and the earth* a merism, i.e., it combines two words to express a single idea. *The heavens and the earth* is equivalent to everything; the universe. A new age will be introduced with a tumultuous shaking in the moral, spiritual, and physical universe. For the fulfillment, see on 2:6. It is still the practice to refer to "earthshaking" events. The establishment of the Davidic dynasty was considered an "earthshaking" event in biblical history (2 Sam 22:8 // Ps 18:8). The re-establishment of that dynasty will be even more earthshaking for it will affect the entire universe.

2. *In political terms (2:22a):* ***I will overthrow the throne of kingdoms...*** Overthrow (r. *hpk*) has its roots in the

action that Yahweh took against Sodom and Gomorrah.[49] Thus the power that totally destroyed the cities of the plain will be unleashed against the kingdoms of this world in that final day. Hebrew grammar permits *throne* to be rendered as a plural.[50] Haggai may have deliberately chosen the singular to convey the thought that behind the kingdoms of the world there is a single organizing power opposed to Yahweh.

The shaking was especially to include the political world. Haggai is not just talking about a change of dynasty in Persia. See on 2:7a.

3. *In general terms (2:22b):* **and shatter the strength of the kingdoms of the nations.** Shatter (r. *šmd*) is part of the conquest vocabulary (Dt 9:3; Am 2:9). Thus the God who destroyed Canaanite nations before Israel will once again intervene on behalf of his people. The term *strength* (*chozeq*) is used elsewhere 4x, three of which refer to Yahweh's power manifested at the exodus. Haggai uses the term ironically. The combined strength of earthly kingdoms cannot compare with the strength of the God of the exodus.

4. *In military terms (2:22c):* **I will overthrow chariot and its riders; horses and their riders will go down...** *Overthrow* is repeated in this v for emphasis. Chariots, horses and riders are symbols of the military weaponry by which nations rise to power. *Go down* (r. *yrd*) was taken from the Red Sea victory over Pharaoh (Ex 15:1, 4-5). Israel saw the Egyptian oppressors no more. So in the final day the God of Red Sea deliverance will again assert his power to remove forever the oppressors of his people.

B. Cause of the Shaking (2:22d):

Each by the sword of his brother. Yahweh will use internal revolutions and invasions by other nations as the means of overthrowing hostile nations. Heathen powers vanquish one another either in the panic that falls upon them or in the strife that develops between them.[51] The point is that the sin

---

[49] Dt 29:23; Isa 1:7-9; Jer 20:16; Amos 4:11; Lam 4:6
[50] The term *throne* might be used distributively for various thrones of several kingdoms. See GKC §124r.
[51] Cf. Judg 7:22; Ezek 38:27; Zech 14:13.

Haggai: 2:1-23

of hating God and his people is self-destructive. Haggai seems to be echoing Dan 2 and 7 which depict symbolically the rise and fall of various empires that precede the manifestation of the kingdom of God on earth.

Heavenly Kingdom Unshaken
Haggai 2:23

A. **God's Day** (2:23a):
In that day... refers to the time when the kingdoms of this world come crashing down. During that same time God will be at work building up his kingdom. *That day* does not refer to the vague future; it refers to that specific time when Yahweh intervenes decisively in human history.

B. **God's Word** (2:23b):
(oracle of Yahweh of Hosts). This powerful attribution of the promises to God's declaration appears 3x in this single v. It emphasizes, authenticates and confirms the three aspects of God's promise: 1) the certainty of the coming day; 2) the selection of Zerubbabel; and 3) his status.

C. **God's Servant** (2:23c):
I will take you, O my servant Zerubbabel son of Shealtiel (oracle of Yahweh)... The language implies special selection for a special mission.[52] It also suggests that Zerubbabel will experience divine protection during those tumultuous times. Zerubbabel is called *my servant*. This is a title given in recognition of past faithfulness, but also in anticipation of greater usefulness in the future. *My servant* is an honorable title used especially of David (21x) and of the Messiah (Isa 42:1; 52:13; Ezek 34:23).

D. **God's Signet** (2:23d):
And I will make you like my signet ring... A signet was worn on the finger or on a cord fastened round the neck. On the stone was engraved either the name or some identifying

---

[52]Cf. Josh 24:3; Ex 6:12; Nm 3:12; 2 Sam 7:8; Amos 7:15.

emblem of the owner. The signet was impressed on the soft clay tablets on which business or legal matters were inscribed. If papyrus or parchment was used, the seal was imprinted on wax or clay disks affixed to the documents. This seal verified the document as an authentic declaration of the persons affixing their seal (Laetsch). A signet was equivalent to a signature in a world where most people did not write.

Thus Zerubbabel will be God's signature, his authoritative leader among the remnant. In similar words Yahweh had rejected Zerubbabel's grandfather, Jehoiachin, from the throne (Jer 22:24). Thus these words attest the reinstatement of the Davidic line. Zerubbabel was Yahweh's pledge that all of the ancient promises made to David (2 Sam 7:12-16) will be fulfilled.

E. God's Chosen (2:23e):

For I have chosen you (oracle of Yahweh of Hosts). Zerubbabel had been chosen not by the people, or by Cyrus, but by the Almighty. This is not to be taken as a personal assurance only to Zerubbabel; he did not rise to any special prominence in the kingdoms of the world. The language reflects what was said of God's Servant in Isa 42:1. The fulfillment must be looked for in Christ, who was a descendant of Zerubbabel (Mt 1:12; Lk 3:27). Promises are often made in Scripture to individuals that are accomplished only in their descendants. Apparently the grand promises made to David are here passed on to Zerubbabel and to his line. From him will spring the Messiah in whom alone these wide predictions find their fulfillment.[53] Yahweh is faithful in his messianic promises.

---

[53] W.J. Deane, *PC*, 23.

ZECHARIAH
PROPHET OF NIGHT VISIONS

INTRODUCTION

Zechariah has been called "the temple builder" and "the seer" (Robinson). Patterson referred to this prophet as "the idealist" while Ward branded him "the enthusiast." Since such a large part of his book centers on eight visions which he received in one night Zechariah might appropriately be called "the prophet of night visions."

Zechariah: the Man

The eleventh of the Minor Prophets had a very common name. At least thirty individuals in Scripture were called Zechariah.[54] The name means "Yahweh has remembered."

A. Ancestry

The prophet is said to be the son of Berekiah the son of Iddo (1:1, 7). In the Book of Ezra (5:1; 6:14) he is called simply the son of Iddo. Berekiah may have died young leaving Zechariah to be raised by his grandfather. In Nehemiah (12:4) a priest named Iddo is named among those who returned from Babylon with Zerubbabel in 538 BC. This Iddo is said to have had a son named Zechariah (Neh 12:16). It is probable but not certain that the author of the Book of Zechariah is being named in Nehemiah 12:16.

B. Personal Life

Concerning Zechariah's personal life little is known. That he was a contemporary of Haggai is clear from the date assigned to his first oracle. Assuming that he is mentioned in Nehemiah 12, he functioned as a priest and head of a father's house in the days of Joiakim who succeeded Joshua as high

---

[54]1 Chr 5:7; 9:37; 15:18, 20,24; 24:25; 26:2, 11, 14; 27:21; 2 Chr 17:7; 20:14; 21:2; 24:20-21 (cf. Mt 23:25); 26:5; 2 Kgs 14:29; 18:2 // 2 Chr 29:1; 29:13; 34:12; 35:8; Isa 8:2; Zech 1:1; Ezra 8:3, 11; 8:16; 10:26; Neh 8:4; 11:4, 5, 12; 12:35, 41.

priest (Neh 12:12, 16). Like Ezekiel, Zechariah reflects familiarity with priestly things.[55]

Zechariah was probably born and educated in Babylon. This may account for his frequent use of visions and allegories. If Iddo his grandfather was among those who as priests went up with Zerubbabel to Jerusalem, and some sixteen years have elapsed (536-520 BC), Zechariah would be comparatively young at his call.

C. Ministry

Haggai had been preaching in Judea since August 29, 520 BC when Zechariah joined him sometime in October or November of that same year (1:1). The last dated message in the book is assigned to December 4, 516 BC. No doubt Zechariah lived to see the temple rebuilt and dedicated (March 12, 515 BC). His ministry, however, probably continued much longer. Zechariah would have been in his sixties when the Persians were defeated in their attempted invasions of Greece in 490 and 480 BC. He would have seen Greece rising steadily on the horizon as a potential enemy of his people.[56]

D. Tradition

In tradition Zechariah is associated with Haggai in the titles of certain Psalms. He is also said to have made a contribution to the liturgical worship of the restored temple. Tradition regarded him as a member of the so-called Great Synagogue, a law-making body which supposedly guided the people of God in postexilic times.

In Patristic tradition Zechariah is said to have exercised his prophetic office in Babylon where he worked miracles. He returned to Jerusalem at an advanced age where he discharged the duties of the priesthood. He supposedly was buried beside Haggai. A careful study of the chronology of the book, however, indicates that Zechariah was a young man when he began to preach.

---

[55]Zech 3:7; 5:3, 6-11; 6:9-15; 9:8, 15; 14:16, 20, 21.
[56]Cashdan, *SBB*, 269-70.

Zechariah: Introduction

E. Death[57]

In Matthew 23:35 Jesus referred to a Zechariah son of Berekiah who was slain in the courts of the temple.

Was Jesus referring to the Zechariah son of Jehoiada (2 Chr 24:17-22)? Evidence supporting this view can be summarized like this: 1) place of death in the temple is similar in Matthew and Chronicles; 2) the account of this Zechariah's death is recorded in Chronicles, the last book of the Hebrew Bible. Jesus was using a beginning-to-end argument—from Genesis to Chronicles—the last recorded murder in the OT; 3) Jewish tradition indicates this murder was a notable event. According to the Babylonian Talmud, the blood of Zechariah boiled for centuries[58] and was avenged by Nubuzaradan who slew 80,000 priests to atone for his death. Against this view is the phrase "son of Berekiah" in Matthew's Gospel for the Zechariah who died in the temple courts was the son of Jehoiada.

Was Jesus referring to the Minor Prophet Zechariah? (McGarvey). There is a Jewish tradition that the Minor Prophet Zechariah also was slain in the temple.[59] The same tradition appears in some early Christian sources.[60] However, a contradictory tradition regarding the death of the Minor Prophet Zechariah appears in *The Lives of the Prophets* to the effect that Zechariah died a natural death.[61]

Was Jesus referring to some other Zechariah, someone who lived nearer the first century and was well known to Jesus' hearers? (John Broadus). In favor of this view are the following facts: Josephus refers to a Zacarihas (the son of

---

[57]J. Barton Payne, "Zechariah who Perished," *GJ* 8 (Fall, 1967): 33-35.
[58]*Sanh.*, 96b; *Gittin* 57b; *Midrash Koheleth* 3:16.
[59]Targum to Lamentations 2:20. The passage reads: "Shall the priest and the prophet be slain in the sanctuary of the Lord?" The Targumist adds the comment: "As you killed Zechariah the son of Iddo, the high priest and faithful prophet in the sanctuary of the Lord on the Day of Atonement because he admonished them not to do what was displeasing to the Lord."
[60]Epiphanius and Sozomenus. See Migne, *Patrological Graeca* 43, p. 411, fn. 55; 67, p. 1628ff.
[61]Cited in *Interpreter's Bible*.

Postexilic Prophets

Baruch) upon whom they fell "in the middle of the temple and slew him" (*Wars* 4.5.4). But when Jesus spoke the words of Mt 23:35 this event was yet thirty-four years in the future, and Jesus used the past tense. Note also "middle of the temple," i.e., the court of Gentiles. Jesus spoke of Zechariah being slain between the temple and altar, i.e., in the court of priests. The church father Origen quotes a tradition that the father of John the Baptist was murdered in the temple.[62]

Most commentators think Jesus was alluding to the death of Zechariah son of Jehoiada (2 Chr 24:17-22). How, then, is the phrase "son of Berekiah" in Mt 23:35 explained? Liberals contend that Jesus simply confused the two Zechariahs (Blank; Peake). For Bible believers, however, there are three viable explanations of the phrase "son of Berekiah" in Mt 23:35.

First, Jehoiada may have also had the name Berekiah ("Blessed of Yahweh"), possibly given to him for saving his country (Clarke). Second, Jehoiada may be the grandfather (he died at age 130 according to 2 Chr 24:15), and Zechariah's father was Berekiah, not otherwise mentioned in the historical books. Third, the phrase "son of Berekiah" may be a scribal addition to Matthew (Alfred). The phrase is omitted in some NT MSS (e.g., Aleph, and four cursives), and the parallel passage in Lk 11:51.[63]

Zechariah: the Book

A. Genre

The Book of Zechariah in its entirety can be classified as apocalyptic literature (Baldwin). Here there is a progression from the local scene to the world scene; from a point in time to the end of time. Visions are prominent along with an angelic interpreter of those visions. Angels are featured prominently. The book reflects determinism—the view that God

---

[62] de la Rue, 4.845.
[63] Jerome found that the Gospel of the Nazarenes read *Jehoiada* rather than *Berekiah* in Mt 23:35. See Jerome's commentary on Matthew, Migne, *Patrological Latina*, 26, p. 180.

Zechariah: Introduction

already had worked out his purposes in heaven, and all that remained was for him to initiate those purposes on earth. Here there is animal symbolism as well as the use of symbolic numbers.[64]

The Book of Zechariah is one of the most difficult of the prophetic books to interpret (Leupold). Much here is obscure and difficult to fit into any system of eschatology. The conflicting interpretations of modern scholars are not just limited to individual words or vv, but to the entire structure of the book.

Why is this book particularly obscure? Jews find the book obscure because of its clear depiction of a suffering Messiah, a view that they find repugnant. Zechariah is obscure to rationalists because they will not admit what is manifestly a prediction of a remotely future event. Simple believers find the book obscure for two reasons: 1) the predominance of symbolical language; and 2) the occasional brevity and conciseness of statement.

One helpful key to interpreting this book is the following principle: What was future to Zechariah's pre-exilic predecessors was now past or present. Zechariah's glowing accounts of deliverance and enlargement of Israel certainly were not fulfilled in the return from Babylon. The return from Babylon was essentially completed by Zechariah's day. So he must have been anticipating another and more glorious restoration yet future to him.

B. Style and Form

Zechariah makes use of direct prophetic speech reflecting a wide range of emotion. For example, there are impassioned imperatives like *cry out* (1:14); *flee* (2:6); *escape* (2:7); *sing and rejoice* (2:10); and *be silent* (2:13).

The prophet records eight visions in which he actively participated. He was fully involved in all that was going on—interjecting remarks, questions, and suggestions.

---

[64]Baldwin, *TOTC*, 70-74.

Zechariah performed at least two symbolic acts reminiscent of similar actions performed by Jeremiah and Ezekiel.

Repetition is a characteristic of this prophet's style, e.g., *you shall know that Yahweh of Hosts has sent me*; and *thus says Yahweh of Hosts*. This prophet uses bold and frequent declarations of his own inspiration in a variety of formats.

Zechariah's Hebrew is pure, free of Aramaisms. He does, however, display certain orthographic peculiarities.[65] Zechariah's poetry, found primarily in chs 9-11, is fine poetry. "But his parallelisms want the neatness and harmony which are found in earlier writings" (Deane).

Baldwin offers this tasty estimate of the contribution of Zechariah: "If Haggai was the builder, responsible for the solid structure of the new temple, Zechariah was more like the artist, adding colorful windows with their symbolism, gaiety and light."[66]

C. Unity

The Book of Zechariah consists of fourteen chapters. The book falls naturally into two divisions. The first part (chs. 1-8) is generally regarded as the work of the postexilic Zechariah who is mentioned with Haggai in Ezra 5:1 and 6:14. The second part (chs 9-14) differs from the first in both style and subject matter. For this reason critics have argued that the last six chs must have been written by a different person. Some even regard these chs—sometimes dubbed Deutero-Zechariah—as having been written prior to the exile! Conservative scholars, of course, have defended the unity of the book ably. No insurmountable difficulty stands in the way of accepting the entire fourteen chs as the work of one prophet, Zechariah son of Berekiah.

---

[65]See 12:7, 8, 10; use of *'achat* for indefinite article in 5:7; unusual position of *'et* in 7:7; 8:17.
[66]Baldwin, *TOTC*, 59.

Zechariah: Introduction

D. Structure

Some of the most creative work on the structure of the Book of Zechariah has been done by Meredith Kline.[67] Kline sees Zechariah as a diptych with 6:9-15 as its primary hinge or center passage.[68] The two side panels are also divided by spines (3:1-10; 11:1-17). The two spines and the primary hinge share these qualities in common: 1) Zechariah personally participates in a prophetic action that involves specific historical individuals. 2) These "spine" passages involve a coronation or some sort of investiture to theocratic office. 3) In each "spine" passage a messianic (pre-)figure is commissioned to the royal-priestly task.

Kline regards 1:1-6 and chs 7-8 as the introductions to the two major divisions of the book. These passages have several things in common: 1) an opening date formula (1:1; 7:1); 2) a recollection of lessons from past covenant history with reference to earlier prophets and the exile (1:2-6; 7:7-14); 3) an exhortation for the postexilic community to fulfill its present duties (1:3-4; 8:16-17); and 4) a promise of future blessings upon their repentance and obedience (1:3; 8:2-23).

Kline sees the first diptych (1:1-6:8) as containing seven visions,[69] rather than the traditional understanding that there are eight visions recorded in these chs. He thinks that ch 5 is a compound vision, rather than two separate visions.[70] He

---

[67]"The Structure of the Book of Zechariah," *JETS* 34 (1991): 179-193.

[68]Meyers and Baldwin (*AB*) treat chs 7-8 as the center of the book in its present form and indeed of the entire Haggai-Zechariah-Malachi corpus.

[69]Meyers eliminates what is traditionally labeled the fourth vision (3:1-10) and joins it to 4:1-14. He regards it as the center of a section consisting of seven visions plus one "prophetic vision." (*AB*, liv-lviii). Dorsey arrives at seven visions by treating the traditional second vision (1:18-21) as the conclusion of vision one. *The Literary Structure of the Old Testament* (Grand Rapids: Baker, 1999), 318.

[70]Klein observes that 5:5 lacks an introduction that combines the use of *ra'ah* (*see*) and *hinneh* (*behold*) as do all the other visions except the fourth (3:1-10).

sees two triads of visions with the fourth vision being the "spine" between the two sets.

Klein sees a similar balance in the second main division of the book (chs 7-14). As noted above, he sees chs 7-8 as an elongated introduction to this section. The introduction is followed by two "burdens" beginning in 9:1 and 12:1 with ch 11 being the "spine" between them. The structure of the book developed in this commentary follows Klein in the main.

STRUCTURE OF ZECHARIAH						
Messages During Temple Construction			Crowning Of Joshua	Messages After Temple Construction		
Intro.	Visions 1-4	Visions 5-8		Intro.	1st Burden	2nd Burden
1:1-6	1:7-3:10	4:1-6:8	6:9-15	7-8	9-11	12-14

E. Predictions

Payne finds seventy-eight predictions in the Book of Zechariah involving some 144 verses or sixty-nine percent of the book.[71] The book is rich in personal messianic prophecy.

---

[71] J. Barton Payne, *Encyclopedia of Biblical Prophecy* (New York: Harper & Row, 1973), 450.

COMMENTARY

PART ONE: MESSAGES DURING TEMPLE CONSTRUCTION
Zechariah 1:1-6:8

Introduction to Part One
Zechariah 1:1-6

Introductory Formula
Zechariah 1:1

A. Chronology of the Prophet (1:1a):
In the eighth month of the second year of Darius... Zechariah's opening message is dated prior to the final oracles of Haggai (Hag 2:10, 20). So the ministry of Zechariah phased in while that of Haggai was coming to an end. The temple reconstruction project had begun on the twenty-fourth day of the sixth month, or at least thirty-six days prior to the delivery of the first message of Zechariah.

B. Claim of the Prophet (1:1b-c):
  1. *Claims divine revelation (1:1b):* **the word of Yahweh came.** This expression is used at least 103x in OT to point to divine revelation. It occurs 6x in this book, two of those times in the first person. The phrase is broad enough to include visional as well as verbal revelation.
  2. *Claims prophetic authority (1:1c):* **to the prophet...** Masoretic accentuation indicates that the title *prophet* belongs to Iddo. A prophet and seer by this name recorded the history of the early kings of Judah (2 Chr 12:15; 13:22); but it is very unlikely that he is the Iddo of this text. NIV is correct, however, in referring the title to Zechariah rather than Iddo (Laetsch; Kimchi; LXX). A *prophet* is a spokesman for another, a messenger (Ex 7:1; cf. 4:11-16).

C. Identity of the Prophet (1:1d):

Zechariah son of Berekiah, the son of Iddo: On the meaning of the name *Zechariah* see the introductory notes. This is a more precise listing of the genealogy of Zechariah than appears in Ezra 5:1 and 6:14 where Berekiah is omitted. If Iddo is the priest mentioned in Neh 12:4, 16 then his name alone would have been sufficient to distinguish Zechariah from others who bore this common name.

Introductory Message
Zechariah 1:2-6

The purpose of the opening message of Zechariah is to set forth the prerequisite for spiritual blessing.

A. Observation (1:2):

Displeased has Yahweh been with displeasure concerning your fathers. *Yahweh* had been greatly displeased with his people. No one could dispute that statement. The remnant had tasted divine wrath in Babylonian captivity. Some may still have been alive who had childhood memories of the devastating destruction of Jerusalem by Nebuchadnezzar.

Your fathers refers to the generation of the Babylonian captivity. Zechariah uses a strong verb (r. *qtsp*) and two grammatical devices[72] to stress the acuteness of the displeasure. This reminder of an unpleasant recent past serves as theme statement for the first oracle. At the same time it is an oblique warning. Should the present generation continue in the same path as their fathers the anger of Yahweh could lash out against them. The unpleasant reminder of v 2 is the backdrop against which the grace of Yahweh in v 3 shines in greater brilliance.

---

[72]The two grammatical devices are 1) the initial position of the verb in the sentence; and 2) the cognate accusative.

Zechariah 1:1-6:8

B. Exhortation (1:3):

1. Authorization (1:3a): ***Therefore tell them: Thus says Yahweh of Hosts...*** Zechariah is authorized, accredited, or called to communicate to his fellows the revelation he had received. *Thus says Yahweh* is strong claim of divine authority, guidance and inspiration that occurs 415x in OT, 18x in this book. Scholars refer to this phrase as the messenger formula. It was used in the secular setting by messengers who first delivered a message orally before handing over that message to the recipient in written form.

The divine title *Yahweh of Hosts* appears for the first time in 1 Sam 1:3. It appears 275x in the OT, 82x in the postexilic prophets, 46x in this book. The term *hosts* can refer to the armies of Israel, the angelic armies or the armies of stars that parade with military precision across the heavens in the night sky. Yahweh is commander of all host. In NIV the translators try to capture the meaning of this term by rendering it *Almighty*.

2. Invitation (1:3b): ***Return to me (oracle of Yahweh of Hosts)...*** God sees in the present generation the same root sin as in the captivity generation, viz. disobedience. Returning to Yahweh in this case will manifest itself in the work on the temple. This gracious invitation indicates that people can escape the dreadful reality of divine wrath by getting back on track with the Lord.

Oracle (n^e'um) is the strongest term used in the OT to claim divine origin for a statement. An *oracle* was (usually) in poetic form. It is equivalent to a direct quote from Yahweh. So the invitation in this v comes from God himself. He invites his wayward people to come back to him in their devotion and allegiance. The oracle formula is used 375x in OT, 20x in this book.

Repetition of the divine name serves two purposes. First, it underscores the divine authority of Zechariah's commission. Second, it stresses the certainty of the result that follows returning to the Lord. The very one who marshals all the forces of heaven and earth is at the same time the blessed God of redemption.

3. **Incentive (1:3c):** *in order that I may return to you, says Yahweh of Hosts.* Now Zechariah explains the value of repentance. This promise begins with Hebrew *vav* (*and*) which here seems to introduce the subordinate idea of purpose, hence *in order that I may return.* The verb is imperfect = progressive action. God will ever and continually return to those who return to him. What condescension! What grace! A change of conduct on the part of the people induces a change of attitude on the part of God. *Says Yahweh of Hosts* is called the declaration formula. It is the third strong claim of inspiration in this single v.

C. Admonition (1:4a):
Do not be like your fathers, i.e., disobedient. Zechariah cites the fathers as an example of apostasy 4x. He thereby warns his generation not to go down the same path. *Fathers* could be rendered "forefathers" (NIV), indicating pre-exilic generations.

D. Description (1:4b-e):
Zechariah describes the previous generation that he discourages his contemporaries from emulating.

1. *They had access to powerful messengers (1:4b):* **to whom the former prophets proclaimed, saying, Thus says Yahweh of Hosts...** These words sound very Jeremiah-like (cf. Jer 25:5; 35:15). The *former prophets* are the prophets before the exile, especially Jeremiah. The message of these prophets was mainly threat. *Proclaimed* is lit., "called." They made themselves heard. Their witness was public, clear, understandable, and authoritative. On *Yahweh of Hosts* see on v 3.

2. *They had received a powerful warning (1:4c):* **Turn please from your evil ways and your evil deeds.** This warning by the pre-exilic prophets had the authority of a divine command, but also an element of tact and grace. Turning to God as in v 3 requires a turning away from what offends God. *Evil ways and deeds* are violations of God's law. Pre-exilic prophetic texts indicate that idolatry was one of the chief offenses against Yahweh.

Zechariah 1:1-6:8

3. They had refused to obey (1:4d): **But they would not listen or pay attention to me...** Their fathers had given no heed to the earnest exhortations and solemn warnings of the pre-exilic prophets. *Listen* suggests warm reception or acceptance. *Pay attention* (*give heed* NASB) suggests implementation or obedience. Rejecting the prophetic word is equivalent to rejecting God himself.

4. They had rejected a direct message of God (1:4e): **(oracle of Yahweh).** The oracle formula underscores the first person pronoun in the previous line. It is Yahweh personally who spoke to the fathers through the pre-exilic prophets; it is Yahweh personally who offers this present assessment of their fathers.

E. Interrogation (1:5-6a): Zechariah directs three thought-provoking questions to his audience.

1. Question #1 regarding the impermanence of life (1:5a): **As for your fathers, where are they?** They were no longer accessible. They had died.

2. Question #2 regarding the impermanence of life (1:5b): **And the prophets, do they live forever?** The prophets who preached to the disobedient fathers had been silenced by death.[73]

3. Question #3 regarding the permanence of God's word (1:6a): **But did not my words and my statutes, which I commanded my servants the prophets, overtake your forefathers?** *But* (*'ak*) introduces the contrast between the impermanence of life and the permanence of God's word. *My words* are the words God put into the mouth of his prophets. *My statutes* are the divine decrees that threatened punishment. God *commanded* the prophets to preach these words and statutes. Essentially *my words* and *my statutes* are a synopsis of the prophetic message. Prophets are called God's *servants* 18x in OT. *Overtake* (*nûg*) indicates "to reach or catch up with" one who has gone away or fled. The word is used in the Bible of both blessing and curse (e.g., Dt 28:2; Ps 69:25).

---

[73] Jewish commentators have suggested that these words are part of a dialogue—the impudent response of the people to Zechariah's question about their fathers.

Postexilic Prophets

One cannot outrun or outdistance the penalties stipulated in God's word. Zechariah saw God's word as an active force in the world.

F. Recognition (1:6b):
1. What they did (1:6b): **Then they repented...** The fathers who experienced exile in Babylon *repented*. This refers to a change of mind or opinion brought about by conviction of the truth of God's word and his judgment (Cashdan). Prior to 586 BC the Judeans based their theology on the miraculous deliverance from Assyria in 701 BC. The false prophets and priests assured the nation that God would never permit Jerusalem to be destroyed. The painful experience of the exile forced them to abandon that theology.

2. What they said (1:6c): **According as Yahweh of Hosts purposed to do to us, according to our way and according to our deeds, so has he dealt with us.** The present desolate condition of Jerusalem testified to the faithfulness of God's word. In addition the fathers themselves had been forced to confess that God had dealt with them according to their sins. They admitted that their exile to Babylon was an appropriate response to their years of stubborn rejection of God's word.

Triad of Visions
Zechariah 1:7-2:13

Introduction to the Visions
Zechariah 1:7

A. Time of the Visions (1:7a):
On the twenty-fourth day of the eleventh month, the month of Shebat, in the second year of Darius... The date of this second message is more specific than the notation in v 1. The day as well as the month is noted. On the modern calendar the date of these visions is February 24, 519 BC. This was three months after the first address and five months after the temple work resumed (Hag 1:14, 15). For five months the people had demonstrated their commitment by their arduous

Zechariah 1:1-6:8

labor. Three months earlier Haggai had delivered his last oracles. The chronological notation in this v underscores the sad circumstances of God's people. The prophet was forced to date revelations of Yahweh to the reign of a Persian king using the Babylonian calendar that the Persians used.[74] Judah was no longer an independent kingdom, not even a vassal state; she was only a miserable province within the region the Persians called Trans-Euphrates.

B. Significance of the Visions (1:7b):

The word of Yahweh came to the prophet Zechariah son of Berekiah, the son of Iddo. The revelation claim (*the word of Yahweh came*) is repeated from v 1 as is the position and ancestry of Zechariah. In vv 2-6 the *word of Yahweh* refers to oral revelation, here the phrase refers to visions. Each vision has an application to the specific situation of Zechariah's day, and a wider application to all God's people. Some of the visions are accompanied by passages that are definitely messianic.

C. Structure of the Visions:

There is some discussion about the number of visions that Zechariah reports, and about the way in which those visions have been arranged in the book. The traditional view is that Zechariah had eight visions.[75] These visions appear to be arranged in a chiastic pattern:[76]

---

[74] Petersen, *OTL*, 139.

[75] Smith, *WBC*, 181; McComiskey, *MPEEC*, 1019; W. VanGemeren, *Interpreting the Prophetic Word* (Grand Rapids: Zondervan, 1990), 193-98.

[76] H.G. Mitchell (*ICC*, 115) argues that the visions are arranged topically: the first three deal with the return from captivity; the fourth and fifth, the anointed of Yahweh, and the last three, the removal of sin. Joyce Baldwin (*TOTC*, 85) arranges the eight visions in a chiastic pattern: a-b-b-c-c-b-b-a. The first and last deal with horses and chariots patrolling the earth and the earth is at rest. The central visions come in pairs: the second and third deal with the threat of the nations against Judah and God's defense of his people; the fourth and fifth deal with Judah's anointed leaders; and the sixth and seventh describe the cleansing of the land.

A. Vision 1: Report of Heavenly Patrol.
B. Vision 2: Nations Meet Retribution.
C. Vision 3: Jerusalem Protected.
D. Vision 4: Priest Encouragement.
D' Vision 5: Prince Encouragement.
C' Vision 6: Jerusalem Purified.
B' Vision 7: Sinners Meet Retribution.
A' Vision 8: Action of Heavenly Patrol.

Vision One:
Report of the Heavenly Patrol
Zechariah 1:8-13

Introduction (1:8a):
I saw in the night and behold... Zechariah saw eight visions in one night at short intervals. It is impossible to tell whether he saw with the bodily eyes or whether he was in rapt ecstasy. The text, however, does not call what he saw *dreams*. *Behold* signals something unexpected, even shocking. The word is used 22x in this book, 14x in the eight visions. The word is usually left untranslated in NIV.

A. Description of the Vision (1:8b-d):
1. A mounted man: (1:8b): **there before me was a man riding a red horse!** This *man* is most likely an angel, probably the angel of Yahweh mentioned again in vv 10, 11. He apparently is the leader of the company of horsemen[77] who follow him. He is not to be confused with the interpreting angel who also appears in this vision. No significance is assigned to the color red here.

---

[77]Mark Allen suggests that the horses Zechariah saw were a miniature breed averaging 9-11 hands that was popular in the Persian Empire. The breed was considered extinct until a herd of miniature horses was found in Iran near the Caspian Sea in 1965. This breed is surefooted. They are excellent jumpers—ideal for the rough mountain roadways of Iran. Allen does not take into account, however, that the horses in Zechariah were seen by a Jew in Palestine, and that they are associated with Palestinian geography. "The Background and Use of Equine Imagery in Zechariah," *SCJ* 3 (Fall 2000): 243-260.

Zechariah 1:1-6:8

2. Myrtle trees (1:8c): **He was standing among the myrtle trees in the bottom.** This kind of tree was once common in the vicinity of Jerusalem. *Myrtle trees* may signify Israel (Leupold, Unger; Laetsch). Prophetic symbolism used the tall cedar to represent arrogant worldly powers. The lowly but fragrant myrtle is an apt symbol for God's people. The *bottom* ($m^e tsul\bar{a}h$) or "ravine" (NIV; NASB) may point to an ordinary valley near Jerusalem (Cashdan). Some think the word is used to denote horrible, inescapable agony, and hopelessness. Thus Israel is in deep humiliation. Perhaps the idea is that in that ravine God's people grow, out of the gaze of the world.

The man astride the red horse was standing among the myrtles, indicating that the Most High condescends to dwell among and identify himself with those of a contrite and humble spirit (cf. Isa 57:15; 66:2).

3. A company of horses (1:8d). **Behind him were red, brown and white horses.** Concerning the company of horses Zechariah makes two observations.

First, they were behind the first rider. This suggests that these horses were under the command of the angel of Yahweh. Horses speak to the swiftness with which God carries out his purposes. Most likely these horses were being ridden by angels. The fact that the riders are not mentioned but the colors of the horses are mentioned suggests that the colors were symbolic.

Second, the horses were of various colors. Some commentators take these colors to signify various lands traversed by them (Keil); more likely the colors point to the different tasks assigned to each group (Barnes). *Red* signifies judgment, blood, vengeance (cf. Isa 63:1; Rev 6:4).

Some controversy exists over the color translated *brown.*[78] *Brown* or "sorrel" (NASB)—a combination of the

---

[78] Heb *sārōq* is rendered *brown* (NIV), *speckled* (KJV) *sorrel* (reddish-brown) in NRSV, NJPS, NASB. The related word *sōrēq* is used of choice vines and grapes (Isa 5:2; Jer 2:21) which hints at reddishness. Cognate words in related languages also are connected with reddishness (*NIDOTTE* 3:1295). Those, like McComiskey, who argue that the word denotes spottedness are pressing too hard to make the horse colors in ch 1 conform to those in ch 6. See Allen, "Equine," op. cit., 50.

first and last colors—perhaps indicates a mission of mixed character—one of both judgment and mercy. *White* is the symbol of victory, triumph and glory.

The point is that God's agents were on the scene. They were about to move against the enemies of God's people. Certainly these horses and riders were "messengers of vengeance and of victory for the good of God's people Israel" (Rignell). This vision is a way of recalling that "the chariots of God are twenty thousand, even thousands of angels (Ps 68:17). He has abundant power to deliver his people from whatever situation in which they might find themselves.

B. Request by the Prophet (1:9):

1. Zechariah's question (1:9a): **Then I said, my Lord, What are these?** The question is probably addressed to an interpreting angel who accompanied the prophet throughout all his visions.[79] Zechariah wants to know the symbolic import of what he sees. *My Lord* (*'adōnî*) is a title of respect without implications of deity. It is used 4x in this book in addressing the interpreting angel.

2. Angel's response (1:9b): **The angel who was speaking with me answered, As for me, I will show you what they are.** The word *angel* is used 24x in the book. This particular angel (*hammal'ākh haddōbhēr bî*) is mentioned 11x. This angel is an interpreting angel assigned to accompany Zechariah through his visionary experience. Some think that this angel is the same as the angel of Yahweh whom the prophet saw standing among the myrtle trees.[80] The preponderance of the evidence, however, indicates that the two are distinct heavenly beings.

To the interpreting angel no divine work is ascribed and no divine name is given. He interprets visions, or at least prepares the mind of the prophet to understand the explanation

---

[79] Others think the question is addressed to the first rider.

[80] The arguments for equating the two angelic beings are these: 1) Zechariah addressed this angel as "my lord" when the only person named previously was the angel of Yahweh; 2) this angel promises to explain the vision, and in the next v it is the angel of Yahweh who gives the explanation; 3) in v 12 the angel of Yahweh offers supplication for Jerusalem, and the answer in the following v is given to the interpreting angel.

Zechariah 1:1-6:8

which is given by the Lord himself. Zechariah's situation is similar to what Daniel and John experienced when they encountered two heavenly beings in connection with the same vision (Dan 8:16; 10:5-13; Rev 1:1).

In his response to the prophet the interpreting angel makes the first person pronoun emphatic—I, and no one else will respond to your request. The angel does not promise to tell Zechariah what he wants to know, but *to show* (r. *r'h* in Hiphil) him.

C. Explanation by the Commander (1:10):

Then the man standing among the myrtle trees explained, These are they whom Yahweh has sent to walk to and fro through the earth. The interpreting angel explains the meaning of the horsemen by causing Zechariah to overhear the conversation of the angel riders.

The commander of the angelic unit explains their function. The riders are a heavenly reconnaissance troop. They have just returned from their mission and are ready to report to their commander. *Walk to and fro* is used in a military sense, to patrol, make careful survey. Cf. Job 1:7. *Earth* in this context refers primarily to the Near East of Zechariah's day.

D. Report of the Patrol (1:11):

Zechariah is now permitted to hear the report of the heavenly patrol. He observed three facets of their report.

1. They reported to the superior angel (1:11a): **And they reported to the angel of Yahweh who was standing among the myrtle trees...** *Reported* is lit., "answered," i.e., the horsemen responded to the unexpressed inquiry of the commander. Here for the first time the rider of the red horse is identified as *the angel of Yahweh*. The OT is full of references to this special angel/messenger. A close examination of the passages where he is mentioned indicates that he is a manifestation of deity, perhaps the second person of the godhead. Yahweh sent these riders out, but they reported to the angel of Yahweh. Here, as elsewhere in the OT, this an-

81

gel/messenger is Yahweh, yet is distinct from Yahweh.[81] On the significance of the myrtle trees see on v 8.

2. *They reported what they had done (1:11b)*: **We have gone to and fro in the earth...** On this language see on v 10. The point is that they had completed their mission.

3. *They reported what they had found (1:11c)*: **and behold all the earth sits still and is at rest.** On the meaning of *behold* see on 1:8. Two participles (continuous action) are used to describe the state of things in all the earth. *Sits still* (r. *yšb*) when used of a place has a passive force, i.e., to be peacefully inhabited (Ezek 16:42; Jer 47:6-7). *At rest* (r. *šqṭ*) is used of one that no one harasses. Therefore it means "to have respite from war." The main point is this: there was no sign yet of Haggai's predicted shaking. Nations were enjoying security while Judah was in a state of misery and oppression. This report brings to the forefront the sorry state of affairs in Israel. While surrounding nations were enjoying peace and security, the sons of Israel were servants in their own land (Neh 4:36). They were struggling to regain their ancestral inheritance from Gentile interlopers.

E. Prayer of the Commander (1:12):

The scene continues to unfold before Zechariah. He next hears the commander respond to the report of the angelic patrol by offering up an intercessory prayer.

1. Intercessor (1:12a): **Then the angel of Yahweh spoke and said...** This special angel/messenger appears not only as the representative of God but as the advocate of Israel. He is identified with his people in their suffering, degradation and woe, i.e., he is standing among the myrtle trees in the deep valley. The angel of Yahweh had not appeared in the OT since the days of Hezekiah some two hundred years earlier. His mere presence among the remnant was comforting news; but the fact that he was Israel's advocate elevated that comfort exponentially.

---

[81] The angel of Yahweh is identified with Yahweh in some passages (Gn 16:11, 13; Judg 6:11, 14; 13:21-22); but in other passages he is distinguished from God because God speaks to him (2 Sam 24:16; 1 Chr 21:18, 27) or because he speaks to God (Zech 1:12).

Zechariah 1:1-6:8

2. Intercessory address (1:12b): ***O Yahweh of Hosts...*** Intercession was offered to the one who had authority over all the armies of heaven and earth, i.e., the all powerful. The angel/messenger now intercedes for Israel.

3. Intercessory method (1:12c): ***How long will you not have compassion on Jerusalem and on the cities of Judah against whom you have had indignation these seventy years?*** Intercession was couched in the form of a question. The question focuses on two circumstances that indicate that the angel of Yahweh was disappointed in the report of his subordinates.

First, the commander's intercessory question focuses on the present pitiful condition of God's people. The present peaceful state of the Gentiles and pitiful condition of the restoration community are regarded as evidence that God had withdrawn his compassion from his people. He had not blessed them as he had promised to do in the restoration promises found in Isaiah, Jeremiah and Ezekiel. The turmoil that surrounded Darius' ascension to the throne did not escalate into the international shake-up and overthrow of Persia as promised by Haggai (2:20-23). Whatever the state of international relations (cf. v 11), the situation is viewed negatively if God's people are not prospering. Saints of all ages can find consolation in the fact that the angel/messenger of Yahweh—the Lord Jesus—intercedes for them with similar compassion and fervency.

Second, the intercessory question focuses on the duration of the pitiful condition of God's people. *Seventy years* is not referring to the seventy years predicted by Jeremiah (Jer 25:11; 29:10) because that ended with the fall of Babylon. This is the period of *indignation* that began with the destruction of the temple in 586 and ended with its rebuilding in 515 BC.

F. Answer of Yahweh (1:13):

So Yahweh spoke with good words, even comforting words to the angel who talked with me. Yahweh responded to the intercessory prayer by speaking to the interpreting angel, not the angel of Yahweh since he already knew the answer.[82] *Good words* indicate that the response to the prayer was positive. *Comforting words* is the plural of abundance indicating the abundant comfort which the words brought to Israel. The essence of these comforting words is summarized in the message that follows.

Vision One Amplification
Zechariah 1:14-17

In conjunction with the first vision Zechariah was authorized to deliver his second public discourse.

A. Commissioning of Zechariah (1:14a, b):
1. By God's angel (1:14a): **Then the angel who was speaking to me said...** Neither Yahweh nor the angel of Yahweh directly addresses Zechariah in this vision. His instructions come from the angel who was assigned as his interpreter/guide during the visions.

2. For proclamation (1:14b): **Proclaim this word: Thus says Yahweh of Hosts...** The interpreting angel gave Zechariah a twofold charge. First, he is to preach forcefully God's word. *Proclaim* is lit., "cry." He is to preach or make public in a forceful way the message that God had for his people in response to their discouragement as voiced in the intercessory prayer of the angel of Yahweh. This strong word *proclaim* appears again in v 17.

Second, Zechariah is to preach authoritatively with a "thus says Yahweh." This is the first of 4x Zechariah was told to assure the people that his message came from God. Three times (vv 14, 16, 17) he was to remind the Jews that the covenant God Yahweh was the Lord of Hosts with inexhaustible resources to carry out his pledges to Jerusalem.

B. Yahweh's Love for Zion (1:14c):
I am jealous for Jerusalem and for Zion with a great jealousy. *Jealousy* is ardent love that cannot bear to see the

---

[82]It is also possible that *Yahweh* here is an abbreviation for *the angel of Yahweh* (Deane).

Zechariah 1:1-6:8

object of love injured. The Hebrew sentence is full of devices that underscore the intensity of God's love for Israel.[83] In this sentence Jerusalem probably refers to the physical city, while Zion refers to the people of God. At the time that these words were uttered Jerusalem was still in ruins except for the work that was being done in the temple area.

C. Yahweh's Hostility to Zion's Enemies (1:15):

1. Declaration (1:15a): **and I am greatly displeased with the nations that are at ease.** *Displeased* is a participle, indicating continuous action.[84] *The nations* are those that oppressed Israel. The adjective *at ease* (*šaʾănān*) sometimes has overtones of being careless, wanton and arrogant (Amos 6:1; Isa 32:9, 11; Ps 123:4). It is not that the Gentiles are free from strife that displeases Yahweh; it is the pride, insolence and sense of false security that is the irritant.

2. Explanation (1:15b): **When, on my part, I was a little displeased then they helped for calamity.** *On my part* indicates the presence of the first person pronoun in an emphatic position in the Hebrew. As terrible as the seventy years of desolation were, they indicated only a little displeasure of the Lord toward his people. Yahweh would unleash the fullness of his wrath against the nations.

They *helped for calamity* is rendered "added to the calamity" (NIV); "furthered the calamity" (NASB). The idea is that these nations had exceeded the limitations of God's instruments of chastisement. They had wished to destroy Israel altogether or to oppress them beyond measure (cf. Isa 47:6).

---

[83]Unger points out seven syntactical devices used in this v to express the intensity of God's love for Israel: 1) the command to *cry out* is to call with energy or spirit; 2) the prefixed *thus says Yahweh of Hosts*; 3) the position of the verb first in the clause *jealous am I*; 4) the meaning of the root *qinn 'tî* = a burning passion; 5) the position of the objects *for Jerusalem and for Zion* before the adverbial idea of *with jealousy*; 6) the use of the cognate accusative; and 7) the use of a qualifying adjective modifying the cognate accusative.

[84]Unger points out three ways v 15 indicates the intensity of God's displeasure with the oppressing nations: 1) the cognate accusative in the first position; 2) the use of the adjective to modify the noun in the adverbial accusative; 3) the use of the participle with separate pronoun *I* indicating continuousness of the anger.

It was not the exile itself that moved Yahweh to compassion for his people, for they deserved that punishment. Rather his compassion was stirred by the inhumane treatment the Judeans had received at the hands of their enemies.

D. Yahweh's Plans for Jerusalem (1:16):

1. Holy presence restored (1:16a): **Therefore, thus says Yahweh: I have returned to Jerusalem with compassions.** *Therefore* signals a connection with what precedes. In view of Yahweh's intense jealousy for Israel and his displeasure with their oppressors Yahweh spoke a word of encouragement to his people. *I have returned* might be taken as a prophetic perfect indicating a commitment to be fulfilled in the future. More likely, however, is the view that Yahweh's return to Jerusalem already has been indicated by the return of the exiles of Judah and the commencement of temple reconstruction. *Compassions* is the plural of abundance. This line makes explicit what was symbolically represented in the vision, viz. the standing of the angel/messenger of Yahweh in the midst of the myrtles.

2. Holy house restored (1:16b): **and my house shall be built in it.** *My house* is the temple. It is mentioned before the verb for emphasis. The temple was already under construction. The project, though facing formidable obstacles, would be brought to completion.

3. Holy city restored (1:16c): **And a line shall be stretched forth over Jerusalem (oracle of Yahweh of Hosts).** The city itself as well as the temple will be rebuilt. *The line* is the measuring line essential in larger building projects. It symbolizes reconstruction efforts. Jerusalem underwent reconstruction and repopulation under the leadership of Nehemiah in 445 BC.

E. Yahweh's Choice of Zion (1:17):

Also proclaim further: **Thus says Yahweh of Hosts...** *Proclaim* or cry is the same verb used in v 14. It connotes energy and enthusiastic proclamation. For the fifth time in this ch the messenger formula is used. Zechariah had an ur-

Zechariah 1:1-6:8

gent and welcomed message from Yahweh to deliver to the Judeans. It involved three assurances.

1. Assurance of prosperity (1:17a): **Yet shall my cities overflow with prosperity.** *Cities* overflowing with prosperity (lit., "good") is a promise grounded in Deuteronomy. *Overflow* (r. *pūts*) is elsewhere used of the gushing forth of a fountain (Prov 5:16). It includes economic prosperity and more—thriving families and national well-being (Dt 28:11; 30:9).

The returnees were anything but prosperous. They were oppressed by the people of the land. They had experienced a period of devastating famine. Haggai explained their plight as due to failure to work on the temple. Even after the temple work resumed, however, the workers had not witnessed any dramatic change in their circumstances. The present message from Yahweh must have lifted their spirits and set their sights on a glorious future.

2. Assurance of comfort (1:17b): **And Yahweh will yet comfort Zion.** *Yet* or "again" (*'od*) recalls earlier unspecified occasions when Yahweh comforted his people. *Zion* here is God's people collectively, or Jerusalem personified as a person. God's people will be comforted by the reconstruction of their temple, and the realization that they once again were playing an important role in God's program.

3. Assurance of selection (1:17c): **And he will yet choose Jerusalem.** The implication is that for a period of time God had ceased to designate Jerusalem as his own. That was about to change. God promised *yet* (or "again") to choose Jerusalem for his dwelling place. This is the first of three references in this book to Yahweh's choice of Jerusalem (cf. 2:12; 3:2; cf. Isa 14:1).

Choose is the language of election. The election of Israel remained unimpaired. The Judeans were destined to play an important role in God's program of world redemption. In fact, salvation would come to the world through the Jews (Jn 4:22).

Some see a "prefillment" of these promises in the rebuilding of the temple, the restoration of Jerusalem by Nehemiah, and the prosperity under the Hasmonean princes of the intertestamental period. In the final analysis, however, these promises were fulfilled in the ministry of Christ. Jerusalem was chosen as spot from which the gospel went forth (Laetsch). Believers have come to the heavenly Jerusalem where God himself has chosen to dwell (Heb 12:22f).

Vision Two: Retribution for Nations Zechariah 1:18-21; H 2:1-3[85]

Introduction (1:18a):

And I lifted up my eyes and I saw and behold... These words signal the start of the second vision. On the significance of *behold* see on 1:8. Zechariah *lifted up* his eyes either because the previous vision had produced drowsiness, he was meditating upon what he had seen, or perhaps because the heavens themselves functioned as a screen on which he saw his visions.

A. First Phase of the Vision (1:18b-19):

1. *He observed four horns (1:18b): four horns!* We are not told whether or not these horns were attached to some object, floating loose in the air, or thrusting about. Some think of the horns attached to an altar. The description of what the horns had done, however, suggests that they may have been attached to rampaging animals like bulls. Horns are symbolic of power.[86] They are sometimes explained by the biblical writers as symbolizing the political powers of the world (cf. Dan 8:3; Rev 17:3-12).

The horns were *four* in number. Four is the universal number, associated with what is world-wide in significance. Scripture speaks of the four corners of the earth or land (Isa

---

[85]At this point the ch and v numbers differ in the Hebrew and English texts. Verse division probably goes back to ca. AD 200; but numbers were not assigned to the vv until medieval times. Ch divisions were not standardized in the Hebrew Bible until the early tenth century AD.

[86]Moses compared the strength of the Joseph tribes to the horns of a wild ox (Dt 33:17). When a wild ox was captured his horns were cut off. So Yahweh will cut off all the horns of the wicked, and exalt the horns of the righteous (Ps 75:10; 92:10). Yahweh promises to give the daughter of Zion horns of iron (Mic 4:13).

11:12; Ezek 7:2) and the four winds of heaven.[87] The number hints that God's people face enemies from all directions.

   2. *He inquired about the four horns (1:19a)*: **I asked the angel who was speaking to me, What are these?** As in 1:9 Zechariah addressed a question to the interpreting angel. This is the fourth mention of the interpreting angel in this ch.

   3. *He learned the meaning of the horns (1:19b)*: **He answered me, These are the horns that scattered Judah, Israel and Jerusalem.** The angel does not mention in the interpretation the number four. This suggests that four is not to taken mathematically, but symbolically. Thus those who take the horns to represent the four great empires of Daniel (i.e., Babylon, Persia, Greece and Rome) are probably reading too much into the vision. The horns represent the totality of enemy nations in every direction that had threatened or will threaten God's people.

   The Piel form of *scattered* indicates unmerciful sifting. This is equivalent to going beyond Yahweh's commission referenced in 1:15. *Judah* was the southern kingdom during the divided monarchy period. It was ruled by the descendants of David. The restoration community is probably viewed as new Judah. *Israel* may refer to the old northern kingdom (Cashdan); but more likely *Israel* is either a further definition of Judah (Watts) or an honorable name for the entire nation (Laetsch). The horns had even scattered the population of *Jerusalem*, the city of the Great King. The basic idea is that the crime of the horns had been against Yahweh's people, hence against Yahweh himself.

B. Second Phase of the Vision (1:20-21a):

   1. *He observed four craftsmen (1:20)*: **Then Yahweh showed me four craftsmen.** The vision is initiated by Yahweh, not the interpreting angel. Craftsmen (*chārāšîm*) or workers are artisans that work with wood, stone, or metal. Again the number four is not to be taken mathematically. The point is that the craftsmen are equal to the horns in number.

---

[87]In keeping with this are the several references to the four winds (Jer 49:36; Ezek 37:9; Dan 7:2; 8:8; 11:4; Zech 2:6).

"For every enemy of God's people God has provided a counteracting power adequate to destroy it" (Lange).

2. *He inquired about the craftsmen (1:21a).* **I asked, What are these coming to do?** This is the third question that Zechariah addressed to the interpreting angel. The question implies that the craftsmen were seen in motion as they entered into the scene.

C. **Interpretation of the Horns** (1:21b):

He answered, These are the horns that scattered Judah so that no man raised his head. The thought of v 19 is repeated, except that here the focus is on Judah with no mention of Israel and Jerusalem. The horns represent those, like the Babylonians and their allies, who had taken advantage of the weakness of Judah. The people of Judah were utterly crushed. No one could stand up to resist the horns.

D. **Interpretation of the Craftsmen** (1:21c-e):

Concerning the meaning of the craftsmen the interpreting angel makes three points.

1. Craftsmen terrify the horns (1:21c): **but the craftsmen have come to frighten them.** *Frighten them* (r. *chrd*) is Hiphil, meaning "to throw into panic, to drive away in terror" (cf. Judg 8:12; 2 Sam 17:2). Perhaps the craftsmen were carrying hammers with which to shatter the horns. The craftsmen symbolize the human agencies employed by God to overthrow the powers hostile to God's people.

2. Craftsmen throw down the horns (1:21d): **and throw down these horns of the nations.** *Throw down* (r. *ydh*) is Piel, indicating the violence of the action. For the first time the text makes explicit what has been implied, viz. that the horns represent *the nations* or Gentiles. All opposition to God's people eventually will be overthrown.

3. Craftsmen punish enemies (1:21e): **who lift up a horn against the land of Judah to scatter it.** *Lift up* is a participle, implying on-going or imminent action. Gentile nations have in the past lifted up a horn against God's people. That may happen again. Whenever a Gentile nation does threaten the land of Judah, however, God will use his agents to throw down that horn or power.

Scatter (r. *zrh*) indicates the intention of the hostile nation. Deane suggests the figure of a bull catching his prey on horns, tossing them into the air, scattering them to the wind. A land is scattered when its population is dispersed. The temple builders could continue their work without fear of that work being disrupted by external intervention.

Vision Three:
Jerusalem Protected
Zechariah 2:1-5; H 2:5-9

Introduction (2:1a):
And I lifted up my eyes and behold... The introduction to the third vision is identical to that of the second in 1:18.

A. Man in the Vision (2:1b-2):
1. A surveyor (2:1b): **a man with a measuring line in his hand!** This *man* may be another angel as in 1:8. There is also, however, the intriguing possibility that this "man" is the same "man" seen in the first vision riding upon a red horse, i.e., the angel of Yahweh, the second person of the godhead (1:8, 11). In 6:12 this figure is again called "the man." There we will discover that he is the builder of the true temple of God. Here he appears as the architect and builder of that Jerusalem of the future (Heb 12:22).

The "man" has a building tool in his hand—*a measuring line*. Here the thought of 1:16 that a line shall be stretched over Jerusalem is further developed.[88] Zechariah seems to be building on concepts set forth by Ezekiel who saw a man "whose appearance was like bronze" who was going forth "with a linen cord in his hand and a measuring rod" to measure the site of the Jerusalem that was to be (Ezek 40:3; ch 43). John the Revelator picks up on this symbolism and ap-

---

[88]In 1:16 the word *line* is *qāvh*, while here *measuring line* is *chebhel middāh*; but doubtless the idea expressed in the first vision is further developed here.

Postexilic Prophets

plies it to the Jerusalem which is above—the city whose maker and builder is God (Rev 11:1-2; 21:15-27).

With enemies destroyed or in check, God's people can grow and develop until the time of their final glory.

2. *A question (2:2):* ***I asked, Where are you going? He answered me, To measure Jerusalem, to find out how wide and how long it is.*** This is an interactive visionary experience. Zechariah could talk with those he saw in the vision. The surveyor is measuring Jerusalem in preparation for the reconstruction of the city.

B. Movement in the Vision (2:3):

1. A departure (2:3a): ***And behold the angel that spoke with me went forth.*** The interpreting angel left Zechariah. Neither his direction nor his purpose is stated. *Behold* indicates that Zechariah found his departure unexpected and perhaps shockingly disappointing.

2. An appearance (2:3b): **and another angel was going out to meet him.** Just as the interpreting angel *went forth* (*yōtsēʾ*) from the side of the prophet, so another angel *was going forth* (*yōtsēʾ*) from the side of the surveyor. Apparently the two met somewhere between the surveyor and the prophet.

C. Message in the Vision (2:4-5):

1. Commission (2:4a): **and said to him, Run, tell that young man...** It is not clear who gives this order and to whom. If the analysis of the preceding v is correct, then most likely the angel who went out from the side of the surveyor gives this order to the interpreting angel.[89] The term *young man* (*naʿar*) denotes a male from infancy (Ex 2:6) to the prime of life. It occasionally is used for a servant without reference to age. The term is inappropriate to use of angels who do not pass through stages of growth as do humans. Some regard the surveyor as the young man, but this only confuses the vision. The *young man* is probably Zechariah (Pusey;

---

[89] So Deane and Laetsch. Cashdan, however, thinks the interpreting angel gave the order to the other angel.

Zechariah 1:1-6:8

Keil; Deane).[90] He is commissioned to convey three promises to the remnant.

2. *Promise #1 (2:4b):* **Jerusalem shall be inhabited as open regions by reason of the multitude of men and cattle therein.** Future Jerusalem will be vast. *Open regions* ($p^e r\bar{a}z\bar{o}th$) is an area in which there is nothing to circumscribe the inhabitants—nothing to prevent them from spreading out in all directions (cf. Ezek 38:11; Esth 9:19). The *cattle* represent the possessions and wealth of the city. Jerusalem will be so extensive that walls will no longer be able to contain its inhabitants. This prediction builds upon several earlier depictions of the burgeoning population of the Jerusalem to come (e.g., Isa 49:19-20). Messianic Jerusalem will resemble a succession of "villages" on the open plains (Baron). The fulfillment is not to be found in physical Jerusalem (Wright) because the walls of physical Jerusalem were rebuilt under Nehemiah. The reference is not to some imagined millennial Jerusalem (Unger), but the messianic Jerusalem, the church of Christ (Heb 12:22).[91]

3. *Promise #2 (2:5a):* **And as for me, I will be (oracle of Yahweh) a wall of fire around it...** Future Jerusalem will be secure. Though inhabited as "villages" on an open plain with no visible fortifications messianic Jerusalem will be protected (cf. Isa 26:1). The messianic kingdom (the church) does not need walls of stone, for God himself will be her wall, a fiery wall that consumes all who attack. He will be a perfect defense for all within messianic Zion, and lethal obstruction to all who would attack her. *As for me* conveys the emphasis on the first person pronoun in the Hebrew. In the short run Nehemiah will build walls to protect Jerusalem; in

---

[90] Others think: the young man is the man with the measuring line (Wright; Perowne; Cashdan). But what indication is there that the surveyor was making a mistake in attempting to define the limits of what would be unlimited? Others think the young man represents the average person of the day. He believes Jerusalem will be rebuilt, but his concept of the city of God is poured into too small a mold (Leupold).

[91] Renewed national welfare and prosperity are prophetic ways of depicting the glorious messianic age. See Isa 54:1; Jer 31:27; Ezek 36:10-11; 37-38; Hos 1:10-11.

the age to come Yahweh will provide the protection by his very presence within Jerusalem.

4. *Promise #3 (2:5b):* **and glory I will be in its midst.** Future Jerusalem will be glorious. Yahweh will be Zion's protection from without; but he will also be her glory from within (cf. Isa 60:19; Rev 21:23). Christ is present in his church. God's providential care for the church reflects his glory. 2 Thess 1 speaks of Christ returning to be glorified in his saints.

Vision Three Amplified
Zechariah 2:6-13; H 2:10-17

The amplification of the third vision takes the form of exhortations with accompanying explanations. In this oracle Yahweh cites four reasons why the captives in Babylon should flee as soon as possible.

A. **Exhortation #1** (2:6):
1. *Presentation (2:6a):* **Ho! ho! Flee from the land of the north (oracle of Yahweh).** *Ho! Ho!* is an onomatopoetic interjection employed to arrest attention.[92] *Flee* (r. *nûs*) does not always connote fleeing from oppression or danger.[93] There is no hint in the text that those addressed were in any immediate danger. *Land of the north* is the region of Assyria and Babylon. Geographically, Assyria and Babylonia were northeast of Palestine. This region is called the land of the north because the normal invasion route against Palestine was from the north.

The land of the north was no longer a threat to the people of God as it had been in the days of Jeremiah. Therefore, Zechariah is probably not thinking of Babylon geographically, but symbolically. The land of the north, source of oppression and grief to the OT people of God, symbolizes the world. God is calling for people to leave the world and come

---
[92]Rendered *Come, come* (NIV); *Ho there* (NASB); *Up, up* (NRSV); *Away, away* (NJPS).
[93]See use of *nûs* in Dt 34:7; 2 Kgs 9:3; Song 2:17; Isa 35:10.

Zechariah 1:1-6:8

to messianic Zion. People flee from Babylon spiritually and psychologically (cf. Isa 48:20; 52:11; Jer 51:6, 45).

The oracular formula is used twice in this one v. On the significance of this formula, see on 1:3.

2. *Explanation (2:6b):* **For as the four winds of the heavens I have spread you abroad (oracle of Yahweh).** *For* (*kî*) introduces the reason people are urged to flee from the land of the north. *As the four winds* denotes the four points of the compass. *Spread abroad* (r. *prs*) in the Piel almost always means "to spread out."[94] Thus Yahweh announces broad geographical expansion. This is a further development of the Zion-without-walls motif of v 4.[95]

B. Exhortation #2 (2:7):

Ho, O Zion, escape you who dwell with the daughter of Babylon. As in the previous v, *ho* indicates an urgent appeal. *Zion* in this v refers to God's people who are dispersed throughout the world. *Escape* (r. *mlt*) is Niphal fem. imperative. Babylon is no place for Zion to dwell. *Daughter of Babylon* personifies the population of Babylon. In this context *daughter of Babylon* is probably equivalent to *the land of the north* in the previous v.

Babylon recently had been involved in two successive rebellions against the Persians—one in 522 and the other in 521 BC. Darius and one of his generals had dealt harshly with the residents. Perhaps the hardships during these wars form the background of what Zechariah is urging. A more devastating assault was administered by Xerxes in 482 BC when he punished a third rebellion by Babylon. Zechariah recognized that people who live in physical or metaphorical Babylon get caught up in the turmoil that surrounds that place.

After 586 BC *Babylon* stood for all lands of the exile and was not confined to the geographical area known as "Babylon" (Baldwin). Zechariah's audience probably understood him to be issuing a call to Jews living in the far corners of the Persian Empire to return to Jerusalem. The appeal of this unit,

---

[94]Ps 68:14 ("scatter") is the single exception.
[95]Promises of territorial expansion also appear in Mic 7:11; Isa 54:2. They are built on the original promise to Abraham in Gn 22:17.

however, is even broader. Babylon is the world that opposes Zion. God is always calling his people out of the world. Cf. Rev 18:4-8.

C. Word of Explanation (2:8-9):

A much longer word of explanation is attached to the second exhortation.

1. Solemn utterance (2:8a): **For thus says Yahweh of Hosts...** For (*kî*) introduces the reason for the summons to escape Babylon. Yahweh, commander of all armies in heaven and on earth, has issued a proclamation that necessitates a hasty departure from Babylon.

2. Visitation of God's enemies (2:8a): **After glory he has sent me unto the nations that spoil you.** The speaker appears to be the angel or messenger of Yahweh who elsewhere is identified as Yahweh himself. *After glory* means "in pursuit of glory." *Glory* means to vindicate and to display the glory of God both in destroying the enemies of his people and in delivering his people from their oppression. *He has sent me* refers to the mystery of mysteries—how Yahweh the Father dispatched Yahweh the Son on his mission into this world. In the Nazareth synagogue Jesus read Isa 61:1-2a—"Yahweh has anointed me to preach good news...*he has sent me*."

Apparently the angel of Yahweh is sent to get glory or honor over the heathen by conquering them.[96] This v anticipates the NT revelation of the Father sending the Son to glorify him (Jn 17:4). The verb *spoil* or "plunder" (NASB) is a participle, indicating the continual plundering of God's people by the nations. The nations that were the most implacable foes of God's people must confront the angel of Yahweh.

3. Vindication of God's people (2:8c): **because the one who touches you touches the pupil of his [God's] eye.** *Because* (*kî*) introduces the reason for God's intervention in the human scene. *Touches* (r. *ngʿ*) has a hostile connotation in this context. *Pupil* is lit., "gate."[97] The gate of the eye could

---

[96]Baldwin (*TOTC*, 109) renders *'achar kābhôd* "with heaviness," i.e., with a burdensome message for the nations (cf. Ecc 12:2; Ps 73:24).
[97]Similar to the common Hebrew expression "the little man of the eye" (Dt 32:10; Ps 17:8), or "daughter of the eye" (Ps 17:8; Lam 2:18.

be the pupil; or it could refer to the opening of the eyelids, which the ancients may have viewed as the entrance to the eye. With bold anthropomorphism the text refers to his, i.e., God's, eye.[98] The point is that God is extremely sensitive to any harm done to his people. It was Moses who first used this eye metaphor to express God's tender compassion for his people (Dt 32:10). David applied this same figure to himself (Ps 17:8).

4. *Vanquishing of hostile nations (2:9):* **For behold I am about to wave my hand against them and they shall be a spoil for those that served them; and you shall know that Yahweh of Hosts has sent me.** In this v there is a divine action, a shocking reversal, and a certain conclusion.

First, Yahweh makes a dramatic gesture. On *behold*, see on 1:8. The angel of Yahweh has only to wave his hand in a threatening gesture and his enemies shrink with fear. *Wave my hand* is similar to modern "shake my fist." This v is a further development of the protection of Zion motif symbolized by the wall of fire in 2:5. The verb (r. *nūph*) is repeated from Isa 11:15 and 19:16 where similar prophecies of deliverance and intimidation of enemies are found.

Second, as a result of the divine gesture there is a shocking reversal. Zechariah builds on a prediction found in Isa 14:1-2. The hostile nations will be a *spoil* or plunder to former servants. The statement could be taken in a general sense, i.e., powerful nations will be overturned and thereafter plundered by former subject peoples. Those in Zechariah's day had witnessed the subjugation of Babylon, the former mistress of the world.

Those that served them, however, probably refers to God's people. This prediction came true only in a spiritual sense when nations were converted to the true faith in the NT age (Deane). The theme that Israel's dominion expands over Gentile nations in the messianic age is a major theme in OT prophecy. Such passages are applied to conversion by NT teachers (cf. Acts 15:15-18 citing Amos 9:11-12).

---

[98] According to Jewish tradition the original reading was "the pupil of MY eye."

Postexilic Prophets

Third, the divine gesture and shocking reversal of circumstances lead to a certain conclusion. *You shall know that* has been called the recognition formula. *Know* refers to experimental knowledge. The mission of the angel of Yahweh[99] in the invisible realm will be as evident as fallen trees are evidence of the invisible wind. When once hostile Gentile nations become servants of Zion then God's people will understand the angel of Yahweh has been at work. This angel or messenger is the representative of *Yahweh of Hosts.* On the divine title, see on 1:3.

D. Exhortation #3 (2:10-12):

1. Call for joy (2:10a): **Shout and be glad, O daughter of Zion.** Anticipating the announcement of Yahweh's coming, God's people are told to rejoice. *Daughter of Zion* is the population of Zion personified. Since physical Jerusalem was uninhabited at this time, the reference must be to Zion as a name for God's people collective. So God's people are designated as a beloved daughter. Four reasons are given for the call for joy.

2. Promise of Yahweh's coming (2:10b): **For, behold, I am about to come and I will dwell in the midst of you (oracle of Yahweh).** *For* (*kî*) introduces the reason for the joy. On the meaning of *behold,* see on 1:8. Zechariah repeats the declaration of Messiah in Ps 40:7 (cf. Heb 10:7). The first person pronouns now refer to Yahweh, as indicated by the oracular formula. Since, however, Yahweh and the angel/messenger of Yahweh are one no change in speaker has occurred.

Yahweh will *dwell* (r. *škn*) in the midst of his people. God is the designated subject of this verb 43x in OT, 4x in this book. God dwells on Mount Zion (Ps 74:2) and among his people (Ex 25:8). On several occasions some symbolic representation of the divine presence is said to do the dwelling: the glory (Ex 24:16; Ps 85:9); the cloud (Nm 9:17, 18, 22; 10:12). The *w*ord used here connotes the idea of nearness and closeness. God once dwelled in the tabernacle (Ex 25:8); then in the temple (1 Kgs 6:13). Ezekiel foresaw his return to

---

[99] Others think Zechariah is the speaker in the recognition formula. He ties his call and commission to the fulfillment of his prophecies.

Zechariah 1:1-6:8

the temple (Ezek 43:2, 4). But this v does not directly connect Yahweh's dwelling with the temple currently being built. The fulfillment of this promise was in the incarnation—when God came in the person of his Son to dwell in the midst of his people. On *oracle of Yahweh,* see on 1:3.

3. *Promise of Gentile conversion (2:11a):* **Many nations will join themselves to Yahweh in that day and will become my people.** *Many nations* probably refers to and explains the nations mentioned in v 8—nations which become plunder in v 9. *Join themselves* (r. *lwh* in Niph.) could also be translated as a passive as in NIV. In either case a mass conversion of Gentiles is indicated. This term is used to describe a military alliance (Ps 83:3), a conjugal joining of husband to wife (Gn 29:34), and the joining of Levites with Aaron for tabernacle service (Nm 18:2-4).

The idea of Gentiles being joined with Jews in a glorious future kingdom echoes a promise that first appeared in Isa 14:1. Such converts are assured that they will not be separated from God's covenant (Isa 56:3-6). The same verb is used of Jews who will join themselves to Yahweh in an everlasting (new) covenant (Jer 50:5). So in each case the r. *lwh* points to a voluntary, solemn and permanent commitment.

Become my people indicates that converted Gentiles become part of the Israel of God. Clearly then the plundering of the nations in v 9 is spiritual and not the result of military conquest. This is further amplification of the promise of v 4 that Jerusalem will be inhabited without walls because of the multitude of people.

Those who first heard these words may have understood Zechariah to say that there would be a massive influx of Gentiles into the postexilic community. The text, however, does not require such an interpretation. Furthermore, history does not indicate that any such influx took place. In the church, however, there is the merging of Jew and Gentile just as is envisioned here (Eph 2:11-16). The existence of the church confirms the angel's words.

4. *Promise of a special relationship (2:11b):* **And I shall dwell in the midst of you.** The promise of v 10b is re-

Postexilic Prophets

peated for emphasis as well as assurance. The speaker clearly is Yahweh.

5. *Promise of verification (2:11c):* **and you shall know that Yahweh of Hosts has sent me.** The recognition formula is repeated from 2:9b where the conquest of hostile nations validates the message and mission of the angel of Yahweh. Here it is the coming of Yahweh in the person of Messiah that validates the message and mission of the angel of Yahweh. The interchange of pronouns referring to the angel of Yahweh and Yahweh anticipates the relationship between the Father and the Son. One might argue that the angel of Yahweh is the second person of the godhead.

6. *Promise of divine election (2:12):* **Yahweh will inherit Judah as his portion in the holy land and will again choose Jerusalem.** *Inherit* (r. *nchl*) often denotes possession by right of succession. This is the only place in the OT where Yahweh is said to *inherit Judah*. *Portion* (*cheleq*) denotes a share of something, i.e., ownership. God will take possession of the true Judah, the church, as his heritage (Laetsch).

This is the only place where the term *holy land* is used in Scripture. The OT land or kingdom of Israel had been defiled and polluted. Messiah's land or kingdom will be holy, for only those who have been set apart by gospel cleansing can dwell in his land. The phrase *holy land*, then, is not restricted to physical Palestine. Cf. the expressions "holy hill" (Ps 2:6; 15:1) or "holy mountain" (Ps 48:2; 99:9). *Holy* (r. *qdš*) denotes separation from the common and profane. Wherever God reveals himself, there is the holy land.

Yahweh chooses Jerusalem as well as Judah. There is a rich tradition in OT that God chose Jerusalem as his special place of habitation.[100] Eventually Jerusalem was rejected and handed over to the Babylonians. The city will again be chosen. All the decisive religious events of the future were to take place in physical Jerusalem. This passage, however, envisions a greater Jerusalem—one that cannot be enclosed with walls. Physical Jerusalem is but a shadow of that heavenly Jerusalem portrayed by the apostle (Heb 12:22).

---

[100]E.g., 1 Kgs 11:32, 36; 14:21; 2 Kgs 21:7; 23:27; Ps 132:13; etc.

E. **Exhortation #4** (2:13)

1. Presentation (2:13a): ***Be silent, all flesh, before Yahweh...*** *Be silent* (*has*) is essentially equivalent to the English "hush," or "keep your mount shut." In the light of the promises made in the first three visions complaints about injustice and God's inactivity should cease. *All flesh* must include both Judeans and Gentiles. The phrase also underscores the weakness and impotence of man in the presence of the Almighty.

2. Explanation (2:13b): ***for he is aroused out of his holy habitation.*** Yahweh is *aroused* (r. *'ūr* in Niphal) when he is about to become actively engaged in the affairs of mankind (cf. Ps 44:23). The arrogance and abuse of his people by the Gentiles had moved him to respond. *His holy habitation* must be heaven, since the earthly temple had not yet been rebuilt. The expression was introduced by Moses (Dt 26:15). It was used in Ps 68:6 and Jer 25:30. These words were an encouragement for the people of God to be patient and to wait in awe for the great day (Laetsch). At the same time these words are a warning to the nations that God was coming to execute judgment upon them. Yahweh was getting ready to fulfill all his promises and threats.

Central Vision Encouragement to the Priest Zechariah 3:1-10

Unlike visions 1-3, vision 4 has nothing mysterious to arouse the attention of the prophet. There is no explanation from an interpreting angel. The vision is explained as it unfolds. The setting of the vision is probably the Jerusalem temple.[101] The vision depicts a scene of legal controversy.

---

[101] Others locate the vision in the heavenly temple or in the city gate where trials were conducted.

Joshua Accused
Zechariah 3:1

A. His Appearance (3:1a):
Then he showed me Joshua the high priest... The subject of the verb *showed* is not indicated. It could be Yahweh, or the interpreting angel. On the other hand, the verb could be taken impersonally and rendered as a passive, *I was shown*. Joshua or Jeshua was the current high priest, having served in that office for the past sixteen years (Ezra 3:2). The use of the official title *the high priest* suggests that Joshua represents not only the priesthood, but the entire nation (Laetsch; Unger; Leupold). His condition is Israel's condition; his acquittal is Israel's acquittal. Words addressed to him are also addressed to the people.

B. His Position (3:1b):
Standing before the angel of Yahweh... Apparently Zechariah saw Joshua rendering priestly service in the temple (Unger; Laetsch).[102] This view is supported 1) by the use of the verb *stand* which often points to ministerial service (Dt 10:8; Ezek 44:15); and 2) the mention of his garments, which implies that he was engaged in official duties at some consecrated spot. The scene may have taken place before the altar (Deane). While the temple was only under construction, pious Judeans could imagine what the full restoration of that facility would entail. On the identification of the angel of Yahweh, see on 1:11.

C. His Adversary (3:1c):
1. His identity (3:1c): ***And Satan...*** Some take *sātān* as a common noun meaning "the accuser" and not as a proper name. They propose that the reference is to a member of the heavenly court who was acting as prosecuting angel (Cashdan). The noun has the article. Sometimes in Hebrew proper names are formed by attaching a definite article to a common

---
[102]Cashdan, Perowne and Baldwin think Joshua was standing in a judicial sense as a defendant (cf. Nm 27:2; 1 Kgs 3:16; Nm 35:12). It is not stated, however, that Yahweh was sitting upon a throne of judgment.

noun. It is probably best to take the reference to be to Satan (Unger; Laetsch).[103]

2. *His position (3:1d)*: **standing at his right hand...** Satan stands at Joshua's right hand which may have been the usual position of an accuser (cf. Ps 109:6). How and why Satan was permitted by God to appear before him is one of the mysteries that Scripture does not resolve for us.

3. *His purpose (3:1e)*: **to accuse him.** The verb *accuse* comes from the same root as the name Satan, which creates a neat paronomasia or play on words. So, lit., *Satan* stood there to *satanize* Joshua, i.e., to do what Satan was best at doing, viz. accusing God's people (Rev 12:10). In this scene Satan is an enemy who is resisting Joshua's efforts to intercede for his people. Satan objects before the angel of Yahweh that Joshua was not qualified to offer up intercession both because of his own personal sin (symbolized by the filthy garments) and because of the transgressions of the people whose burden he bore.

Joshua Defended
Zechariah 3:2

A. **Accuser Reprimanded** (3:2a, b):

In response to the accusations against Joshua (and by implication, Israel) a double rebuke is administered to Satan.

1. Initial rebuke (3:2a): **And Yahweh said unto Satan, Yahweh rebuke you, O Satan!** The text does not reveal the actual accusation of Satan. Perhaps this rebuke is administered even before he spoke. Yahweh utters the rebuke, and administers it in his own name.[104] Baldwin has this cogent comment: "When the Lord rebukes there is no gainsaying His word." The power of the rebuke is enhanced in that it was spoken directly to Satan. He is addressed by name.

---

[103] On the doctrine of Satan in the OT see Appendix B in Perowne's commentary on Zechariah.

[104] According to the Syriac version, it is the angel of Yahweh who is speaking. It is not uncommon for Scripture to interchange Yahweh and the angel of Yahweh.

Postexilic Prophets

2. Repeated rebuke (3:2b): **Yea, Yahweh rebuke you...** Repetition underscores the seriousness of the rebuke. The Judge himself pleads the cause of his people. The verb *rebuke* (r. *g'r*) means "to reprove;" but when applied to God this verb includes the idea of the power to suppress.[105] When Jesus rebuked the demonic spirit he departed out of his victim.

B. Basis of the Reprimand (3:2c, d):

The text sets forth two reasons for the stern reprimand of Satan: Yahweh's immutable choice (3:2c) and Israel's marvelous salvation (3:2d).

1. Yahweh's immutable choice (3:2c): **the Chooser of Jerusalem!** In the repetition of the reprimand of Satan Yahweh began to set forth the reason for it, viz. God's choice of Jerusalem. This first basis of reprimand looks forward to what God had in store for Jerusalem. To criticize the chosen is to impugn the wisdom and foresight of the Chooser.

Chooser of Jerusalem is a participle + the article, i.e., the one who chooses or has chosen Jerusalem. This confirms the conclusion reached in v 1 that the vision has something to do with the remnant as a whole, not just Joshua personally. Twice earlier Zechariah had declared that Yahweh will yet choose Jerusalem (1:17; 2:12). As both a physical city and as a designation of God's people Jerusalem will yet play a significant role in the plan of God. Therefore, neither Satan nor any of his earthly agents should regard the present pathetic condition of the City of the Great King as indicating that the Judeans were still under God's wrath. What God has chosen let not Satan or man regard lightly. Humble circumstances are no barrier to future glory.

2. Israel's marvelous salvation (3:2d): **Is not this a brand plucked out of the fire?** The second reason for Satan's reprimand is based on what God already had done for his people. A *brand* (piece of charred wood) plucked out of the fire is a metaphor for deliverance from total destruction. *This* is a masculine singular demonstrative pronoun. It could refer

---

[105] Ps 9:5; 18:15; 80:16; 106:9; 119:21; Isa 17:13; Nah 1:4; Mal 2:3.

to Joshua personally, or to the people of Judah as in "this people."[106]

Proof that Joshua and the people he represents stand in God's favor is seen in the fact that they had been delivered from the fire of exile where they might well have been destroyed (cf. Amos 4:11). Therefore, neither Joshua nor the people he represented should be the victim of malicious slander. The principle is that those who have been saved by God from judgment are not subject to condemnation by anyone (cf. Rom 8:1, 33, 34).

Joshua Pardoned
Zechariah 3:3-5

A. Cleansing Needed (3:3):

Now as for Joshua, he was dressed in filthy clothes as he stood before the angel. Although Satan's verbal accusation against Joshua is not recorded in this vision, this v supplies a clue as to the kind of vitriol which it must have contained. Satan might well have been arguing for the complete repudiation of Israel as the priestly nation. *Filthy* (*tsô'îm*) points to excrement-soiled garments that were offensively smelly as well as dirty. The garments are symbolic of sins of the entire nation (cf. Isa 64:6). *Dressed* is a participle, indicating that the moral and spiritual filthiness was a continuing problem. *The angel* is the angel of Yahweh as in 3:1. On the significance of the participle *standing*, see on 3:1. This v adds to the picture painted in v 1. It gives the reason Satan was accusing Joshua (and his people) of being unqualified to enter into the presence of the holy God.

B. Cleansing Ordered (3:4a):

And he answered and spoke to those who were standing before him, Take off his filthy clothes. Joshua was unable to answer. He was aware of his unworthiness. Only God can remove our sin and guilt. The speaker in this v is the angel of

---

[106]The phrase "this people" appears 78x in OT, 3x in this book, 2x in Haggai.

Postexilic Prophets

Yahweh. He addresses the attendant angels who wait upon him. These attendant angels are mentioned for the first time. On the *filthy clothes*, see on the previous v.

C. Symbolism Explained (3:4b):
And unto him he said: Behold, I cause your iniquity to pass from you... The removal of the garments is symbolic of the remission of sins or cleansing. *Iniquity* is the whole sinful disposition which leads to distress and guilt. Removal of the filthy garments silenced the accuser. The most holy Judge had done the unthinkable. By an act of his sovereign grace he had removed the guilt of his people.

D. Glory Restored (3:4c-5):
1. Promise of the angel (3:4c): **and I will clothe you with festal garments.** *Clothe* (Hiph. inf. absolute) indicates the continuation of the action of the previous finite verb.[107] *Festal garments* are lit. "garments that are put off or taken off" before going to work; hence, a precious, costly, beautiful garment. Undoubtedly the *holy garments* of the high priest (Ex 28) are intended. These garments are symbolic of righteousness and glory (cf. Isa 61:10). The Aaronic priesthood has been reinstated in anticipation of the completion of the temple and the resumption of temple services. This promise illustrates the principle of Rom 8:30, "those whom he justified he also glorified" (cf. 2 Cor 3:18).

2. Petition of the prophet (3:5a): **Then I said: Let them place a clean miter upon his head.** Zechariah is so excited by what he sees that he gives vent to his feelings. The *miter* or turban was the headgear of the high priest.[108] The golden plate on the front of that miter was called the holy crown (Ex 29:6; Lv 8:9).

---

[107] On this function of the infinitive absolute in later Hebrew, see GK §113 z. There is no need to follow the lead of LXX which suggests the reading "and they clothed him" or "let them clothe him."

[108] The priest's headdress is called *mitsnephet,* while here the word is *tsānîp,* a word elsewhere associated with fine apparel. Clearly the high priestly turban is intended. Perhaps the implication is that even greater glory will be added to the reinstated priesthood.

3. Implementation of the order (3:5b): **So they set a clean miter upon his head and clothed him with garments.** *They* must be the servant angels who stood before the angel of Yahweh (v 4). These angels are part of the trappings of the vision, not part of its symbolism. The request of the prophet is immediately carried out apparently even before the other garments were completely in place. This action signifies complete reinstatement of Joshua in the high priestly function. The *miter* (*tsānîp*) was the headdress of princely persons and kings.[109] It declared the priest to be *Holy to Yahweh*, i.e., qualified to intercede for the people. The garments with which Joshua was clothed are those special garments referenced in the preceding v.

By way of application, one thinks of the crown of glory that completes the Christian's process of glorification (1 Pet 5:4; 2 Tim 4:8).

4. Approval of the whole transaction (3:5c): **while the angel of Yahweh stood by.** He was watching the transaction, sanctioning and directing what was being done. On the identification of the angel of Yahweh, see on 1:11.

Fourth Vision Amplified
Zechariah 3:6-10

A. Covenant with the Priesthood (3:6-7):

1. Transition (3:6-7a): **And the angel of Yahweh solemnly testified unto Joshua, saying, 7 Thus says Yahweh of Hosts says:** The verb (r. *'ûd*) is rendered "gave this charge" (NIV) or "charged" (NJPS); "admonished" (NASB); "assured" (NRSV). The term is intended to express the solemnity and importance of the charge about to be made.[110] This v marks the transition from the symbolic vision to the practical application to Joshua. The solemn testimony to Joshua is introduced with the messenger formula. On the angel of Yahweh, see on 1:11. On the title Yahweh of Hosts, see on 1:3. This is the seventh use of the messenger formula in this book.

---

[109]McComiskey (*MPEEC*, 1074) thinks these figures represent the agencies by which God expunges guilt, viz. the Levitical sacrifices and rituals.
[110]Cf. 1 Kgs 2:42 where the term is used of Solomon's warning to Shimei.

2. *Two conditions (3:7b)*: **If in my ways you walk and if my charge you keep...** Re-instatement of the priesthood and nation symbolized by the change of garments is conditioned on obedience—personal and national.

The first requirement is that Joshua must *walk* in God's ways, i.e., observe God's commandments governing his life. Word order emphasizes *in my ways*. The high priest was expected to model the holiness that he represented by his garb and by the rituals he performed.

The second requirement is that Joshua must keep God's charge, i.e., be faithful in his ministerial duties. Word order places emphasis on *my charge* (*mišmeret*). To "keep the charge" is an idiom used at least 27x of an office or function, especially that of a priest or Levite. The word connotes certain responsibilities to be performed, certain rules to be kept, certain traditions to maintain.

3. *Three-fold blessing (3:7c)*: **then you will judge my house and will also keep my courts and I will give you free access among these who stand by.** If Joshua meets the two-fold requirement put forth in v 7 he will be granted a three-fold blessing.

First, Joshua will be given the privilege of superintending the temple of God. *Judge* (r. *dîn*) is used in the sense of rule or govern. *My house* may be used metaphorically of God's people (cf. Nm 12:7). If this be the sense, then Joshua will function as the supreme judge in all matters of controversy among the people (Dt 17:8-10). Probably, however, *my house* refers to the physical temple. Joshua will rule and order divine worship in the temple, i.e., he will govern the ministers of the sanctuary. Formerly kings had assumed a large measure of authority over worship. Now the rights of the high priest will be indisputable. This promise assumes the successful completion of the building project currently underway.

The second blessing is that of authority. If faithful to the Lord, Joshua will *keep my courts*. This line confirms the interpretation given to *my house* in the previous line. Joshua will have the authority to guard the temple courts from being desecrated by ungodliness and frivolity, idolatry or anything that defiled (2 Chr 23:19).

Zechariah 1:1-6:8

The third blessing is access to the presence of God. *Free access* is lit., "walking places." *These who stand by* must be a reference to the serving angels mentioned in vv 4-5. So the essence of this promise is that Joshua will have direct communication with God, like the angels. The glory of the future priesthood will exceed that of previous generations of priests who only had access to the Most Holy Place once a year. Thus Joshua will have access through intercessory prayer to the very throne of God himself. The ultimate fulfillment of this promise may be in Christ, Joshua's ministerial successor. The priesthood of messianic Joshua/Jesus has the right to enter boldly before the throne of grace (Heb 4:14-16).

B. Coming of the Messianic Priest (3:8-9a).

1. Call for attention (3:8a): **Hear now, O Joshua the high priest, you and your fellows that sit before you...** Yahweh himself is speaker. The summons to hear kindles expectation of further information about the significance of the vision just described. Once again Joshua is addressed as *the high priest* to remind the reader that it is in his official capacity that Joshua is addressed. Joshua is addressed along with *your fell*ows or "friends" (NASB) or "colleagues" (NJPS), i.e., associate priests (cf. NIV).

Sit before you may indicate that the associate priests were merely spectators in the vision just described. On the other hand, *sit before* is used of pupils sitting before a teacher (1 Kgs 4:38; Ezek 33:31; cf. 1 Sam 19:20). Perhaps Joshua was conducting training sessions for the priests in anticipation of the restoration of temple ministries.

2. Sign of Messiah's coming (3:8b): **for they[111] are men that are a marvelous sign.** In v 3 Joshua individually was declared to be a *sign* standing for the nation that God had snatched like a brand from the fire. Now Joshua's colleagues are said to be *men that are a marvelous sign.*[112] Here the term

---

[111] In the Hebrew the pronoun appears at the end of the clause, probably for emphasis: they, too, are men of a sign.

[112] *A marvelous sign* (*mōphēt*) is rendered "symbolic of things to come" (NIV); "a symbol" (NASB); "an omen of things to come" (NRSV); "a sign" (NJPS).

Postexilic Prophets

refers to men who arouse the attention of the people to a coming event. Cf. Isa 8:18. The OT priests were types prefiguring the NT high priesthood and royal priesthood.[113] The restored priesthood is a sign of the advent of the Messiah. The purified priesthood is typical of greater purification to come.

3. *Messiah as Servant (3:8c):* **for behold I am about to bring my servant...** *For* introduces the reason Joshua and his fellows are such types. They foreshadow the eternal priest who will by his vicarious suffering obtain full forgiveness for mankind. *Behold* is an attention getting device that conveys excitement (cf.1:8). This is the only use of the word *servant* (*'ebhed*) in this book. The phrase *my servant* is used in conjunction with ten named individuals.[114] Without a proper name attached, the phrase is used 4x in Isaiah to refer to a coming Servant par excellence who will die for the sins of mankind (42:1; 49:3, 6; 52:13). The NT understands this Servant to be Christ (Mt 12:18; Acts 8:32-35). He is called *my servant* because of his willing, patient, perfect obedience to his Father (Laetsch).

4. *Messiah as Shoot (3:8d):* **the Shoot.** The term *tsemach* is translated "Branch" in the standard English versions. The term refers to a small shoot poking its head up from the soil, not a large branch of a tree. *Shoot* was used messianically by Isaiah (4:2) and Jeremiah (23:5; 33:15) of a royal Davidic figure.[115] Ancient interpreters, both Jewish and Christian, agree in explaining the *Shoot* as the Messiah. In this passage the term *tsemach* does not have the article. It appears to be a proper name.[116] *Shoot* points to the miraculous origin of Messiah and to the mystery of his person as one implanted by God in the world.

---

[113] "They are men who foreshadow some future events, whose persons, office, duties, typify and look forward to good things to come" (Deane).

[114] Abraham (Gn 26:24); Moses (Nm 12:7 + 5x); Caleb (Nm 14:24); David (2 Sam 3:18 + 17x); Job (Job 1:8 + 3x); Isaiah (Isa 20:3); Eliakim (1 Sam 22:20); Nebuchadnezzar (Jer 25:9 + 2x); Zerubbabel (Hag 2:23); and Jacob = the nation Israel (Isa 41:8-9 +10).

[115] Isa 11:1 uses the word *netser* for the Messiah, which appears to be synonymous with *tsemech* used here.

[116] "If this well-known prophetic epithet of the coming of the Messiah was not a proper name by the time of Zechariah, he makes it one" (Pusey).

5. Messiah as Stone (3:9a): **For behold, the Stone which I have set before Joshua. There are seven eyes on that one stone. Behold, I will engrave the engraving of it.** *For* introduces further explanation of the Shoot-Servant of the previous v. On the meaning of *behold* see on 1:8. Joshua is told to focus his attention on a stone that presumably was placed before him at some point in the vision. This action indicates that *the Stone* (*hā'ebhen*) was a rather large object, not a small gem stone as imagined by some commentators.

That the stone is another symbol for the coming Messiah seems clear enough.[117] By Zechariah's day *Stone* was quite familiar as a messianic title (Isa 28:16; Ps 118:22; cf. Mt 21:42; Eph 2:20). Three points are made concerning the Stone in this vision.

First, the words *upon one stone* suggest that the stone is unique. There was but one stone before Joshua. It was marked in a most unusual way. This suggests that the coming Messiah was to be absolutely unique.

Second, the stone was covered with eyes. *Eyes* is the traditional and likely rendering of (*'ēnāyim*).[118] The eyes were engraved *on* the Stone, they were not looking *at* the Stone.[119] *Seven* eyes are symbols of perfect intelligence or omniscience. The number seven recalls Messiah's sevenfold anointing by the Holy Spirit foreseen by Isaiah (11:2). John the Revelator seems to build on these passages when he depicts the Lamb which had been slain having seven horns (omnipotence) and seven eyes (omniscience) which are the seven spirits of God (Rev 5:6).

---

[117] Leupold lists nine interpretations of the stone. For example, it is the capstone of the temple (Cashdan), the spiritual temple or church (Leupold, Laetsch, Deane), a symbol of the current building project (McComiskey) or the Messiah himself (Unger, Wright, Pusey).

[118] The term is rendered "facets" (NRSV; Cashdan) representing the beauty of the stone; but a stone with seven facets would be difficult to use either in the foundation or as a cap stone in the temple. Others render "fountains" (Baldwin), symbolizing cleansing; but *'ayin* never occurs elsewhere as a metaphor for cleaning.

[119] Others think the eyes are God's eyes which are directed toward the stone in watchful care.

Third, the Stone will be engraved. Prophetic excitement escalates with the use of another *behold* (see on 1:8). *I will engrave the engraving of it.* The pronoun refers to God. The text does not indicate the nature of the *engraving* on the Stone. The engraving is something God does to the Stone, or at least permits to be done. The reference is not to the polishing and inscribing of some literal stone to go into the temple.

The purpose of engraving a stone is to make it all the more beautiful the precious cornerstone of Isa 28:16. If the Stone is Messiah, then the engraving must be what was cut into his sinless humanity. The scars in his body are what make him beautiful to the believer.

C. Results of Messiah's Coming (3:9b-10):

Two wonderful blessings result from the coming of the messianic Servant-Shoot-Stone.

1. Day of forgiveness (3:9b): **And I will remove the iniquity of that land in one day.** In these words one finds the key to the entire vision (Baron). The result of the engraving or deep cutting into the Stone is the removal of iniquity. *Remove*[120] recalls the removal of the filthy garments from Joshua earlier in the vision (v 4). *That land* refers to the messianic land of Promise, the kingdom of Christ. *One day* in which sin is removed has as its backdrop the Mosaic Day of Atonement. On that day sin was removed from the land (actually rolled forward until the next Day of Atonement). If the Stone is Messiah, and his engraving is his sacrificial death, then this single day of sin removal must be Calvary day—the once-and for-all-time messianic Day of Atonement.[121] Later Zechariah will have more to say about that special day (12:10; 13:1).

2. Day of peace (3:10): **In that day, says Yahweh of hosts, you shall call every man his neighbor under the vine and under the fig-tree.** The reference is not to the day when the temple is complete (Cashdan), but to the glorious day

---

[120] *Remove* comes from the r. *mûš*, meaning "to yield, give way;" in the Hiphil, "to cause to yield, or give way," hence, "to remove."

[121] Others think that with the completion of the temple God will remove the people's sins.

Zechariah 1:1-6:8

ushered in by the coming of the Shoot, i.e., the NT era. The idiom of sitting under vine/fig-tree signifies security and prosperity. Cf. the description of the kingdom of Solomon in 1 Kgs 4:24-25. Micah used a similar language to describe the messianic age in Mic 4:4.

Quartet of Visions
Zechariah 4:1-6:8

Vision Five:
Encouragement for the Prince
Zechariah 4:1-14

A. **Preparation for the Vision** (4:1-2a):
   1. *Angel returned (4:1a):* **Then the angel who talked with me returned.** Perhaps the interpreting angel had departed for a time.[122]
   2. *Prophet aroused (4:1b):* **and wakened me, as a man is wakened from his sleep.** This sleep is probably actual sleep rather than spiritual lethargy or exhaustion. This v seems to indicate that these visions were not dreams.
   3. *A stimulating question (4:2a):* **He asked me, What do you see?** A question like this from an angelic being helps a prophet to focus, to look for more than what meets the eye.

B. **What the Prophet Saw** (4:2b-3):
   1. *A lampstand (4:2b):* **And I said, I have seen, and behold a lampstand all of gold with its bowl over the top of it and its seven lamps thereon. There are seven even seven pipes to each of the lamps which are upon the top of it.** Zechariah responded to the probing question of the angel. He acknowledged seeing what he perceives that the angel wishes for him to see. On the significance of *behold*, see on 1:8.

---

[122]Others think that *returned* (*šûbh*) here has an auxiliary function answering to "again" in 5:1 and 6:1. They translate: "roused me again." This understanding, however, encounters the problem that there is no prior rousing recorded in the book.

Postexilic Prophets

The central feature of the vision was a *lampstand* (*mᵉnôrāh*). Lampstands of this period came in various configurations and with varying numbers of oil lamps.[123] Zechariah paints a word picture of what he saw by listing four major features of the lampstand.

First, Zechariah noted the value of the lampstand. Like the lampstand of the tabernacle, this lampstand was all of gold. On a least two points, however, this visionary lampstand differed from the Mosaic lampstand. Nothing here indicates that this lampstand was made of *pure gold* (*tāhôr*) or that it was hammered out of one piece of metal (Ex 25:31). In any case, gold indicates that this lampstand was precious.

Second, the lampstand had a bowl over it. Nothing is said about a bowl upon or over the top of the Mosaic lampstand. The *bowl* (*gullāh*) that Zechariah saw upon or over the top of the lampstand was the oil reservoir.

Third, Zechariah speaks of seven *lamps* (*nērôt*) on the lampstand. The text does not make clear how many spouts or lips each lamp had. Excavated lamps suggest that each lamp in the vision had seven outlets for wicks. A lampstand with forty-nine provided maximum illumination.[124]

Finally, the prophet observed that each of the seven lamps atop the lampstand had a number of *pipes* (*mûtsāqôt*) or "channels" (NIV).[125] The exact number of pipes is in dispute. The Hebrew could be read 1) seven times seven (Leupold), 2) seven plus seven, or 3) seven even seven. The latter interpretation is probably correct. *Seven* is the number of perfection.

---

[123] Surrounding nations employed multi-tiered and multi-legged lamps and lampstands. This description does not resemble the tabernacle lampstand which had three branches extending from either side of the central tier (Ex 25:31-40). What type of lamps each branch contained is not made explicit in Exodus.

[124] Beyond this obvious symbolism, some have tried to be more specific about the lamps. E.g., Josephus thought that the seven lamps represented the seven planets including the sun (*Ant.* 3.6, 7; 3.7, 7; *Wars* 5.5, 5).

[125] Some think that *mūtsāqōt* refers to spouts or lips on each saucer-like lamp. Such seven-lipped lamps have been discovered in excavation. This reconstruction, however, provides no explanation of how the oil flowed from the bowl over the lampstand to the lamps.

Zechariah 1:1-6:8

2. Two olive trees (4:3): **Also there are two olive trees by it, one on the right of the bowl and the other on its left.** On either side of the lampstand was an olive tree. The olive trees signal that the vision is not describing some piece of furniture for the soon-to-finished temple. This lampstand was outside the temple, i.e., in the world. Zechariah shortly will inquire as to the meaning of these two trees.

C. What the Prophet Asked (4:4-5).

1. Prophet's question (4:4): **I asked the angel who was talking with me, What are these, my lord?** Zechariah did not grasp the significance of what he had seen. He probably understood the meaning of the lampstand as a symbol for the people of God.[126] The meaning of the two olive trees, however, eluded him. *My lord* in this case is a title of respect, not an indication of deity. A student who is eager to learn inquires about what he does not understand.

2. Angel's response question (4:5): **He answered, Do you not know what these are?** The angel considered the symbols so clear that the prophet should have grasped them. The interpreting angel twice delays his reply (cf. v 13). The effect is to concentrate interest on the final v of the ch. This messenger from heaven is not the first teacher of heavenly things who had high expectations of his students. A good teacher forces students to become precise in their questions. He builds anticipation before answering. He tries to get his students to discover answers for themselves.

3. Zechariah's response (4:5b): **No, my lord, I replied.** On his part young Zechariah did not try to bluff. He frankly admitted that the scene had him baffled. A wise sage said: Ignorance is correctable; stupid is forever. Zechariah was ignorant, but not stupid.

D. General Application (4:6):

Before explaining the details of the vision the angel gave to the prophet a global application of it. Viewing this oracle as an intrusion into the vision account, some modern versions

---

[126]Cf. the figure of light in Isa 51:4; Mt 5:16f, Phil 2:15; Rev 1:12, 20.

have opted to rearrange the text.[127] Such rearrangements are both unnecessary and exceed the prerogatives of a translation.

1. *Addressee (4:6a):* **This is the word of Yahweh unto Zerubbabel:** Joshua had been given a special word in the previous vision, hence the focus here on Zerubbabel. Something that Zechariah saw in this vision was designed to bring comfort to Zerubbabel. This is the first mention of Zerubbabel in this book.

Zerubbabel was a prince from the house of David (1 Chr 3:17-19). He had been appointed by the Persians to lead the first contingent of Jews back from exile in Babylon in 538 BC (Ezra 2:2). As governor of the province Zerubbabel was currently leading out in temple reconstruction (Hag 1:12). The lampstand vision was intended to show that Zerubbabel will accomplish his work through the grace of God alone.

2. *Negative emphasis (4:6b)* **Not by might, not by power**... This is an unusual construction in the Hebrew. It lacks any verbal element that might drain strength from the powerful nouns. It looks like the angel intended these words to be like a slogan for the postexilic community. Though the immediate application is to the temple project, this slogan is applicable to the work of God in any age.

The slogan begins with a negative emphasis on the complete insufficiency of human strength and resources to accomplish any work of God. The repetition of the negative heightens the emphasis. The work of the Lord is not accomplished by means of armies of workers such as had enabled Solomon to build the first temple. *Might* (*chayil*) is a general word for human resources such as physical strength, ability, wealth, military power, and force. *Power* (*kōach*) is used in Nehemiah for the strength of the burden bearers (Neh 4:10). Again the word denotes human strength—physical, mental, material, etc.[128]

---

[127]E.g., NEB, JB, TEV. Similar textual rearrangements were proposed originally by Wellhausen, S.R. Driver, J.M.P. Smith, and H.G. Mitchell.

[128]Baron distinguishes between *might* and *power*, taking the former to refer to the strength of many, the latter to the strength of one person. The two terms together signify human strength of every description. *The Visions & Prophecies of Zechariah* (2d ed. London: Morgan & Scott, 1919), 137.

Zechariah 1:1-6:8

3. Positive emphasis (4:6c): **but by my Spirit, says Yahweh of Hosts.** The positive key to spiritual success is set forth in these words. The lampstand in Zechariah's vision was fed with oil not by man's hand and without human effort. So the temple will be restored not by the strength of Zerubbabel's hands but by the Spirit of God. Clearly the ceaseless supply of oil to the lampstand symbolizes the inexhaustible supply of God's Spirit available to those engaged in God's work. This assurance echoes the assertion of Zechariah's contemporary (Hag 2:5; cf. Isa 59:21).

This powerful utterance[129] is signed, as it were, by Yahweh himself in the words *says Yahweh of Hosts*. It is a slogan born in heaven. For spiritual success no truer words were ever spoken.

E. Specific Application (4:7):

Following the slogan Yahweh gives three specific promises to Zerubbabel.

1. Obstacles removed (4:7a): **Who are you, O great mountain? Before Zerubbabel ... a plain.** With God's Spirit at work in the restoration community, nothing could stand in the way of the completion of the temple task. Any difficulty impeding the progress of Zerubbabel in the rebuilding of the temple will be removed. Again the Hebrew uses an emphatic construction. *Mountain* is a figure for the opposition that was stood in the way of completing the temple.[130] These obstacles

---

[129]The powerful expression in the Hebrew is enhanced by 1) the unusual Hebrew construction in which both subject and predicate are omitted—an abbreviated sentence containing only the adverbial modifier of the predicate. So stated it is ideal as a slogan—the expression of a truth applicable to all the work of God; 2) the negative emphasis on the complete insufficiency of human strength and resources; 3) the repetition of the negative *not* (*lō'*) heightens the emphasis; 4) the emphatic positive statement follows the emphatic negative and is introduced by *kî 'im*, the strongest possible adversative; 5) the impact of the words themselves; 6) the addition of the formula *says Yahweh of Hosts*.

[130]Some interpreters take the *mountain* as a symbol for the Gentile world power which is the major obstacle to the restoration of the theocratic kingdom. The idea of moving mountains of opposition to the kingdom of God is prominent in the NT (Mt 17:20; 21:21-22; Mk 11:22-23; Lk 17:6; 1 Cor 13:2).

Postexilic Prophets

are personified and addressed as if they were a single person. Perhaps the governor's chief problems came from human obstructionists.

2. *Project completed (4:7b)*: **Then he will bring out the capstone...** The pronoun refers to Zerubbabel the governor. *Capstone* is lit., "the stone of the head." This was the richly ornamented stone that crowned the building. Thus the hands of the man who had laid the foundation will also complete the task.

3. *Joyous acclaim (4:7c)*: **amid shoutings, Grace, grace to it!** Zerubbabel will lead the festive celebration that accompanied the positioning of that final stone. The people will cheer when the job is done. *Grace* here indicates loveliness or elegance. Syntactically *grace* refers to the top stone, but by extension to what the top stone adorned.

Fifth Vision Amplified
Zechariah 4:8-14

Introduction (4:8):
Then the word of Yahweh came to me, saying... This formula has been used 3x before. Twice Zechariah referred to himself by name (1:1, 7), once the word came to Zerubbabel (4:6). Now for the first time Zechariah uses the formula in the first person. Four additional times the prophet will make this same claim. Zechariah exhausts the vocabulary of inspiration to bolster his claim to be a spokesman of Yahweh.

A. Contemporary Application (4:9-10):
1. *Zerubbabel rewarded (4:9a)*: **The hands of Zerubbabel have laid the foundation of this temple; his hands will also complete it.** What is implied in v 7 is now made explicit. This word of Yahweh stresses the certainty and immediacy of the completion of the temple. The Hebrew emphasizes that Zerubbabel's own hands and no one else will finish the work. It is rare in the work of the Lord that the person who starts a project is permitted also to finish that project, especially a project that was as important, controversial and complex as was the rebuilding of the temple. Documenta-

Zechariah 1:1-6:8

tion of the fulfillment of this prediction about four years later is recorded in Ezra 6:14-15.

2. God's word vindicated (4:9b): **Then shall you know that Yahweh of Hosts has sent me.** This is the third use of the recognition formula in the book. For the meaning of this formula, see on 2:9. The completion of the temple by Zerubbabel will vindicate the message and mission of the angel of Yahweh (Unger; Laetsch).

3. Critics silenced (4:10a): **Who despises the day of small things? They will rejoice when they see the plumb line in the hand of Zerubbabel, viz. these seven.** The beginning of the work of temple reconstruction had been mocked by some. Perhaps this explains the mountain of opposition referenced in v 7. Anyone who has engaged in establishing a new work for the Lord knows the sting of mocking words from those who should be applauding the efforts.

The sentence following the rhetorical question is strange. It delays the identification of the subject of the verb *rejoice*. Initially one might think that *they* refers to the despisers referenced in the first line of the v. The subject of the verb, however, is *these seven*. While there are some that look down on Zerubbabel's efforts, there are some who rejoice over the progress.

The *plumb line* (lit., "the stone, the lead") was simply a stone on a cord that helped builders to get perfect right angles for construction. Unless we are to understand this v as a figurative description of the foremost temple builder, we must conclude that Zerubbabel was not just a cheerleader in this effort. He was a hands-on leader. His princely birth and governor's office did not deter him from getting his hands dirty.[131]

The celebration of the glorious completion of the building was noted in the previous word from Yahweh (v 7). Success puts to shame all those who despised meager beginnings. This v, however, is intended to give encouragement during the difficult days of the construction effort.

---

[131] Another possibility is that Zerubbabel was holding the plumb line ceremonially for the laborers as they set the final stone in place, squaring it with the adjacent stones (McComiskey).

4. Surprising explanation (4:10b): **(these seven are the eyes of Yahweh; they run to and fro through the whole earth).** Even more encouraging to Zerubbabel than the supportive enthusiasm of his fellow citizens, the governor can be assured that Yahweh himself was rejoicing over the progress in the temple project. The continuing rebuilding effort was carried out under divine auspices. The *eyes of Yahweh*, symbols of his knowledge, are said to be *seven*, i.e., he has perfect knowledge. Yahweh is omniscient. God beholds the progressing temple work with joy and gladness. How can the doubters continue their campaign of ridicule?

The eyes of Yahweh are said to *run to and fro* (r. šūṭ) *through the whole earth.* The verb connotes eager and wide-ranging searching for something that is desirable. It is used for the searching for manna in the wilderness (Nm 11:8), for those capable of military service (2 Sam 24:8), or men in time of spiritual famine searching for God's word (Amos 8:12). Jeremiah roamed through the streets of Jerusalem looking for one honest man (Jer 5:1). The verb is used with the eyes of Yahweh previously in an utterance by the prophet Hanani (2 Chr 16:9). There Yahweh was looking for those who were fully committed to him. The same is true here. That is why his eyes were focused on Zerubbabel.

The eyes of Yahweh are mentioned 21x in OT. They are associated with evaluation whether bad (e.g., 1 Kgs 16:25) or good (e.g., Gn 6:8), with judgment (Amos 9:8), and with blessing (Dt 11:12; Ps 34:16; Isa 49:5). This is the only passage in which Yahweh is said to have *seven* eyes. The messianic Stone in Zech 3:9 is said to have seven eyes on it, perhaps indicating deity.

B. Request for Additional Details (4:11-13):

1. General question (4:11): **Then I asked the angel, What are these two olive trees on the right and the left of the lampstand?** Zechariah's question is a bit more specific than the one he asked in v 4. He seems to have understood the lampstand as a symbol of God's people. He was still perplexed, however, by the olive trees positioned on either side of the lampstand.

2. *More precise question (4:12):* **And a second time I said to him, What are these two olive branches which by means of the two spouts empty from over them the gold.** Zechariah's third question to the angel makes clear three aspects of the vision that have not previously been mentioned. First, two branches from the olive trees apparently hung over the lampstand. Second, coming out of those two branches were two spouts that connected the fruitful olive boughs to the bowl over the lampstand. Third, flowing through those spouts was *the gold*, i.e., oil that was so clear that it looked like gold. The finest olive oil might resemble liquid gold, especially as seen flowing along the golden pipes. The verb *empty* suggests that the oil was flowing in profusion, not simply dripping from the spouts. The olives were automatically processed into oil. The oil flowed through the golden spouts, and then into the bowl. From the bowl the oil was distributed to the lamps on the lampstand.

3. *Confession of ignorance (4:13):* **He replied, Do you not know what these are? No, my lord, I said.** The angel again administers a mild rebuke to Zechariah as he did also in v 5. God expects us to understand his revelation.

C. Messianic Application (4:14):

So he said, **These are the two sons of oil who stand alongside the Lord of all the earth...** Oil (*yitshār*) is not the word (*šemen*) for the oil used in ritual ordination of priests and kings. It is the word for oil as a staple and a symbol of abundance.[132] The two *sons of oil* must be Joshua and Zerubbabel. They were the channels through which the divine empowerment flows to the postexilic community. The text avoids naming individuals so as not to limit the application of this vision to specific personalities. It is doubtful that Zerubbabel ever underwent the ceremony of anointing. Still he was a Davidic prince by ancestral right. The two olive *trees* then represent the regal and priestly powers. These two offices foreshadow the Messiah who was to be both king and priest.

---

[132] So McComiskey, citing Dt 7:13; 14:23; Neh 5:11.

Postexilic Prophets

Stand alongside points to the fact that kings normally sat, servants stood. The civil and priestly representatives were at hand to obey the behest of the King. This is similar to 3:1 where Joshua was depicted standing before the angel of Yahweh. *Lord* is *ᵃdôn*, i.e., Sovereign, Ruler. The title *Lord of all the earth* is used 6x in the OT.[133]

Christians are also both kings and priests. God uses us as his channels through which the oil of the Holy Spirit is conveyed to mankind through the preaching of the gospel (Laetsch). Rev 11:4 is a reference to this passage.

To summarize: the emphasis in this vision is upon the automatic and spontaneous supply of oil for lighting without human agency. The lampstand undoubtedly signifies the people of God. Consider: its value (gold); its design (to give light); its vitality (endless supply of oil). The oil symbolizes the Holy Spirit or grace of God. The seven spouts accentuate the increased supply of oil to make possible an abundance of light.

Vision Six
Jerusalem Purified
Zechariah 5:1-4

A. What the Prophet Saw (5:1-2):

1. Introductory formula (5:1a): **And I returned and I lifted up my eyes and looked and behold...** *I returned* is equivalent to English "again," and is so rendered by most versions. Zechariah uses the same introductory formula as in second and third visions (cf. 1:18; 2:1). On the meaning of *behold*, see on 1:8.

2. Observation (5:1b): **a flying roll.** The *scroll* (*mᵉgillāh*) was not rolled up in a case, but flying like a banner for all to read. The participle indicates continuous action, i.e., the scroll was hovering. The flying scroll suggests not only its speed but its source. The scroll was in the air, suggesting that it came from God. A scroll is the symbol of a message or

---

[133] Josh 3:11, 13; Ps 97:5; Mic 4:13; Zech 4:14; 6:5.

pronouncement of solemn import from God to man (cf. Ezek 2:9-10).

3. *Interrogation (5:2a):* **He asked me, What do you see?** The angel used the same question to introduce the fifth vision (4:2). His purpose is to alert Zechariah to a new vision and help him focus on what he sees. As the prophet answers the angel's question he reveals the vision to his readers.

4. *Response (5:2b):* ***I answered, I see a flying scroll, thirty feet long and fifteen feet wide.*** The scroll was overwhelming and fearful. It was the size of the holy place of the tabernacle (Ex 26:15-25) and porch of the temple (1 Kgs 6:3); but no significance is given to that fact.[134] The main point is that the scroll was large enough to be seen; none could plead ignorance.

B. God's Curse (5:3a):

And he said to me, This is the curse which is about to go out over the face of the whole land. The scroll symbolizes the curse (i.e., the punishment) against those who violate God's word. Previous visions had promised divine intervention; but here moral conditions had to be met.

This is the curse (*hā'ālāh*) might refer specifically to the awful catalog of curses which Moses predicted would fall upon Israel because of disobedience (Dt 28:15-68). This catalog is called simply *the curse* in Dt 30:1. The curse is *about to go out*, i.e., be set into motion by Yahweh of Hosts.

People in the ancient world were afraid of curses. The *curse* is the punishment or judgment that falls upon those who violate God's word (the scroll). The term is used several times in conjunction with covenant (Gn 24:41; 26:28; Dt 29:12; Ezek 16:59 etc.). The law taught that those who kept it would prosper; those who broke it would meet with disaster. The scroll represented the law with its specific curses on lawbreakers within the covenant family.

---

[134]Some envision the curse going forth from the porch of the temple, the spot at which God was supposed to commune with his people (cf. 1 Kgs 7:7). Others think that the curse or judgment against sin was to be meted out in accordance to the standards of Yahweh's holiness as symbolized in the tabernacle.

Postexilic Prophets

Land (*'erets*) could be translated *earth*; but in view of the teaching of this book concerning national cleansing the former translation is probably correct (cf. ch 13). God's word of judgment has a cleansing effect.

C. Subjects of the Curse (5:3b-c):

The scroll was inscribed on both sides. One side stipulated punishment against thieves, the other against blasphemers.

1. Removal of thieves (5:3b): **for every thief shall be cleansed out (as) from this (side of the scroll) according to it...** The *thief* represents all who were engaged in the act of stealing. Such people will be *cleansed out* (r. *nqh* in Niphal) or "banished" (NIV), i.e., they would no longer be part of the covenant people, hence "cut off" (KJV) from covenant benefits. Violation of the eighth commandment represents all sins against man. *From this* (*mizzeh*) refers to one side of the scroll.[135]

2. Removal of blasphemers (5:3c): **and everyone who swears (as) from that side according to it shall be cleansed out.** The reference is to swearing falsely, for using Yahweh's name in oaths was a commendable practice in the OT. Swearing falsely blasphemed the name of God, for it called on the Holy One of Israel to sanction a lie. Only those who have been cleansed from sin can avoid being *cleansed out* by God's judgment.

D. Severity of the Curse (5:4):

Yahweh makes four statements that underscore the severity of his flying curse (punishment) against the sinners in Judea.

1. Curse dispatched (5:4a): **I will cause it to go forth (oracle of Yahweh of Hosts).** This v sets forth the certainty with which God's judgments shall finally overtake the

---

[135]*Mizzeh* has been taken by others to mean "from this time" (RSV), i.e. henceforth; "from this place," the church of God (Laetsch). The double use of *mizzeh* in v 3 recalls Ex 32:15 where the same construction is used to indicate that the two tables of the Ten Commandments were written front and back.

wicked. There is no escape. God's words are often personified and said to go forth on his errands (Ps 147:15; Isa 55:11). This is the fourteenth use of the oracle formula in this book. See on 1:3.

2. *Curse penetrating (5:4b):* **and it will come into the house of the thief and the house of the one who swears to a lie by my name.** The transgressor may think that he is safe within his house. Bolted doors, strong walls, and locked windows cannot keep out the avenging justice of God. These words were no doubt an encouragement to those who tried to administer justice in the postexilic community. Yahweh's law-curse would consume all that belonged to these lawbreakers. *Swears to a lie* recalls the language of Lv 19:12.

3. *Curse abiding (5:4c):* **And it shall abide in the midst of his house...** The curse will not pay sinners a passing visit. It will *abide* (r. *lūn*) or lodge or spend the night in his house. Yahweh's curse will completely destroy the house of the evil doers. The point is that God's word found its way where the judicial machinery could not go, viz. the privacy of the home.

4. *Curse demolishing (5:4d):* **and shall consume it with the timber thereof and the stones thereof.** This is the climax of the calamities that God's judicial curse will bring upon the house of the wicked. How terrible is the punishment that sin brings down upon itself. The word of God will utterly consume sinners. The language here is virtually identical to that used of the leprous house in Lv 14:45 which also had to be destroyed.

This vision of the flying scroll was meant to be encouragement to the temple builders. The entire nation will not be held accountable for the sins of some or many citizens. God's promise to make them a kingdom of priests will not be frustrated by the waywardness of the few.

Vision Seven
Sinners Meet Retribution
Zechariah 5:5-11

A. **First Phase** (5:5-6):

1. Command (5:5): **Then the angel who was speaking to me came forward and said to me, Lift up now your eyes, and see what this is going out.** The interpreting angel *came forward*, i.e., he drew near to Zechariah. His purpose may have been to underscore the importance of what follows, or to point out more clearly what was emerging on the visionary scene. *Lift up now your eyes* suggests that the night of visions was exhausting the prophet.

2. Question (5:6a): **I asked, What is it?** Zechariah probably wanted to know what the vision meant.

3. Identification (5:6b): **And he said, This is the ephah that goes forth.** The *ephah* was the largest of the dry measures used in ancient Israel. It was about two-thirds the size of a bushel. A literal ephah could not contain a woman. This ephah may have been enlarged as was the scroll in the preceding vision (Baldwin). *Goes forth* (participle) may indicate either that the ephah was flying (like the preceding scroll) or about to fly. The participle anticipates the use of the ephah to remove something, as it turns out, wickedness. As in 3:1-5 and 5:1-4 the sin that was hindering the people from accomplishing worthy goals will be removed. Some regard the ephah as a symbol of godless commercialism; but the ephah may simply be a container used to depict the removal of sin.

4. Explanation (5:6c): **And he said, This is their eye in all the land.** *And he said* suggests that what follows advances the thought beyond the ephah that was identified in the previous saying. *This* (*zō't*) could refer to the ephah again; but *zō't* usually points forward in discourse. It probably refers to what is about to be revealed within the ephah, viz. a woman. *Their eye* refers to the way they looked, their appearance.[136] The

---

[136] "This is the iniquity" of the people (NIV) is based on a slight emendation of the text. This reading is probably not correct because then the woman is twice identified as a personification of evil.

Zechariah 1:1-6:8

reference is to the covenant-breakers of vv 4-5, whom the crouching figure in the ephah represents.

B. Second Phase (5:7-8):
   1. Zechariah observed a lid lifted (5:7a): **And behold a lid of lead was lifted up.** The *lid* (lit., "a circle") of the ephah was raised so that the prophet could see its contents. Here the term refers to a disk or circular plate which formed the cover of the round shaped ephah (Unger). Who or what lifted up the lid is not indicated; its rise is completely mysterious.
   2. Zechariah observed a woman in the ephah (5:7b): **and this (is) a woman sitting in the midst of the ephah.** All sin is united and concentrated in this woman. She may represent specifically the lawbreakers of vv 3-4.[137] The fact that she was confined in the ephah beneath a heavy lid suggests that God already had taken care of the sin problem of his people.
   3. Zechariah hears an explanation of the woman (5:8a): **He said, This is Wickedness.** *Wickedness* in Hebrew is a feminine noun, hence it symbolized by a woman. Cf. Rev 17-18 Babylon has both religious and commercial dimensions.
   4. Zechariah observed the confinement of the woman (5:8b): **and he cast her into the midst of the ephah and pushed the lead cover down over its mouth.** Evidently the woman tried to arise from her ephah basket. She is flung back down by the angel. She knows her doom is at hand. The verbs indicate a struggle. Thus wickedness is confined within the ephah.

C. Third Phase (5:9):
   1. Two women appear (5:9a): **Then I looked up, and behold there came forth two women and the wind was in their wings, and they had wings like the wings of a stork.** Perhaps the sound of beating wings caused the prophet to look up to the air above the ephah. *Behold* introduces the unexpected. These two women represent angelic agents of God.

---

[137]Unger probably goes too far in suggesting that the woman represents ecclesiastical sin contentedly sitting in the ephah, thus at home in her secular surroundings.

Usually in Scripture angels are represented as men. Perhaps here they are depicted as *women* to balance the representation of wickedness as a woman. The *wind* could also be translated *Spirit*. If so, the vision emphasizes that the removal of wickedness was God's doing (Baldwin). Storks were common in Palestine. They had strong wings. The word for *stork* also literally means "faithful one." This may give added significance to this feature.

2. *Ephah is raised (5:9b):* **and they lifted up the ephah between heaven and earth.** The two women soared heavenward with stork-like wings. Obviously they were about to transport the ephah somewhere.

D. Final Explanation (5:10-11):

1. *Question of the prophet (5:10):* **And I said unto the angel that was speaking with me, Where are these bearing the ephah?** Zechariah inquires about the final destination of the ephah since it was obviously about to be taken some place.

2. *Destination of the ephah (5:11a):* **And he said unto me, To build for her a house in the land of Shinar...** The angel answers the prophet's question. The two winged women will build a *house* for wickedness personified. The *house* may be a temple (Pusey; Baldwin). *Shinar* ("Babylonia" NIV) is the ideal land of unholiness where the world power first reared itself against God. Cf. Nimrod's empire (Gn 10:10) and the tower of Babel (Gn 11:1-9). The basic thought is that wickedness is removed from Zion. Cf. Ps 103:11-12. Wickedness belongs in a place where idolatry, oppression and cruelty already abide.

3. *Permanent abode of the ephah (5:11b):* **and it shall be established and they shall set it there upon its base.** *Established* (Hophal perf. 3ms) refers to the house that is built for wickedness personified. *They shall set it* involves a slight but necessary alteration in the vowel points in order to make sense of the v. *Its base* may refer to a pedestal for an idol. The two winged women are the subject of this verb. Wickedness becomes a virtual idol to be worshipped in the land of

Shinar, symbol of the lost world (Baldwin). The language has a note of finality. Wickedness is removed permanently.

In postexilic Judaism the ideal of this prophecy was never realized, as the later invectives of Zechariah and Malachi indicate. The ephah vision anticipated the new covenant where sin is removed from messianic Israel. God can absolutely remove sin because his law is written upon the hearts of all his people (Jer 31:31-34).

Vision Eight
Action of the Heavenly Patrol
Zechariah 6:1-8

The eighth and final vision is similar in some respects to the first vision of the series. Colorful horses appear in both, howbeit not of identical colors. The setting of vision one—a valley full of myrtles—is similar to the locale of vision eight—between two mountains. In both cases the horses patrol the earth (1:10; 6:7). The phrase *walking through the earth* appears twice in the first vision, three times in the last vision (1:10-11; 6:6-7).

Vision eight is distinct from the first vision in these respects: The horses in vision one are mounted; those in vision eight are attached to war chariots. In vision one the horses are standing still; those in eight are in motion. The horses in vision one were involved in surveillance; those in vision eight execute judgment. The horses in vision one went about their business as a group; those in vision eight go in various directions. If vision one emphasizes Yahweh's awareness of the earthly situation, vision eight underscores his action on the stage of human history.

A. What the Prophet Saw (6:1-3):

1. Transition formula (6:1a): **And I returned and I lifted up my eyes and behold...** The language introducing the fifth vision is repeated (cf. 5:1).

2. He saw chariots (6:1b): **and there before me were four chariots going forth from between the two mountains**

Postexilic Prophets

of bronze! Zechariah brings out three points regarding the chariots he saw in vision eight.

First, Zechariah notes that the chariots were four in number. *Four* is the number of universality. *Chariots* (*markābhôt*) are almost always war chariots, the storm troops in ancient warfare. They sometimes symbolize the vast might of Yahweh (Hab 3:8; Isa 66:15). Here they represent God's intervention in international affairs, especially judgment.[138] These four chariots are representative of thousands of chariots that carry out the will of God (Ps 68:17).

Second, Zechariah saw the chariots being dispatched between two mountains. *Going forth* (r. *yts'*) is the first of seven uses of this verb in this vision. The verb frequently has the connotation of going out to confront an adversary, especially in a military sense. Thus Yahweh is not an impotent observer; he is active in pursuing justice on the international scene.

Third, Zechariah notes that the mountains in the vision were made of bronze. The mountains that (symbolically) guard the approaches to God's heavenly throne are imposing and impregnable. The imagery may be taken from the situation of earthly Jerusalem in respect to Mount Zion and Mount Olivet. The suggestion also has been made that the two huge bronze pillars, which stood at the front of Solomon's temple (1 Kgs 7:13-22), were symbolic representations of these two bronze mountains.[139]

3. *He saw horses attached to the chariots (6:2-3):* **Hitched to the first chariot were red horses, to the second black, 3 to the third white and to the fourth spotted, strong horses.** The horses were of various colors as in vision one. It is not clear whether these colors have special significance, or are simply used to designate the various groups of God's agents.

---

[138] Based on their analysis of 1 Kgs 10:29 where the value of a chariot is four times that of a horse, the rabbis concluded that a chariot had a team of four horses.

[139] Mason, *CNEB*, 59; Baldwin, *TOTC*, 131. Others think that the two mountains represent Mount Zion and the Mount of Olives. Thus God's judgments on the world go forth from Jerusalem. In support of this view Baron observes that the Valley of Jehoshaphat, which lies between these two mountains, is also associated with God's judgment on the nations.

Zechariah 1:1-6:8

The first chariot had red horses. The preposition *beth* on the word *chariot* indicates accompaniment, i.e., the red horses were *hitched* to the chariot. Emphasis is placed on the fact that the chariots are in immediate readiness to execute the judgment. Some of the horses in vision one were also *red* (*'edōm*). *Red horses* are perhaps symbolic of war and bloodshed. Cf. Rev 6:4.

As for the symbolism of the colors hitched to the second, third and fourth chariots, these suggestions can be made: *black* (*shāchōr*) may symbolize famine and death (cf. Rev 6:5-6) and w*hite* (*lābhān*) victory and triumph (Rev 6:2). The spotted horses perhaps are symbolic of plagues (Rev 6:8).

The word *strong* dangles at the end of the clause. Its exact significance in relation to *spotted* is unclear. *Strong* might accentuate the spottedness of the horses, or be descriptive of their physical strength. If the latter, it is not clear why the strength of these particular horses is mentioned. In the light of the use of the same term in v 7, NIV is probably correct to take the adjective *strong* as descriptive of all the horses in the vision not just those hitched to the fourth chariot.

B. General Explanation (6:4-5):

1. Zechariah's request (6:4): **I answered and said to the angel who was speaking to me, What are these, my lord?** Zechariah requests an explanation. In visions 1, 2 and 5 Zechariah asked this same question (1:9, 19; 4:4). Zechariah addressed the interpreting angel with respect as *my lord* 5x.

2. General explanation (6:5): **The angel answered me, These are the four winds of heaven which are about to go forth from standing before the Lord of all the earth.** In response to Zechariah's query the interpreting angel offers three statements of explanation.

First, the angel explains the symbolism of the chariots, howbeit cryptically. The angel used a symbol to explain a symbol. *Winds* (*ruchōt*) are frequently used in OT as a symbol for divine activity.[140] *Winds* could also be rendered *spirits*

---

[140]Isa 11:15; 17:13; 41:16; 57:13; 59:19; Jer 51:1; Ezek 1:4; Dan 7:1-3. The *four winds* are symbolic of God's destructive power in Jer 49:36. Cf. Rev 7:1.

Postexilic Prophets

of heaven. So there is a marvelous ambiguity in the word. Are they literal winds? More likely they are angelic beings (Unger) who go forth with the swiftness of the winds in willing obedience to the Creator (Ps 103:20-21; 104:4).

Second, the angel explains that the chariots are about to begin their mission. *About to forth* renders a participle that suggests imminent action. Initially Zechariah saw the angelic chariots before their mission.

Third, the angel explains the present location of the chariots. They are standing before the Lord. This phrase seems to confirm the interpretation of "angels." Servants always stood in the presence of the king they served. The chariots (winds = angels) are under the authority of the Sovereign. They will do his bidding when he sends them forth.

C. Chariot Jurisdictions (6:6):

Having indicated the general significance of the chariots, the angel now explains the significance of the various colors of horses.

1. Black-horse chariot (6:6a): **[As for] the one with the black horses [they] were about to go forth to the land of the north...** The v begins with *the one* (*'ashēr*), obviously referring to one of the chariots. The construction is unusual, but not without precedent.[141] *With* (lit. "on it") is the preposition *beth* + the 3fs suff. referring back to the word *chariot* in v 3. This construction emphasizes the connection between each team of horses and a chariot.

About to go forth is a plural participle, referring to the horses. The pronoun for this participle must be supplied.[142] The *north* probably should not be limited to Mesopotamia or Persia (cf. Jer 46:10; 50:9). In Jeremiah "the land of the north" refers to the lands of the exile (e.g., Jer 3:18) or the direction from which Israel's enemies attack (Jer 10:22).

---

[141]McComiskey points out several similar usages of the particle *'ashēr* in Jeremiah (14:1; 46:1; 47:1; 49:34). There is no need to emend the text as in NRSV; NEB, and JB.

[142]OT frequently uses a participle with an unexpressed pronoun when the pronoun's referent is clearly indicated by the context.

2. *White-horse chariot (6:6b)*: **and the white will certainly go forth after them.** *Will certainly go forth* is perfect, which following a participle has a future orientation. The perfect also connotes the certainty of the departure. The chariots do not actually depart until v 7. *After them* (lit., "to/at the rear of them") indicates both direction and sequence. Two chariots were dispatched to the north[143] to symbolize a double blow against the ancient enemies of Israel (Babylon and Assyria?).[144]

3. *Spotted-horse chariot (6:6c)*: **and the spotted will certainly go forth unto the land of the south.** The verb (r *yts'*) in the perfect is repeated from the previous clause with similar connotation. *Land of the south* points in the direction of Egypt, Israel's traditional enemy. North and south are highlighted in this vision because those were the two main concerns of the postexilic community.

What happened to the red-horse chariot mentioned in v 2? Perhaps the red horses were held in reserve until judgment had been executed on the land of the north and south.[145]

Why are east and west omitted? Palestine is bordered on the west by sea and on the east on desert. Any judgment on the world would have to depart north-south.

D. Preparation of the Chariots (6:7):

1. *Positioning (6:7a)*: **and as for the strong ones, they came forward.** *Strong ones* (*hā'ᵃmutsîm*) stands first in the clause to highlight a new development in the scene. The term seems to be a reference to all of the horses of whatever color. *Came forward* is again the r. *yts'*, but in this new clause the

---

[143] The NIV follows a slight emendation of *after them* (*'achᵃrehem*) and reads "toward the west" (*'achᵃre hayyām*) This understanding involves the addition of one Hebrew consonant (cf. NEB, NRSV, NJB, TEV).

[144] *After them* could also simply indicate sequence, i.e., the white-horse chariot went out after the black-horse chariot, but perhaps in a different direction.

[145] Another possibility is that two different chariots go south just like two go north. Perhaps the strong horses are the red horses mentioned earlier. Leupold sees five chariots here. Baldwin unnecessarily adds a clause to account for the missing red horses: "The red horses went towards the east country."

perfect has its regular connotation of completed action. In preparation for departure the horse-drawn chariots *came forward* from their previous position of standing before the Lord of all the earth (v 5).

    2. *Eagerness (6:7b):* **And they sought to go that they might walk to and fro through the earth.** They sought to go in NIV is "they were straining to go," i.e., the horses pawed the ground and strained at their harnesses until the command was given. The reference is probably to all the horses (Unger) not just the strong horses. The agents of the Lord are anxious to carry out their ultimate mission, viz. the suppression of all enemies of God's people. *To walk to and fro through the earth* is to patrol the earth with a view to suppressing all opposition to God's program.

E. Dispatch of the Chariots (6:7c-8):

    1. *Divine commission (6:7c):* **and he said, Go! Go to and fro in the earth.** The Lord of all the earth is the speaker. At the proper moment he unleashes his heavenly warriors to do battle with his enemies upon the earth. The basic lesson is that from first to last the affairs of nations are under God's directions, not that of men.

    2. *Divine declaration (6:8):* **Then he cried out to me and said unto me, Look, those going toward the north have quieted my Spirit in the land of the north.** *Cried out* may indicate that the interpreting angel shouts to the prophet so as to be heard over the roar of the thundering hoofs of the horses. On the other hand, the shouting may indicate the good news which he is about to announce. The angel is apparently speaking directly for the Lord of all the earth. *Those going toward the north* refers to the black and white horse chariots. *My spirit* refers to the angel of Yahweh; but he is closely related to Yahweh. *Quieted my spirit* is an idiom meaning, to cause God's anger to cease.

TRANSITIONAL EPISODE: SYMBOLIC CORONATION
Zechariah 6:9-15

Action Parable
Zechariah 6:9-11

Introduction
Zechariah 6:9

The word of Yahweh came to me, saying: On the meaning of this formula see on 4:8. The prophet uses this standard prophetic formula to indicate that the series of visions is now at an end.

The Prophet's Taking
Zechariah 6:10a, b

A. **Contribution Authorized** (6:10a):
Take (offerings) from (them of) the captivity... Babylonian Jews were accustomed to sending gifts to the temple in Jerusalem. Zechariah was told to take these offerings because normally the offerings would be given to temple personnel. This is the first of two action parables performed by Zechariah during his ministry.

B. **Contributors Named** (6:10b):
From Heldai, from Tobijah, and Yedaiah who have come from Babylon. These are the names of individuals who headed the delegation from Babylon. Each of the names expresses a relationship to Yahweh.[146] Thus one would assume they were men of faith. This delegation probably arrived in Jerusalem on the very morning after the night of visions.

---

[146] Heldai = "Yahweh's world"; Tobijah = "Yahweh is my good;" Yedaiah = "Yahweh knows." Others think Heldai means "mole."

Postexilic Prophets

The Prophet's Making
Zechariah 6:10c-11

A. **Location** (6:10c):
You go that day to the house of Josiah son of Zephaniah. *That day* suggests the prophet was to go the same day, i.e., at once. There was urgency in this mission. Since Joshua the high priest was found in the house of *Josiah son of Zephaniah* it is possible that Josiah was a ranking priest who, along with Joshua, lived in the temple precincts. Josiah is called *Hen* (Gracious) in v 14.

B. **Construction** (6:11a):
And take silver and gold and make a crown. The offering of the visitors was in the form of gold and silver. *Crown* (*^{a}tārōth*) is lit., "crowns."[147] The term refers to a crown of royalty. Unger unnecessarily insists on emending the Hebrew plural to the singular. More likely the plural indicates a composite crown. Eastern crowns were circlets which could be worn singly or fitted together to make a composite crown (Baldwin). Cf. Rev 19:12. So the plural crowns could be a plural of excellence; or even a Phoenician singular.[148]

C. **Crowning** (6:11b):
And set it on the head of the high priest, Joshua son of Jehozadak... Under OT law Joshua could not wear a royal crown. There was a rigid distinction between kingly and priestly offices in the OT, the one confined to the house of David, the other to the house of Aaron. Cf. Uzziah's attempted intrusion in 2 Chr 26:16-21. Thus the crowning of Joshua must be typical of priestly kingship (Heb 7:1-3; Ps 110:4).[149] He was a type of Christ (cf. 3:8) in whom the two dignities of priesthood and kingship were to be united.

---

[147] The plural reading is confirmed by the Greek and Latin versions. The ancient Syriac version, however, has a singular.

[148] So Baldwin calling attention to a comment by Kidner on Prov 1:20; 9:1; 14:1. The plural *^{a}tārōth* is used in Job 31:36 for one crown.

[149] Liberals insist that originally a crown was placed on the head of the prince Zerubbabel. For this there is no support in the text. To have placed a

Zechariah: 6:9-15

Action Parable Explained
Zechariah 6:12-15

Messianic Significance of the Event
Zechariah 6:12-13

A. Promise of Messiah (6:12a):
And say unto him, Thus says Yahweh of Hosts: Behold, a man! As Zechariah crowns Joshua he is to say these words to him. On *Yahweh of Hosts* see on 1:3. On the meaning of *behold* see on 1:8. The words explain the significance of the crowning. The action points to a man, not this particular man as would have been suggested had Zechariah spoken of *the* man. The one to whom God calls attention is the man *par excellence*—the ideal representative of the human race—the One who after wearing the crown of thorns is crowned with glory and honor (Heb 2:9). This dramatic "behold" statement recalls three other such statements that introduce the same wonderful figure in other aspects of his character: "Behold my Servant" (Isa 42:1; 52:13; "Behold your King" (Zech 9:9), "Behold your God" (Isa 40:9).

B. Name of Messiah (6:12b):
Shoot is his name and from his place he will shoot up. The man symbolized by the newly crowned Joshua is called *Shoot* ("Branch" in most English versions). *Shoot (tsemach)* was used in 3:8 for the Messiah. Zechariah builds on Jeremiah's theology of the coming royal Davidic Shoot (Jer 23:5; 33:15; cf. Isa 11:1). The title *Shoot* denotes the lowly origins of this coming ruler.

The Shoot will *shoot up*. This indicates the obscurity of his origin. He will come where there is little promise of new life—like a root out of dry ground (Isa 53:2). *From his place* is lit., "from under him," i.e., from his own root. As to race and nationality he will be of the seed of the Abraham, of the

---

crown on the head of Zerubbabel would have been misleading, pointing to the immediate reestablishment of the Davidic kingdom.

tribe of Judah, of the family of David and of the line of Zerubbabel. Geographically, he shall spring forth in Immanuel's land, out of Bethlehem Ephratha (Baron).

If Zerubbabel the Davidic descendant entertained any thought of being restored to the throne (there is no indication that he did) those hopes were crushed by this symbolic action. Zion's future king will have priestly office as well as Davidic ancestry. During the intertestamental period the Hasmonean dynasty of priest-kings arose in Judea; but they were not of the Davidic line. Only Jesus of Nazareth fills out the requirements of the symbolism of this passage.

C. Work of Messiah (6:12c-13a):

And he will build the temple of Yahweh. Yes, he himself shall build the temple of Yahweh. The reference is not to the temple currently under construction. This prophetic temple is to be built by a future Davidic priest-king while the present temple was to be finished by Zerubbabel (4:9). The reference must be to a greater temple of the future, the spiritual temple of the new covenant age depicted in great symbolic detail by Ezekiel. That temple is a present reality (Eph 2:19-22; 1 Pet 2:5).

The repetition of the promise functions to underscore certainty. It is also a device to distinguish between *he* (Joshua) and *he* (the Shoot), as well as between the contemporary temple and the one to come (Baldwin). The announcement of a coming ruler who will build God's temple served as encouragement to the current temple builders Zerubbabel and Joshua in two ways. First, they were encouraged to know that the current somewhat humble temple effort was a type and pledge of the greater temple to come. Second, Zerubbabel and Joshua were honored to realize that in their respective offices they foreshadowed the greater Builder of the future.

D. Glory of Messiah (6:13b):

And he himself shall bear the glory. The pronoun in Hebrew is again emphatic, i.e., he and no other. The word *glory* (*hōd*) is used 23x in OT. It is used most frequently of divine splendor (12x) or splendor bestowed by God on persons or things.[150] The term is used of the messianic king in Ps 45:4. Christ will bear the regal majesty as none other has borne it. His is the glory of the only begotten of the Father (Jn 1:14; Heb 2:9).

E. **Offices of Messiah** (6:13c-e):

1. Kingly office (6:13c): **and he will sit and rule on his throne.** The Shoot will *sit...on his throne.* He possesses the dignity and honor of royalty for he is the rightful monarch. David prophesied that God "would raise up Christ to sit on his throne" (Acts 2:30). The angel said concerning Mary's child: "He shall be great, and shall be called the Son of the Highest: and the Lord God shall give unto him the throne of his father David" (Lk 1:32). Not only will he occupy the throne as rightful monarch, he will actually *rule*, i.e., he will exercise all royal power and authority. His rule is autocratic and absolute. His blessed rule results in the most wonderful blessing for the righteous (Ps 72).

2. Priestly office (6:13d): **and he will be a priest on his throne.** This significant sentence is only four words in the Hebrew. They effectively summarize in large measure the messianic expectation that was gradually revealed through the former prophets. The Shoot will be a royal priest, the greater Melchizedek of Ps 110. This statement builds on Jer 33:15 where the term Shoot is used in a context where kingly and priestly functions merge. Christ exercises his high priestly office as the Advocate with the Father (Jn 2:1), the only Mediator between God and man (1 Tim 2:5). It is this royal priest that has compassion upon the ignorant and erring (Heb 5:2).

3. Perfect harmony (6:13e): **and peaceful counsel shall be between the two of them.** *Peaceful counsel* is counsel planning or procuring peace. *Between the two of them* is difficult. Some believe that the reference is to the concord existing between the offices of priest and king. Only when the two offices are united in one person can there be total harmony between them. Cf. 1 Tim 6:15; Heb 8:1; Rev 19:16.

---

[150]E.g., Moses and Joshua (Nm 27:20), kings like Solomon (1 Chr 29:25), olive trees (Hos 14:6), a battle horse (Job 39:20).

Postexilic Prophets

A less popular view, but one with much to commend it, is that the peaceful counsel is between Messiah and Yahweh, i.e., between the Son and the Father. In favor of this second view are the following considerations. First, the phraseology *two of them* points in the direction of persons, not things or abstract offices. Second, only two persons are mentioned in this v, viz., Yahweh and Yahweh's Christ. Third, communication between Yahweh and his Christ is plainly referred to in Ps 110 where Messiah is also depicted as both king and priest. The will of the Father and the Son is one. Both have as their focus the salvation of the world resulting in peace through our redemption (Eph 2:14, 16, 17).

Memorial to the Event
Zechariah 6:14

A. Persons Honored (6:14a):
The crown shall be for Helem, Tobijah, Jedaiah and Hen son of Zephaniah... The crown was not a gift to Joshua; it was merely a prop in a symbolic act. The crown was temple property which now would serve another function. *Helem* (*strength*) appears to be a new name bestowed on Heldai. Perhaps his generosity is being rewarded by use of this new name. *Hen* (*grace*) is substituted for *Josiah* the gracious soul in whose house the symbolic act was conducted. He may also have provided lodging for the three who had returned from exile.

B. Place for the Memorial (6:14b):
A memorial in the temple of Yahweh. The crown in the temple served two purposes. First, it served as a memorial to the generosity and kindness of the three visitors from Babylon and the local resident who opened his home to them. A *memorial* (*zikkārôn*) is an object designed to recall an event. Second, the crown was a pledge of the coming of Messiah and the building of an even greater temple. According to Jewish tradition the crown was hung in the windows in the height of the temple.

Zechariah: 6:9-15

Final Messianic Note
Zechariah 6:15

A. **Conversion of Gentiles** (6:15a):
And those afar shall come and build in the house of Yahweh. These words explain the significance of the three guests from distant Babylon in the symbolism of Joshua's crowning. There is no reason to limit *those afar* to Jews remaining in the lands of exile. As early as Isaiah there was a strong current of prophetic thought that envisioned Gentiles coming to Zion. So here it is best to interpret *those afar* as Gentiles who will bring their gifts to the temple that Shoot will build (cf. 2:11). Both Peter and Paul speak about those from afar who became part of Messiah's kingdom (Acts 2:39; Eph 2:13). *The house of Yahweh* is not the temple currently under construction, for it was well on its way to completion. This *house (temple) of Yahweh* is the kingdom over which the Shoot will rule (cf. Hag 2:6). The Gentiles will build *in* the temple, but the Lord will be the builder.

B. **Vindication of God's Word** (6:15b):
And you shall know that Yahweh has sent me unto you. The recognition formula is used for the fourth and final time in the book (cf. 2:9, 11; 4:9). The fulfillment of the messianic predictions regarding the union of Jews and Gentiles in the messianic kingdom will confirm the role of the angel of Yahweh as representative of Yahweh.

C. **Condition of Experience** (6:15c):
And it shall come to pass if you diligently hearken to the voice of Yahweh your God. The thought is similar to Dt 38:1. These words do not say that the coming of Messiah is conditional upon the obedience of the Judeans. The idea is that individuals will not be able to share in the glories of the messianic age unless they faithfully obey the commandments of the Lord. Unbelieving Jews will not be part of the glorious future temple-building effort with converted Gentiles. The Shoot will preside over a house, temple or kingdom of Jews and Gentiles truly converted and devoted to him.

Postexilic Prophets

PART TWO: MESSAGES AFTER TEMPLE CONSTRUCTION
Zechariah 7-14

According to Klein, the second diptych of the book begins here. This section consists of two "burdens" with a lengthy introduction prefixed. The gist of these chs is set forth concisely in 8:11, viz. Yahweh will no longer deal with his people as he had done in the past.

Response to the Bethel Query
Zechariah 7-8

A concrete event triggered Zechariah's most poetic and dramatic revelation concerning the distant future of God's people. This event and Zechariah's fivefold response to it (chs 7-8) constitute an introduction to the second division of the book. The similarities between this introductory section and the six vv that introduce the first diptych were pointed out in the discussion of the structure of Zechariah in the introduction. There are also a number of similarities between the previous episode (6:9-15) and the present section.[151]

Circumstances
Zechariah 7:1-3

A. **Date** (7:1):

In the fourth year of King Darius, the word of Yahweh came to Zechariah on the fourth day of the ninth month the month of Kislev. On the modern calendar the date of this episode is December 4, 518 BC. This is nearly two years after the

---

[151] R. Smith (*WBC*, 22). These similarities include: 1) a delegation coming to Jerusalem; 2) difficulties concerning the names of the visitors; 3) assurance that the temple will be rebuilt (6:12; 8:3, 9); 4) stress on obeying God's voice (6:15c; 7:8-14; 8:16); 5) the vision of Gentiles coming to Zion to share in the blessing of the messianic age.

Postexilic Prophets

night visions. The temple reconstruction effort is about at its midpoint. Outside of Jerusalem some Jews had leisure to engage in religious disputation. Questions were being raised about how the community will be affected by the completion of the temple.

B. Delegation (7:2):

1. Delegates (7:2a): **Bethel had sent Sharezer and Regem-Melech, together with his men...**[152] The leaders of the Bethel community had selected certain men to convey their query to the national religious leaders in Jerusalem. The two leaders of the delegation are named.[153] *Sharezer* is a Babylonian name meaning "protect the king."[154] *Regem-Melech* means "friend of the king."[155] The foreign names suggest that these two men may once have occupied positions of prominence in the courts of Assyria or Babylon. Perhaps like Shadrach, Meshach and Abed-nego these two men also possessed proper Hebrew names (Dan 1:6).

2. Purpose (7:2b): **to entreat the face of Yahweh.** The phrase lit., means "to stroke the face," hence "to mollify, appease, or entreat the favor." It is used of entreating the favor of the rich with gifts (e.g., Job 11:19). When used of God (12x) the phrase is anthropomorphic. One entreats the favor of Yahweh through gifts and offerings. The language hints that the inquirers anticipated a favorable response to their request to be relieved from annual fasts.

---

[152]Other translations of the v: "Bethel-Sharezer sent" (Baldwin); "Sharezer and Regem-melech sent to the house of God." Baldwin understands the delegation to have come from Babylon, not Bethel. Personal names with Bethel as a constituent appear in the Babylonian texts of this period. But v 5 seems to make the resolution of the question a matter of concern to Palestinian rather than Babylonian Jews.

[153]So most English versions. McComiskey argues that the two individuals named are in apposition with *Bethel*, hence were senders, not sendees.

[154]*Sharezer* was the name of one of the parricide sons of Sennacherib (Isa 37:38). The full name was Nergal-Sharezer, with Nergal being a Mesopotamian god. One of the princes of Babylon who desolated Jerusalem was named Nergal-Sharezer (Jer 39:3-13). It appears that the delegate from Bethel had dropped the name of the false god from his personal name.

[155]Regem is found as a proper name in 1 Chr 2:47.

Zechariah 7:1-8:23

C. Question (7:3):

1. Authorities questioned (7:3a): **by asking the priests that were at the house of Yahweh of Hosts and the prophets...** The *priests* were the logical group to whom to address a question about ritual. Priests were experts in the Law of Moses (Dt 33:8-10; Mal 2:5-7). The *prophets* were those who might make known a revelation from heaven on points where the law was not crystal clear. In the postexilic community the hostility that often characterized the relationship between priests and prophets disappeared. In particular the prophets Haggai and Zechariah may be intended, for they were the most influential prophets of this period.

2. Question posed (7:3b): **Shall I weep in the fifth month being separated, as I have done these—how many years?** The town of Bethel is personified and speaks as a single person (Unger). *Weep* points to the ritual lamentation of a fast day. Fasts over national calamities were not God-ordained. There were periodic calls for national fasting, but these were not intended to be annual occurrences. The Day of Atonement was the only annual fast. *Being separated* (r. *nzr* in Niphal) or "separating myself" is the same root used of the Nazirite vow in which a person took a vow of abstinence from strong drink and other bodily indulgences.

The fast of the fifth month commemorated the destruction of the temple (2 Kgs 25:8-9).[156] Among the exiles in Babylon that day had become a day of fasting. Now, however, the temple was nearing completion. Was it necessary to continue to mark the day of the temple's destruction after the place had been rebuilt? One might judge this question to be sincere were it not for the way the petitioners refer to the length of time they had observed the fast. The wording betrays weariness with the privations imposed by the fast.

---

[156]This fast is commemorated by Jews to this day on the ninth day of Ab (July/August). Jewish legend suggests five other disasters that fell on the same day of the month: 1) the decree of Yahweh in the wilderness that his people were not permitted to enter Canaan; 2) the destruction of the second temple by the Romans; 3) city of Bethar fell to the Romans in the Bar Cochba revolt; 4) Bar Cochba himself, whom many thought to be Messiah, fell into the hands of the Romans; and 5) Turnus Rufus ploughed up the temple mount.

Postexilic Prophets

In response to the query of the delegation from Bethel Yahweh gave Zechariah five messages of response.

First Response Message
A More Basic Issue
Zechariah 7:4-7

Introduction (7:4):
Then the word of Yahweh of Hosts came to me: Zechariah was led by the Holy Spirit to speak yet another word on behalf of Yahweh. The first response message is built around three rhetorical questions.

A. First Rhetorical Question (7:5):
1. Those to whom the question is directed (7:5a): ***Say unto all the people of the land and the priests, saying ...*** The question raised by the Bethelites had implications for the entire population—*the people of the land.*[157] Zechariah can authoritatively speak to the priests on the subject at hand because he received direct communication from Yahweh.

2. Question itself (7:5b): ***When you fasted and mourned in the fifth and seventh months even these seventy years, did you at all fast unto me, even me?*** Yahweh's word came in the form of a counter-question to the inquirers. The answer demolishes the mistaken notion that fasting in itself is a meritorious work.

The prophet begins with an acknowledgment that the fasting by the remnant was real, that it was intense, and that it was a custom of long duration (seventy years). Not only had they abstained from food from sunup to sunset as was customary in fasts, they had *mourned* (r. *spd*) during that day. This word is used for mourning over the dead or over great

---

[157] The phrase *people of the land* is used over 60x in the OT with various meanings: 1) the indigenous people of a land (e.g., Gn 23:7); 2) the entire population of a country (Lv 20:1, 4); 3) property owners of Israel who were instrumental in the nation's political life (e.g., 2 Kgs 11:18); 4) the peoples surrounding postexilic Judea (Ezra 4:4).

Zechariah 7:1-8:23

public calamities. The linkage between fasting and (ritual) weeping is frequent in OT.[158]

Not only did the remnant fast in the fifth month (see v 3), they observed a similar fast in the *seventh month*. The fast of the seventh month commemorated the death of Gedaliah (2 Kgs 25:25), the governor for a few months after the fall of Jerusalem to the Babylonians. *Even seventy years* indicates that the fasts began to be observed immediately after the fall of Jerusalem. They had been observed for almost seven decades.

In spite of the faithful observance of their fast days, the effort was totally in vain. *Did you at all fast unto me, even me?* indicates that the fasts were not being observed to please the Lord. Their fasts were man-centered, not God-centered. The fasts expressed sorrow for their national misfortunes, but not for the sin that brought on those misfortunes. The question probes the motives for their fasting.

B. Second Rhetorical Question (7:6):

And when you eat, and when you drink do you not eat for yourselves, and drink for yourselves? This question, like a surgeon's scalpel, exposes a serious cancer in the attitude of the Bethel citizens. Even in their celebratory feasts these people gave no thought to God.[159] They did not recognize him as the provider of their daily bread. These people were indifferent to God in all aspects of their lives.

C. Third Rhetorical Question (7:7):

Are not these the things that Yahweh cried by the former prophets when Jerusalem was inhabited and in prosperity, and the cities thereof round about her, and the Negev and the Shephelah were inhabited? Far more important than whether they continued with their man-made fasts was the issue of whether or not this people finally would listen to the word of God. *The former prophets* are those who preached

---

[158] Judg 20:26; 1 Sam 1:7; 2 Sam 1:12; Ezra 10:1; Neh 1:4, etc.

[159] Other views: the eating and drinking in v 5 refers to regular meals; or perhaps the fasts mentioned in this ch were not total, i.e., some food and drink were permitted.

prior to the destruction of Jerusalem. What God had to say to the pre-exilic generation still applied. The implication is that the Jews lost their prosperity and land by failing to listen to those prophets.

The rejection of previous prophetic voices is a theme taken up from Jeremiah.[160] Reference to the preaching of the former prophets is relevant in the present situation because those great preachers had practically nothing to say about fasting! Fasting was not the foremost concern of Yahweh (but cf. Isa 58:1-9).

The three geographical regions of ancient Judah are named in this v. The *Negev* is the southern region of Judah which extended as far as Beersheba (Josh 15:21). The *Shephelah* is the region of rolling hills on the western side of Judah. *Jerusalem* and *the cities round about* refer to the third geographical region of Judah, viz. the hill country.

Second Response Message
Focus on God's Word
Zechariah 7:8-14

Introduction (7:8-9a):

And the word of Yahweh came to Zechariah: 9 Thus says Yahweh of Hosts, saying: The second message begins with a claim of divine revelation, but this time Zechariah speaks in the third person (cf. 7:4). The reception of the divine revelation was translated immediately into a message for the people. The messenger formula, last used in 3:7, is now used for the seventh time. See on 1:3.

A. Summary of the Divine Word (7:9b-10):

For the biblical prophets social justice was a requirement, not as an end in itself, but as an expression of submission to the rule of Yahweh.

1. Just judgments (7:9b): **With true judgment, judge...** Yahweh always had required fairness in the courts. Judgments were to be rendered without partiality or bias (cf. Jer

---

[160]Jer 7:25; 26:5; 29:19; 35:15; 44:4.

Zechariah 7:1-8:23

5:28). This admonition is not aimed at the public in general, but at those in positions of authority who had the fate of the poor in their hands. *True judgment* refers to legal decisions that accord with facts, not twisted decisions rendered for illicit gain.

    2. Compassion (7:9c): **With kindness and abundant mercy deal each man with his brother.** Their personal dealings with one another were to be marked by kindness (*chesed*). Here is the only use of this important OT word in Zechariah. The term is about as close as the OT comes to the NT concept of *agape* love. *Mercy* in the Hebrew is a single word, but it is in the plural, hence *abundant mercy*. A *brother* is a fellow citizen.

    3. No oppression (7:10a): **Do not oppress the widow or the fatherless, the alien or the poor.** These are the four categories of disadvantaged people that appear often in the law. The first three are regularly grouped in Dt.[161] The *widow* (*'almānāh*) has no husband (and probably no son) to take her part. The *fatherless* (*yātōm*) has no parents to love and care for him. The *alien* (*gēr*) has no country to protect him. The rough economic times may have necessitated the listing of *the poor* (*'ānî*) among the oppressed. These folks had no money to purchase life's basic necessities. Furthermore, human law does not require merchants to dispense goods without compensation. God expected his people, however, to live by a higher standard of compassion.

    4. Guilelessness (7:10b): **In your hearts do not think evil of each other.** Here Zechariah literally gets to the heart of the matter. Outward conduct reflects inner values. In this way social justice is a reflection of true piety. So the prophets admonished Israelites not to plot or devise evil. God's law forbids even a thought of revenge or injury against a brother. Cf. Jer 5:26; 6:13.

B. Prior Attitude toward God's Word (7:11-12a).

    1. Deliberately rejected (7:11a): **But they refused to pay attention.** *Pay attention* (r. *qšb* Hiphil inf. const.) is the

---

[161]Dt 14:29; 16:11, 14; 24:19, 20-21, 26:12-13; 27:19.

Postexilic Prophets

same verb used in 1:4 to describe how the previous generation had responded to the proclamation of the former prophets.

2. Stubbornly resisted (7:11b): **stubbornly they turned their backs...** like an ox that refuses to have the yoke put on its neck. Cf. Neh 9:29; Hos 4:16.

3. Actively opposed (7:11c): **and made their ears heavy.** Isaiah was told that his preaching would make the ears of the people heavy so they could not hear (Isa 6:10). The term *heavy* or hard (r *kbd*) is also used 6x of the hardening of Pharaoh's heart (e.g., Ex 7:14).

4. Hardened hearts (7:12a): **Yea, they made their hearts as a diamond, lest they should hear the law and the words which Yahweh of Hosts had sent by his Spirit by the former prophets.** Their heart was hard like a stone (*shāmîr*) that could receive no cutting or engraving.[162] Probably the *diamond* is in view. Authoritatively the prophets were on the same level as the Law of Moses. The former prophets spoke words that were inspired by God's Spirit. This is a clear statement of inspiration. Cf. Mic 3:8. *Former prophets* include both literary and non-literary prophets.

C. Result of Disobeying God's Word (7:12b-14):

1. They incurred the wrath of God (7:12b): **Therefore there came great wrath from Yahweh of Hosts.** Disobedience always stirs God's *wrath* (*qetseph*). The word literally means "outburst." This is the third usage of the term in the book (cf. 1:2, 15).

2. They experienced unanswered prayer (7:13): **And it came to pass that, as he cried, and they did not hear so they cried out, and I did not hear, says Yahweh of Hosts.** The subject of the first verb *cried* is Yahweh who spoke through the pre-exilic prophets. The Judeans did not listen. During the period of the *great wrath* (v 12)—the seventy years—the distraught people continually cried out to God but he continually

---

[162]The term *shāmîr* is used 3x in the OT, in each case in reference to the hardness of the hearts of the people of God (cf. Jer 17:1; Ezek 3:9).

Zechariah 7:1-8:23

did not answer their prayers.[163] This is one of the ways that Zechariah saw the wrath of God manifested. The point is that fasting and temple-building will not gain access to the ear of God apart from daily obedience to his word. On *Yahweh of Hosts*, see on 1:3.

3. *They were scattered in foreign lands (7:14a):* **that I might scatter them**[164] **among all the nations which they did not know.** Exile is another way in which the wrath of God expresses itself. If this is future (as the standard text reads) then what happened in the past was a sign of what shall befall them in the future in punishment of similar obduracy (Deane). *Scattered* (r. *s'r* Piel impf 1cs + 3rd mp suff.) means "to toss about (by whirlwind)"; BDB renders it "storm them away" (cf. NIV). *Nations that they did not know* are foreign nations whose gods and/or language were unknown to the Israelites.[165]

4. *They caused their land to become desolate (7:14b):* **And the land was made desolate after them from passing over and returning, for they made the pleasant land a desolation.** This is the third, and perhaps worst, manifestation of the wrath of God. After the Judeans were carried away captive their land was *made desolate. From passing over and returning* indicates that the land was deprived of travelers. The text does not mean that no one could travel over the land, only that they had no desire to do so. By their stubborn disobedience to God's word the guilty fathers were responsible for the desolation of the land of Canaan.

---

[163]The tense changes from perfect to imperfect. They continually cried out to God. Others take the imperfects to be future tense, i.e., present disregard for God's word will have similar results.

[164]A small adjustment of vowel pointing of the initial *vav* yields a more understandable "and I scattered them."

[165]The phrase is connected with foreign gods in the following passages: Dt 11:28; 13:2, 7, 13; 28:26; 32:17; Jer 16:13. It seems to be equivalent to "strange gods" (Ps 44:20; 81:9; Isa 43:12; Jer 5:19; Dan 11:39; Mal 2:4) and "strange tongue" (Ps 114:1; Ezek 3:5, 6).

Third Response Message
Potential for Blessing
Zechariah 8:1-8

In ch 8 there is a Decalogue of promises each with the words *thus says Yahweh of Hosts* at (or near) the beginning. All ten promises made to Zion come from the Lord himself. The promises appear in three separate messages arranged in the pattern of five promises in the first, and two in the second and three in the third.

Introduction (8:1-2a):
And the word of Yahweh of Hosts came, saying, 2 Thus says Yahweh of Hosts ... The introduction to the third message is identical to that of the second except that the name Zechariah is missing here. On *Yahweh of Hosts*, see on 1:3.

A. Promise #1: Yahweh's Zeal for Zion (8:2b, c):
1. Initial declaration (8:2b): **I am zealous for Zion with great zeal.** This strong affirmation echoes the assurances of the angel of Yahweh in 1:14-15. Apparently the postexilic community still doubted Yahweh's commitment to them as much as they did at the outset of Zechariah's ministry. Although the temple work was continuing apace, still the economic hard times continued. Discouragement was prevalent.

In Hebrew the same word (*qin'āh*) means zealous or jealous. The word suggests intolerance of all rivals. Yahweh is often represented as a jealous God in the OT.[166]

2. Declaration reinforced (8:2c): **Yea, with great fury I am zealous for her.**[167] Yahweh's zealous good will toward

---

[166]He is called a jealous God at least 7x. Yahweh is said to have manifested jealous anger in a number of passages, e.g., Dt 29:20-28; Ezek 5:13; 16:38, 42; 23:25.

[167]Unger points out the devices used in this passage to underscore Yahweh's undying love for Israel: 1) by divine revelation (v 1); 2) the repetition of the divine appellation *Yahweh of Hosts*; 3) by the extremely emphatic assertion *I am zealous* which is a present perfect; 4) by the use of the cognate accusative *with zeal*; 5) by use of the adjective *great* with the cognate accusative; 6) by the use of the uncognate accusative strengthened by the

his people is so intense that it burns with fury against their enemies. One side of God's love for Zion is shown in the punishment of Zion's enemies.

B. Promise #2: Yahweh's Return (8:3):
1. Declaration (8:3a): **This is what Yahweh says: I have returned unto Zion.** This promise echoes the words of 1:16 and 2:10. Yahweh had deserted the city prior to the Babylonian conquest (Ezek 10:18; 11:23). But now the restoration of the exiles, the rebuilding of the temple, and the voice of prophecy showed that God had returned to Jerusalem. The theme of Yahweh's return to Jerusalem is also developed in Ezekiel 43:1-5 and Hag 1:8.

2. Yahweh's presence (8:3b): **And will dwell in the midst of Jerusalem.** The line of thought parallels 2:9-10 where the enemies are plundered and God dwells in the midst of his people. *Dwell* (r *shkn*) means to "settle down, abide, or remain." This is the same word used of Yahweh's abode among his people in the Wilderness Period (Ex 25:8; 29:45; etc.).

3. Jerusalem's new name (8:3c): **Then Jerusalem will be called the City of Truth, and the mountain of Yahweh of Hosts the holy mountain.** Renaming a person or place in biblical times signaled a change of status.[168] *City of Truth* could also be rendered "Faithful City." Whereas Jerusalem once had been unfaithful, now she would be faithful. On the significance of this name see Zeph 3:13.

In OT times the temple in Jerusalem was the center for instruction by the priests about the Law of God. Most of the great prophets of God had walked the streets of this city announcing current revelations from God. In Zechariah's day Jerusalem was still in ruins. This prophet, however, foresaw a day in which Jerusalem would again be the center for dis-

---

adjective *great*, i.e., "with great heat, i.e., anger, wrath; 7) by the repetition of the verb zealous; 8) by repetition of the object of the fierce love.

[168] Other new names for messianic Jerusalem: Yahweh Shammah ("Yahweh is there") in Ezek 48:35; Hephzibah ("my delight is in her") and Beulah ("married") in Isa 62:2-4.

Postexilic Prophets

seminating the truth about the one true and living God and his expectations for man.[169]

The mountain of Yahweh is Zion, one of the prominent hills of Jerusalem. Subsequently Zion became a name for the city itself and for the people of God. Zion had been considered God's holy mountain for centuries. *Holy* means separated from the common and profane. During the exilic period when the land was desolate Zion was not considered holy or special to God. By virtue of Yahweh's habitation, however, the place would again be called the holy mountain. The messianic Jerusalem will be the exclusive realm of Yahweh.

The promises in v 3 find complete fulfillment in the church of Christ which is the spiritual Jerusalem (Heb 12:22). This Jerusalem is the center for God's truth about the Messiah, and the habitation of a holy people (1 Pet 2:9). God once again dwells in an earthly temple (2 Cor 6:16).

C. Promise #3: Jerusalem's Peace (8:4-5):

1. First peace picture (8:4): **Thus says Yahweh of Hosts: Once again men and women of ripe old age will sit in the streets of Jerusalem, yes each man with his staff in his hand by reason of days.** At the time these words were spoken Jerusalem was still in ruins. Yet Yahweh reassures the Judeans that *once again*[170] (cf. 2:4) the beloved capital will be repopulated. Zechariah paints a beautiful word picture of the safety and tranquility of the new Jerusalem of which the physical Jerusalem is a type. New Jerusalem will be a safe and tranquil city. Elderly people generally do not desire to be present in public places when there is danger to them. Yet they will sit in the streets of messianic Jerusalem without fear that they will be endangered by raging mobs or racing war chariots.

2. Second peace picture (8:5): **And the streets of the city shall be filled with boys and girls playing in her streets.**

---

[169] Another view is that City of Truth means that Jerusalem will once again enjoy conditions consistent with God's promises in the past.

[170] *Once again* (*'ōd*) appears to be a special prophetic formula used to introduce salvation oracles (cf. Hag 1:6; Zech 1:17). Earlier uses: Isa 14:1; 49:20; 56:8; Jer 31:23; 32:15; 33:10, 12, 13.

Zechariah 7:1-8:23

Zechariah sketches a second picture of peace and tranquility. Little children would not be playing in the streets if there were danger from raging chariots, thugs or enemy soldiers.

Long life and children were thought of in the OT as blessings from God (Prov 3:2; 9:10-11; Pss 127:3; 128:3-4). So the new Jerusalem will be a city much blessed. It is by the well-being of children and aged that Zechariah measures the greatness of the city, not by industry, professional sports, art and culture by which cities are usually measured today.

D. Promise #4: Marvelous Promises (8:6):

1. Future blessings are marvelous to men (8:6a): **Thus says Yahweh of Hosts: It may seem marvelous to the remnant of this people at that time...** *Marvelous* points to something too difficult to do. *Remnant* refers to those Judeans who have returned to Palestine from the exile in Babylon. More narrowly, the term refers to the nucleus of true believers. These faithful ones are unable to comprehend how such miraculous things just promised in vv 3-5 could come to pass.

2. Future blessings not marvelous to Yahweh (8:6b): **should it also be marvelous in my eyes? (oracle of Yahweh of Hosts).** Scholars have classified this question as "a disputation question"—a questions that raises a question about Yahweh's power to deliver on his promises.[171] Apparently the Judean remnant had doubts about earlier promises of peace and restoration for Jerusalem. But man's extremity is God's opportunity. The interrogative force is only indicated by the context.[172]

In the most solemn of utterances—an oracle from the lips of God himself—Zechariah wants the remnant to know that Yahweh has infinite power at his disposal. He can fulfill all his promises. So the fourth promise is a promise to fulfill all marvelous promises!

---

[171] Similar questions are raised in Gn 18:13-14; Jer 32:17.

[172] The interrogative *hey* is sometimes omitted when the context makes the interrogative force obvious or something more than a question is intended, as the expressing of strong feeling or something incredible to imagine. Here it is incredible that anything should be thought to be impossible for God. The less suitable alternative is to regard these words as irony: "If it seems like a marvel to you, it even seems like a marvel to me also."

E. Promise #5: Dispersed Gathered (8:7-8):

1. Deliverance from bondage (8:7): **Thus says Yahweh of Hosts: Behold, I am about to deliver my people from the land of the east and from the land of the west.** Though a few thousand brave souls had returned to the desolation in Judea, God had many more people throughout the world that one day will join with faithful Jews in the kingdom of God. *East* and *west* are symbols for the whole world (cf. Ps 50:1; 113:3; Mal 1:13 where the same idiom is used). The participle *deliver* denotes continuous performance of the act. The promise here echoes Isa 43:5-6.

In the OT God refers to "my people" some 169x., 23x in conjunction with "Israel." The theme is prominent in Jeremiah (42x). Even before the Exodus and the covenant at Sinai he referred to the descendants of Jacob as "my people." Thus those who are designated "my people" may be those who are potentially God's people. Even Gentiles in the messianic age will become "my people" (Isa 19:25). These considerations suggest that "my people in Zech 8:7 who are gathered from the lands of the east and the west may include Gentiles as well as descendants of Jacob.

2. Restoration to Jerusalem (8:8a): **And I will bring them, and they shall dwell in the midst of Jerusalem.** The gathering of the remnant is a theme that appeared as early as the eighth century (e.g., Isa 11:11-12; Mic 2:12-13; 4:6-7). The promise relates to the physical Jerusalem as long as the OT was in effect. But the ultimate reference is to the spiritual Jerusalem, the church of God (Gal 4:26; Heb 12:22; Mt 8:11). That this does not refer to the return from Babylon entirely is indicated by two facts: 1) the return from Babylon came from only one direction, usually designated north; 2) the bulk of restoration from Babylon was past by the time of Zechariah.

In v 3 God dwells in Jerusalem; here it is the people of God who dwell there. They are drawn as to a magnet to the place where their God has chosen to dwell.

Clearly here Jerusalem has become a symbol of something much larger than the physical city of Jerusalem, for by no means could all the redeemed throughout the earth and throughout the ages fit into the physical parameters of ancient Jerusalem. Those who discern the true depths of this promise understand that God is presently in the process of gathering his people through the gospel into the kingdom of Christ. This v recalls the summons in 2:6-7 for people to leave the nations and come to Zion.

3. *Reconciliation to God (8:8b):* **and they shall be my people and I shall be their God in truth and in righteousness.** *Shall be my people* implies that prior to the time of the gathering they were not God's people—they were Lo-ammi (Hos 1:10). The language here points to a new covenant relationship (cf. Jer 31:31). Those who become part of the new Jerusalem will enter into a new covenant with the Lord. *In truth and righteousness* refers both to the people and to God.[173] The promises made to Jerusalem will be seen to be true. He will deal with them according to his nature. On their part, God's people will have true allegiance to the Lord. Furthermore, they will reflect in their conduct the right relationship with him.

Fourth Response Message
More Promises
Zechariah 8:9-17

The sixth and seventh sayings in the Decalogue of promises come within a sermon of sorts. The sermon is similar in form to 7:4-14. The first part of the sermon begins and ends with the exhortation to *let your hands be strong*.

Introduction (8:9):
Thus says Yahweh of Hosts: The messenger formula signals the beginning of a new word from the Lord. By way of introduction to the fourth response message Zechariah presents a wordy description of the addressees and then his opening exhortation. The promises then come in support of the exhortation.

---

[173] These same two words are used to describe the messianic Jerusalem in Isa 1:26, and the messianic Ruler (Isa 11:5; using a synonym for *truth*).

Postexilic Prophets

1. Addressees (8:9a): **Those of you who are hearing in these days these words from the mouth of the prophets who (were) in the day when the foundation of the house of Yahweh of Hosts was laid to the end that the temple might be built...** Zechariah seems to turn from the Bethel representatives to the postexilic community as a whole. He addresses those who had been listening to the prophetic word since the resumption of the temple work. *These words* refer particularly to the words of promise that had just been uttered by Zechariah in the preceding vv, and by Haggai. The *prophets* are those that ministered to the community since the return from Babylon, including Haggai and Zechariah.

The day when the foundation was laid refers to the day nearly two decades earlier when the returning exiles prepared to rebuild the temple (Ezra 3:6; Hag 2:18). *To the end that the temple might be built* anticipates the completion of the project. The point is that the same prophets that speak words of promise now are those who have encouraged you throughout the time when the temple was under construction.

2. Opening exhortation (8:9b): **let your hands be strong.** This idiom, meaning "be of good courage," is derived from the context of the holy war.[174] The exhortation is aimed at the older generation that had seen the temple project proceed by fits and starts. It also is directed to those young adults who had been born in the past two decades.

A. Promise #6: Conditions Reversed (8:10-13b):

1.. Reminder of former conditions (8:10): **For before those days the wages of man did not exist, nor the wages of the cattle; and to the one who went out and came in there was no peace because of the adversary; and I set every man against his neighbor.** In this recounting of pre-temple construction miseries this v is reminiscent of Haggai. The prophet focuses on three conditions.

First, Judea's economy was in depression (cf. Hag 1:4-11). *Before those days* looks back to the time before the reconstruction effort was renewed about two years previously.

---

[174]Cf. Judg 7:11; 1 Sam 23:15-17; Isa 35:3; Ezek 22:14.

Zechariah 7:1-8:23

Wages probably refers to crop yield which was so small that men and even cattle found it difficult to subsist.[175]

Second, the land was insecure. *Going out and coming in* is an idiom that can refer to military activity; but here the reference is to everyday activity (2 Kgs 19:27; Ps 121:8). The Judeans could not go about their usual occupations or move from place to place with safety on account of their enemies that compassed them about. *The adversary* might refer to those living around Judea who harassed the farmers and herders who went out to labor in the fields (cf. Ezra 4:4). The *adversary* might also be the regional Persian officials who threw up roadblocks to reconstruction work in Jerusalem (Ezra 4-6).

Third, the Judean community had become embittered. Pre-construction hard times led to internal dissension as well as outward opposition. *I set* reveals the prophetic viewpoint that everything that happens is either caused by direct action of Yahweh, or is at least permitted by him.

2. *Divine pledge (8:11)*: **But now not as in former days will I be to the remnant of this people (oracle of Yahweh of Hosts).** *Now* (*'attāh*) signals that Yahweh is ready to reverse the fortunes of the Judeans. *The remnant of this people* points to the limited population and resources of the restoration of community. Yahweh will not deal with his people as in former days. The title *Yahweh of Hosts* reminds the listeners of all the power and authority of their God.

3. *Increased production (8:12)*: **For the seed of peace, the vine, shall give its fruit, and the land shall give its increase, and the heavens shall give their dew; and I will cause the remnant of this people to inherit all these things.** *For* (*kî*) is used for the second time in this discourse (cf. v 10) to introduce a reason for optimism. *The seed of peace* is *the vine*.[176] Viticulture is a product of peaceful conditions. The basic idea: the crops will be safe and secure. *Increase* points to abundant harvest. *Dew* represents moisture essential in summer to produce crops. *Inherit these things* refers to the

---

[175] Another view: the poverty was so bad that the hired man could not be paid and the beast could not be given its share of the grain.

[176] Others think the v refers to seed time marked by absence of war (Unger, Perowne, Deane).

land, abundant harvests, and security. Agricultural abundance symbolizes God's provisions for his people.

4. *Changed reputation (8:13a):* **As you were a curse among the nations, O house of Judah and house of Israel, so I will deliver you, and you will become a blessing.** *Curse* indicates that the fate of God's people had been used as a formula of imprecation among the heathen, e.g., May your fate be that of the Judeans. Both *Israel* and *Judah*—the entire nation—experienced exile; both were also represented in the return from Babylon; both are represented in the present kingdom. *Deliver you* refers to deliverance from their national calamity and national sin. *Blessing* indicates that observers will begin to use God's people as a formula of blessing. Thus God reverses the fortunes of his people and fulfills the blessing promise made to Abraham (Gn 12:2; cf. Isa19:24; Ezek 34:26).

5. *Concluding exhortation (8:13b):* **Do not be afraid.** This admonition seems to mark the end of the first part of the sermon. In essence these words repeat the opening admonition in v 9 to be courageous. They need not fear failure if they will put their hands to the task of completing the temple and rebuilding the city.

B. Promise #7: Good Things to Come (8:13c-17):

1. *Introductory admonition (8:13c):* **Let your hands be strong.** The injunction of v 9 is repeated. This is the only one of the ten promises in ch 8 where some element precedes the declaration *thus says Yahweh of Hosts*. Knowledge of what God had done and would do for Israel should encourage them in their work.

2. *God's past purpose (8:14):* **For thus says Yahweh of Hosts: Just as I proposed to do evil to you when your ancestors provoked me to anger and I did not relent, says Yahweh of Hosts...** The opening admonition is followed by the messenger formula (see on 1:3). *For (kî)* indicates the reason for the strengthening of the hands. This conjunction is omitted in NIV. The promise has to do with the purpose of Yahweh.

Babylonian captivity was no accident. This *evil* was a result of deliberate, purposive divine planning. God carried

Zechariah 7:1-8:23

out the dreaded decrees that he had given forth against the apostate nation. The word *provoked to anger* (r *qtsp* Hiph.) was used in 1:2 in connection with the fathers, i.e., the previous generation. Here he explains why that anger was appropriate. Yahweh did not *relent* (r *shūbh*), i.e., he did not change his mind.

3. *God's present purpose (8:15a):* **so again I have purposed in these days to do good to Jerusalem and to the house of Judah.** The thought recalls Jer 32:42. *So again* (*kēn*) introduces a change in God's purpose, but a purpose nonetheless. From former days Zechariah turns to *these days*, i.e., the days in which he lived. God is true to his purpose. Previously he carried out his purpose to bring judgment on his people. Now God purposes to bring blessing. God's purpose toward them has changed because they have sought him.

The *good* that Yahweh proposes to do for the Judeans was outlined in v 12. Those who lived in the outlying regions will be beneficiaries of these blessings as well as Jerusalem. The past chastisement which happened as it was threatened is a guarantee of the fulfillment of the promised blessings (Deane). Furthermore, the benefits that were immediate did not exhaust the full scope of these sweeping prophetic previews (Unger).

4. *God's encouragement (8:15b):* **Do not be afraid.** The admonition from v 13 is repeated. Primarily fear of failing in the rebuilding efforts is in view. Fear of failing leads to discouragement.

5. *God's requirement (8:16-17a):* **These are the things you shall do: speak truth every man with his neighbor. Judge truth and the judgment of peace in your gates. 17 And let none of you devise evil in your hearts against his neighbor, and love no false oath** The future blessing is assured; but the time and place of its fulfillment are conditioned by the people's response (R. Smith). The prophet now lists some fundamental moral requirements that must be met if the Judeans are to experience the promised blessing. This sounds very much like the preaching of the previous prophets which Zechariah summarized in 7:9-10.

First, as to their words, they must always speak the truth. *Truth* is what is consistent with the facts as one knows them.

Second, in respect to legal judgments there must be perfect equity. Such decisions secure peace and concord between the parties concerned. Local judges sat in the city *gates* (cf. Dt 16:18; 21:19; Amos 5:10).

Third, they must not devise evil in their hearts. Cf. 7:10. Micah 2:1. The Mosaic Law forbade covetousness in the heart. Such covetousness evolves into concrete plans to defraud and deceive one's neighbor.

Fourth, they must not love false oaths, i.e., employ them as a standard business tool. The prevalent sins of this period were not idolatry but cheating, lying, and injustice—vices perfected in Babylon, the land of commerce. *A false oath* is one that is not honored—a promise that went unfulfilled.

6. God's holy will (8:17b): **For all these are things that I hate (oracle of Yahweh).** The ultimate reason for avoiding the sins named in the previous vv is that they are contrary to the holy character of God. Yahweh hated what he observed taking place in the postexilic community. Because God hates these sins, we too must hate them.

Fifth Response Message
A Glorious Future
Zechariah 8:18-23

Introduction (8:18):
And the word of Yahweh of Hosts came unto me, saying... These words signal the beginning of a new message. The message, however, completes the Decalogue of promises that commenced in the third message.

A. Promise #8: Fasts become Feasts (8:19):
Thus says Yahweh of Hosts... These familiar words introduce the eighth promise that came in response to the question about fasting. For the first time the message directly addresses the issue posed by the delegation from Bethel.

1. Current fasts (8:19a): ***The fast of the fourth month, and the fast of the fifth month, and the fast of the seventh***

Zechariah 7:1-8:23

month, and the fast of the tenth month... Among the most pious Jews, the four fast days named in this v are observed even to this day.

The fourth month fast was mentioned in 7:5. On the Jewish calendar this is the 17th of Tammuz. This fast commemorated the day when a breach was made in the walls of Jerusalem by the Chaldeans. See 2 Kgs 25:3; Jer 52:6, 7; 39:2.

The fifth month fast was mentioned in 7:3. On the Jewish calendar this is known as the 9th of Av. This fast commemorated the day the Jerusalem temple was burned in 586 BC. See 2 Kgs 25:8-9; Jer 52:12.

The seventh month fast commemorated the death of Gedaliah, although the Scriptures do not specify the day on which he was slain. See 2 Kgs 25:25; Jer 41:1, 2, 4, 5. It is possible, but not likely, that the fast of the seventh month was the Day of Atonement.

The tenth month fast—the 10th of Tebeth—commemorated the beginning of the siege of Jerusalem by the Babylonians. See 2 Kgs 25:1; Ezek 24:1-2.

2. *Feasts of the future (8:19b):* **shall be to the house of Judah joy and gladness and cheerful feasts**. Former miseries will be forgotten in the presence of the blessings showered upon them by the Lord. The painful experiences commemorated by the fasts can even become occasions of celebration when the redeemed realize how these events propelled them into a more wonderful relationship with Yahweh.

3. *Conditions of this promise (8:19c):* **Therefore truth and peace [you must] love**. The word order highlights the objects of the verb *love*. In order to share in the blessing that will unfold for God's people an individual Jew must certainly practice truth and peace (8:16); but he must also *love* these ideas as well. There must be an inward compulsion always to say and do the right thing. There must be inward striving for a peaceful relationship with neighbors.

B. Promise #9: Gentile Conversion (8:20-22):

Thus says Yahweh of Hosts... The messenger formula introduces the ninth promise in the Decalogue of promises.

Postexilic Prophets

1. Gentiles will seek Yahweh in great numbers (8:20): **[It shall yet come to pass] once again that there shall come peoples, and the inhabitants of many cities...** The glorious blessings bestowed on God's people will attract surrounding nations to join in the worship of Yahweh. On *once again* (*'ōd*) see on 8:4. *Peoples* is a representative name for all peoples.

2. Gentiles will seek Yahweh earnestly (8:21): **And the inhabitants of one city shall go to another, saying, Let us go speedily to entreat the favor of Yahweh, and to seek Yahweh of Hosts. I will go also.** The Hebrew syntax (imperf. + infin. abs.) implies, "Let us go on and on continually" (Pusey; Wright). On *entreat the favor of Yahweh,* see on 7:2. Not merely will the Gentiles make pilgrimages to the great annual festival, they will desire to seek to know Yahweh and worship him acceptably. The scene is the same as that portrayed in the eighth century by Isaiah (2:2-4) and Micah (4:1-4). *I will go also* has been taken to be the words of 1) some straggler or doubter; 2) the city exhorted; 3) Zechariah himself; and 4) those who give the exhortation, i.e., they will encourage people by their example.

3. Gentiles will seek Yahweh in messianic Jerusalem (8:22): **Yea, many peoples and strong nations will come to seek Yahweh of Hosts in Jerusalem and to entreat the favor of Yahweh.** This v expands on the previous v. *Strong* nations are those numerically strong. As in 2:5-7 these Gentiles come to *Jerusalem.* A literal fulfillment is not to be looked for (Deane). These words declare the future conversion of the Gentiles and their being made one with Israel in the church of Christ. One *entreats God's favor* through prayers and godly living. See further on 7:2.

In prophetic literature there are two opposite pictures of the relation of the Gentiles to messianic Jerusalem. In one picture the Gentiles are gathered to Jerusalem for battle. Their intent is plunder. This picture is sketched most vividly in chs 12 and 14 of this book. In the other picture Gentiles come to Jerusalem for worship on a holy pilgrimage. Both traditions have deep roots in the prophetic tradition, the first in Joel 3:9-17, the latter in Isa 2:1-4 and Mic 4:1-5.[177]

C. Promise #10: Prominence of Jews (8:23):

Thus says Yahweh of Hosts... For the tenth time the messenger formula introduces a promise in this ch thereby completing the Decalogue of promises. This v provides a concrete example of Gentiles desperately seeking the blessing of being associated with Jerusalem.

1. Zeal of Gentiles (8:23a): **In those days ten men from the nations of all languages and nations shall take hold, shall take hold of the robe of a Jew...** *In those days* refers to the time when Gentiles in great numbers turn to Yahweh, i.e., in the NT age. The number *ten* is symbolic of a large, indefinite number. Cf. Gn 31:7; Lv 26:26; 1 Sam 1:8. *Languages and nations* is lit., "tongues of nations." Diversity of language and ethnic background will not hinder unity in the faith. The verb *take hold* means "to grasp, seize, grab." The verb indicates the zeal of those who will seek Yahweh. The verb is repeated for emphasis. The metaphor of the many taking hold of one appears also in Isa 4:1.

The v is an amplification of Isa 66:13. The spiritual magnetism of messianic Zion overcomes the confusion of tongues at the Tower of Babel (Gn 11).

2. Declaration of Gentiles (8:23b): **and say, We will go with you...** The picture is one of a Jew coming from some far country to celebrate the festivals. He has a number of Gentiles clinging to him, asking permission to accompany him on his journey. Gentiles want to join faithful Jews in their devotions to the Lord. In Christ Gentiles declare their allegiance to the God of Abraham, Isaac and Jacob. Jew and Gentile march together in the great new covenant pilgrimage to the heavenly Jerusalem.

3. Explanation of Gentiles (8:23c): **because we have heard that God is with you.** Gentiles will observe how well

---

[177] Other passages reflecting this tradition: Isa 45:14; 49:22-23; 60:1-3.

Postexilic Prophets

favored the Jews are and conclude that God is with them.[178] Salvation is of the Jews. The gospel began to be announced in Jerusalem, preached by Jewish apostles. The founder of Christianity was of the seed of David. True Israelites are all true Christians (Rom 4:11; Gal 3:7, 29; 4:26). So the Gentiles have become convinced that they must join these faithful Jews if they are to experience the blessings of the gospel age.

Preliminary Note to Chs 9-14

Critics generally contend that Zechariah 9-14 was not written by the same hand that wrote chs 1-8. Some critics allege that chs 9-14 are pre-exilic. Yet there are clear indications that these chs were written after the exile. For example, governors are mentioned in chs 9-14; but there is no hint that there was any king in Judea. Judah and Israel had been in exile; some were still there (9:11, 12; 10:6-10). Judah and Ephraim together shall wage successful war against Javan, i.e., the Greeks (9:13). The pre-exilic jealousy between the two divisions of the chosen people has ended. There is one nation.

Whereas critics allege that chs 9-14 are by a different author (called Deutero-Zechariah) a strong case can be made for the unity of the book. First, similar expressions, some rather rare, are found in both sections of the book. Second, similar concepts are developed in both sections. Third, there is a predilection for the number four throughout the book. Fourth, the negative critics themselves cannot decide between a pre-exilic and post-exilic origin of chs 9-14. Fifth, in both sections there is liberal use of the earlier prophets.

The following dissimilarities to chs 1-8 have been noted by Chambers. First, chs 9-14 came at a later time in the ministry of Zechariah. Second, no dates are present in the last six chs. Third, the first eight chs communicated the revelations that bore immediately upon the interests of people living in the sixth century; the last six chs have a wider range, focusing on the kingdom of Messiah. These final chs are intended for

---

[178]The Philistine Abimelech was the prototype of the Gentiles who recognize that God is with the descendants of Abraham in a special way (Gn 26:28).

Zechariah 7:1-8:23

all people of all times. Fourth, in the Book of Isaiah there is a precedent for a book with an initial section focused on issues in the days of the prophet, and a concluding section focusing on the more distant future.

A few other points about chs 9-14 should be emphasized. First, these chs are extremely difficult—the hardest in the OT. Second, as to style, some of the grandest and most powerful passages in Zechariah are found in chs 9-11. These are as fine as any in Hebrew poetry (Deane). Third, the influence of these final six chs is substantial (Baldwin). Chs 9-14 are the most quoted section of the prophets in the passion narratives of the Gospels. Furthermore, next to Ezekiel, Zechariah has influenced the author of Revelation more than any other OT writer.

First Burden
Zechariah 9:1-10:12

In the first "burden" Zechariah juxtaposes the images of donkey and horse to describe the salvation and transformation God's people will experience in the future.[179]

Coming World Conqueror
Zechariah 9:1-8

Zechariah describes a divine judgment that sweeps southward through the regions of Syria, Tyre, and Philistia. Although Israel seldom occupied these territories, these areas fell within the ideal borders of Israel.[180]

A. Judgment on Syria (9:1-2a).

1. Introductory formula (9:1a): ***A burden.*** Burden (*massā'*) refers to something uplifted (Ex 23:5) or an utterance. Thus a *burden* is an authoritative divine utterance which contains a weighty pronouncement of judgment. The

---
[179]Allen, "Equine," op. cit. *SCJ* (Fall, 2000): 254.
[180]Nm 13:21-24; 34:1-12; Dt 1:7; Josh 1:3-4; 1 Kgs 4:21, 24; 2 Kgs 14:25, 28.

167

term is often used in the OT in a technical sense to introduce an oracle of a prophet. [181] The word connotes the idea that the prophet feels an obligation to deliver his message to others.

2. *Initial object of God's judgment (9:1b):* **The word of Yahweh is in the land of Hadrach, and Damascus is its resting place.** Hadrach is mentioned only here in OT, but it does appear in Assyrian inscriptions.[182] The place was situated between Hamath and Riblah. The idea is that God's word of judgment will fall upon this area of Syria.

The oracle is describing a judgment that is moving from north to south. The word of Yahweh's judgment next rests upon *Damascus*, a major trade center in Syria during the Persian period. The details of this prediction are adequately fulfilled by Alexander the Great whose armies march south from Asia Minor through Syria and eventually to Egypt.[183]

3. *Reason for divine judgment (9:1c):* **for Yahweh's eye**[184] **is on mankind and all the tribes of Israel.** *For* (*kî*) introduces the reason for the divine judgment on the land of Hadrach and Damascus. *Yahweh's eye* is lit., "to Yahweh is an eye." The thought is parallel to Jer 32:19. The first vision (1:7-17) proclaimed Yahweh's knowledge of world events and his loyalty to his people. This v makes the same claim. *Mankind* (*'ādām*) is the world of the Gentiles.[185] God sees their evil doing and oppression of Israel. Therefore judgment

---

[181] Isa 13:1; 14:28; 15:1; 17:1; 19:1; Ezek 12:10; Nah 1:1; Hab 1:1.

[182] Among the fanciful interpretations of Hadrach are these: 1) a name for Messiah; 2) symbolic of the Persian Empire; 3) an Aramean king; 4) an Assyrian fire-god; 5) a scribal error for Hauran, a district south of Damascus. It is now generally accepted that there was a city named Hadrach in greater Syria.

[183] R. Chisholm, *Interpreting the Minor Prophets* (Grand Rapids: Zondervan, 1990), 260. Cf. Hanson (*DA*, 316-19) who divorces these vv from any historical battles. He thinks Zechariah was using stock prophetic formulae and locations to represent stereotypically Yahweh's redemptive actions for his people. *The Dawn of Apocalyptic* (Philadelphia: Fortress, 1975), 316-19. R. Smith (*WBC*, 252) concurs with Hanson.

[184] So NIV note. But NASB has "for the eyes of men, especially of all the tribes of Israel, are toward the LORD." The line then points to the consternation into which men will be thrown at the approach of the conqueror who is Yahweh's agent of judgment.

[185] The slightest of emendations yields "Aram" (*'ārām*) for *mankind* (*'ādām*). But MT makes sense as it stands.

falls upon them. Cf. Jer 32:19 (Deane). *All the tribes of Israel* speaks of the theocracy in its ideal form represented in Zechariah's day by Judea.[186] Yahweh sees the condition of his people and intervenes in history on their behalf.

4. *Subsequent object of the judgment (9:2a):* **and Hamath also shall border on it.** Hamath was both the name of an important Syrian city and a province of the Persian Empire. This v suggests that the province of Hamath bordered on that of Damascus. Apparently this city/territory will share in the judgment on Hadrach and Damascus. Hamath survives today under the name Hama with 50,000 population.

B. Judgment on Phoenicia (9:2b-4).

1. Reason for the judgment (9:2b): **Tyre along with Sidon for she is very wise.** The judgment continues to move southward from Syria to the two most important cities of Phoenicia. Sidon is mentioned parenthetically. *She is very wise* refers to Tyre, a city noted for wisdom (Ezek 27:8; 28:3, 4).

2. Inevitability of the judgment (9:3): **though Tyre build a tower, though she heap up silver like dust and fine gold like the mire of the streets.** Any doubt that vv 1-2 are describing a military judgment are removed by this v. Description of the judgment on Tyre almost certainly was influenced by Amos 1:10. Zechariah makes two points designed to squelch any hope that Tyre may escape this divine judgment.

First, fortifications will not avert judgment. Zechariah employs paronomasia. *Tyre* (*tsōr*) will build a *tower* or "fortress" (*mātsôr*), an obvious word play on *tsōr*. This may be an allusion to the island fortifications of Tyre located about seven hundred yards off the mainland. Isaiah 23:4 referred to it as "the fortress of the sea." It is said that this island fortress had a wall 150 feet tall. The city had been besieged by the Assyrians for five years and by the Babylonians for thirteen years without success. Nonetheless, Tyre's mighty fortress will not stand up to Yahweh's judgment. Alexander the Great

---

[186]Other views: 1) all peoples as well as the tribes of Israel will recognize God in the future. Cf. 8:22 (Cashdan); 2) the eyes of mankind and Israel are upon the agent of Yahweh, viz. Alexander the Great.

was able to construct a mole out to the island in a matter of weeks.

Second, wealth will not avert judgment. Through her commercial enterprises Tyre amassed wealth as easily as one would sweep dust from a house and gather dirt from the street. Her vast wealth, however, will not enable her to bribe enemies.

3. Result of the judgment (9:4): **Behold Yahweh will dispossess her, and smite her wealth into the sea, and she will be consumed with fire.** On the meaning of *behold*, see on 1:8. *Yahweh will dispossess* implies conquest at the hands of her enemies. Cf. Josh 8:7; 17:12. On the smiting of Tyre into the sea, see Ezek 26:4. All of Tyre's wealth will be buried in a watery grave. On the burning of fortress Tyre, see Amos 1:10. The passage is probably predicting the fall of Tyre to Alexander after of a siege of seven months.

C. Judgment on Philistia (9:5-6a):

1. Fear of the Philistine cities (9:5a): **And Ashkelon will see and fear, and Gaza shall be exceedingly mournful along with Ekron, for her trust shall be ashamed.** Four cities of the famous Philistine pentapolis are mentioned in this v in the same order that appears in Jer 25:20.[187] *Ashkelon* fears the same fate as Tyre. *Gaza* is in anguish over the impending confrontation with Alexander. Tyre was Ekron's hope or trust. Perhaps there was a mutual defense pact between the two cities. When Tyre fell, Ekron knew there was no hope. Cf. Zeph 2:6-7.

2. Fate of the Philistine cities (9:5b-6a): **And the king will perish from Gaza, and Ashkelon will not be inhabited, 6 and a mongrel race will dwell in Ashdod.** One by one Zechariah predicts the fate of three prominent Philistine cities.

First, *Gaza* will cease to be independent. This statement is important in setting the stage for a contrast with the coming of a future great king for God's people in vv 9-11. No special

---

[187]This is the case also in Amos 1:6-8 and Zeph 2:4. Gath is missing from the list because it had been destroyed in the days of King Uzziah (2 Chr 26:6).

Zechariah 9:1-10:12

mention is made of Ashkelon, Ekron or Ashdod in the records of Alexander's march south from Tyre. The fate of Gaza, however, is fully documented. The city fell to Alexander after a siege of five months. Ten thousand of its inhabitants were slain and the rest were sold into slavery. Batis, the king, was bound to a chariot with thongs thrust through the soles of his feet. He was then dragged through the city.

Second, *Ashkelon* will gradually fade from the scene. During the Greek period, Ashkelon became a Hellenistic center of culture. The city did not apparently have hostilities with the Maccabean rulers in Jerusalem (1 Macc 10:36; 11:60). In fact, many Jews lived there. In 104 BC Rome granted to Ashkelon the status "free allied city." Herod the Great built some beautiful buildings there, including a palace. He left the city to his sister, Salome, at his death. The city was attacked by the Jews in the first Roman Revolt (AD 66) but survived and was faithful to Rome. It later became a Christian city. The Moslems conquered Ashkelon in the seventh century. It was taken by the Crusaders, then retaken by Saladin in 1187. The city was systematically destroyed by the Mamelukes in 1270.

Third, *Ashdod* will be inhabited by a foreign people. *Mongrel race* (*mamzēr*) is used in Dt 23:2 where the word is often interpreted to mean one born of incest or adultery. Here the thought is that Ashdod shall be overrun by people not native to the area.[188]

In the Greek period Ashdod was known as Azotus. It was a flourishing city until being captured by Judas Maccabeus. He destroyed altars and images in Ashdod (1 Macc 5:68). Judas' brother Jonathan later burned the temple of Dagon, those who took refuge there, and ultimately the city itself (1 Macc 10:84-87). In 63 BC the Romans separated Ashdod from Judea. Gabinius rebuilt the city, and it was joined to the province of Syria. The Emperor Augustus granted it to Herod the Great. Ashdod's greatness as a city ended with the Roman destruction of AD 67, although it was occupied at least through the sixth century.

---

[188]Targum and LXX take the word to mean "stranger" or "foreigner." Therefore here the threat is that aliens will inherit Ashdod.

Postexilic Prophets

D. Conversion of the Philistines (9:6b-7):

The switch from third person to first person in the remaining vv of this oracle signals a change in tone from judgment to hope.

1. Humbling (9:6b): **and the pride of the Philistines I will cut off.** The humbling of Philistine pride is the first of a series of actions taken by Yahweh to incorporate Gentiles into the family of God. The four great cities of the coastal plain were the pride of the Philistines. When prophets speak of the pride of a nation, they refer to the magnificence of that nation—its history, wealth, territory, unique culture. All of this Yahweh will *cut off,* i.e., destroy. That, however, is not bad. The humbling of Philistine pride paves the way for conversion.

2. Cleansing (9:7a): **And I will remove his blood from his mouth and his abominations from between his teeth.** The Philistines are depicted as a single individual perhaps signaling that the focus is no longer upon political Philistia but on individual Philistines. The text does not require that this conversion comes as a direct result of Alexander's conquests, only that these conquests are the prelude to transformation on the part of some Gentiles.

The *blood* (lit., "bloods") probably refers to the drinking of sacrificial blood as an act of worship or eating of sacrificial animals with their blood. Cf. Ezek 33:25; Lv 3:17; 7:26; 17:10, 12. The *abominations* are animals forbidden by Mosaic Law (Dt 14:3ff.) or sacrifices offered to idols and afterward eaten. The prophet paints the disgusting picture of pieces of the abominable meat still lodged between the teeth of this pagan Philistine.

Yahweh announces his intention to *remove* (Hiph. r. *swr*) this abomination from the mouth of the Philistine. He does not say when or how this will happen, except that one may conclude from the sequence of the prophecy that it occurs after Alexander's conquests. The verb is generally used of a gracious response of Yahweh to a petition or to an obedient response on the part of people. Divine removal is generally not associated with force. So one can probably postulate here

Philistine petition or repentance to which Yahweh responds by removing the taint of idolatry.

3. *Recognition (9:7b):* **he also shall be a remnant to our God...** This statement builds on the teaching of Zech 2:11 and 8:23. At some point *he*, i.e., the corrected Philistines, will no longer be considered aliens. They as much as penitent Jews will be considered a *remnant to our God*, i.e., a people belonging to God. *He also* expresses the prophet's personal shock about what he is announcing.

4. *Exaltation (9:7c):* **and he shall become as a governor in Judah**...Their worldly pride humbled, the Philistines are ready for honor within the family of God (cf. Jam 4:10). *Governor* is lit., "a chief."[189] *Judah* here has spiritual rather than political connotations. It refers to the church. Cleansed of past abominations and counted among God's people former Philistines (Gentiles) rise to positions of leadership within the redeemed community. The prototype of Philistines rising to leadership among God's people was Ittai the Gittite (2 Sam 18:2).

5. *Integration (9:7d):* **and Ekron shall become like the Jebusite**. *Ekron* represents the entire Philistine people, and perhaps all Gentiles. The *Jebusites* were the ancient inhabitants of Jerusalem. They were conquered by David and incorporated into the nation of Israel. Cf. 2 Sam 5:6; 24:22; 1 Chr 21:23. The basic idea is that Gentiles will be completely integrated with Jews so as to become indistinguishable.

Perhaps using this passage as justification, some people of Philistine extraction were forced to circumcise and convert to Judaism during the intertestamental period (1 Macc 5:68; 10:84; 13:47, 48). Forced conversion, however, is far removed from the spirit of this passage. Only in Christ do former Gentiles and former Jews sit down to share a common meal around the Lord's Table.

E. Protection of God's People (9:8):

1. *Divine protection (9:8a):* **And I will encamp about my house...** *Encamp* (r. *chnh*) is a word that often has mili-

---

[189] LXX has "head over a thousand."

tary connotations. The idea is similar to Isa 31:4 where Yahweh of Hosts comes down "to fight for Mount Zion, and for the hill thereof." *My house* could be the temple; but more likely this is a figurative description of the remnant or Judah mentioned in the previous v. The point is that while the heathen world suffers judgment, God protects his own people. This promise is illustrated by the hosts of angels encamped on hills around Dothan, protecting Elisha (2 Kgs 6:17).

2. *Necessary protection (9:8b):* **because of an army, because of the one passing through and the one returning.** The word translated *because of an army* (*mitssābhāh*) probably is the preposition *min* + an odd spelling of the word for *army* (*tsābhāh*).[190] *The one passing through and returning* seems to describe someone who passes through a land en route to another destination.[191] The picture is of an army marching back and forth. It is tempting to see in this v a reference to Alexander the Great who by-passed Jerusalem en route to Egypt. He later returned through Palestine without doing harm to the holy city. See Josephus *Ant.* 10.1.8. Probably, however, the text refers more generally to the fact that Yahweh protects his people in all ages (cf. 2 Thess 3:3; 1 Pet 1:5).

3. *Promise of future peace (9:8c):* **and an oppressor will not again pass over them.** This line is very difficult to interpret. *Oppressor* (*nōgēs*) can refer to one who drives men or beasts, i.e., a taskmaster; an arbitrary ruler; foreign oppressor; tyrant; exactor of tribute (Ex 3:7; 5:6-10). The term here further describes the *army* that passes through and returns. *Pass over them* depicts the steamroller effect of the oppressor. He tramples God's people in order to sweep on to further conquests.

Probably the meaning is that a day will come when there will be no more oppressors with their armies to harass the people of God. Historically a foretaste of that day came when

---

[190] Some take the word to mean "as a guardian" (referring to Yahweh) deriving the word from the r. *ntsb*, "to take one's stand" BDB. NIV opts to render all of v 8b as "against marauding forces."

[191] The phrase elsewhere, however, merely indicates the overrunning of a land by an invading army. See Ezek 35:7.

Alexander the Great bypassed Jerusalem on his way to and from Egypt.[192] Palestine, however, remained under the oppressor's heel for centuries following Alexander. Only the appearance of the great king in the following v ushered in the age when the ultimate oppressor (Satan) has been defeated.

4. Reason for God's promises (9:8d): ***for now I have seen with my eyes.*** The opening vv of this unit set forth the proposition that Yahweh's eyes are upon the nations as well as Israel. The previous six vv illustrate his awareness of what will transpire among the Gentile nations. This v demonstrates that his eyes are also on Israel. During Israel's past calamities God had not looked upon them; but now he will notice the plight of his people and will intervene on their behalf.

Coming Prince of Peace
Zechariah 9:9-11

At the time these words were uttered the Judeans had no king. The people were ruled by Persian-appointed governors and high priests. Judea was only a tiny sub-province within the Persian Empire. There was little prospect that they would ever have even a vassal king, not to mention an independent ruler.

A. Promise of the Coming Ruler (9:9a, b):

In contrast to the surrounding nations (cf. v 5), God's people will find deliverance through a native-born king.[193] No one denies that this v is messianic. The Gospel writers apply it to Jesus (Mt 21:5; Jn 12:15).

1. Double call for joy (9:9a): ***Rejoice greatly, O daughter of Zion! Shout, daughter of Jerusalem!*** The exhortation

---

[192]Other views: 1) partly fulfilled, partly yet to be fulfilled (Unger): Yahweh protects his people in the days of Alexander, and at some future time there will be no more oppressors to bother the land; 2) presently being fulfilled: the entire v has nothing to do with Alexander, but rather looks forward to the protection of God's people in the future; 3) partly fulfilled, partly being fulfilled. The Alexander episode only partially fulfilled the prophecy. It continues to be fulfilled until finally no more oppressors shall bother the people of God (Keil).

[193]Chisholm, op. cit., 266.

Postexilic Prophets

to *rejoice/shout* grows out of the previous thought that Yahweh's eyes are upon his people. The *daughter* of a place is the population of that place personified as a youthful female. *Zion* and *Jerusalem* are parallel.

2. *Cause for joy (9:9b)*: **Behold your king shall come to you**. *Behold* introduces the unexpected. *Your king* is a king of your own race. This king will fulfill the promise of the end of oppression which was set forth in the previous v.[194] The reference is to the Coming One who had been foretold by prophets. *To you* (fem. sing.) refers to Zion. The expression does not indicate a mere geographical approach; the phrase indicates "for your good." He comes as a Deliverer. He is Zion's King, yet he *shall come* to Zion. This may point to his deity. He was *of* Zion, yet not *of* Zion; he was human, yet divine.

B. Description of the Coming Ruler (9:9c-f):

Zechariah intends for his readers to see the messianic king as the exact opposite of the great military conquerors of antiquity

1. *His character (9:9c)*: *[He is] righteous*, i.e., just, impartial in judgment. He exemplifies the right relationship with both God and man. By implication, he is the ideal king. All of his decisions and actions are motivated by what is right. Such action on the part of the king will result in rain (fertility) and peace (Ps 72:1-7).

2. *His work (9:9d)*: *and showing himself a savior...* The verb (*nôšā'*) is a Niphal which can be rendered as reflexive. The term could also be rendered as a passive: *endowed with salvation* (Keil; Deane).[195]

3. *His demeanor (9:9e)*: *gentle...* The term also means "afflicted," a translation that might be justified on the basis of what is reported about him in chs 11-13 and in Isa 53. The following clause, however, tilts the scale in favor of *gentle* or "lowly." The LXX render "meek."

---

[194]Isaiah also foretold the end of oppression under the reign of the messianic king (Isa 9:4).
[195]The LXX wrongly rendered the term *sōzōn*, "saving" or "savior."

4. His transport (9:9f): **and riding on a donkey, on a colt, the foal of a donkey.** From the time of Solomon, the donkey was a lowly animal.[196] It was also a symbol of peace (Deane). *Colt* (*'ayir*) denotes a young male donkey (Gn 49:11; Job 11:12) that bore burdens (Isa 30:6) and labored in fields (Isa 30:14). Yet the mount is also a *foal of a donkey*, lit., "the son of she-donkeys," i.e., young animal still running behind the she-donkeys. This phrase is added to show that whereas the mount was an ordinary beast of burden (= humility), it was still an appropriate mount for a king in two ways. First, it was purebred.[197] Second, it was so youthful that it had never before been ridden or used in ordinary work. The donkey imagery linked the coming king to hopes for Davidic monarchy (Gn 49:11). At the same time it dashed expectations of military deliverance.[198]

The exact fulfillment of this prophecy was arranged by Jesus (Mt 21:1-7) as he made a public claim of messiahship. The prophecy would have been truly fulfilled, however, had Jesus never made those arrangements. The prophet's portrayal most likely referred to the entire range of events connected with Messiah's first coming.

C. Nature of the Ruler's Kingdom (9:10):

1. Peace within the nation (9:10a): **And I will cut off the chariot from Ephraim, and the horse from Jerusalem; and the battle bow shall be cut off.** Zechariah indicates the peaceful nature of the messianic kingdom by portraying the removal of three types of military equipment.

First, Zechariah speaks of war chariots. The verb *cut off* (r. *krt*) when used metaphorically means to eliminate, remove, excommunicate or destroy by violent means if necessary. Chariot (*rekebh*) is a collective noun used in reference to horse-drawn vehicles used for warfare and royal travel. War chariots were used in Mesopotamia before 3000 BC.

---

[196]Pre-Solomon the donkey had been a royal mount (Judg 5:10; 10:4; 12:14; 2 Sam 16:1-2). David apparently had a mule for his royal mount (1 Kgs 1:33).
[197]Baldwin, *TOTC*, 166; Meyers & Myers, *AB, Zechariah 9-14*, 131.
[198]Meyers & Myers, *AB*, Zechariah 9-14, 129-30.

Postexilic Prophets

During the Conquest and Settlement periods Israelite infantry went up against powerful chariot forces on numerous occasions (e.g., Josh 11:4; Judg 4:3). David seems to have introduced chariot forces in Israel (2 Sam 8:4; 1 Chr 18:14). Assyrian records indicate that King Ahab (of Ephraim) was able to furnish two thousand chariots at the battle of Qarqar (853 BC).

Since Messiah's kingdom is one of peace, a chariot force will not be needed. The success of God's kingdom does not depend on instruments of war (cf. Mic 5:10-15; Zech 4:6). Through the coming messianic king Yahweh will launch a war on war. *Ephraim* (northern tribes), formerly declared to be Gentiles by Yahweh (Hos 1:9), is part of the messianic kingdom.[199]

Second, Yahweh removes the war horse. The verb *cut off* governs this phrase. The battle *horse* mentioned without article or verb jumps out at the reader in this truncated sentence. Zechariah surely intended a contrast to the donkey upon which Jerusalem's king entered triumphantly into the city. Humility, not pride is the mark of the coming King. Zechariah views Jerusalem as the capital of Messiah's kingdom. As the ancient capital of Judah, Jerusalem also stands for the Jews. So Jews and Ephraimites (Gentiles) will be united in Messiah's peaceful kingdom.

The *battle bow* (*qešet*) is the third apparatus of war that will be *cut off*. The bow and arrow were effective arms from long-range (300-400 yards). This weapon was used widely by the nations of the Bible. Israel had expert archers in men from Benjamin (1 Chr 8:40; 2 Chr 17:17) and the eastern tribes of Reuben, Gad, and Manasseh (1 Chr 5:18). Bows were constructed with single pieces of wood, or more effectively with glued layers of wood, horn, and sinew, and sometimes even with added bronze (2 Sam 22:35; Job 20:24). The size varied from approximately three to six feet in length.

---

[199]A major theme in prophetic literature is the healing of the rift between Israel (Ephraim) and Judah. See Ezek 37:16-17; Jer 31:31; Isa 11:13. This theme is further developed in ch 11. Cf. Jer 3:18; 23:6.

Zechariah 9:1-10:12

Messiah's kingdom is to be established without physical force. Zechariah's words reflect the longings of earlier prophets (Ps 72:7; Isa 2:4; 9:4-7; Mic 5:10-11).

2. *Peace among the nations (9:10b)*: **for he shall speak peace to the nations.** The messianic reign of peace is not to be confined to the Jews and to the physical land of Canaan. It will extend to the nations as well. This prophecy builds upon Isa 2:4 and Mic 4:3. Peace means "blessing" and "total well-being." To *speak peace* means to announce peace and the removal of hostility (cf. Ps 85:8). The peace he announces is not just the absence of external hostility. It is that deeper peace of the soul in which men have assurance that all is well with their Creator. To announce peace implies that this Ruler has the authority and power to bring about this peace.

3. *Peace under the coming ruler (9:10c)*: **His rule shall be from sea to sea and from the River unto the ends of the earth.** *From sea to sea* is an idiom meaning, from the sea to the end of the world where the sea begins again. *The River* is the Euphrates, the most remote eastern boundary of the Promised Land (Gn 15:18; Ex 23:31). The thought is that the Holy Land will extend from the furthest limits of the OT Promised Land *to the ends of the earth*. This is an OT way of referring to Messiah's kingdom as world-wide (cf. Ps 72:8; Mic 7:11-12).

D. Redemption of the Coming Ruler (9:11):

1. Basis of coming redemption (9:11a): **Also you in your covenant blood...** *Also you* (fem. sing.) means "as regards you, O daughter of Zion." Cf. v 9. *In your covenant blood* means that redemption is possible "for the sake of" blood that has been shed for the daughter of Zion, i.e., population of messianic Jerusalem. The messianic context suggests that it is the blood of the eternal covenant (Heb 13:20) that is in view—the blood of the new covenant (Mt 26:28).[200]

---

[200] Others think the reference is to the covenant with Abraham (Gn 15:9-12, 17ff) which guaranteed the preservation of "Israel" and the eventual incorporation of Gentiles into that holy nation The Sinai covenant was also sealed with blood (Ex 24:5ff); but it was a covenant conditioned upon obedience.

Postexilic Prophets

2. Depiction of coming redemption (9:11b): **I shall send forth your prisoners out of a pit in which there is no water.** The verb *send forth* (r. *šlk* in Piel) is prophetic perfect, indicating what God said was certain to happen. The *pit* is a symbol for subservience to hostile powers. The *prisoners* (lit., "bound ones") are Zion's citizens. The background of the figure is the experience of Joseph at the hands of his brothers (Gn 37:22). Cf. Jer 38:6. In such a pit the prisoners would inevitably perish if they were not drawn out.

Since the context is messianic, the bondage spoken of must be spiritual rather than physical. The waterless pit, then, is figurative for the disgusting bondage of sin. In Isa 61:1 the Servant liberates prisoners (same word used here) from their prisons.

Coming Divine Warrior
Zechariah 9:12-17

A. **Summons to Exiles** (9:12):
1. Exhortation (9:12a): **Turn to the fortress...** The daughter of Zion will not automatically be liberated from the waterless pit. *Turn* points to repentance. The imperative is plural because it is addressed to individuals. *The fortress* is messianic Jerusalem in which believers are protected by the power of God through faith (1 Pet 1:5).[201] Only those who choose to be part of messianic Jerusalem will enjoy the liberation just described.

2. Address (9:12b): **You prisoners of the hope.** The reference is not *the hope* (*hattiqvāh*) of deliverance from captivity; but the hope of Israel, viz. the messianic King and kingdom. See Acts 26:6-7; 28:20.

3. Incentive (9:12c): **even today I declare: Double I will return to you.** *Even today* suggests Yahweh's immediate resolve to dispense blessing on the daughter of Zion. A *double* measure of blessing compensating for past suffering is offered as an incentive to get people to turn to the fortress (cf. Isa 40:2; 61:7).

---

[201] Another view is that the *fortress* is God himself (Joel 3:1-6).

Zechariah 9:1-10:12

B. Mission for God's People (9:13):

1. Preparation for a holy war (9:13a): **For I will tread Judah my bow, I will fill (it) with Ephraim.** *For* (*kî*) introduces the explanation of how Yahweh will return double to Zion. God uses his people as his weapon. *Judah* and *Ephraim* constitute Zion. Some citizens of the northern tribes (Ephraim) joined the restoration community in Judea. In biblical prophecy, however, Ephraim was declared to be "not my people," i.e., Gentiles. So prophecies envisioning the reunion of Judah and Ephraim point to the eventual union of Jews and Gentiles in one body.

As Zechariah develops the figure, Judah is the *bow*, Ephraim the *arrow*. Both together—a unified people—are essential to having a lethal weapon.[202] *Tread...my bow* references the Hebrew custom of using the foot to string the bow. In 9:10 Yahweh cut off the battle bow from his people because they will not need physical weapons of war. The holy people will not use weapons for defense or advancement; but they will be a weapon in the hands of their God.

2. Adversaries in the holy war (9:13b): **and stir up your sons O Zion, against your sons, O Greece.** The Jews were protected from the rampaging army of Alexander, although he had every reason to punish Jerusalem for assisting Tyre during the siege (cf. v 8). Eventually, however, Zion will have a showdown with Greece.

Is Zechariah referring to the Greek empires of antiquity? Or is he using Greece as earlier prophets used Assyria, Egypt, Edom, et al as symbols for all the enemies of God's people? The prediction pertains initially to Maccabean victories over the Greek Seleucids during the intertestamental period. These victories, however, were typical of the Messiah's victories over his enemies.

---

[202]McComiskey (*MPEEC*, 1171) follows the Hebrew accents and renders: "For I will bend Judah for myself, as a bow, I will fill [the hand with] Ephraim." This translation has the text speak of two bows.

Postexilic Prophets

C. Yahweh's Intervention (9:14):

This v depicts the assistance that Yahweh gives his people in their struggles with hostile powers.

1. Yahweh defends his people from above (9:14a): **And Yahweh will appear over them, and like lightning his arrow will go out.** In the time of battle against enemies *Yahweh shall appear over* his people. *Lightning* is Yahweh's weapon. The figure is of a storm cloud hovering over the people. Yahweh uses a lightning bolt as a signal arrow to initiate the battle.[203] Divine assistance appears to have been present during the wars with the Greeks in the second century BC. That same assistance has also been present in every assault against the kingdom ruled by the lowly King of v 9.

2. Yahweh joins with his people from below (9:14b): **And the Lord Yahweh with the trumpet will blow, and he will come with the whirlwinds of the south.** Along with the signal arrow, the *trumpet* signals the approach of Yahweh and the start of battle; it also directs the movement of troops during the conflict. Yahweh is in charge. Perhaps in the poet's imagination, thunder is being compared to a battle trumpet. The *whirlwinds of the south,* the most violent, may be viewed as the war chariot of Yahweh in which the mighty King leads his troops into battle.[204] Cf. Isa 21:1. The *south (tēmān)* might be rendered as a proper name, referring to one of the major Edomite cities. If this is so, then Yahweh comes from Teman as in Hab 3:3.

D. Results of Yahweh's Intervention (9:15):

Zechariah identifies four specific results of Yahweh's intervention on behalf of his people.

1. God's people protected (9:15a): **And Yahweh of Hosts shall be a shield over them.** The title *Yahweh of Hosts* has military connotations. It emphasizes the unlimited power God has to protect his people. *A shield over them* reflects the

---

[203] Alternatively, lightning bolts going forth from the cloud are the arrows of God's judgment.

[204] Alternatively, Yahweh is depicted as marching triumphantly in the midst of the roaring winds.

Zechariah 9:1-10:12

language of Isa 31:5 where Yahweh promises to protect Jerusalem.

   2. God's people strengthened (9:15b): **and they shall eat...** Some think the picture is that of a lion devouring the prey (Cf. Nm 23:24). This, however, is probably reading too much into the verb. More likely those who were once prisoners in the waterless pit are now strengthened by the consumption of food.[205]

   3. God's people emboldened (9:15c): **and they shall subdue sling stones.** Strengthened by heavenly food, God's people go boldly on the attack. They will *subdue* (r. *kbš*), lit., "tread down," *sling stones,* probably a symbol for the enemy that is trodden underfoot.

   4. God's people victorious (9:15d): **and they will drink and make a noise as through wine and will become full, like the sacrificial bowls, like the corners of the altars.** The picture is that of a boisterous feast.[206] God's people will celebrate their redemption even while under attack by their enemies.

Those who were released from the waterless pit will be refreshed. *They will drink* of the water of life that God himself provides. Refreshed by their drink, the redeemed of the Lord *make a noise* (r. *hmm*). This verb is used of the roar of waves (Jer 5:22) and the din created by multitudes or armies (Isa 17:12; Jer 6:23). *As through wine* suggests boisterous, uninhibited noise like that resulting from the consumption of intoxicating drink. *Become full* is another reference to their eating. Those who once were emaciated and dying in the waterless pit are now depicted feasting until they want no more. The *sacrificial bowls* and *corners of the altars* are both used to underscore the degree of fullness.[207]

There are numerous examples of God's special intervention on behalf of the Maccabees in the second century BC. See

---

[205] Others think the reference is to the messianic celebration banquet referenced in Isa 25:6.
[206] Others (e.g., McComiskey) think the picture is that of a violent destruction of enemies in which God's people are spattered with blood.
[207] Cf. NASB "they will be filled like a (sacrificial) basin, (drenched) like the corners of the altar."

1 Macc 3:16-24; 4:6-16; 7:40-50; 2 Macc 2:21-22; 3:24; 5:2-4; 11:8; 12:11, 15, 22, 28, 37 etc. These victories, however, were only the foretaste of the spiritual conquest of those who march under the banner of cross.

Coming Triumphant Savior
Zechariah 9:16-17

A. Reason for the Promise (9:16):

1. Yahweh will act (9:16a): **And Yahweh their God will deliver them in that day...** Whenever his people come under attack God will be there for them. The down payment on this promise came during the war with the Greek kingdoms in the second century BC. The promise, however, embraces the rescue of his people in the messianic era when the lowly King of v 9 rules from sea to sea.

2. Glory of God's people (9:16b): **as a flock, his people, for (they are) stones of a crown displayed upon his land.** Zechariah offers two pictures of how those saved by God reflect his glory.

First, God's people are depicted as a flock. The picture is of God the Good Shepherd who battles all beasts that attempt to molest the flock. The term *flock* is used 9x of God's people in this book.

Second, God's people are crown jewels. *For* (*kî*) introduces the reason Yahweh will deliver his people. While the enemies are sling stones trodden underfoot, God's people are *stones of a crown*, i.e., jewels in a king's crown. They are *displayed*[208] upon Yahweh's land, elsewhere called Immanuel's land (Isa 8:8). The land is the crown—symbol of Yahweh's sovereignty—in which the precious stones, the redeemed people, are placed.[209]

This v has given reassurance to God's people in every age. The enemy may enjoy temporary success. In the end, however, the divine Warrior-King will deliver his people

---

[208]English versions generally take *mitnōssōt* (r. *nss* = displayed; prominent; raised) as a biform of *mitnōtstsōt* (r. *ntsts* = sparkle, glitter).

[209]Others think the white sheep grazing under the brilliant oriental sun on a small field might be figuratively called "jewels."

Zechariah 9:1-10:12

from every foe. It is not the inherent worthiness of this people that triggers heavenly intervention. It is the fact that they are the symbols of Yahweh's sovereign rule.

B. Results of the Promise (9:17):
1. Exclamation (9:17a): **For how great is its goodness and how great is its beauty.** *For* (*kî*) introduces the reason the land can be compared to a crown. The suffix *its* refers to the nearest masculine antecedent, *crown*, which is a metaphor for the land. A land is said to possess *goodness* (*tûbh*) when it produces abundantly, i.e., it is good to its inhabitants.[210] A land that possesses *goodness* can also be said to possess *beauty.* Nothing was more beautiful to the eyes of ancient man than lush vineyards and undulating fields of grain. So Israel is a productive and appealing land. As such it is an appropriate symbol for the NT land of promise (Heb 3, 5), the kingdom of Christ.

2. Explanation (9:17b): **Grain shall make the young men flourish and new wine the virgins.** The land abundantly produces *grain* and *new wine*, the linchpins of ancient Israelite agriculture. Those who were once prisoners in the waterless pit (v 11) now will *flourish*, i.e., they will find nourishment and refreshment in the messianic land of promise.

Grain (*dāgān*) is a general word for cereals. Common grains in the biblical world included wheat (Gn 30:14), spelt or emmer (Ex 9:32), barley (Ex 9:31), and millet (Ezek 4:9). *New wine* (*tîrôš*) refers to the first pressings of the grapes, not fermented wine. In Christ's kingdom the grain and new wine have their counterparts in the loaf and cup of communion, the fruit and symbol of the abundant salvation that believers have in Christ. *Young men* and *virgins* point to the vitality and abundant life of those who inhabit the messianic land.

---

[210]*Goodness* is sometimes a figure for spiritual blessing as well (Ps 65:4).

Need for Messianic Salvation
Zechariah 10:1-2

Zechariah returns from future messianic salvation to the present evil age.

A. Need Implicit in Exhortation (10:1):
1. Exhortation to pray (10:1a): **Ask from Yahweh rain in the time of the latter rain.** *Ask* is a general command to the people (cf. Ezek 36:37). Fertility depends upon rain; rain (*mātār*) depends upon God. Zechariah may be suggesting that the prosperity predicted in 9:17 will only come when the people began to beseech God for it. The early rain occurred at the autumnal equinox; *the latter rain* (*malqôš*), at the vernal equinox. The presence of this exhortation implies that the postexilic community was drifting back into the same sins that marked previous generations. This conclusion is confirmed by the follow v.

A prayer for rain is most appropriate in the midst of a drought. Haggai (1:5-6, 10-11) mentions a drought, but it cannot be the one to which Zechariah refers. That drought was connected with lack of temple progress. This drought must be a much later occasion.

2. Exhortation reinforced with promise (10:1b): **Yahweh who makes the lightning; and showers of rain he will give to them, to everyone grass in the field.** Zechariah further describes Yahweh to whom they should address their prayers for rain. These words serve as an encouragement to ask for rain in three ways.

First, Zechariah affirms that Yahweh is in the rainmaking business. *Lightning* (*chazîzîm*) is used elsewhere only in Job (28:26; 38:25). This *lightning* is not a weapon of God as in 9:14; it is an accompaniment of the welcomed showers. In fact the term may refer to storm clouds rather than lightning per se. Earlier prophets struggled mightily to make God's people understand that the rains came from the Lord.[211]

---

[211] Isa 30:22-23; Jer 5:24; 14:22; 51:15-19.

Zechariah 9:1-10:12

Second, Zechariah promises a positive response to a sincere request for rain. These words bring to mind the ask-and-receive promise of Jn 16:24. *Showers of rain* (*tᵉmar gešem*) is lit., "rain of plenty" or "pouring rain." The phrase indicates the abundance of the response of Yahweh.

Third, Zechariah stresses that everyone will benefit from the rains that Yahweh will send. *To everyone* (lit. "to a man") suggests abundant provision for man and beast. *Grass of the field* (*'esebh bassādeh*) in this context refers to edible vegetation.

B. Need Explicit in Explanation (10:2):

In pre-exilic Israel there was an on-going debate about who gives the rain, Yahweh or Baal. There is no mention now of Baal; but still there was a reluctance on the part of the community to rely completely on Yahweh for the annual rains.

1. Undependable guidance (10:2a): **For the teraphim have spoken vanity, and the diviners have seen a lie and speak dreams of deceit; they comfort in vain.** *For* (*kî*) introduces the explanation for the previous exhortation. Zechariah identifies two sources to which people in the community looked for rain or at least predictions as to when the rain would fall.

First, some looked to the *teraphim* for rain. *Teraphim* are mentioned 7x in OT. They were images, sometimes in human form and sometimes life size. They were kept at shrines, but were also found in private houses. Evidently they were among the instruments used by some to predict or influence the future (cf. 2 Kgs 23:24; Ezek 21:21). Those who spoke by making use of the teraphim have spoken *vanity* (*'āven*), i.e., an empty, worthless message.

Second, others looked to diviners. *Diviners* (*haqqōsᵉmîm*) are those who pretend to predict the future. What they see in various omens or dreams is *a lie* (*šeqer*), i.e., untrue and therefore a deception (cf. 8:17).[212] Their dreams were *deceit* (*šāv'*) both to themselves and to those with whom those

---

[212] Other prophets as well accused these self-appointed prophets of lying: Jer 27:9-10; 29:8-9; Mic 3:7.

dreams were shared. *Comfort in vain* indicates that their promises of rain and prosperity, for example, were not fulfilled.

2. *Unrestrained sheep (10:2b):* **Therefore they have gone their way like sheep.** *Therefore* introduces the consequences of following lying oracles and deceptive diviners. Without proper guidance the people *have gone their way*, i.e., wandered aimlessly, like a flock of sheep.[213] Zechariah is not looking back on the exile to Babylon; he alludes to the wandering away from God by the post-exilic community following the completion of the temple.

3. *Unworthy leaders (10:2c):* **they are continually oppressed because there is no shepherd.** *Continually oppressed* is imperfect. It can refer to continuous action in the past. The imperfect can also be rendered as a present tense implying that the oppression continued in Zechariah's day. *No shepherd* must mean there was no true or godly shepherd. The phrase again distances the setting of this pericope from the earlier chs of the book which were written in the days of godly Zerubbabel and Joshua. It appears that after the deaths of this godly duo the spiritual and civil leaders were no longer worthy to bear the title "shepherd."

Provisions for Messianic Salvation
Zechariah 10:3-4

A. **Removal of Tyrannical Leaders** (10:3a):
Against the shepherds my wrath is kindled and upon the he-goats shall I visit (my wrath). The *shepherds* are the leaders of the Judeans in the period after the completion of the temple. It is possible that the term also includes the foreign rulers who dominated Israel during the postexilic period. *My wrath* is lit. "my nose" the redness of which indicated the state of burning anger to the ancients. *He-goats* are a figure for leaders or chieftains. Cf. Isa 14:9; Ezek 34:17. The verb *visit* (r. *pqd*) has the connotation of turning the attention to

---

[213]The *like sheep* comparison is used 5x elsewhere: Ps 44:11; 49:14; 78:52; Isa 53:6; Jer 12:3.

someone or something. The focusing of God's attention results in either judgment or blessing.

B. Empowerment of his People (10:3b, c):

1. He visits his flock (10:3b): **For Yahweh of Hosts shall visit his flock the house of Judah...** *For* (*kî*) introduces the reason for the divine outburst in the first half of the v. The corrupt, incompetent and worthless shepherds of the first half of this v must be removed before Yahweh can bring forth to his flock the Good Shepherd of the following ch. The verb *visit* (r. *pqd*) is used for the second time in this v, this time in a positive sense. When Yahweh visits his flock he sees their misery and focuses on their needs. *Flock* is defined by *house of Judah*, all that survived of the Israel of the exodus. Depicting God as the shepherd of his people is a common motif in biblical literature.[214]

2. He transforms his flock (10:3c): **and he shall make them as a majestic horse in the battle**. In 9:10 the horse is removed from Jerusalem in the messianic age, for the kingdom of Messiah will not advance by physical arms. Now the shepherdless sheep are transformed into a majestic warhorse on which God rides to battle against his foes. This is a figure that promises strength and courage to God's people (Dods). The figure also reminds them that Yahweh advances against the enemy only so far as they carry him. God does not accomplish his work on earth without the church but by means of it. The allusion may be to the Maccabean victories over the Syrian Greeks which were a preparation for the coming of Messiah.

C. Provision of a Divine Prince (10:4):

Divine visitation of the flock results in the appearance of a great ruler. *From him,* referring to Judah, is used 4x in this v to emphasize that the great future ruler and his associates will come from the very same people that were used as Yahweh's majestic horse in battle. The first three expressions are

---

[214] In the Psalms: 23:1; 74:1; 78:52; 79:13; 80:1; 95:7; 100:3. The theme of a ruler as a shepherd is common in the prophets: Isa 40:11; 44:28; Jer 6:3; 23:2-4; Ezek 34; 37:24.

Postexilic Prophets

verbless, setting them apart from the fourth clause where a finite verb appears. By the time of Zechariah it was well established in messianic prophecy that Messiah would come from the family of David within the tribe of Judah.

  *1. Corner (10:4a): **From him the Corner...** The Corner (pinnāh)* is used in Isa 19:13 and Ps 118:22 of present or future rulers. This construction term refers to the stone that is at the junction of two walls. It is probably the same as the Cornerstone in Isa 28:16. "Comparing a ruler to a cornerstone emphasized the stability and the adhesive power that a good ruler gives to his people."[215] The *Corner* probably refers to Messiah, the prince upon whom the whole edifice of God's house (people) shall rest. In the NT God's great temple is the church which is built on the foundation of the apostles and prophets, Jesus Christ himself being the chief cornerstone. Cf. Mt 21:42; Eph 2:20; Heb 7:14; Acts 4:11; 1 Pet 2:5-8.

  *2. Nail (10:4b): **from him the Nail...** Nail (yātēr)* is used of 1) the stake that fastens the cord of a tent; 2) a nail used in building with timber; and 3) a peg used for hanging arms and utensils on a wall. Thus, the Nail is one who holds or holds together the nation. This is another title for Messiah. The term suggests security and reliability in a leader. There is a possible allusion in this title to Isa 22:22-24 where Eliakim of the house of David was compared to "a nail in a sure place."

  *3. Battle Bow (10:4c): **from him the Battle Bow...** Battle Bow (qešet milchāmāh)* is used only here in the OT, but it was a common royal designation in the Near East.[216] This is a figure for the King as a warrior. In 9:10 the physical battle bow is removed from the messianic kingdom, for it will not be needed. The humble King who comes in peace during his first coming, comes to aid his people against their adversaries as a mighty warrior.

  *4. All Ruler (10:4d): **from him shall go out the All Ruler...** The verb is imperfect, setting the temporal framework for the assertion as future with respect to Zechariah. The rendering *All Ruler (kol nôgēs)* is based on two observa-

---

[215] R. Smith, *WBC*, 264.
[216] Mason, *CNEB*, 100.

tions of the context. First, the first three titles in this v seem to refer to a glorious individual ruler.[217] Second, the previous titles are positive, at least in respect to God's people.

Most take *kol nôgēs* to refer to a number of officers, perhaps those who aid Messiah in administering his kingdom.[218]

The term *ruler* (*nôgēs*) is used in the OT for a taskmaster or exactor. If the word has this meaning here it would indicate that the people of God shall subjugate their enemies, oppress them and exact tribute from them. But the term apparently is used in a more general sense of "ruler" in Isa 3:12; 60:17.[219]

5. *Unity of authority (10:4e):* ***together.*** The significance of the adverb *together* (*yachdāv*) is unclear.[220] Perhaps it is best to regard the adverb as referring to all four elements in the v collectively, not as separate entities that come together. All these together come from Judah at the same time for they are all part of a messianic package. All of the qualities portrayed in the four preceding titles come together in Messiah.

Salvation as Military Victory
Zechariah 10:5-7

In these vv Zechariah sets forth the change that will come over God's people after Yahweh of Hosts, in the person of Messiah, visits his flock (cf. v 3).

A. Description of the Victory (10:5):

1. Victory over infantry (10:5a): ***And they shall be like mighty men trampling in the mire of the streets in the battle...*** The scene shifts now from battle preparation to the thick of battle. The plural verb has as it antecedent the house

---

[217]Cf. NJPS which takes the first three titles as collectives.
[218]The phrase is rendered "every ruler" (NIV; NASB); "every commander" (NRSV).
[219]Unger thinks that what is meant is that the *noges*—oppressors—will depart from Judah under the reign of Messiah, i.e., there will be no more oppressor for the people of God. Cf. 9:8.
[220]NIV emends the text to move *yachdāv* to the beginning of the next v. NASB translates *yachdāv* with *kol nōgēs* = "every ruler together."

of Judah in v 3. The *mighty men* are the citizen soldiers in the army of the Ruler who comes riding a donkey (9:9). These warriors are united; they are on the march. They are not deterred by any obstacle or opposing force. The gates of Hades will not prevail against the army of the King.

Surely, however, *in the mire of the streets* means more than a depiction of the armies of God marching out to battle. *Mire* may be a figure of contempt for the adversary (cf. Mic 7:10); or the thought may be that Messiah's troops trample their enemies into the mire. The thought is similar to 9:15 where God's people trample sling stones.

2. *Victory because of God's presence (10:5b):* **and they will fight because Yahweh is with them.** God's people are successful in battle because Yahweh is fighting alongside them. God's people overcome enemies through the power God supplies (cf. 4:6). The appearance of the Corner, the Nail, the Battle Bow and the All Ruler (v 4) is Yahweh's doing.

3. *Victory over cavalry (10:5c):* **and the riders of horses will be put to shame.** Israel's force mainly was infantry; that of her enemies in Zechariah's period was mostly cavalry. *Put to shame* (r. *bôš* in Hiphil) is often coupled with military defeat in the OT. The people of God will prevail over those better armed.

B. Focus on Judah (10:6a):

I will strengthen the house of Judah... Again we are reminded of the mighty defender who hovers over his people (9:15). Again we see the principle that God fights with and through his people, not in their stead (cf. v 3).

C. Focus on Ephraim (10:6b-7):

Judah already had returned from exile. But what was the future of Ephraim—those Israelites who were carried away into exile by the Assyrians in 722 BC? Zechariah now addresses that issue.

1. *Salvation (10:6b):* **and the house of Joseph I will save.** The *house of Joseph* is the old northern kingdom. It is so called because Joseph was the father of the two leading

Zechariah 9:1-10:12

tribes in the north, Ephraim and Manasseh. In biblical prophecy Ephraim or the house of Joseph is a symbol for those who are not God's people (Hos 1:9), i.e., Gentiles. The theme of messianic salvation for Ephraim as well as Judah recalls 9:10, 13). Gentiles will experience deliverance or salvation, which is parallel to the strengthening of the house of Judah in the previous clause. This suggests that strengthening and salvation support and explain each other. Gentiles will join Jews in the conflict and share in the victory. The salvation is not merely deliverance, but positive salvation as in 9:16 (Keil).

2. *Restoration (10:6c):* **and I will restore[221] them...** Apparently the pronominal suffix refers to Ephraim since Ephraim is the subject immediately before and in the following v. *Restore* is the opposite of *cast off* in the following clause. Thus the restoration envisioned is one of spiritual position, not geographical possession. Those of ethnic Ephraim who desired to return to the homeland had done so already by the time these words were penned. So the promise here is of a restoration to divine favor. Not since Noah walked with God (Gn 6:9) had there been any spiritual relationship between Yahweh and someone outside the Abrahamic covenant family.

3. *Reconciliation (10:6d):* **because I will have compassion on them and they will be as though I had not rejected them...** *Because* (*kî*) introduces the reason or basis of Ephraim's restoration to divine favor. The basis of messianic salvation is Yahweh's *compassion* and mercy. When God *cast off* (r. *znch*) Ephraim he expelled them from the land, declared them not to be his people, cut them off from covenant promises, and declared that he was not their God (Hos 1:4-9). Ephraimites were scattered among the Gentiles. For all intents and purposes, they were Gentiles.

The separation between God and Ephraim will end because God takes the initiative in bringing it to an end. *As though I had not cast them off* underscores the completeness of the restoration. *Rejected* (r. *znch*) means to spurn. It ex-

---

[221] Some prefer to take the verbal form from the r. *yšb*, "to sit, dwell." The context, however, weighs in favor of the r. *šūb*, "to return, restore."

193

presses God's strong abhorrence of sin, and of those caught up in it.

4. Reformation (10:6e): ***for I am Yahweh their God, and I will respond to them.*** *For* (*kî*) introduces an explanation of an explanation. There are two reasons given why God so completely restores Ephraim (= Gentiles) that their past repudiation and humiliation is completely forgotten.

First, it is the very nature of God to become involved in redemption, salvation, deliverance and forgiveness. That is what the name *Yahweh* implies. Yahweh is in the forgiveness business. He does it better than anyone else. The essence of his nature is compassion, and compassion knows no finer demonstration than in forgiveness.

Second, Yahweh's exercise of compassion is a response to Ephraim. The verb *respond* or answer (r. *'nh*) has God as the subject 67x in the OT.[222] In the majority of these occurrences, the divine response comes as a result of a person's call or request. The present passage is one of only five where God answers without someone's request; but in each of these cases the greater context suggests that petition had indeed been made prior to the response by the Lord. Furthermore, the suffix *them* suggests a response to a petition on the part of those that Yahweh promises to answer rather than Yahweh's general response to their miserable condition. So the clause suggests that God is reconciled to those who petition for reconciliation, i.e., those who repent and seek his mercy.

5. Transformation (10:7a): ***and Ephraim will be like a mighty man...*** In v 5 the house of Judah was compared to *mighty men* (*gᵉbhôrîm*). Here the singular of the same word is used (a collective in NIV) to portray converted Ephraim. The men of Ephraim shall prove themselves mighty heroes in the spiritual conflict of the messianic age.

6. Jubilation (10:7b): ***and their heart will rejoice as through wine, and their sons will see and rejoice; their heart will exult in Yahweh.*** Ephraim shall hasten to the battle like men refreshed and strengthened by *wine*. Reference to *their sons* suggests two things. First, the jubilation over the

---

[222]In Psalms God is the subject of *'nh* 31 of 33 uses.

restoration of "Ephraim" may be a long time in the future from Zechariah's day. Second, the jubilation of restored Ephraim is not a passing emotion. The children of restored "Ephraim" will be led to a joyful relationship with Yahweh by observing the courageous actions of their fathers. This joy is generated by association with the humble King of 9:9 and the privilege of participation in his glorious kingdom.

Salvation as Gathering
Zechariah 10:8-12

These vv develop a different picture of the same events depicted in vv 3-7. Having spoken of "the house of Judah" and the "house of Joseph" separately, Zechariah now sets forth the purpose of God in respect to the unified nation.

A. Promise of the Gathering (10:8):

1. Means of it (10:8a): ***And I will whistle for them, and I will gather them...*** The imagery of shepherd and sheep is suggested by the verb *whistle* or "pipe" (r. *šrq*). The subject of the verb is Yahweh. This same verb was used twice by Isaiah to describe God's signal in calling together nations to accomplish his purposes (cf. Isa 5:26-27; 7:18-19). The whistle is parallel to *gather* (r. *qbts*). So the shepherd attracts his sheep by his distinctive whistle.[223]

2. Explanation of it (10:8b): ***because I have redeemed them...*** *Because* (*kî*) introduces the explanation for the whistling metaphor. Yahweh had *redeemed* (r. *pdh*) his people (cf. Isa 62:12; Jer 31:11). Those who are gathered are the redeemed. From what they are redeemed is not made explicit. Originally this verb had commercial connotation, referring to the payment of a sum for the transfer of ownership (e.g., Lv 19:20). It is frequently associated with the deliverance from Egypt. As time went on the term broadened until it came to be equivalent to "deliver" or "save." In the Psalms a person might be redeemed from danger, the hand of human oppres-

---

[223]Isaiah depicted Yahweh whistling to summon the invaders of Judah. Cf. Isa 5:26; 7:18, 19.

sion, death, or sin (e.g., Ps 130:7-8). The messianic context of the present passage suggests that Yahweh delivers his people from sin and its consequences.

3. Result of it (10:8c): ***and they will increase as they have increased.*** The gathering and redemption in this v most likely refer to the gathering of the people of God out of the world by the gospel. The result of this gathering is the multiplication of the holy nation in which all the redeemed are citizens (1 Pet 2:9). Just as the Israelites grew so much in Egypt (Ex 1:7, 12), so will NT Israel grow through the evangelistic proclamation of the gospel. The multiplication of the nation by the inclusion of those from distant lands is a prominent theme in this book (cf. 1:17; 2:6-11; 6:15; 8:7-8; 9:7).

B. Prelude to the Gathering (10:9):

This v is the most difficult one in the ch due to the fact that an explicit subject is not stated for any of the four verbs.

1. Sowing (10:9a): ***And I will sow them among the peoples...*** Yahweh will *sow* his people—those who are gathered and redeemed in the preceding v—as one sows seed in expectation of a bountiful harvest, i.e., population growth. This is a theme introduced originally by Hosea.[224] The entire Christian age is characterized by this sowing. *Among the peoples* indicates the sphere of the sowing. The church has been gathered out of the world so as to be sent into the world to preach the gospel.

2. Remembering (10:9b): ***and in far distant places they will remember me...*** *Remember* in the OT means more than merely recalling to mind. This verb has the sense of responding positively to God, even making mention of God (cf. Ezek 6:9). But who remembers Yahweh, those who are sown (the gathered/redeemed) or those among whom they are sown (the peoples)? Either interpretation is possible. The nearest antecedent is *peoples*. This suggests that the remembering of Yahweh is the response of the peoples to the sowing of the gathered/redeemed. Those outside the family of God begin to

---

[224]Cf. Hos 1:11; 2:23; Jer 31:27; Ezek. 36:9-10. It is unlikely that the r. *zrʻ* here connotes scattering as in NIV. The verb is never used of scattering or dispersing in a bad sense (Baron).

acknowledge him as their Creator and God as a result of the evangelistic witness of new covenant Israel.

3. *Thriving (10:9c):* **and they will live with their children...** *Live* (r. *chyh*) connotes enjoying the blessings of God's covenant. It is a word that describes the condition that follows repentance (Amos 5:4, 6). Gentile peoples come to fully enjoy the privileges of new covenant Israel. This is equivalent to the abundant life of which Jesus spoke—spiritual renewal—that results from the new birth. Mention of *their children* indicates that the witness in distant places is on-going from one generation to the next.

4. *Returning (10:9d):* **and they will return.** The *return* (r. *šûbh*) is not geographical (as in return from exile) but spiritual. The verb suggests a return to God with all that entails. This return is not a result of the new birth to life, but is concurrent with it. Gentile peoples will return to the God they abandoned early on in the history of mankind (Rom 1:19-21). Reconciliation and restoration to fellowship are involved.

C. Picture of the Gathering (10:10):

1. Release from captivity (10:10a): **And I will bring them from the land of Egypt, and from Ashur will I gather them.** At the time Zechariah wrote the bondage in Egypt was a distant memory, and Assyria no longer existed. It is, then, highly unlikely that this v refers to the physical lands of Egypt and Assyria. Rather God's people are pictured being gathered out of the great historical lands of captivity (cf. 2:6). In this context these lands symbolize the bondage of sin. In the messianic age no oppressor can separate God's people from their spiritual inheritance. As in v 8, the words point to a general reassembling and reorganization of the people of God (Dods).

2. Bulging population (10:10b): **And unto the land of Gilead and Lebanon I will bring them, and no (place) shall be found for them.** In this line Yahweh makes a commitment regarding the location and multiplication of his people in the messianic age.

First, as to location God's people will inherit the best of lands. Yahweh brings his people out of bondage (Egypt or

197

Postexilic Prophets

Assyria) and into the Promised Land of salvation. *Gilead* and *Lebanon* are the antithesis of Egypt and Assyria. As such they represent for God's people emancipation from Satan's bondage whatever form that might take.

In addition to liberation, Gilead/Lebanon symbolizes expansion, for neither area was considered part of the Promised Land envisioned by Moses.[225] Messiah's kingdom includes both, and more.

Gilead/Lebanon also symbolizes God's provision in the messianic kingdom. Both regions were noted for their fertility. *Gilead*, noted for its lush pastures, symbolizes the Good Shepherd's provision for his flock (cf. Jer 50:19-20; Mic 7:14). *Lebanon* is associated with restored Zion as a provider of resources (Isa 60:13; 35:2, 10).

Second, the promise of multiplication from v 8 is amplified. There will not be enough room in Gilead and Lebanon for the swelling numbers of converts (cf. Isa 49:20-21). The point is that the kingdom of God cannot be confined to Greater Palestine any longer. The Abrahamic promise of innumerable offspring finds ultimate fulfillment in the kingdom of Christ.

D. Power in the Gathering (10:11-12):

Zechariah now depicts five manifestations of the divine power that will be evident in the great gathering of the messianic age.

1. Intervention (10:11a): **And he will cross over the sea (which is) affliction...** The subject is Yahweh. A metaphorical sea of affliction momentarily separates him from his people. The reference is not to affliction in general but to the suffering of God's people at the hands of oppressors. Yahweh crosses that sea to come to the aid of his people—to join them in their suffering. The metaphor may have been suggested to the writer's mind by the Red Sea incident in Exodus.

2. Confrontation (10:11b): **and will smite waves in the sea; and all the depths of the river will dry up...** Smite

---

[225] The northern border of the Promised Land stretched to Lebanon (Dt 1:7; 11:24; Josh 1:4).

Zechariah 9:1-10:12

waves[226] indicates that God will make a way through the sea of affliction for his people. *The river*, either the Euphrates or Nile, is a symbol of humiliation by the ruling power (Assyria or Egypt). The oppressive power can no longer hold God's people captive.[227]

3. *Liberation (10:11c):* **and the pride of Assyria will be brought down and the rod of Egypt will be removed**. *Pride of Assyria* and *rod of Egypt* symbolize oppression. The oppressors of God's people shall pass from the scene (cf. 9:8). It is the gentle King riding a donkey (9:9) that brings this deliverance from oppression.

Messiah's kingdom is spiritual; it cannot be taken captive. Its capital—heavenly Zion—can never be assaulted. Messiah smashes the power of sin, the greatest oppressor (Rom 6:9). Death is conquered (1 Cor 15:55). Inner peace that can never be shattered is ushered in (Jn 14:27). Zechariah's hope is a reflection of the same hope articulated by Isaiah over two centuries earlier (Isa 9:4, 6).

4. *Empowerment (10:12a):* **And I will make them strong in Yahweh...** The oracle formula at the end of the v indicates that the first person speaker is Yahweh. He speaks of himself in the third person so the redemptive implications of the name *Yahweh* will be underscored in the minds of the auditors. Those rescued from bondage will be a strong people, or to use the words of Paul, they will be "strong in the Lord and in the power of his might" (Eph 6:10). They will be ready to undertake mighty exploits in his name.

5. *Sanctification (10:12b):* **and in his name they will walk (oracle of Yahweh).** *Walk* (r. *hlk* in Hithpael) means "to walk up and down" or "walk to and fro." It is the same form used to describe the walk of Enoch and Noah with the Lord (Gn 5:22; 6:9). The word suggests a way of life. Converts

---

[226] The imagery of smiting the waves may have been inspired by the actions of Xerxes when his double bridge across the Hellespont was destroyed by a storm in 480 BC. Xerxes ordered that the Hellespont receive three hundred lashes in punishment for destroying his bridges (Herodotus, *Persian Wars* 7.35).

[227] Another possibility is that the river is the Jordan, the allusion being to the crossing of the Jordan by Joshua. Thus God leads his people out of oppression and into the messianic Promised Land.

will live their lives by the principles and power symbolized by the *name* or attributes of God. Cf. Mic 4:5; Col 3:7.[228] In Messiah the name of Yahweh was personified. He was the image of the invisible God (Col 1:15). This v further develops the theme of empowerment previously encountered in 4:6.

Central Action: Rejected Shepherd Zechariah 11:1-17

Ch 11 brings the first burden to a climatic conclusion. The King who enters Jerusalem riding on a lowly donkey is now rejected. The ch has a peculiar structure which summarized looks like this: Result—Reason—Further Result.

Judgment on Judah's Leaders Zechariah 11:1-3

These vv form a bridge from ch 10 to 11:4-17. The term *Lebanon* has been picked up from 10:10, and the term *shepherds* prepares the reader for the rest of the ch.

A. Tree Metaphor (11:1-2):
Three strong and valuable types of trees (cedar, cypress, oak) are used to represent proud rulers. Some sort of judgment is sweeping southward through Lebanon, Bashan and the Jordan valley. The idea is similar to 9:1-6 where the invasion is of Hadrach, Tyre and Philistia. Zechariah is utilizing the language of Jer 25:34-38; Isa 10:34; and Ezek 27:5-6.

1. Cedars of Lebanon (11:1): **Open, O Lebanon, your doors that the fire may consume your cedars.** The *doors* are the mountain passes which gave access to Palestine from the north. The *cedars* of northern Palestine probably represent the

---

[228]Another possibility is that *walk* means that the converts go about as messengers and representatives sharing the blessings of Messiah's gospel (Baron).

Zechariah 11:1-17

highest ranking members of society (cf. Ezek 17:3).[229] The *fire* is symbolic of judgment. Thus a judgment sweeps into Palestine from the north.

2. *Fir trees (11:2a):* **Howl, O cypress trees, for the cedar has fallen. (Those) that are mighty ones have been spoiled.** *Fir trees* grow south of Lebanon. They too should wail for they are about to suffer the same fate as the northern cedars. Since the cedars (the nobles) have fallen there is no hope for the cypress trees (common people). *Mighty ones* indicates that trees are being used metaphorically of the chiefs of Israel. Given the context and what unfolds in this ch, the invading army is likely that of the Romans who crushed Judea in war AD 66-70.

3. *Oaks of Bashan (11:2b):* **Howl, O oaks of Bashan, for the inaccessible forest has been brought down.** If the inaccessible forest of Lebanon was not spared, much less shall Bashan escape. The destruction is now sweeping into the Jordan valley. Bashan was famous for its oak trees. These proud trees, like the cedars and firs of the preceding v, are metaphorical for leaders of the region. The Roman army is coming closer to Jerusalem.

B. Tree Metaphor Explained (11:3):

The less common metaphor of the trees is explained by the more common metaphor of shepherds and lions.

1. *Howling shepherds (11:3a):* **The sound of the howling of the shepherds, for their glory is spoiled.** The howling of the trees now becomes the howling of the shepherds, a frequent metaphor for national leaders. These are the same shepherds that were introduced in 10:2-3. The *glory* (*'aderet*) of *shepherds* is their pasture, a metaphor for the land over which the shepherds rule. The verb *spoiled* (*šudd^edāh*) links the destruction of the trees in metaphor (v 2) to the destruction of the glory of the shepherds (rulers).

2. *Roaring lions (11:3b):* **The sound of the roaring of young lions for the pride of Jordan is spoiled.** Above the wailing of the shepherds, Zechariah now hears the roar of

---

[229] Lofty cedars sometimes stand as an emblem of the glory of the kingdom of Judah (Isa 14:8; Jer 22:6-7).

young lions. These lions, like the howling shepherds, symbolize national leaders. The lions roar because their habitat has been destroyed by the judgment fire. The *pride of Jordan* was the jungle[230] that lined the River Jordan from north to south. It was a habitat for many wild animals including lions. Here the pride of Jordan symbolizes the land over which the young lions (rulers) have dominion. The third use of *spoiled* creates a verbal link between the ruination of the forests in v 1 and that of the pride of Jordan. Thus the fire of judgment (Roman army) has now reached the southern extremity of the land of Palestine.

In the opening three vv of this ch the physical destruction of Palestine has been in the forefront. The subtext of these vv is that a destructive judgment will fall upon the people of the land. This of necessity must be, because the desolation of the land involves the destruction of the peoples living in it.

Judgment on Judah's Citizens
Zechariah 11:4-6

This prophecy is one of the most enigmatic in the OT. The prophet performs an action parable, but he does not explain it. The interpretations are almost as numerous as the commentaries. The passage appears to be an explanation of the causes and manner of the judgment that were sketched in broad outline in the first three vv.

A. Commission (11:4):

Thus says Yahweh my God: Shepherd the flock of slaughter. Zechariah is directed to act the role of a shepherd (ruler) to national Israel. This is an action parable in which Zechariah plays the role of the Good Shepherd. Prophetic action parables always pertain to the future; so any idea that Zechariah is portraying some past event or present circumstance cannot be entertained. Zechariah acts as a representative of God. In carrying out this assignment In this action

---

[230]Because of hostilities between the countries of Jordan (east of the Jordan River) and Israel (west of the river) the tangled brush known as the pride of Jordan in biblical times has been defoliated in recent decades.

Zechariah 11:1-17

parable Zechariah was emulating the methods of his illustrious predecessor Ezekiel.[231]

A *flock of slaughter* is a flock destined for and exposed to destruction at the hands of their present shepherds. The reason for this commission becomes clear in the following vv. The people of Israel will be treated unmercifully by their leaders or human shepherds. The slaughter flock represents the entire nation. Israel is prophetically viewed as given over to judgment for reasons that will be made clear as the ch unfolds.

Ch 11 amplifies ch 9 in which Messiah rides triumphantly into the city of Jerusalem. It sketches his labors and ministry in trying to seek and to save the lost sheep of the house of Israel (Mt 10:6).

B. Description (11:5):

This v illustrates the truth of the designation *flock of slaughter* in the previous v. The ruthless ways of the leaders of Judah are described under three figures.

1. Purchasers (11:5a): **Those who purchase them, slaughter them and are not considered guilty.** Zechariah paints a picture of a sheep market with buyers and sellers negotiating prices. Those who have taken possession of the sheep do not intend to graze and grow them, but to *slaughter them* wholesale. The buyers and sellers represent those who are in charge of the flock. The flock thus is threatened with extinction. Yet these reckless purchasers *are not considered guilty*, i.e., no one calls them to account. "They go unpunished" (NIV).[232] They have gained control of the flock, but with no intent of nurturing it. They make decisions that lead to the slaughter of the common people. Worst of all, they get by with this malfeasance in office.

2. Sellers (11:5b): **Their sellers say, Blessed is Yahweh for I am rich.** Some sell the sheep out and piously thank God for their ill-gotten gain. Perhaps these are leaders that abuse the public trust then leave office to enjoy the riches they have piled up by placing personal interests ahead of national inter-

---

[231]Ezekiel's role-playing is reported in Ezek 4:1-17; 5:1-4; 12:1-7.
[232]The language in this v is similar to that of Jer 50:6-7.

ests. The verb *say* is singular, the subject is plural. This grammatical dissonance emphasizes that each individual seller acts in the way indicated.

   3. *Shepherds (11:5c):* **Their shepherds have no compassion upon them.** The buyers and sellers are now identified as *their shepherds* or national leaders.[233] They have no *compassion* (r *chml*) on the flock to protect them from those who aimed to abuse and mislead the community. Again the prophet uses grammatical dissonance between the singular verb and the plural subject to emphasize that each individual shepherd acted in the way indicated. One thinks of the calloused attitudes of Pharisees, Sadducees, Zealots and High Priest during the years leading up to the war with Rome in AD 66.

C. **Declaration** (11:6a):

   For I will no longer spare the inhabitants of the land (oracle of Yahweh). For (*kî*) introduces the explanation for the command to play the role of a shepherd in v 4. *No longer spare* (r. *chml*) indicates that God will no longer protect the flock from abuse. *Inhabitants of the land* is used in the Pentateuch and Historical Books to refer to the Canaanites; but in the prophetic books, beginning with Joel, the phrase is used at least 8x to refer to the current occupants of the land, viz. the Israelites. Here the phrase refers to the postexilic community that was now occupying the land promised to Abraham some fifteen hundred years earlier. God will permit this abuse of the flock for at least one generation of those who occupy *the land*. The abuse by the leaders is a manifestation of God's anger with his people—part of their punishment for some as yet unspecified act of unfaithfulness. On *oracle of Yahweh*, see on 1:3.

---

[233]McComiskey (1191-92) thinks the buyers and sellers represent the wealthy and influential members of the community who mistreat the flock with the approval of the shepherds or leaders. Baron (384) identifies the buyers and sellers as Gentile power (i.e., Romans), while the shepherds are the native rulers.

Zechariah 11:1-17

D. Announcement (11:6b-d):

1. Divine intervention (11:6b): ***And behold, I will deliver men up...*** **Behold** serves to arrest attention and signal an unexpected turn of events. The verb *deliver up* (r. *mts'* in Hiphil) is lit., "causing to be found" (cf. 2 Sam 3:8). *Into the hand* points to a struggle in which one party gains ascendancy over another usually by physical means.

As in 8:10 Zechariah identifies two factors leading to the ruin of the nation following the rejection of Messiah: strife within and assault without.

2. Internal strife (11:6c): ***each man into the hand of his neighbor.*** Neighbor (*rē'a*), also meaning "friend, companion, associate", appears 8x in Zechariah, 6x in the reciprocal phrase (*'iš rē'ēhû*) used here (lit. "a man his neighbor"). The situation described in this v is similar to what transpired during the siege of Jerusalem by the Chaldeans (Jer 19:9).

The first result of the withdrawal of divine pity is internal strife. The population living in the land when God withdraws his compassion will be rent by civil war. The confusion, strife, hatred and mutual destruction within the Jewish population following their rejection of their true Messiah is chronicled in all its ugly detail by Josephus.

3. External oppression (11:6d): ***And into the hand of his king...*** The second source of ruin for those that rejected Messiah came from the foe without. *Into the hand* suggests military defeat. This entire ch is about the repudiation of Messiah; so the *king* who inflicts military defeat on the Judeans here is certainly not Messiah.

His king indicates that this passage looks to the distant future when a king acknowledged by God's people will oppress and defeat them. This king is the one to whom the flock of God have given their allegiance, i.e., their chosen king. In this case, the Roman emperor is intended. One is reminded of the words of the Jewish leaders in Pilate's judgment hall: "We have no king but Caesar" (Jn 19:15).

E. Prediction (11:6e):

And they will smite the land and I will not deliver from their hand. The subject of the verb *smite* (r. *ktt* in Piel) is *his*

205

neighbor and *his king*. The verb has a range of meanings including "beat, crush by beating." The Piel form is intensive, thus "beat or crush fine." It is used here as a figure for devastating the land. Thus internal strife and external assault will crush the land where God's flock resides. *I will not deliver from their hand* implies that the smiting of the land will be non-stoppable and therefore total.

The Roman war against the Jews in AD 66-70 is in view. That war resulted in the complete destruction of Jerusalem and the dismantling of the Judean state.

Rejection of the Good Shepherd
Zechariah 11:7-14

A. Ministry of the Good Shepherd (11:7):
Zechariah carried out his assignment to shepherd the flock as directed in v 4.

1. General compliance (11:7a): **And I became the shepherd of the flock of slaughter, therefore the poor of the flock.** *Became the shepherd* can also be translated "fed." He "*fed the flock*" by his ministry of teaching and preaching. The *flock* is national Israel. By shepherding the flock in its entirety Zechariah (symbolizing the Good Shepherd) ministered to *the poor of the flock* as well. This phrase invariably refers to the godly within the nation that are persecuted and abused by the godless.[234] Although rejected by the flock as a whole there will be within the nation a remnant of believers who love and embrace Messiah (Jn 1:11).

2. Two staffs (11:7b): **And I took for myself two staffs: the one I called one Favor and the other I called Bands and I proceeded to shepherd the flock.** To make his role as a shepherd to the nation more authentic Zechariah acquired or fashioned two staffs. Shepherds often carried a rod and a staff (Ps 23:4)—a rod to ward off wild beasts; a crooked staff with which to guide the flock and rescue the straying. Zechariah

---

[234]Ps 10:2-9; 14:6; 35:10; 37:14; 11:17; 70:5; 72:4; 86:1; 104:16-22; Isa 10:2; 14:32; 41:17.

gave names to the two staffs, perhaps carving the names into the wood.[235]

Favor (*nōʻam*) can be translated "beauty" and "pleasantness".[236] The staff called *Favor* symbolized the loving, gracious care of the Good Shepherd. The staff called *Bands* (*chōbhlîm*) or "Union" (NIV) symbolized the unifying mission of the Good Shepherd. Cf. Jn 10:16. *I proceeded to shepherd the flock* again indicates that Zechariah acted out the role of the Good Shepherd using the two staffs. Just exactly what he did is left to the imagination of the reader.

B. Rejection of the Shepherds (11:8):

1. Cutting off (11:8a): ***And I cut off three shepherds in one month...*** The verb *cut off* (r. *kchd* in Hiphil) has the sense of cutting off or annihilating in seven passages (e.g., 2 Chr 32:21). In this context, however, the word may mean "removed" or "expelled." Many different interpretations of the *three shepherds* have been offered.[237] Perhaps the easiest is to regard this as a reference back to the three classes of shepherds mentioned in v 5—buyers, sellers, shepherds.[238] It is as shepherds that they are cut off, i.e., they were so discredited that they could no long serve effectively as national leaders. *One month* symbolizes a short space of time. Cf. Hos 5:7.

The key question is how did Zechariah carry out the cutting off of the three shepherds? Did the prophet have enough political clout that he could "fire" three actual leaders? Is the cutting off of the shepherds part of a visionary experience?

---

[235] The actions of Zechariah are similar to those of Ezekiel who took two sticks and wrote the names of Ephraim and Judah upon them. There is this difference: Ezekiel's sticks speak of saving events, while Zechariah's speak of judgment.

[236] The LXX translate *kallos*—favor, grace, protective care or graciousness.

[237] In 1912 Mitchell found at least forty conjectures about the identity of the three shepherds. (R. Smith (*WBC*, 270) suggests that "three shepherds" is like the "three transgressions" of the nations in Amos 1-2. Three is a complete number. So the text simply means that all the evil shepherds were removed.

[238] Other views of the three shepherds: 1) kings, priests, prophets; 2) three nations which oppressed Israel; 3) the number three used indefinitely; 4) Moses, Aaron, Miriam (Talmud); 5) three actual leaders in Zechariah's day.

Postexilic Prophets

Did Zechariah verbally cut them off with threats and denunciations? In some unspecified manner Zechariah acted out the cutting off of the national leaders or at least some of the national leaders.

The cutting off of the shepherds seems to point to the time predicted in vv 1-3 when trees, shepherds and lions—all symbols of national leaders—agonize over their fate and the fate of their nation. In terms of fulfillment, the cutting off of the shepherds seems to precede the foreign invasion depicted in the vv that follow.

2. *Cutting short (11:8b):* **and my soul was cut short with them...** Soul (*nepheš*) describes humans as conscious beings; but numerous times the term refers to what one may call the heart, emotions or feelings. *My soul was cut short* (r. *qtsr*) *with them* is the testimony of the Good Shepherd regarding the national leadership. The verb indicates that the Good Shepherd had reached the limits of his patience.

3. *Response (11:8c):* **and also their soul abhorred me**. Abhorred (r *bchl*) expresses intense disgust. The national leaders despised the Good Shepherd. Did Zechariah lose patience with the national leaders, and did they come to detest the prophet? Or does this symbolically represent the attitude of Jesus toward the national Jewish leaders, i.e., the Pharisees, Sadducees, and Herodians, and their attitude toward him? Perhaps both questions can be answered in the affirmative. What happened to Zechariah the type will be repeated in the relationship between Jesus and the national leaders.

C. Rejection of the Flock (11:9-11):

1. Good Shepherd announces his intentions (11:9): **And I said, I will not be your shepherd. The one that dies, let it die. The one that is cut off, let it be cut off. And let the rest eat each one the flesh of another.** Because the Good Shepherd has been rejected by the national leaders, he abandons the flock (national Israel) to its fate. *The one that dies* probably refers to plague. Plague did kill many during the Roman war of AD 66-70. *The one that is cut off* probably refers to those who died in violent conflict with the Romans. *Eat ...the flesh of another* points to cannibalism. Many died in famine

Zechariah 11:1-17

during the siege of Jerusalem. Josephus documents that some turned to cannibalism to survive.

The passage anticipates an invasion of Palestine from which God will not deliver his people. In the years following Zechariah there were two major Gentile incursions into Palestine—that by Antiochus Epiphanes in the second century BC, and that by the Romans under Titus in the seventh decade of the first Christian century. God did intervene to bring deliverance to his people in the former ordeal, but not in the latter invasion. Thus the Roman invasion of Palestine that resulted in the destruction of the temple and the Jewish state must be in view.

2. Breaking of the first staff (11:10): **And I took my staff, Favor, and I cut it in two to break my covenant that I made with all the peoples...** God symbolically withdraws his gracious protection of national Israel because the Good Shepherd was rejected by the flock. In the first person pronouns in v 10 the first two refer to the prophet, the second two refer to the Good Shepherd which he symbolizes in this action parable. The explanation by the actor glides over into the declaration of the one being portrayed.

My covenant...with all the peoples refers to restrictions placed on Gentile nations to prevent them from afflicting postexilic Israel. These restrictions were now removed, opening up the land to invasion by enemy nations.

3. Significance of the action (11:11a): **and it was broken in that day.** *In that day* refers to the day that the national leaders showed contempt for the Good Shepherd, not to the day when Zechariah broke his staff. So an action performed by Zechariah in his day forecast an action by God over five hundred years in the future. *It was broken* is feminine, referring to the covenant, not to the staff which is masculine.

4. Good Shepherd's prediction is recognized as the word of God (11:11b): **And the poor of the flock, those who watched me, knew that it was the word of God.** The *poor of the flock* are the faithful remnant who received the Good Shepherd. This believing remnant consisted of *those who watched* (r. šmr) *me*. The verb implies careful, perceptive observation. The believing remnant kept their eyes constantly

209

fixed on the Good Shepherd, ready to act according to his directive. These faithful followers *knew that it was the word of God,* i.e., they knew that national Israel was doomed to attack by the nations (Gentiles). In AD 66-70 the Christians saw the abomination of desolation (Roman legions) approaching Jerusalem. They fled Jerusalem as Jesus had directed (Mt 24:15-22) and took refuge in the town of Pella beyond the Jordan.

D. Rejection of the Good Shepherd (11:12-14):

1. Good Shepherd asks the flock to evaluate his services (11:12): **And I said unto them: If it is good in your eyes give (me) my hire, and if not, desist. So they weighed for my hire thirty pieces of silver.** The Good Shepherd had the right to demand his wages; but he left it up to the flock to express appreciation in the way they deemed appropriate. His request for his "wages" after the first staff was broken was in reality a call for repentance. The wages that the Good Shepherd desired were repentance, faith, obedience (cf. Mt 21:34). Unlike the wicked shepherds, he puts no constraint on the flock. Here was the opportunity to show their gratitude for all God had done for them. Instead of wages, however, they offer the Good Shepherd an insult (Keil). *Thirty pieces of silver* was the value of a slave (Ex 21:32). Thus the flock (represented by their leaders) mocked the Good Shepherd. Their evaluation demonstrated their ingratitude.

2. Directive to the prophet (11:13a): **And Yahweh said unto me, Cast it unto the potter, the goodly price with which I was evaluated by them.** *Cast it* (r *šlk* Hiphil impv.) is the verb used for casting torn flesh to the dogs (Ex 22:31), of discarding a corpse left unburied (Isa 14:19), and of idols cast to the moles and bats (Isa 2:20). Thus the silver was to be flung down with an air of disgust and revulsion.

Zechariah is told to cast the paltry silver pieces *to the potter.* Perhaps the reason for this directive is that a potter was considered one of the lowliest professions. A potter's labor was estimated as being of relatively little value. It could be that "cast to the potter" was a proverbial expression for contemptuous treatment. *Goodly price* (*'eder hay^eqār*) is sarcas-

Zechariah 11:1-17

tic, meaning something like "magnificent sum" (lit., "the magnificence of the price"). Yahweh takes the treatment of the Good Shepherd as a personal insult. He contemptuously rejected the sum.

    3. *Execution of the directive (11:13b):* ***So I took the thirty pieces of silver and threw them to the potter in the house of Yahweh.*** The declaration of execution complies with the directive except now it becomes clear that the potter to whom Zechariah cast the silver was *in the house of Yahweh*. This phrase could simply indicate the venue for the entire symbolic drama. More likely, however, a potter was actually in the temple at the time Zechariah acted out this parable. The potter may have been a temple functionary who made vessels for use in the various rituals. In any case, the announcement of the repudiation of Israel was announced publicly in the very place where the covenant people assembled before Yahweh.

    In the fulfillment of this prophetic drama the national leaders were willing to pay Judas thirty pieces of silver for information leading to the private arrest of Jesus. After the betrayal, Judas had a change of heart. The thirty pieces of silver by which Jesus was betrayed was first cast down in the temple by Judas, then was used to purchase a potter's field. Thus the blood money ultimately wound up in the pocket of a potter. It is no wonder that the Gospel writer cites vv 12-13 as a direct prophecy of what happened to Jesus on the night of his betrayal (Mt 27:9-10).[239]

    4. *Breaking of the second staff (11:14):* ***And I cut in two my second staff, Bands, to break the brotherhood between Judah and [between] Israel.*** For some time after the breaking of the first staff the Shepherd retained his second

---

[239] The passage from Zech 11 is cited as coming from Jeremiah. Matthew seems to be citing the passage by section of Scripture rather than by book. Jeremiah at one time stood at the head of the latter prophets, and for that reason the section may have been cited as "Jeremiah." Another view: Matthew's intent in using the name "Jeremiah" was to signal a connection between this passage in Zech 11 and prophecies concerning the Valley of Hinnom in Jer 18-19, the potter chs. The Apostle saw a connection between the "field of blood" purchased with thirty pieces of silver and the prediction that the Valley of Hinnom would become the Valley of Slaughter.

staff. This may point to the Shepherd's reluctance to give up the flock that had been so dear to him. To the very end he wanted to be gracious to them if they would but turn unto him. In the absence of any manifestation of repentance he not only had to give them over to Gentile enemies (first staff), but also to the terrible calamity of internal strife.

This ch has previously announced that the future of God's people will be marked by internecine fighting (v 6) and even cannibalism (v 9). The dramatic cutting of the second staff by the Good Shepherd (portrayed by Zechariah) indicates that the time had come for the implementation of this aspect of national judgment. The breaking of the second staff symbolized the dissolution of all bands that held the nation together, the civil and social disunion that paved the way for the victory of the Romans.

Brotherhood (*'achavāh*) is used only here in the Hebrew Bible. At the time of the schism in 931 BC the Judeans were forbidden to go to war against their "brothers" the Israelites (1 Kgs 12:24). So the term here refers to the fraternal bond that blinds together people of common ancestry.

Between (*bēn*) is regularly repeated in the Hebrew text to indicate the space separating two distinct objects. Here, however, the text emphasizes the brotherhood that previously existed between Judah and Israel. So it may be that in this case *bēn* has the meaning "among," i.e., "among Judah and among Israel" (Baron).

Judah and Israel is the traditional way designating the tribes descending from Jacob as a whole.[240] In this case the unified nation refers to the people living in Palestine at the time of the rejection of the Good Shepherd.

On the fulfillment of the prediction portrayed in the breaking of the second staff, see on v 9.

---

[240]"Judah and Israel" is used 11x in the OT. In addition the two names with descriptors appear an additional 38x. Sometimes (e.g., Josh 11:21) the dyad is used geographically.

Zechariah 11:1-17

Coming False Shepherd
Zechariah 11:15-17

A. Second Shepherd Commission (11:15):
And Yahweh said to me, Yet again take for yourself the equipment of a foolish shepherd. Yet again (*'ōd*) connects this action with the previous one. It implies that the prophet already had acted out the rejection of the Good Shepherd. It is not clear what the *equipment* of the foolish shepherd was, or how it may have differed from that of the Good Shepherd. Perhaps the text simply means that Zechariah was to again take up the garb, rod, staff, etc. of a shepherd.

Foolish (*'evilî*) occurs only here in the Hebrew Bible; but it is equivalent in meaning to a noun/adjective which is used 25x. A "fool" is always morally bad. He despises wisdom and discipline (Prov 1:7), mocks guilt (Prov 14:9), is quarrelsome (Prov 20:3), and licentious (Prov 7:22). It is useless to attempt to instruct such a person (Prov 16:22). The word is frequently used as a synonym of ungodliness (e.g., Ps 14:1). So this time Zechariah was acting the role of one that is the direct opposite the Good Shepherd.

B. Coming of the False Shepherd (11:16a):
For behold I will raise up a shepherd over the land. For (*kî*) introduces the explanation of the commission of the previous v. Zechariah's second shepherd drama, like the first, is prophetic. *Behold* demands attention and indicates something unexpected. The first person pronoun is emphatic. *I will raise up* is a Hiphil participle (r *qûm*). This is the only time in the OT where the first person declaration of raising up someone is used of a negative figure.[241] God raises this shepherd up in the same sense that he raised up the adversaries of national Israel at various points in OT history. The reference is to the permissive will of God. *Over the land* refers to the land where the Good Shepherd was rejected.

---

[241] First person declarations using the verb *raise up* appear 8x, six of which refer to the messianic prophet (Dt 18:18), priest (1 Sam 2:35) and king (Jer 30:9). This phrase is used once of Cyrus the deliverer (Isa 45:13).

Postexilic Prophets

This shepherd must represent some person or power subsequent to rejection of Christ and the Roman invasion of Palestine. The foolish shepherd is not further identified. He is probably the same as *his king* in v 6. A possible candidate is Titus, commander of the Roman forces that destroyed the temple and ruthlessly mistreated Jerusalem's survivors.[242] The lesson is that if people will not follow good leaders they are doomed to suffer under bad ones.

C. Character of the False Shepherd (11:16b, c):
  1. What he will not do (11:16b): ***The cut off one he will not visit, the young he will not visit; the broken he will not heal; the one who stands still he will not feed...*** The false shepherd will be totally unconcerned about the flock. He will not go after the *cut off* or straying sheep. He will show no particular concern about the young. The sheep that stand still are those too feeble to move. They get no food. This leader is ruthless and heartless.
  2. What he will do (11:16c): ***but the flesh of the fat he will eat and their hoofs he will break.*** The false shepherd uses the flock for his own purposes. *Hoofs he will break* suggests that their hoofs will be torn by driving them mercilessly over rough places.[243]

D. Condemnation of the False Shepherd (11:17):
  1. Warning (11:17a): ***Woe to the worthless shepherd who forsakes the flock.*** This is the only *woe* (*hōy*) in the book. The word warns of judgment to come. *Worthless* (*ʾelîl*) is used 20x in OT. It is used to describe physicians (Job 13:4), utterances of false prophets (Jer 14:14), and gods or idols (Lv 19:4). This is God's estimate and description of the second shepherd. He is designated as worthless because he *forsakes the flock*, thus proving himself to be a false shepherd (Jn 10:12-13).

---

[242] Other proposals include the Romans in general, Antichrist, Herod, false christs, and false prophets.

[243] Another interpretation: he will tear their hoofs in pieces in his attempts to consume every last morsel of meat or fat (Baron).

Zechariah 11:1-17

2. Description (11:17b): ***A sword will be against his arm and against his right eye.*** The false shepherd falls under the judgment of God. *Arm* and *right eye* represent power and understanding.[244] God will deprive him of the power and understanding that he has abused. *Sword* symbolizes judgment by any means. The sword is against the shepherd's arm because he did not reach out to assist the needy sheep. The sword is against the right eye because this shepherd did not search out the lost.

3. Result (11:17c): ***His arm shall be completely dried up and his right eye shall be utterly dimmed.*** A withered arm and a blind eye will be the result of the divine judgment against this shepherd. If the foolish shepherd is Titus and the emperors he represented, then history records the gradual withering of Roman might and blindness to the needs of the masses within the Roman Empire.

Second Burden
Zechariah 12-14

The second "burden" in Zechariah focuses on great attacks against the messianic Jerusalem from which the Jerusalem that is from above emerges as the center of a new creation.[245]

Introduction
Zechariah 12:1

A. Subject (12:1a):
The burden of the word of Yahweh concerning Israel (oracle of Yahweh). National Israel has been rejected in the previous ch; this is addressed to the messianic theocracy—the

---

[244]The right arm and right eye may also be linked with ability to defend his subjects. According to R. Smith (*WBC*, 272) the arm of the leader represented strength for defense and the right eye was the one used to see over the shield in aiming his arrow. Under the foolish shepherd the people will be defenseless.

[245]W. Dumbrell, *The Faith of Israel: Its Expression in the Books of the Old Testament.* (Grand Rapids: Baker, 1988), 198.

Postexilic Prophets

people of God in contradistinction to the world of nations that is estranged from God.

B. Speaker (12:1b-d):

These words are probably taken from a hymn or doxology.[246] The purpose of this description of Yahweh is to assure the reader that Yahweh has the power to carry out whatever it is that he promises. Yahweh is presented as Creator in a threefold way.

1. Creator of the heavens (12:1b): **Yahweh, who stretches out the heavens...** *Stretches out* poetically points to the vastness of the heavens (Job 9:8; Ps 104:2; Isa 40:22). The heavens as known to the ancients were what was visible to the naked eye. That in itself is impressive. How much more magnificent are the heavens as seen through telescopes. *Stretches* (r. *nth*) is the first of three participles in this v. The participle form is intended to stress the continuous display of Yahweh's power and wisdom in the universe which he created (Baron).

2. Creator of the earth (12:1c): **who lays the foundation of the earth...** *Lays the foundation* is a participle (r. *ysd*). The OT references the foundations of the earth 17x. This is a figurative way of referring to the mountains.

3. Creator of man (12:1d): **and who forms the spirit of man within him, declares:** The *spirit of man* is referenced 2x previously in the OT (Ecc 3:21; Isa 57:16). The reference is to the inner being of man, what some call the soul.

Great Siege
Zechariah 12:2-9

Spiritual Jerusalem in this paragraph comes under intense attack. Even so Yahweh will in the end rescue his people.

---

[246]The words of Zech 12:1b are similar to Isa 42:5; 44:24; 45:12; 51:13; Amos 4:13.

Zechariah 12:1-14:21

A. Picture #1: Bowl of Reeling (12:2):
1. Jerusalem's strength (12:2a): **Behold, I am about to set Jerusalem a bowl of reeling...** *Behold* (22x in Zechariah) serves to introduce statements that are shocking, or at least unexpected. The first person pronoun is emphatic in the Hebrew. *About to set* renders a participle that indicates imminent action. Earthly Jerusalem has been crushed in the attack by the Romans at the end of ch 11; but Jerusalem lives on—the Jerusalem that is from above—the church of Christ.

Bowl of reeling develops a figure used several times in Scripture as a symbol of the judgment of God that makes its recipients as helpless as those impaired by intoxicants. Elsewhere it is a "cup" (*kōs*) from which men drink.[247] Here, however, it is a *bowl* (*saph*) or basin. The term is used of the vessel used to collect the blood of the Passover lamb (Ex 12:22); it is used of certain temple vessels (Jer 52:19) as well as basins used in a domestic setting (2 Sam 17:28). The use of the word *bowl* may point to the larger dose of intoxicating judgment that Jerusalem's enemies must consume. On the other hand, the bowl may indicate a vessel that is large enough for attackers to drink out of either together, or one after another in succession.

2. Jerusalem's attackers (12:2b): **to all the peoples round about...** *The peoples* are hostile powers of the world. *Round about* suggests that the attackers in this first picture are those in closer proximity to Jerusalem. *Under siege* depicts the worldly enemies of heavenly Jerusalem coming against the city of God with murderous intent. Their attacks, however, only lead to confusion. The hostile forces that try to drink from the Jerusalem cup will reel about like drunken men. Thus they will be unable to take the city. Unlike the physical type, this Jerusalem will be impregnable.

3. Jerusalem's siege (12:2c): **even (when) Judah shall be under siege (and) Jerusalem.** A literal rendering of the Hebrew is: "and also upon Judah shall be in the siege against Jerusalem." Some take this to mean that Judah—at least initially—joins the Gentiles in the attack upon Jerusalem. In vv

---

[247]Ps 75:8; Isa 51:21-23. Cf. Jer 25:15.

5-6, however, Judah and Jerusalem are allies against the attackers. Some 31x in the OT Judah and Jerusalem are named together as comprising the southern kingdom. So the words "also upon Judah" most likely mean that Judah experiences the same siege as Jerusalem. *Siege* implies a time of hardship for God's people. For a time the attackers may have the upper hand. The point is, however, that God's people collectively will survive the attacks of hostile forces.

B. Picture #2: Burdensome Stone (12:3):

In several ways the second picture intensifies and amplifies the first.

1. Jerusalem's strength (12:3a): **And it will come to pass in that day that I will set Jerusalem as a stone of burden...** *In that day,* used 6x in this ch, is the day of the attack against spiritual Jerusalem. *A stone of burden* is a burdensome stone, a weight too heavy to lift—a weight that wounds and injures those who attempt to carry it.

The origin of the burdensome stone image is disputed. According to some it is taken from construction operations. Another view is that the figure is derived from the efforts of the plowman to remove large stones from his field. The most ancient view is that of Jerome who claimed that large stones were used by young men as weights to be lifted in exercise.[248]

2. Jerusalem's attackers (12:3b): **to all the peoples...** The description of the attackers does not have the restricting phrase *round about* attached as in picture #1. Zechariah considers the possibility that *all the nations of the earth* will converge to attack Jerusalem. These words point to a larger and potentially more devastating gathering of hostile forces. Is this the same attack envisioned in the previous v? Or is Zechariah anticipating the final all-out assault against NT Jerusalem? (Rev 16:14; Joel 3:9-12). Throughout history there have been from time to time concentrated attacks against the Christian faith. All of these point forward to that final assault which the Bible depicts being in process when the Lord returns.

---

[248]Cited by Baron, op. cit., 428-29.

Zechariah 12:1-14:21

3. Jerusalem's deliverance (12:3c): **All who burden themselves with her will surely be lacerated, even if all nations of the earth gather against her.** In the previous picture the deliverance of Jerusalem was implied; now that deliverance is explicitly mentioned. The attackers reeled but were not injured in the previous picture; now those who attack spiritual Jerusalem will injure themselves. Previously Zechariah alluded to a siege against Jerusalem and Judah, i.e., prolonged operations. *Burden themselves with her* may be equivalent to siege; but here the enemy seems to be injured as they approach the city. *Lacerated* (r. *srt*) means "to incise, scratch." Use of this term suggests that the stone is jagged as well as heavy. The size of the attacking force is of no consequence. The attackers will themselves be injured *even if all the nations of the earth gather against her.*[249]

C. Picture #3: Place of Befuddlement (12:4):

In this v Zechariah uses three rhyming words (*timmāhōn; shiggāʿōn; ʿivvārōn*) to show how Yahweh totally befuddles those who attack his people.[250] Seven features of this picture suggest an escalation of imagery: 1) the oracle formula; 2) the triple set of terms 3) the representation of the attackers as a cavalry unit; 4) specific mention of the affliction; 5) the more serious nature of the affliction; 6) the direct involvement of Yahweh; and 7) the expansion of the affliction to the attackers' horses.

1. Horses (12:4a): **In that day (oracle of Yahweh) I will smite every horse with confusion…** As was the case with the second picture, the third is specifically set *in that day*, i.e., in the day of the attack against spiritual Jerusalem. The enemies of God's people are depicted as a cavalry unit assaulting the city.

---

[249]The verb is a perfect + *vav*. McComiskey (1210) points to passages where this construction has a concessive force.

[250]The three rhyming words appear together in Dt 28:28 where they denote divine judgments to be sent upon unfaithful Israel. Petersen, *OTL*, 113-14. Curses once pronounced on Israel are now directed against Israel's enemies. Barker, *EBC*, 7:681.

Postexilic Prophets

Yahweh intervenes to *smite every horse*. This frequently used verb (r. *nkh*) is a strong one. It sometimes connotes hitting an object with one non-fatal blow (e.g., Nm 22:23). It is sometimes used for a beating, i.e., multiple blows (e.g., Neh 13:25). Many times it means to slay (e.g., Ex 21:12). In other passages the verb indicates to attack and/or destroy (e.g., Amos 3:15). In many cases God is the subject of this verb. He smites people with blindness (2 Kgs 6:18), plagues (Dt 28:22), even death (2 Sam 6:7).

Confusion (*timmāhōn*) is rendered "panic" (NRSV; NJPS; NIV) and "bewilderment" (NASB). The horses charge as ordered by their riders, only to shy away in terror. Cavalry thus become useless as a battle weapon.

2. *Riders (12:4b):* **and its rider with madness...** The riders of the horses will not be able to continue the attack on foot, for they will be smitten with *madness* (*šiggāʿôn*). This noun is used but 3x in OT. In Dt 28:28 it is used of a divine judgment on Israel. It is also used to describe the wild and erratic chariot driving of Jehu (2 Kgs 9:20). On foot the horsemen can do no better than their horses. Coordinated attack is impossible for the attackers go racing about in all directions.

3. *Victims (12:4c):* **but upon the house of Judah I will open my eyes...** House of Judah refers to those who are true descendants of Judah and Abraham, i.e., those who have put their faith in Christ. Since Judah and Jerusalem together describe the Kingdom of Judah in the type, there is no reason to think that in the antitype some subtle distinction is to be made between the two designations. Both refer to Messiah's kingdom, the church of Christ. To open the eyes is a metaphor meaning to show favor towards. God will show his people favor in the terrifying scene.

4. *Horses (12:4d):* **and every horse of the peoples I will smite with blindness.** Zechariah returns to the *horses*, the major weapon of the enemy. The strong verb *smite* is repeated for emphasis. The confusion of the horses is now attributed to *blindness* (*ʿivvārôn*) which renders the horses ineffective as instruments of waging war.

Zechariah 12:1-14:21

The three pictures depict those who attack spiritual Jerusalem as reeling (implied), lacerated, and rendered incapable to pressing the attack. It is perhaps important that Zechariah does not see them at this point as slain.

D. Picture #4: Confidence under Attack (12:5):
While the enemy has launched an all-out attack against spiritual Jerusalem, within the city the scene is one of calmness and confidence.

1. Object of confidence (12:5a): **And the princes of Judah will say in their heart, The inhabitants of Jerusalem are my strength...** The *princes of Judah* are the leaders of God's people. These princes are not outwardly boasting of their strength. They have quiet confidence. *Say in their heart* refers to a reasoned conclusion based on evidence. The leaders recognize that the *inhabitants of Jerusalem are my strength,* not walls or gates, but the citizens of spiritual Jerusalem. There is no indication that the inhabitants of Jerusalem engage in the battle; only the leaders do that. So the strength the inhabitants give must be moral support and prayer support.

2. Basis of confidence (12:5b): **in Yahweh of Hosts their God.** The people under attack believe that God is on their side. The survival of spiritual Jerusalem is a token of divine favor.

E. Picture #5: Fire Pan (12:6a, b):
1. Empowered leaders (12:6a): **In that day I will make the chiefs of Judah like a pan of fire in the wood and like a torch of fire in the sheaves...** *In that day* is repeated from v 4. The phrase refers to the day when messianic Jerusalem comes under attack. *The chiefs of Judah* are the leaders of spiritual Jerusalem. In the day of attack they will contribute to the defense of Jerusalem. The leaders are compared to *a pan of fire* and *a torch of fire* exposed to combustible material (the enemy).

2. Victorious leaders (12:6b): **and they will consume upon the right and left all the people round about...** The metaphor underscores the ease with which the leaders, em-

221

powered by the Lord, will subdue all those who intend to do harm to spiritual Jerusalem. *Consume upon the right and left* refers to the slaughter of those who are the enemies of God's people. *All the people round about* refers to all those who attack spiritual Jerusalem.

F. Picture #6: Secure City (12:6c):

But Jerusalem shall be inhabited yet in its (own) place (even) in Jerusalem. Jerusalem had not been repopulated in Zechariah's day; but he envisioned a new *Jerusalem*. This spiritual city *shall be inhabited* no matter how fierce the assaults against her. *Yet in its (own) place (even) in Jerusalem* refers to the period after or during the siege of spiritual Jerusalem. Spiritual Zion will remain settled on her site unmoved by whatever hoards of hell come against her.

G. Picture #7: Yahweh's Intervention (12:7):

This ch previously has stressed the equality of Judah and Jerusalem (vv 2, 5) in the messianic age. That point is now made even more forcefully. Earlier Zechariah depicted the messianic kingdom as a combination of Judah and Ephraim (9:13). Now he portrays that kingdom as consisting of Jerusalem plus Judah (cf. 2:12).

1. *Priority in salvation (12:7a):* **Yahweh will save the tents of Judah first...** The verb *save* is used in conjunction with Yahweh at least 48x in the OT. He is preeminently the God of salvation. Yahweh's people are known as the saved (Dt 33:29). From the time of the wilderness wandering the traditional designation for Israelite dwellings was *tents*.[251] In OT times open towns and villages could offer no effectual resistance to an enemy. So the point is that Yahweh will intervene on behalf of the defenseless.

Citizens who lived in the rural regions of Judah were the first to feel the effects of invasion; now they are portrayed as

---

[251] *Tent* (*'ōhel*) is used for the animal skin dwelling of nomadic people (e.g., Gn 4:20), shepherds (Jer 6:3), women (Gn 31:33), warriors (1 Sam 17:54), and cattle (2 Chr 14:14). It is also used for a bridal tent (2 Sam 16:22). The term continued to be used for a habitation or home (e.g., 1 Kgs 8:66).

Zechariah 12:1-14:21

the first to experience Yahweh's salvation.[252] In the days of Messiah it will no longer be necessary for citizens living in the outlying areas around Jerusalem to take refuge behind the massive walls of the capital when the nation was faced with invasion.

The word *first* suggests priority. The defenseless land will be delivered sooner than the well-defended capital.

This line establishes the following points: 1) the salvation of which Zechariah is speaking is not physical in nature; it does not depend upon walls. In effect this v says the same thing as 2:5 that Yahweh will be a wall of fire around Jerusalem. 2) The citizens of the messianic kingdom are those who enjoy Yahweh's salvation. 3) There is no such thing as second class citizens in Messiah's kingdom.

2. *Glory in salvation (12:7b)*: **in order that the glory of the house of David and the inhabitants of Jerusalem does not exalt itself over Judah**. The *glory of the house of David* consists in the fact that it is the God-appointed royal line in Israel. The Davidic house survived the exile to Babylon and was prominent in the restoration community in the person of Zerubbabel. Since Messiah was to come from the Davidic line there was some reason to think that Yahweh's priority concern would be the royal family. The glory of *the inhabitants of Jerusalem* probably consisted in the fact that they considered themselves exalted above others because they lived in the city Yahweh had chosen as the seat of his earthly government.

Throughout the centuries the prophets of God predicted a restoration of the house of David. The one who rules the future kingdom is a son of David. Those who assist him in his rule are called *the house of David*. God will see to it that every citizen of Messiah's kingdom will have divine protection. The point is that each part of the chosen nation will have its share in the glory of salvation. The ground at the foot of the cross is level. Christians are sinners saved by grace. There is no place for boasting, save in the cross of Christ.

---

[252]Cf. Isa 9:1-2 where the region most subject to oppression and darkness is the first to see the messianic light.

Postexilic Prophets

H. Picture #8: Yahweh's Empowerment (12:8):

1. Certainty of it (12:8a): **In that day Yahweh will defend the inhabitants of Jerusalem...** *In that day* again refers to any time of attack on spiritual Jerusalem. As Yahweh will save the tents of Judah, so will he also *defend the inhabitants of Jerusalem.* The entirety of Messiah's kingdom is protected from on high.

2. Description of it (12:8b): **and it will come to pass that the stumbler among them in that day (will be) as David and the house of David (will be) as God, like the Angel of Yahweh before them.** Zechariah now describes the strength God's people will possess because of Yahweh's empowerment. The *stumbler* (*hannikshāl*) is the person so weak that he cannot even stand much less fight in the battle. He represents the weakest among the citizens of Jerusalem. This person will become a mighty war hero like David. The *house of David,* probably led by a prince or governor, *will be as God (Elohim),* i.e., God in his might and majesty. These words suggest that the leaders of spiritual Jerusalem will be endowed with supernatural strength and discernment. *Like the Angel of Yahweh before them* indicates that the leaders will lead God's people into battle like the Angel of Yahweh led the ancient armies of Israel.[253]

I. Picture #9: Enemy Destruction (12:9):

And it will come to pass in that day that I will seek to destroy all the nations that come against Jerusalem. The *peoples* of v 2 are now called *nations* or Gentiles. *I will seek* means "I purpose." God's purpose is *to destroy* (r. shmd in Hiphil) the enemies of the church. This verb occurs 68x in OT in the Hiphil. Sometimes it has the meaning "to annihilate" (Josh 11:14). When used of a group, however, this verb often has the meaning "to remove from the scene" (Dt 6:19) and "to destroy as a functioning entity" (Isa 10:7; Am 9:8; Jer 48:42) or simply "to subdue" (Dt 9:3; 28:63). When a nation is destroyed, it ceases to function as a political entity. This verb is used most frequently with God as the subject (41x).

---

[253]Ex 23:20, 23; 32:34; 33:2; and possibly Josh 5:13-15.

Zechariah 12:1-14:21

Here God promises to destroy *all the nations that come against Jerusalem. Come against* means to come in martial array to attack the people of God. The coalition of attackers is destroyed in that it is no longer effective as an attacking army. The attackers are neutralized and removed from the scene. Ideally such attacking coalitions are broken up when key members are converted. Sometimes they are destroyed through the overturning of the arguments with which they assault Jerusalem. When necessary, the Lord will intervene to destroy the enemies physically.

Great Savior
Zechariah 12:10

The prophet now begins to show how the new covenant people came to be such—how the church commences the Christian life and obtains the right to the divine protection mentioned in the preceding paragraph (Chambers).

A. Outpouring of God's Spirit (12:10a-c):
 1. *Action (12:10a):* **And I will pour...** This v begins with a *vav* conjunction (*and*) which suggests that what follows is directly related to what immediately precedes. The speaker is Yahweh. The verb *pour* (r. *špk*) suggests lavish provision. The concept of pouring out God's Spirit was introduced by Joel (2:28) and further developed by Isaiah (44:3 using the r. *ntsq*) and Ezekiel (39:29).
 2. *Recipients (12:10b):* **upon the house of David and upon the inhabitants of Jerusalem...** Again as in v 7, *the house of David* refers to the leaders of spiritual Jerusalem, the *inhabitants of Jerusalem* are the citizens of Christ's kingdom. Jerusalem is used as the designation for the whole of God's people in accord with the custom of regarding the capital as the representative of the whole nation (Keil).
 3. *Gift (12:10c):* **the Spirit of grace and supplication.** *Spirit* refers to the Holy Spirit. *Grace* (*chēn*) is what God manifests and the Holy Spirit communicates through his word to the heart of sinners. The Spirit teaches that God is favorably disposed toward those who have violated his law. Cf. Heb

225

10:29; Jn 16:8. *Supplication* (*tach^{a}nūnîm*) refers to the fruit of grace—entreaty for a specific application of God's favor. There is a hint in the remaining part of the v that the favor that they seek is forgiveness.

B. Looking unto the Pierced One (12:10d-f):

1. Action (12:10d): **and they shall look...** The verb *look* (r. *nbt* in Hiphil) refers to what one does with the eye (Ps 94:9). The term embraces everything from a mere glance (1 Sam 17:42) to a careful, sustained, and favorable contemplation (Isa 5:12; Ps 74:20; 119:6, 15). It is used of both man's looking to or upon God (Ex 3:6; Nm 12:8) and God's looking upon man (e.g. Ps 33:13). The subject of the verb is the house of David and inhabitants of Jerusalem. Zechariah does not refer to an ordinary or mere passing look, but a look of faith and hope that is part of the supplication. The same verb is used in the story of the bronze serpent on a pole (Nm 21:9), a passage that Zechariah may have had in mind as he penned these words. It is this verb also that is used in Nm 12:8 when Moses looked upon the form of Yahweh.

2. Direction (12:10e): **unto me...** The first person singular pronoun identifies the object of the contemplation as the speaker. There has been no indication of any change of speaker. Therefore the object of contemplation is Yahweh. The Holy Spirit leads sinners unto God through the gospel. The emphasis in the passage is upon return to Yahweh. There is no need to emend MT as some have proposed.[254]

3. Identification (12:10f): **whom they have pierced...** The speaker identifies himself as one *whom they have pierced*. Yahweh had been pierced through. *Pierced* (r. *dqr*) means "to slay by any kind of death whatever" (Keil). Jewish interpreters generally give this word a metaphorical meaning. This, however, is unlikely. In all of its occurrences this verb has a concrete sense, referring to actual piercing, usually by a sword. A shepherd is smitten with a sword in the following ch (13:7). Most likely this v refers to that shepherd, the same

---

[254]S.R. Driver (*CB*, 264-66) pointed out that some fifty MSS support "unto him."

Zechariah 12:1-14:21

Good Shepherd rejected by the flock in 11:4-14 (McComiskey).

The record in the Gospels indicates that it was a Roman soldier who did the actual deed of piercing. The responsibility for the piercing, however, rested upon the Jewish leaders who delivered him over to Pilate. In an even deeper sense, the piercing of the Christ was vicarious, i.e., he was pierced to the death on behalf of sinners (Isa 53:5). So in that sense, all of us were responsible for the piercing.

Some identify the Pierced One as some unknown martyr of Zechariah's time. This passage, however, invites consideration of a connection with the Suffering Servant of Isa 53 who suffers vicariously for the sins of mankind. This may suggest the nature of the supplication with which the inhabitants of Jerusalem look unto the Pierced One.

Both the Babylonian and Palestinian Talmud take the reference to be to the Messiah.[255] The Apostle John sees this as a prediction of the piercing of Christ at his crucifixion (Jn 19:37; Rev 1:7). Faith is implied in this look upon the Pierced One, otherwise it would not be possible to account for the intense emotional response to the look that is described in next line.

C. Mourning for the Pierced One (12:10g):

And they will mourn for him, as one mourns for an only son, and they will weep bitterly over him like the bitter weeping over a firstborn son. The change in person mid-verse should be noted. They look *unto me*; they mourn *for him*. Yahweh speaks of Pierced One as distinct in person from himself. So the Pierced One is Yahweh the speaker; yet he is distinct from Yahweh. This identification/distinction motif prepares the way for the NT doctrine of the Father and the Son.

The bitterness of the mourning is emphasized by two similes. The mourning over the Pierced One is compared to the mourning over *an only son*. The preservation of the family

---

[255] F.F. Bruce, *New Testament Development of Old Testament Themes* (Grand Rapids: Eerdmans, 1969), 112.

ily was deemed of vast importance. The death of an *only son* was the heaviest blow that could happen (cf. Jer 6:26; Am 8:10). The death of a son is bad enough, but the death of *a firstborn son* is even a more intense loss.

The designations "only son" and "firstborn" are particularly appropriate for the mourning over Messiah. He is the "Firstborn" of all creation.[256] He was also the "only begotten" Son of God (Jn 3:16).

If looking unto him whom they have pierced suggests faith in the Pierced One, morning over him implies repentance for the deeds that led to his being pierced. Repentance follows faith. When we come to realize that our sins made his death necessary—that in a very real sense we are responsible for his death—the realization leads to godly sorrow and godly sorrow to repentance (2 Cor 7:10).

Great Salvation
Zechariah 12:11-13:5

A. **Lamentation** (12:11-14):
Clearly the text highlights the mourning that follows correct apprehension of why the Pierced One died. Zechariah already has compared the grief of the penitent to that grief experienced by a family over the loss of an only son or a firstborn son. Now he adds another comparison—that of a grief stricken nation.

1. Intensity (12:11): **In that day the mourning shall be great in Jerusalem like the mourning of Hadad-rimmon in the valley of Megiddo.** *In that day* refers to the messianic era. *Jerusalem* should be given its spiritual connotation—the people of God of the messianic era. There was little mourning among the residents of physical Jerusalem when they observed the piercing of Christ. Jerusalem here consists of all those who look on the Pieced One and mourn in repentance. *Hadad-rimmon* is the location where Josiah, a beloved king, died. For years there was a national lamentation over this

---

[256]Rom 8:29; Col 1:15, 18; Heb 1:6; Rev 1:5.

Zechariah 12:1-14:21

event. See 2 Chr 35:25. Hadad-rimmon may have been a city in the valley of Megiddo.[257]

2. *Universality (12:12a):* ***And the land shall mourn...*** *The land*, like Jerusalem, is defined contextually as those who look on the Pierced One and mourn in repentance.[258] Once people realize that their sin put Jesus on the cross they plunge into intense mourning and repentance.

3. *Individuality (12:12b):* ***every family apart, with their wives apart...*** This language suggests that the mourning will extend to every individual of every family. This is not like the organized national mourning occasions that one reads about at various junctures of OT history. All who reside in the messianic land or kingdom are penitent.

4. *Illustrations (12:12c-13):* ***the family of the house of David apart and their wives apart; the family of the house of Nathan apart and their wives apart; 13 the family of the house of Levi apart, and their wives apart; the family of the Shimeites apart, and their wives apart...*** Zechariah cites four families as illustration of the general principle stated above, two royal families, two priestly families. In each set the first family named is the trunk family, the second a branch. This is Zechariah's unique way of representing the entirety of both the royal and priestly lines.

Jeremiah prophesied that both the Levitical and royal families would be represented in the messianic age (Jer 33:17-22). In the NT age Christians are regarded as brothers of the King of Kings, hence of the house of David. They are also regarded as priests to God (Rev 1:6).

Even the family at the top of the social/economic ladder will mourn. *House of David* is the royal family. *Their wives apart* suggests that women as well as men will look upon the Pierced One and be brought to repentance. Following the custom of the time, they will mourn apart from the men, express-

---

[257]The name Hadad-rimmon does not occur elsewhere in the OT. R. Smith (*WBC*, 278f) argues that this was the name of a god. In this case the meaning is that the messianic weeping will be as loud and deep as the pagan wailing for a fertility god.
[258]*The land* (*hā'ārets*) sometimes, as here, refers to the inhabitants of the land (cf. Lv 19:29; 1 Sam 14:25; Ezek 14:13).

ing in their own unique feminine way the sorrow they feel. *House of Nathan* was a branch of the royal family (2 Sam 5:14; Lk 3:31.

House of Levi indicates that the priests will join in the mourning. *House of the Shimeites* is a specific family within the tribe of Levi (Nm 3:18).

5. *Reiteration (12:14):* **all the families that remain, every family apart, and their wives apart.** The universality of the mourning is again emphasized. *All the families that remain* are the rest of the population within the messianic kingdom. None can reside in Messiah's kingdom that has not looked on the Pierced One. *Apart* points to private, individual mourning in which people wish to express in their own ways the mourning for the Pierced One. The mourners seek to avoid the eyes of others, even members of their own family, including their spouses. This is a good and godly sorrow that leads to repentance and flows from it.

The text gives the impression that looking on the Pierced One is not a onetime proposition. Some who were physically present at the site of the piercing looked, then went away and rejoiced that he was dead. Those who mourn, however, are those who see him in their mind's eye again and again.

B. Purification (13:1):

Yahweh will make provision for the cleansing of those who mourn over the Pierced One. The cleansing described in this v proves that the mourning of the previous vv is not the anguish of despair, but the godly sorrow that leads to repentance.

1. Provision (13:1a): **On that day a fountain will be opened...** *On that day* sets the time of the cleansing as concurrent with the preceding mourning. Since the mourning appears to be an on-going response to the recognition of the Pieced One, so also must the cleansing be an on-going provision. *The fountain* is not forgiveness itself (McComiskey), but the means of procuring forgiveness. The fountain will *be opened*, i.e., made available. No amount of weeping alone can cleanse. Only God can provide the cleansing. The fountain was *opened* when, on the day of Pentecost, the first presentation of the gospel directed penitent sinners to "repent and be baptized." Sinners buried in the baptismal pool contact the blood of Christ which cleanses them from all sin (Rom 6:3; Jn 1:7).

2. *People (13:1b):* **to the house of David and the inhabitants of Jerusalem.** The fountain is opened to the very ones who were mourning in the previous vv. Whether the penitents come from the highest levels of society or the lowest, they secure forgiveness in the same way, i.e., at the fountain. All citizens of spiritual Jerusalem share the common experience of the fountain. This is not a fountain filled with blood, but, like most fountains, with water. To this fountain the penitent will come in humble obedience to the command of the Pierced One to repent and be baptized (Acts 2:38).

In this passage Zechariah builds on Ezekiel's prophecy that Yahweh will cleanse his people, give them a new heart, and put a new spirit within them (Ezek 36:25-26).

3. *Purpose (13:1c):* **for sin and for uncleanness.** Fountain (*māqōr*) is used metaphorically in Ps 36:9 for the abundant life that Yahweh provides to those who turn to him. In Jer 2:13 and17:13 the term is used as a figure for Yahweh himself. He is the fountain of living waters. Here, however, the fountain is a means of purification. The connection between water and purification is firmly established in the law[259] and in the earlier prophets.[260] What Zechariah envisions, however, is not mere cleansing from ceremonial uncleanness, but from the devastating and contaminating effects of moral impurity.

The penitents who plunge into the fountain find complete forgiveness, not because the water is efficacious, but because by divine appointment that is the time and place of cleansing. The forgiveness is total. It removes their *sin* or guilt (*chatta't*). It also removes every stain of *uncleanness* (*niddāh*) caused by their overt disobedience. This OT sketch of the salvation to come calls to mind the admonition of the

---

[259]E.g., Nm 8:7 which speaks of "the water of cleansing" (lit., "sin water," i.e., water that removes sin).
[260]Ezek 36:25 "I will sprinkle clean water upon you, and you will be clean."

Postexilic Prophets

preacher to the penitent Saul of Tarsus, "Get up, be baptized and wash your sins away, calling on his name" (Acts 22:16 NIV).

C. Consecration (13:2):

Having been cleansed from all sin in the fountain, the penitents rise to walk in newness of life (Rom 6:4). They now live in a new land—the kingdom of God—in which God does not tolerate the vices that too often marred the history of national Israel.

1. Introduction (13:2a): **It shall come to pass in that day (oracle of Yahweh of Hosts)...** Again Zechariah sets the timeframe for what he is about to assert as *in that day,* i.e., the day of mourning over the Pierced One, and cleansing in the fountain. Before making the dramatic announcement that follows, the prophet again reminds his readers that this is an *oracle*—a most solemn first person utterance—of the all-powerful *Yahweh of Hosts.* See on 1:3.

2. Idolatry removed (13:2b): **I will cut off the names of the idols from the land, and they shall not be remembered any more.** Yahweh declares some 45x in the OT that he will *cut off* (r. *krt*) something. In addition to the literal meaning of this root, there is a metaphorical meaning "to root out, eliminate, remove, excommunicate or destroy by a violent act of man or nature."

In the present passage an act of overwhelming grace—the sacrificial death of the Pierced One—leads to the total banishment of idolatry from the land, i.e., from the citizens of the messianic kingdom. God's grace wins over hearts that in the past were all too eager to invest physical objects with divine qualities. *Names of the idols* are all of the attributes that are associated with idols.

The names of the idols will no longer *be remembered,* i.e., honored, celebrated, worshiped (cf. Hos 2:17). Those who experience messianic cleansing will have no association with the old idols.

3. False prophecy removed (13:2c): **And also the prophets and the unclean spirit I will remove from the land.**

Zechariah 12:1-14:21

Prophets are the false prophets. There is no word in the Hebrew language for "false prophet."

In 12:10 Zechariah mentioned "the spirit of grace and of supplications," i.e., the Holy Spirit. Now the unholy spirit is introduced. *The unclean spirit,* mentioned only here in the OT, is probably the lying spirit that works in the false prophets. Cf. 1 Kgs 22:19-23. In the Gospels demonic spirits are referred to "unclean" 10x. Unclean spirits will be particularly active in the last days of the Christian age.[261]

The false prophets and the unclean spirit Yahweh will *remove* (r. *'br* Hiphil) from the land, i.e., his kingdom of redeemed people. The removal is not accomplished by some violent act, but by the overwhelming act of divine grace referenced in the preceding ch. Citizens of Messiah's kingdom want nothing to do with false prophets any more than they desire to cling to idols. This v is the OT equivalent of "All to Jesus I surrender."

In the days of Zechariah neither idolatry nor false prophets were current issues. This makes it likely that these two areas of Israel's earlier transgressions are here used to symbolize the total consecration that follows the cleansing of the messianic age. Those who respond in faith to the Pierced One, who repent, and are cleansed in the fountain, will serve the Lord with single-focus commitment. They will not serve other gods; they will not listen to other voices.

The reference to this consecrated land recalls earlier references to the messianic land: Yahweh will remove the guilt of the land in the day that the Shoot appears (3:9). That Shoot is the Pierced One of the present context. Likewise the visions of the flying scroll (5:1-4) and the ephah (5:5-11) depict the removal of evil from the land. Zechariah uses these symbols to depict the purity of the people of God—his land—in the messianic age.

D. Commitment (13:3):

Zechariah devotes the next four vv to amplifying his announcement that false prophecy and idolatry will be removed

---

[261] 2 Thess 2:4; Rev 13:1-6; 16:13-14.

Postexilic Prophets

from the messianic land. These vv illustrate the change in perspective and extreme commitment of those who are citizens of Messiah's kingdom.

1. Hypothetical situation (13:3a): **And it shall come to pass if a man shall prophesy yet again...** To underscore the assurance that false prophetism will be at an end, Zechariah pens a hypothetical scenario. *Shall prophesy* indicates that someone claims prophetic inspiration. There is an attempt to revive false prophecy. The language hints that the prophetic powers will cease.

2. Declaration (13:3b): **then his father and mother (who) gave birth to him will say unto him, You will not live for you have spoken a lie in the name of Yahweh.** *Father/mother* points to the nearest relatives of the false prophet. Those who love him most will not tolerate his prophetic claims. The law required the execution of those who prophesied falsely. See Dt 13:6-10; 18:20. The son had *spoken a lie in the name of Yahweh* by pretending to deliver a message from God. That was a capital crime.

3. Execution (13:3c): **And his father and mother, to whom he was born, shall pierce him through when he prophesies.** *Pierce him through* means to stab or pierce him, i.e., put him to death. This is the same verb used in 12:10. Under the Law of Moses parents were required to stand against their offspring when the latter were violation of God's Law; but they were not required to participate in the execution (Dt 21:19-21). So what is envisioned here is a zeal for truth and righteousness that exceeds anything envisioned in Mosaic Law.

E. **Conscience** (13:4-5):

The messianic community will not tolerate false prophecy; but even the pretended prophets themselves will be ashamed of their actions.

1. Inward shame (13:4a): **On that day every prophet will be ashamed of his prophetic vision.** Prophetic pretenders will be ashamed of their visions. So strong will be the popular feeling against false prophecy that the false prophets will be

Zechariah 12:1-14:21

ashamed to make any pretense to visions. See Acts 19:13-20 for the conversion of false prophets.

2. *Public restraint (13:4b):* **He will not put on a prophet's garment of hair in order to deceive.** *A garment of hair* is a rough garment meant to deceive. [262] This garment was a sign of frugality and abstinence from worldly pleasure; it was also on occasion a symbol of grief. The hairy garment had become the badge of the prophets. For the false prophet it was a cloak of hypocrisy for it was meant *to deceive.* The point is that in previous times the population warmly embraced the false prophets. In the messianic land prophetic pretenders will not wish to be publicly identified as prophets. In the age to come there will be among the redeemed abhorrence of anything that appeared to be untrue.

3. *Forthright denial (13:5):* **But he will say, No prophet am I. A man who serves the ground am I; for a man has made (others) buy me from my youth.**[263] Fearing for his life the suspect emphatically denies that he is a prophet. The suspect professes to belong to a vocation that precludes the prophetic call. Cf. Gn 4:2 ("a tiller of the ground"). *Made others buy me* (r. *qnh* in Hiphil) suggests that the tiller was indentured (sold) to a farmer or hired out to farmers. *From my youth* suggests that the tiller had been an indentured servant for his entire life. Thus the suspect's point is that he had never had the time to play the role of a prophet.

Great Savior
Zechariah 13:6

A question is asked of someone in this v. The usual interpretation is that the suspected false prophet is being grilled about certain wounds upon his body, wounds hitherto unmentioned. Some take the wounds to have been self-inflicted in idol worship with idolatrous *friends* or "lovers." In this case

---

[262] Cf. the mantle of Elijah (1 Kgs 19:13, 19; 2 Kgs 1:8; 2:13, 14) and of John the Baptist (Mt 3:4).

[263] Other translations: 1) "for a man made me a possessor (of land) from my youth" (Targum); 2) "for man taught me to keep cattle from my youth" (Rashi; Kimchi); 3) "I have been made a bondman from my youth" (ASV).

this case the false prophet of the previous v is admitting his guilt. Others take the wounds to have been inflicted by the righteous parents who disciplined their wayward son as he pretended to be a prophet; *friends* then would be family or relatives.

Unger and Gill argue for a messianic interpretation of the conversation in this v. In the immediate context the only "wounds" of which the text speaks are those of the Pierced One in 12:10. So the main theme of the Pierced One is reintroduced with dramatic abruptness (Unger). The intervening paragraph is in the nature of an extended parenthesis.

A. Question (13:6a):

If someone asks him, What are these wounds between your hands? Who asks this question? The Hebrew uses the indefinite third masculine singular. Each individual among those who look unto him whom they have pierced (12:10) asks this question. Like Thomas (Jn 20:25) they examine his wounds and acknowledge him as their redeemer. The question is probably addressed to the Pierced One.

The question focuses on certain *wounds*. The term denotes any "wound" whether unhealed or healed and remaining only as a "scar." The wounds might be the result of an accident or violence done to someone by another. For this reason the question is asked. The wounds are located *between your hands*, which are envisioned as stretched out. Hence the wounds were on the back (Rashi) or chest (Wright; Chambers).[264]

B. Response (13:6b):

And he will answer, With these I was wounded in the house of friends. The answer comes from the lips of the Pierced One of 12:10. *With these* refers to the wounds. The term *friends* is masculine, lit., "my lovers, or those who love me." The term is not used here of idolatrous "lovers" for

---

[264]The phrase occurs in Ugaritic in parallel with the word for shoulder. McComiskey citing Gordon, *Ugaritic Texts*. Chambers cites 2 Kgs 9:24, which is "between the arms" not "between the hands." Unger thinks the phrase is equivalent to "in your hands."

Zechariah 12:1-14:21

when it has this meaning it uniformly occurs under the metaphor of male and female. Hence (male) friends of a male figure are in view. The speaker was not wounded *by* those who loved him, but in their *house*. The reference is to the house of Abraham, Isaac and Jacob, the house of those who longed for his coming.

Great Smiting
Zechariah 13:7-9

Having re-introduced the Pierced One, and having raised the question of the origin of his wounds, the prophet now expands upon that theme A brief poetic oracle indicates how the wounding took place, and the consequences of it.

A. Call for this Smiting (13:7a):

O sword awake! Cf. Jer 47:6. The imperative implies 1) that the sword is an instrument under the control of God; and 2) that the sword has for a time been inactive.[265] The *sword* represents any kind of instrument that inflicts physical harm (Zech 11:17) or death. Cf. Ex 5:21; 2 Sam 12:9; Isa 27:1. The text does not clearly state that the victim of the smiting dies; but this fact is strongly suggested by the intensity of the mourning over the Pierced One in ch 12.

The sword is God's will being exercised. Peter explained the matter this way: "This man was handed over to you by God's set purpose and foreknowledge; and you, with the help of wicked men, put him to death by nailing him to the cross" (Acts 2:23 NIV). It was "not the sword of Caiaphas or the priests or Pilate or Romans or the sword of impending justice, but the sword of righteous retribution for sins of Israel and the world" (Meyer).

---

[265]The idea of a sword as a symbol of judgment can be traced back to Jeremiah. The expression "sword, famine, and pestilence" was a favorite of his (14:12, 13, 15, 18; 21:7, 9; 24:10). Ezekiel adapted with slight addition this same expression (Ezek 14:1-23). In Ezek 21:1-22 there is a "song of the sword" predicting judgment on Judah.

Postexilic Prophets

B. Object of this Smiting (13:7b, c):

1. Yahweh's shepherd (13:7b): **against my shepherd...** Zechariah returns to the motif of the shepherd (9:16; 10:2-3; 11:3-17). *My shepherd* is not the foolish shepherd of 11:15-17 or the kings who have oppressed Israel (11:5). *My shepherd* is the shepherd of Yahweh mentioned in 11:4 etc.—the Messiah who is identified as the Pierced One in 12:10. He is also the shepherd and pierced one of Isaiah 53:5, 6. Ezekiel prophesied that Israel's divine Shepherd will set up over his people "one shepherd" who is identified as "David my servant" (Ezek 34:23). So Yahweh performs his work as Shepherd through Messiah. Therefore, in this passage God calls him *my shepherd,* for he is in the fullest sense God's representative.

2. Yahweh's fellow (13:7c): **against the man that is my fellow (oracle of Yahweh of Hosts).** *My fellow ('amîtî)* means "my equal." The word occurs only here and in Lv (11x) where it is usually rendered "neighbor." The term suggests one united to another by the possession of common nature, rights and privileges (Deane). The term implies equality between persons.[266] The language could refer only to Christ. Cf. Jn 10:30. The shepherd who is smitten is the Good Shepherd of 11:4-14 who is mysteriously identified with Yahweh. This identification is proved by the application of the following clause to Jesus in Mt 26:31.

C. Result of this Smiting (13:7d):

Smite the shepherd, and the sheep will be scattered... The imperative again indicates that the sword serves the purpose of God. For this reason when this v is paraphrased in Matthew's Gospel it reads: *I [God] will smite* (Mt 26:31).

A scattered flock is a flock without a shepherd, a flock destined for misery and destruction. The scattering due to smiting began in Gethsemane and at the cross when even his

---

[266]Baron (*op. cit.,* 478f) cites the Jewish commentators Aben Ezra, Kimchi, Izaak of Troki, and Abarbanel who admit that the word *ᵃmūthî* indicates equality of persons. They identify the "man my equal" as arrogant Gentile kings. Abrabanel identifies the "man my equal" as Jesus of Nazareth to whom Christians, wrong in his view, attribute equality with God.

disciples forsook him and fled (Mt 26:31). But like ripples in a pond, there were ever wider circles of people affected by the smiting of the shepherd. The dispersion of Jews and their denationalization were also results of this smiting. This v builds on the theme of the flock of slaughter and the abandonment by the Good Shepherd depicted in 11:7, 9.

D. **Aftermath of this Smiting** (13:7e):
But I will return my hand over the little ones. The idiomatic expression "return the hand" is used in a good and bad sense.[267] Cf. Isa 1:25; Amos 1:8. Here the phrase seems to be used in the sense of assistance or protection, otherwise there would be no sheep left to constitute the remnant that is mentioned in v 9. Jesus may have been interpreting this idiom for us when he paraphrased the previous sentence of this prophecy, then added: "but after I have risen, I will go ahead of you into Galilee" (Mt 26:32). Jesus was announcing re-gathering after scattering.

The term *little ones* ($tsō^{a}rîm$) is used only here in the Hebrew Bible. In this context it refers to the humble and meek, those who embraced Messiah. They are to be identified with "the poor of the flock" in 11:7 and "the little flock" in Lk 12:32.

E. **Result of this Smiting** (13:8a):
And it shall come to pass, that in all the land (oracle of Yahweh) two parts therein will be cut off and die. In discussing the effect of the smiting of the shepherd upon the flock, Zechariah follows a pattern introduced by Ezekiel. He divides the flock into thirds (cf. Ezek 5:12).

The land here is used geographically for the v speaks of those who dwell *in* the land. *The land* is Palestine where the Good Shepherd tended his flock in ch 11. *Two parts* of the land is not to be taken mathematically. The figure simply indicates that a remnant will survive. Of those living in Palestine after the smiting of the Good Shepherd the vast majority will be *cut off and die*. On the verb *cut off,* see on 9:10. *Die*

---

[267] Cf. NASB rendering, "I will turn my hand against the little ones."

defines the sense in which the two parts will be cut off. The fulfillment came in those who perished in the war with Rome.

F. Future of the Remnant (13:8b-9):

Concerning the remnant that embraces Messiah the prophet predicted five things.

1. Their initial salvation (13:8b): **But the third part shall be left in it.** A third of the flock will escape the great tribulation that comes upon the land. This third represents all those who embraced the Messiah. Through this remnant God will continue to work out his redemptive purposes. The existence of this remnant ensures the continuation of God's promises to Abraham.

2. Their further purification (13:9a): **And I will bring the third part into fire, and I will refine them as the refining of silver, and I will try them like the trying of gold.** While the third part of the flock survives a devastating attack on the land, they will yet pass through the *fire*. Presumably this fire represents persecution. Through much tribulation the early believers were refined and purified.

3. Their full access to God (13:9b): **As for it, it shall call upon my name and as for me, I will answer it.** The third person singular pronoun refers to the third part of the flock that survived being cut off from the land. Collectively this small flock will turn to God. The flock will have full access to God throughout the persecution. The Hebrew emphasizes the first person singular pronoun. God responds positively to the petition of the believers in their times of distress.

4. Their acknowledgment by God (13:9c): **And I will say, It is my people.** The surviving flock (NT believers) collectively will be acknowledged by God as his people.

5. Their living testimony (13:9d): **And it will say, Yahweh is my God.** The surviving third part of the flock will collectively testify to everyone of their commitment to the Lord.

Zechariah 12:1-14:21

Final Glimpses of the Coming Day
Zechariah 14:1-21

Commentators of all schools of interpretation recognize the difficulties of the final ch of Zechariah. The prophet appears to employ highly symbolic, even apocalyptic language, to highlight certain leading features of the coming day of Yahweh. He seems to group his thoughts around the phrase *in that day* which appears 7x in the ch. To assume that these snapshots are presented in chronological sequence is probably a mistake. The focus of activity is Jerusalem which is mentioned 11x in ten vv.

A. Picture #1: Assistance in Battle (14:1-3):
1. Jerusalem ravished: a general statement (14:1): **Behold a day will come to Yahweh when your spoil will be divided in your midst.** **Behold** introduces something unexpected and shocking. In the previous chs Jerusalem has been depicted as impregnable. Now suddenly the city is pictured as subject to a terrible invasion. This is the apocalyptic equivalent to the persecution depicted in the closing v of the previous ch.

A day will come to Yahweh means that Yahweh's day is coming. In prophetic thought the day of Yahweh is any time when Yahweh steps on the stage to implement his purposes. In this case, a devastating attack against Jerusalem provides Yahweh with the opportunity to crush once and for all time the enemies of his people.

Your (fem.) *spoil* refers to spoil of a city or land. The subsequent v identifies Jerusalem as the city under attack. *Divided in your midst* depicts the enemy as successful early on. They will penetrate the city. Spoil is divided after a battle has been won. The enemy will feel so secure they will divide the spoils in the midst of the subjugated city. So the enemy thinks he has been triumphant over God's people. As will shortly appear, however, the situation is not what it appears to be.

It is impossible to fix the historical situation for this prophecy. It seems to depict the kingdom of God in its trial,

Postexilic Prophets

development, and triumph (Deane). Perhaps there is a mingling here of the first destruction of Jerusalem and the last attack in the times of Antichrist (Pusey). Laetsch thinks the work of the papacy in ravishing the spiritual Jerusalem is being described.

2. Jerusalem ravished: specific details (14:2): **And I will gather all nations unto Jerusalem to fight. And the city will be captured, and the houses will be plundered, and the women raped, and half the city will go out into captivity; but the rest of the people will not be cut off from the city.** In this v the general picture of the preceding v is fleshed out with three details.

First, the v explains how the enemy came to attack Jerusalem. God claims responsibility for what takes place. *I will gather* suggests an active mobilization of the enemy forces. *All nations* indicates at the very least that the enemies of God's people are numerous. The phrase probably refers to all Gentiles who are not part of the holy nation. *Unto Jerusalem* indicates the venue of the coming showdown. These Gentiles approach Jerusalem, not with the idea of conversion (2:11; 6:15; 8:20-22), but with hostility. They come *to fight*. There is no indication that Jerusalem is being punished for transgression. It appears that God has orchestrated this advance to Jerusalem in order to highlight a dramatic salvation of his people and an equally dramatic crushing of his enemies.[268] The final such attack against God's people is generally designated as Armageddon (cf. Rev 20:7-9).

Second, the v depicts the capturing of the city. *The city* is Jerusalem. The sufferings described are the usual fate of a conquered city in antiquity. The enemy is pictured within the walls. *Half the city will go out into captivity* does not contradict the 2/3 that are destroyed in 13:8. The 2/3 refers to the entire land; the 1/2 refers to the city alone.

Third, the v depicts the deliverance of a remnant. By orchestrating the attack on Jerusalem God did not intend to terminate his people. A remnant will be left in spiritual Jeru-

---

[268]The motif of Yahweh leading foreign armies against Jerusalem only to destroy them is fairly common in the OT. See Joel 3:9-14; Isa 10:5-19; 29:1-8; Mic 4:11-13; Jer 25:8-14; Ezek 38:1-23.

Zechariah 12:1-14:21

salem following the assault by the Gentile nations. This cannot refer to destruction of AD 70, for the city was razed, its inhabitants were slain or sold as slaves (Josephus *Wars* 6.9).

3. *Explanation (14:3):* **Then Yahweh shall go out and fight against those nations as in the day of his fighting in a day of battle.** When things are most desperate for spiritual Jerusalem the Lord appears. *Go out* is military terminology. It is not likely that the Lord goes out of Jerusalem, for the city has been captured. Yahweh goes out of his heavenly abode. He will *fight* against the Gentiles (unbelievers) who are warring with great success against Jerusalem. The Lord will fight for his people with the fervor and intensity of a mighty warrior in battle.[269]

B. Picture #2: Deliverance (14:4-5):

The intention of this paragraph is to indicate how God will preserve the remnant when Jerusalem comes under attack.

1. *Intervention (14:4a):* **And his feet shall stand in that day upon the Mount of Olives which is beside Jerusalem on the east...** When the Lord goes out from his place, he walks upon the high places of the earth (Mic 1:3; Amos 4:13; 9:5). That concept is here particularized. The first step down from God's heavenly abode is the Mount of Olives. *His feet* are the feet of Yahweh. This anthropological expression intersects with history when Messiah's trod upon the Mount of Olives on numerous occasions.

The *Mount of Olives* is mentioned many times in the OT (e.g., 2 Sam 15:3), but only here by this name. This mount rises 600'—187' over Mount Zion; 295' above Mount Moriah. The Mount of Olives is *beside Jerusalem on the east*. It is separated from Jerusalem by the deep Kidron valley.

2. *Result (14:4b):* **and the Mount of Olives will be split in two (toward) the east and west a very great valley, and half of the mountain will move to the north and half to the south.** Micah saw mountains melting when the Lord went out

---

[269] Some think a specific intervention in Israel's history is alluded to in the phrase *the day of his fighting in a day of battle,* e.g., the intervention at the Red Sea (Rashi; Targum).

Postexilic Prophets

of his heavenly abode to tread upon the high places of the earth (Mic 1:4). Clearly the Micah passage is not to be taken literally; neither is the present passage. Here the coming of the Lord results in a gigantic earthquake affecting topographical changes. *A very great valley* is the result of the splitting of the mountain. The mountain splits so as to form an east-west valley. This prediction amplifies the promise of 4:7 that Yahweh will level whatever mighty mountain that might stand in the way of accomplishing God's purpose. The basic idea is that Christ makes a way of escape for his people when they come under attack.

3. *Flight (14:5a):* **And you will flee by means of the valley of my mountains for the valley of my mountains will reach unto Azel. Yes, you will flee as you fled before the earthquake in the days of Uzziah, king of Judah.** God's people will flee from the assaulted city by means of the ravine made by the cleaving of Olivet. *My mountains* refers to the two halves of the Mount of Olives created when Yahweh forms the great ravine. *Azel* is perhaps Beth-ezel (Mic 1:11), a village on the east of Olivet.[270] Azel may be mentioned to indicate the size of the valley, i.e., adequate to protect all who flee; or the destination of the valley miles from the scene of the attack. The imagery of the v may have been suggested by David's "valley of the shadow of death" (Ps 23:4).

The earthquake in the days of Uzziah is referenced in Amos 1:1. This earthquake was long remembered. Josephus (*Antiquities* 10.4) connects it with the attempt of Uzziah to burn incense (2 Chr 26:19).

The valley symbolizes every means by which God intervenes in the upheavals of history for the benefit of his people. It is not clear whether the valley is viewed as an avenue of escape from the vicinity of rampaging Gentiles or whether the valley itself is the refuge from the conflict. Either interpretation fits with the context.

4. *Return (14:5b):* **And Yahweh my God will come (and) all the holy ones with you.** This is the third reference to

---

[270]*Beth* (lit., "house') is frequently omitted from place names constructed with it. Some take *Azel* to mean "union." They see here a union of law and gospel, Jew and Gentile.

Yahweh's coming in this passage. He goes out to fight against those who are attacking Jerusalem in v 3; his feet stand on the Mount of Olives in v 4. Now *Yahweh my God shall come*. Is this coming one of the two previous comings personalized (*my God*) and reiterated? Or is this coming referring to an event that follows the coming to fight and the coming to deliver? The latter is probably the case. Where does Yahweh come? In the light of the rest of the ch, Yahweh comes with his people to reclaim Jerusalem.

This coming is glorious, for the Lord is accompanied by *all the holy ones*, presumably a reference to angels. *With you* (fem. sing.) is the reading of the Hebrew text. Most English versions have opted to follow the ancient versions and some Hebrew MSS translating *with him*. But such changes in person are not uncommon (Deane).[271] So this line refers to "a triumphant entrance procession into Jerusalem by Yahweh, his holy ones, and the remnant that was saved in the battle with the nations."[272]

C. Picture #3: Hope (14:6-7):

1. Dark day (14:6): **And it shall come to pass in that day it shall not be light. The glorious things shall shrink.** *In that day* refers to the day of the Lord mentioned in v 1. *It shall not be light* indicates that it will be a dark day when the Lord comes to rescue his people. Darkness is frequently associated with the day of Yahweh's intervention against Israel (e.g., Amos 5:20) and other nations (e.g., Isa 13:9-10). *Glorious things* ($y^eq\bar{a}r\bar{o}t$)[273] are probably the heavenly bodies. *Shrink* (r. *qp'*)[274] always denotes drawing together, thickening, solidifying, losing some of the characteristic attributes or functions. Thus, the luminaries lose their function of being light bearers.[275] They cease to shine; they grow dim so that

---

[271] Jewish interpreters take *with you* as referring to Jerusalem and give it the meaning *for your sake*.
[272] R. Smith, *WBC*, 287.
[273] *Qere* reading is *vqrot* (r. *qrr*, to be cold), hence plural of coldness.
[274] The *Qere* reads as a noun, "congelation," probably referring to frost.
[275] Other translations: 1) Greek, Syriac, Latin versions: "There shall not be light, but cold and ice," i.e., without sun-light terrible cold will prevail on earth. 2) Heidenbeim: "There shall not be light, either the bright (light of

dusk, gloom, and darkness take the place of light on the earth. Cf. Joel 3:15; Mt 24:29; Rev 6:12, 13.

2. *Hidden day (14:7a)*: **And it will be a unique day which is known to Yahweh**. The day of the Lord's intervention on behalf of spiritual Jerusalem is *a unique day*, an unparalleled day. It is beyond human experience. The character and time of arrival of that day are known only to God. Cf. Mt 24:36.

3. *Hopeful day (14:7b)*: **Not day and not night; but it will come to pass at evening time there will be light**. The time of the Lord's intervention will not be wholly day or wholly night, but a mixture of both. This has been explained symbolically: There will not be altogether consolation or affliction in that day. *At evening time there will be light* suggests that in the midst of trouble and danger deliverance will come.

D. Picture #4: Abundant Life (14:8):

1. *Source of blessing (14:8a)*: **And it will come to pass in that day that living waters will go out from Jerusalem...** *In that day* refers to the day of mingled rebukes and promises. *Living waters* is fresh, pure, perennial, flowing water. This is a figure for the spiritual blessings—especially God's Spirit (Jn 7:38-39)—bestowed by God upon his people. The figure of a river symbolizing God's presence and blessing can be traced back at least to the Psalmist Korah: "There is a river whose streams make glad the city of God" (Ps 46:4). Isaiah used the waters of Shiloah that flow softly as the symbol of divine government (Isa 8:6). Joel, Ezekiel and now Zechariah build on that figure, and picture water flowing *out from Jerusalem*. Jerusalem is the kingdom of God, the messianic kingdom. Cf. Joel 4:18; Ezek 47:12. These passages anticipate the description of the river of life flowing from the throne of God and the Lamb (Rev 22:1).

2. *Abundance of blessing (14:8b)*: **half of them unto the eastern sea and half of them unto the hinder sea.** *The eastern sea* is the Dead Sea. *The hinder sea* is the Mediterra-

---

the sun) or the cold (light of the moon) for God's glory will illumine the world."

Zechariah 12:1-14:21

nean Sea. These two seas served as boundaries of the Promised Land (Nm 34:12; Dt 11:24; 34:2). The Promised Land and Jerusalem depict the kingdom of God. Ezekiel also depicted this river of life issuing forth from the temple in Jerusalem, bringing life even to the waters of the Dead Sea (Ezek 47). The gospel river brings life and refreshment wherever it flows.

   3. *Permanence of blessing (14:8c):* **In the summer and in the winter it will be there.** This stream of blessing will not dry up in summer as most brooks in Palestine, or be frozen in the winter. "Alike in times of peace and of persecution those waters shall continue in their course" (Jerome). The gospel is preached until east and west meet each other.

E. Picture #5: Exaltation (14:9-11):

The coming day of Yahweh is a time of exaltation for the people of God.

   1. *Wonderful Ruler (14:9):* **And Yahweh will be king over all the land. In that day Yahweh will be one and his name one.** Yahweh is sole king in that day. The consensus among commentators and translations is that this v affirms that Yahweh will be king over "all the earth," i.e., universally recognized as king throughout the world. The phrase *kol hā'ārets* can be translated "all the earth" It seems to have this meaning in 1:11 and 6:5. Here, however, it probably is used in its more restricted sense of *all the land*, referring to the messianic kingdom. It is extremely important to correctly understand what this v asserts because it is the key element in assigning the balance of the ch to the post Armageddon Millennium.[276]

Is this v affirming that Yahweh is king over all the land or over all the earth? Context must decide. This v is bracketed by vv that refer to the messianic land, not the entire earth. Furthermore, it is clear that *kol hā'ārets* in v 10 is used in the

---

[276] The Psalmist saw Yahweh as king over all the earth in his day (Ps 47:2, 7). So even if the phrase in question had its more universal connotation, it would not necessarily point to universal recognition of Yahweh in some future Millennium. Christ's authority in heaven and earth in the present age (Mt 28:18) does not mean that he is universally recognized.

Postexilic Prophets

restricted sense. It is very unlikely that back-to-back uses of the same phrase have different connotations.

What is the point of affirming that Yahweh will be king over all the land? There was no monarchy in Zechariah's day, and no prospects of seeing the monarchy restored. Nonetheless, this prophet foresees a kingdom in the future age ruled by Yahweh himself. It is allegiance to this king that unifies the citizens of this kingdom. Earlier prophets spoke of a future in which God's people are led by "David their king" (Hos 3:5; Jer 30:9). Perhaps without understanding the matter fully himself, Zechariah affirms that this future Davidic king will in some unique way be Yahweh himself.

In that coming day Yahweh's nature will be recognized. The language echoes Dt 6:4. *One* (*'echād*) stresses unity while recognizing diversity within that oneness. The notion of uniqueness also is found in the usage of the term.[277] Yahweh's *name* is used in the OT to refer to all that the Lord has revealed about himself.

In pre-exilic times many professed followers of Yahweh recognized him only as tribal deity, one among many. Throughout the history of Israel a large number of Israelites—perhaps the majority—saw no inconsistency in worshiping Yahweh and at the same time observing the rituals in honor of other gods. Zechariah, however, envisions a time when the people of God no longer compromise on such a vital issue. They unashamedly and boldly proclaim the singularity of Yahweh. He alone is God—the only God. In his name only is there salvation to be found (Acts 4:12).

2. *Elevated city (14:10a):* **And all the land shall be turned as the Arabah (a plain) from Geba to Rimmon south of Jerusalem and it shall be lifted up.** *The land* refers to the mountainous region of Judah. The *Arabah* is the flat Jordan valley, the deepest depression on the face of the earth. It was a fertile valley. The basic idea is that all the land Judah becomes flat so that the holy city becomes all the more prominent. *Geba* is six miles northeast of Jerusalem, the northernmost limit of Judah (cf. 2 Kgs 23:8; Josh 18:24). *Rimmon*

---

[277] *TWOT*, 30.

Zechariah 12:1-14:21

south of Jerusalem is the En-rimmon of Neh 11:29, a town on the southern border of Judah near Beersheba.

Jerusalem will be exalted on its hill. This is a way of stressing the spiritual exaltation of the messianic kingdom. Micah and Isaiah also foresaw the day when the mountain of Yahweh's temple would be established as chief among the mountains; it would be raised above the hills (Isa 2:2; Mic 4:1).[278]

3. *Permanent city (14:10b):* **And it shall remain in its place from the Benjamin gate unto the place of the first gate, unto the corner gate and from the tower of Hananel unto the winepresses of the king**. The land transformations envisioned in the previous line will not affect the holy city. Jerusalem will occupy her ancient limits. Cf. Jer 31:38-40; Ezek 48:15. *It shall remain* sounds a note of permanence.

Zechariah has already made clear that the Jerusalem he envisioned is a city without walls (2:4). So in this v the various landmarks of the old wall of Jerusalem must serve a symbolic purpose. The four corners of the ideal city are given. *The Benjamin gate* was in the northeast corner (Jer 37:12).[279] *The first gate* is in the eastern part of the wall.[280] *The corner gate* was in the northwest corner, west of the Benjamin gate. *The tower of Hananel* was on the north wall (Neh 3:1; 12:39). *The winepresses of the king* were probably near the king's garden (Neh 3:15) at the southeast extremity of the city. So Zechariah has sketched an imaginary circumference of the walls of Jerusalem.

Why does Zechariah focus on the gates of a city that he previously described as wall-less? Clearly these landmarks must be regarded as symbolic. There are at least three possible functions of this symbolism. First, in this v Zechariah may simply be illustrating the growth and stability of the church by the figure of the earthly city Jerusalem, firmly ordered and built (Deane). Second, gates speak of access; messianic Jerusalem is easily accessible to all who might desire

---

[278] Pss 48:1-2 and Ezek 40:2 also depict messianic Zion as a city on a very high mountain.
[279] This is probably the gate elsewhere called the gate of Ephraim.
[280] This is probably the same as the *old gate* of Neh 12:39.

to enter. Third, gates and towers also speak of security, a thought further developed in the following v.

4. Inhabited city (14:11a): **And they shall dwell in it...** Jerusalem was not inhabited at the time of Zechariah except for the few priests who lived in the precincts of the newly built temple. The antecedent of the pronoun *they* is not clear because no plural subject precedes it. The NASB inserts the noun "people"; NIV elects to render the verb as a passive. Both approaches are defensible, and amount to the same thing. The point is that those in Zechariah's day who were distressed over Jerusalem's continued desolation even after the exile could be assured that the Jerusalem of the future will be inhabited.

5. Secure city (14:11b): **and utter destruction shall be no more, and Jerusalem will dwell in trust.** *Utter destruction* (*cherem*) is extermination of a population in a holy war. The term is usually translated "curse" or "ban." The citizens of Jerusalem will not incur the curse that was inflicted on transgressors, idolaters and their cities by the old law. Cf. Ex 22:20; Dt 7:2; 13:12-15; 20:17. Ralph Smith puts it: "There will be a ban on the ban."[281] This means that *Jerusalem will dwell in trust* (*lābhetach*), i.e., in security. Trusting Yahweh is the identifying mark of all citizens of messianic Jerusalem. Because sin has been removed there will be no more need for chastisement. The spiritual Jerusalem will never be destroyed (Deane). Cf. Zeph 3:12-15.

F. Picture #6: Protection (14:12-15):

Messianic Jerusalem will need protection from time to time, for there will be those who fight against the place. Zechariah now spells out four additional sources of protection.

1. Protection by means of plague (14:12): **And this will be the plague with which Yahweh will smite all peoples who fight against Jerusalem: his flesh will be consumed while he**

---

[281] R. Smith, *WBC*, 288. Smith, however, probably goes too far in asserting that the removal of the ban means there will be no more war, because it is Jerusalem's safety that is at issue in this v. The peaceful nature of Messiah's kingdom is portrayed in much clearer pictures elsewhere.

Zechariah 12:1-14:21

is standing upon his feet and his eyes will rot in their sockets and his tongue will rot in his[282] mouth. An assault against spiritual Jerusalem forms the background for this v. Most likely this is the same assault depicted in vv 1-2. *All peoples who fight against Jerusalem* are probably the same as *all the nations* that Yahweh gathers to Jerusalem to in v 1. *The plague* is mentioned as though it has been previously referenced but is now about to be described. In v 3 the prophet stated that Yahweh would go out and fight against those nations that come against Jerusalem. The means of Yahweh's fighting has been left unclear until now.

God will send a contagious affliction upon all peoples (nations; Gentiles) who attack Jerusalem. *His flesh* refers to the flesh of each one of them. The suffixes are singular to indicate that no one will be overlooked. All individually and collectively will be punished (Laetsch). The flesh of the attacker will putrefy and molder away while he is *standing upon his feet,* i.e., was in the very act of attacking Jerusalem. Yahweh's enemies cannot stand before his might. *Eyes will rot...tongue will rot* indicates that a supernatural plague is in view. The point is that no force, however great, will be successful in wresting the inheritance of the saints from them.

2. *Protection by means of mutual slaughter (14:13):* **And it will come to pass in that day great tumult from Yahweh will be upon them, and they will seize each man the hand of his neighbor, and his hand will go up against the hand of his neighbor.** *Great tumult from Yahweh* refers to a general panic or confusion sent from God. Cf. Judg 7:22; 1 Sam 14:20. Perhaps this panic is the result of seeing what Yahweh did to the first wave of attackers in the previous v. As a result of the panic the enemy begins to fall upon one another with the weapons intended for the people of God. The enemies of God's people defeat themselves. The point is the same as in the previous v. No force will be successful in depriving Messiah's people of their inheritance.

3. *Protection by the sword of Judah (14:14):* **And also Judah will fight [in the battle] in Jerusalem; and the wealth**

---

[282] The suffix is actually plural.

of all the surrounding nations will be gathered: gold and silver and garments in great abundance. Again Judah is pictured on the same footing with Jerusalem (cf. 1:12, 19; 2:12; 8:15; 12:2, 5, 6). Judah will fight in the battle in Jerusalem,[283] i.e., God's people will be unified in the defense of their inheritance. *The wealth of all surrounding nations* is the spoil abandoned by the enemy in the confusion. This wealth *will be gathered*, but the text does not say by whom. The implication is that this spoil will fall to God's people. *Gold, silver and garments* are examples of the spoil. The nations had come to spoil Jerusalem; now the wealth of the heathen will be gathered to requite her. The church emerges victorious from persecutions. She is enriched and adorned by means of those who planned her overthrow.

The theme of Gentile wealth coming over to Zion is part of the larger theme of Gentiles coming to Mount Zion in the last days (Isa 2:2-4; Mic 4:1-4). Isaiah depicted Gentiles bringing their treasures by land and sea to the holy city (Isa 60:6-9). The development of the wealth-to-Zion theme in Zechariah (2:11; 8:22-23; 14:14, 16) differs from these earlier portrayals in one respect. Here the wealth is not voluntarily brought to Jerusalem. .

4. *Total defeat of attackers (14:15):* **And the plague of the horse, the mule, the camel, the donkey and all the cattle which shall be in those camps will be as this plague.** The devastating plague of 14:12 falls on the animals as well. *Those camps* are the camps of the attacking armies. The animals named are a mixture of war and pack animals. The animals may have been assigned to units for military or supply purposes; or they may have been plunder seized in prior campaigns. By *cattle* Zechariah may be referring to food supplies.

Two thoughts are conveyed by this v. First, the wealth that does not fall to God's people will be destroyed. Second, the triumph over the forces of evil will be complete.

---

[283]The preposition could be translated "against," but that does not seem to fit the context. Nothing else in this section suggests that Judah and Jerusalem are at odds with one another.

Zechariah 12:1-14:21

H. Picture #7: Celebration (14:16-19):
1. Pilgrimage for worship (14:16a): ***And it will come to pass that all who are left from all the nations (that) went up against Jerusalem...*** In vv 12-15 the forces attacking spiritual Jerusalem appear to be totally destroyed; but this v suggests that some of the attackers survive. Another possibility is that this v refers to the rest of Gentiles who did not actually participate in the attack against Jerusalem, i.e., the non-combatants. In either case Zechariah foresees a day when Gentiles who were once hostile to the people of God are converted.

2. Place of worship (14:16b): ***even they shall go up...*** As Gentile armies once went up against Jerusalem, so would Gentile converts *go up* to the heights of Zion for worship purposes. The language is suggested both by the elevation of physical Jerusalem, and by the enhanced elevation attributed to spiritual Jerusalem (cf. v 10). Where once they (or their brethren) had attempted to exterminate Yahweh's worshipers these converts will now be numbered among those devoted to the Lord.

3. Regularity of worship (14:16c): ***from year to year...*** Under the Mosaic system males were required (and females were welcome) to attend three annual festivals at the Jerusalem temple—Passover and Pentecost in the spring, and Tabernacles in the fall. Zechariah portrays Gentiles streaming to Jerusalem from distant lands every year. This is the OT way of depicting worship that results from a lifetime commitment—worship that is both faithful and regular.

4. Focus of worship (14:16d): ***to worship the King, Yahweh of Hosts...*** The primary purpose for the annual arduous and expensive pilgrimages to Jerusalem is *worship*. This is the only usage of the verb *worship* (r. *šchh* in Hithpa.) in Zechariah. The verb means to "bow down, prostrate oneself before a superior; to worship." The pilgrimage recognizes Jerusalem as the proper place for the worship of *the King* of all the earth (cf. v 9). The King is identified as *Yahweh of Hosts* (see on 1:3). No longer will the Gentiles venerate Molech—the divine king—to whom they had offered their children as sacrifices in OT times.

Postexilic Prophets

5. *Occasion of worship (14:16e):* and to celebrate the Feast of Tabernacles. *Tabernacles* was the last of the three annual feasts and perhaps the most important. The feast commemorated Israel's sojourn in the wilderness and divine protection there. It is called *the* feast par excellence (cf. 1 Kgs 8:2). Tabernacles celebrated the harvest vintage. During temple times sacrifices were brought on this festival on behalf of the nations of the world and prayers were offered for rain. It was the most ecumenical feast of the Mosaic system.

It is a mistaken application of this v to assume that Christians should observe the Mosaic feast of Tabernacles, or that such Mosaic practices will be revived at any point in the future. In prophetic literature Christian worship is consistently represented under the symbols of OT worship. The basic idea is that under Messiah's reign the Gentiles are converted to true religion; they worship God in regular, orderly fashion (Deane).

6. *Punishment for failing to worship (14:17):* And it will come to pass that if any from the families of the earth will not go up unto Jerusalem to worship the King, Yahweh of Hosts, even upon them there will be no rain. Failure of periodic rain in Eastern countries meant drought, famine, and distress. In a spiritual sense, rain represents the grace and blessing of God. These are withheld from people who refuse to worship the Lord. Cf. Isa 60:10-12. The v assumes that in the age envisioned by Zechariah believers and unbelievers will live side by side, the former blessed, the latter deprived of blessing.[284] Such is the situation during the Church Age.

7. *Specific example: Egypt (14:18-19):* And if the family of Egypt neither goes up nor enters, then (rain will not come) upon them. It will be the plague with which Yahweh will plague the nations that do not go up to celebrate the Feast of Tabernacles. 19 This shall be the punishment of Egypt and the punishment of all the nations which do not go up to celebrate the Feast of Tabernacles. In these vv Ze-

---

[284] A number of commentators stumble on this v. Supposedly Zechariah uses a hypothetical situation to convey a sense of absoluteness. In their view, no non-believing nations will exist at this time, i.e., during the so-called Millennium or the new heavens and earth.

Zechariah 12:1-14:21

Zechariah cites a specific example of the principle that he set forth in the preceding v. He makes three points about God's judgment.

First, the text depicts God's judgment negatively. *Egypt*, the ancient land of bondage, is cited as a representative of all Gentiles who will not submit to the King of Kings. This sentence is difficult to translate; it appears to be elliptical, hence the words supplied in parenthesis. *Goes up* follows the motif of the two previous vv. *Enters* ("take part" NIV) seems to be redundant, for if the Egyptians did not go up they could not enter the city and share in the worship. Perhaps the thought is that to avoid the punishment, the Egyptians must not only start out, but enter whole heartedly into the worship of Yahweh in spiritual Jerusalem.

Second, the text depicts God's judgment positively. Zechariah refers again to the plague that strikes those who attack Jerusalem (vv 12, 15). That plague will come upon Egypt if they refuse to acknowledge the King.

Third, the text speaks of God's judgment judicially. *Punishment* (*chātā'*) is lit., "sin." The word, however, often bears the meaning of the consequence or effect of sin, hence, *punishment*. The word means to miss the mark and face the consequences. The Feast of Tabernacles symbolizes conversion and submission to the Yahweh. So those who do not go up for Tabernacles will be punished.

I. Picture #8: Holiness (14:20-21):

Whether in public life, religious life or private life holiness will pervade every aspect of the life of God's people in the messianic age.

1. Previously unholy becomes holy (14:20a): **In that day there will be upon the bells of the horses HOLY TO YAHWEH...** *Bells of the horses*[285] are probably small metallic plates suspended from the necks or heads of the animals for the sake of ornament and making a tinkling noise when striking against each other. They may have had the names of the owners inscribed on them. *HOLY TO YAHWEH* was the

---

[285]The LXX translates "bridle" and, by extension, the Hebrew word may have this meaning.

Postexilic Prophets

inscription on the golden miter of the high priest (Ex 28:36). The basic idea is that the ornaments of worldly pomp and warlike power become as truly consecrated as the very miter of the high priest. These horses may be viewed as providing transportation to Jerusalem for the feast.[286]

2. *Previously holy becomes holier (14:20b):* **and the pots in the house of Yahweh will be like the bowls before the altar.** Under the Mosaic system the *pots in the house of Yahweh* were vessels of inferior sanctity. They were made of bronze rather than gold. They were used to remove ashes from the altar (Ex 27:3). *The bowls before the altar* were vessels of superior sanctity. They were used to hold the blood for sprinkling upon the altar and for libations. These vessels were made of gold.[287]

3. *Previously common becomes holy (14:21a):* **And every vessel in Jerusalem and in Judah shall be HOLY TO YAHWEH OF HOSTS and all that sacrifice will come and take of them and will boil in them.** In the messianic age all distinction between sacred and secular comes to an end, because all shall now be equally holy (Perowne). All vessels will be consecrated and used in divine service. The basic idea is that the old Levitical distinctions in degrees of holiness in society (priests, Levites, people), temple (outer court, holy place, holy of holies), animals (clean and unclean) disappear. Cf. 2 Tim 2:21.

4. *Irreclaimably profane forever shut out (14:21b):* **And in that day there will be no longer a Canaanite in the house of Yahweh.** The picture of the holiness of the messianic Israel continues in this statement about the exclusion of the Canaanite. Cashdan thinks *Canaanite* refers to a merchant. Jesus twice drove out of the temple courts the money makers who exploited pilgrims with the sale of animals and vessels. For this use of *Canaanite* see Prov 31:24; Job 40:30. Probably it is best, however, to regard *Canaanite* as a proper name—a reference to an unclean person who had not consecrated him-

---

[286]Baldwin, *TOTC*, 207.

[287]Cashdan thinks the v is saying that the pots normally used for cooking consecrated flesh will be used as sprinkling bowls, so numerous will the sacrifices be.

self to the service of God. Such a person will be excluded from the house of God in the messianic age. Cf. Joel 3:17. *The house of Yahweh* is God's temple, the church, and heaven itself. Cf. Rev 21:27.

MALACHI
PROPHET OF INTERROGATION

INTRODUCTION

Because he was the last of the OT prophets Malachi has been dubbed "the seal of the prophets," or more poetically, "the last flush in the sunset of Hebrew prophecy" (Farrar). The style that is manifested in this book has caused others to call Malachi "the prophet of didactic-dialectic," or "the lecturer" or "the Hebrew Socrates" (Robinson). The message of this man of God has earned him the title "the prophet of universal worship" or "the prophet of the coming and the return of the Messiah."

Background

Over three quarters of a century elapsed between the completion of the temple and the ministry of Malachi. The key political figures in this period were the Persian King Xerxes and his son and successor Artaxerxes.

Reign of Xerxes

The death of Darius triggered new rebellions, especially in Babylon and Egypt. Xerxes (485-465 BC) was finally able to consolidate his power. He then determined to expand his empire into Europe. A great assembly was called to plan the invasion of Greece. Esther 1 probably alludes to that planning session.

In 480 BC the expedition to Greece was undertaken. Xerxes met with devastating defeats in a sea battle at Salamis, and in land battles at Thermopylae and Plataea. The Persian king then retreated to his capital at Shushan (Susa) to rebuild his forces. As a diversion for the shattered ego of their king, Xerxes' advisors suggested that a new queen be selected to replace Vashti. The former queen had been deposed prior to the invasion of Greece when she refused to obey a command of her husband.

Postexilic Prophets

In 478 BC, after a lengthy search process, the Jewess Esther was selected to be Xerxes' queen, i.e., the leading wife of his harem. Some five years later Esther was able to use her influence with the king to foil the plot of Prime Minister Haman to exterminate the Jewish people.

In 466 BC Xerxes made one last attempt to invade Greece. This effort was even more disastrous than the first. The following year Xerxes was assassinated.

Reign of Artaxerxes

A. Ministry of Ezra

In his seventh year of rule Artaxerxes (465-424 BC) commissioned Ezra, a Jewish scholar, to be secretary of state for Jewish affairs in the entire region "beyond the river," i.e., west of the Euphrates. Ezra was given the authority to enforce the law of God among his people even to the extent of executing those who resisted him.

After a perilous journey of four months, Ezra and a group of returnees arrived in Judea in July of 457 BC. The reformer discovered almost immediately that several of the leading Jewish men had cast aside their Jewish wives to marry heathen women. Ezra organized a procedure for investigating and resolving all alleged cases of religious intermarriage.

Apparently Ezra also attempted to rebuild the walls of Jerusalem (Ezra 4:11-23). Since this was not part of his commission the effort failed. Under pressure from the people of the land Artaxerxes ordered that the work cease. Ezra, somewhat discredited by this failure, disappeared from public life.

B. Nehemiah's First Governorship.

Thirteen years after Ezra's mission, Nehemiah became governor of Judea. He had royal permission to rebuild the city. In spite of a determined effort by the people of the land to stop the project, the walls of Jerusalem were rebuilt in fifty-two days. Completion of the walls was celebrated with a dedication service in which two groups of leaders walked the

Malachi: Introduction

walls in opposite directions. Nehemiah led one of those groups; Ezra led the other.

Jerusalem was then repopulated to further protect it from the local enemies. At the same time Nehemiah instituted other reforms designed to bring the postexilic community into compliance with the law of God.

C. Nehemiah's Second Governorship.

After twelve years Nehemiah returned to the Persian court perhaps to have his commission as governor renewed. In his absence many of the abuses which Nehemiah and Ezra had corrected reappeared. Most likely the ministry of Malachi should be assigned to this period of Nehemiah's absence from Jerusalem.

About 420 BC Nehemiah returned to Jerusalem. He dealt decisively with the problems of Sabbath abuse and intermarriage with the heathen. Nehemiah discovered that in his absence Tobiah the Ammonite had been assigned a chamber in the temple. This man had been one who had bitterly opposed the rebuilding of Jerusalem. Nehemiah threw Tobiah out of his chambers.

Thus OT history concludes with a dramatic effort by Nehemiah to purge Jerusalem of the corrupting influence of nonbelievers.

Malachi: the Man

A. Name

The name *Malachi* means "my messenger." Malachi is not mentioned in the NT or Josephus. The name is not found elsewhere in the OT either. The name stands alone in v 1 without any further definition as to family or hometown. For these reason a tradition arose in ancient times that "Malachi" was not a proper name. The Targum, for example, attributed the authorship of this book to Ezra. Jerome echoes this opinion. Other traditions attributed the book to Nehemiah or Zerubbabel or Mordecai. Because Mal 1:1 parallels Zech 9:1 and 12:1 some modern scholars have suggested that Malachi originally may have been a third appendix to the Book of

Postexilic Prophets

Zechariah. This idea is surely incorrect. The content and style of Malachi have nothing in common with the style and content of Zechariah 9-14.

None of the above arguments for the anonymity of the last book of the Minor Prophets has that much weight. Other prophets, for example, also are mentioned without further definition in the opening vv of their books. If there was a Jewish tradition that this book was written by someone other than Malachi, there was also a parallel tradition that Malachi was a personal name. Malachi appears as a proper name in 2 Esdras 1:40, the Talmud, and the heading of the Septuagint. Epiphanius and other church fathers accepted Malachi as the name of an individual.

Probably Malachi should be taken as the proper name for the last OT prophet. It would be very strange if the last book of the prophetic canon were the only book not to have the name of its author in the opening v. In the final analysis there is no valid reason for rejecting Malachi as a proper name.

B. Biography

Nothing is known of the life of Malachi except what can be deduced from the book itself. He was an excellent teacher. He was deeply devoted to sincere worship of the Lord. Tradition held that Malachi was a Levite who was born at Supha and who lived in the region of Zebulun.

C. Ministry

1. Chronological setting. The Book of Malachi fits the situation amid which Ezra and Nehemiah worked "as snugly as a bone fits its socket."[288] Yet no uniformity of opinion exists as to the precise relationship between the prophet and the governor. Five different positions have been proposed. Malachi prophesied 1) before the coming of Ezra in 457 BC; 2) between Ezra and Nehemiah's coming in 445 BC; 3) as a coworker with Nehemiah; 4) between the two governorships of Nehemiah, i.e., after 432 BC; and 5) just after Nehemiah's return to Jerusalem for his second governorship.

---

[288] J.M.P Smith, *ICC*, 7.

Malachi: Introduction

Only one small piece of evidence exists to help narrow down the range of possibilities. Malachi challenged his audience to present an offering to their governor (Mal 1:8). Yet the Scriptures declare that Nehemiah did not require gifts from those he governed (Neh 5:15, 18). Therefore one might conclude that Malachi ministered at a time when Nehemiah was absent from Jerusalem. On this solitary piece of evidence the position has been taken here that Malachi ministered between the two governorships of Nehemiah, sometime between 432 and 425 BC.

2. *Spiritual setting.* Malachi's mission was to correct the abuses and attitudes of the Jewish community in the last half of the fifth century before Christ. He furthermore was commissioned to announce the coming of the Sun of Righteousness and the day when men throughout the world will worship God in spirit and in truth.

Jerusalem in Malachi had just been rebuilt and repopulated, but the temple had been functioning for almost a century. The Persians ruled the world at the time. Their philosophy generally was to grant religious freedom to subject peoples. While some of the neighboring peoples made life difficult for the Jews, for the most part during this period the Jews were free to practice their faith.

Spiritually the Jews of the fifth century had lost the joy of their salvation and their zeal for the Lord. The priesthood was degenerate. The people brought faulty sacrifices, and the priests approved them for presentation before God. Religious apathy and skepticism were widespread. Tithes were neglected. Divorce was common. Yet the people and priests refused to admit that anything was wrong. Into this environment Malachi marched. With these hypocrites and apostates he engaged in public debate. When he was finished he had laid bare the rotten foundation upon which their relationship to God rested.

Malachi: the Message

In his message Malachi reaches back to clasp the hands of Moses, and reaches forward to clasp the hands of Messiah and his forerunner.

A. Structure
The fifty-five vv which constitute the Book of Malachi are arranged in three chs in the Hebrew Bible. The ancient versions, however, organized the same material into four chs. The English translations have followed the four-chapter arrangement.

STRUCTURE OF MALACHI			
Introduction Yahweh's Sovereign Love	Priests Sin Against Love	People Sin Against Love	Final Exhortation
1:1-5	1:6-2:9	2:10-4:3	4:4-6

B. Style
Malachi is more prosaic than any other prophetic book. The parallelism is less pronounced. The imagery lacks force and beauty. Perhaps this is the reason that at least one liberal writer sees in Malachi "the hardening of the spiritual arteries of the prophetic faith which reached its apex in Pharisaism."[289] Malachi was not, however, a formalist; the book breathes the genuine prophetic spirit. His was an incisiveness that is unequaled by any other.

C. Method
The method of this prophet has been called didactic-dialectic or dialogistic. Seven times in the book this pattern recurs: Malachi makes an affirmation or assertion about some sin or problem in the community; then the people object to the charge by interrogating Malachi. They demand in effect

---

[289] W. Neil, "Malachi" in *IDB*, vol K-Q, 231.

Malachi: Introduction

that Malachi explain the charge and present his evidence. Thus the dominant pattern in this book is assertion, objection and refutation. To put the matter another way, the literary pattern in Malachi is affirmation, interrogation and rebuttal. Again and again the prophet refutes the objection of his auditors by lawyer-like arguments. Certainly this is the most argumentative of all OT books. A courtroom atmosphere prevails throughout the book.

D. Theme

The theme of Malachi is "the sovereign love of God" (1:1-5). Both the priests (1:6-2:9) and the people (2:10-4:3) had sinned against that love.

Postexilic Prophets

COMMENTARY

Heading and Prologue
Malachi 1:1-5

Announcement
Malachi 1:1a, b

A. Proclamation (1:1a):
A burden. The term *massā'* ("what is lifted up") became a technical term for a prophetic proclamation. The term has been explained in two ways. First, as a messenger of God it was the prophet's "burden" to transport the message from sender to recipient. Second, since the term often introduces a prophecy of judgment, *massā'* may originally have indicated a weighty woe against the wicked. The NASB and NIV rendering "oracle" perhaps is too technical.[290] In most prophetic contexts the term *massā'* probably is equivalent to "revelation."[291]

B. Source (1:1b):
The word of Yahweh... An oracle or proclamation contains a direct utterance of God. Thus Malachi opens with the claim that what follows is a proclamation of the word of Yahweh. Like Haggai, Malachi does not hesitate to claim that he has been inspired by God to present his message.

---

[290]In prophetic literature the term *massā'* is used about 34x in reference to a prophetic utterance. The term previously has appeared in the headings of the books of Nahum and Habakkuk. Zechariah titled chs 9-11 and chs 12-14 respectively with this term. For this reason the final editors placed Malachi after Zechariah because of the "catchword" principle. See Stuart, *WBC*, xlii-xlv.

[291]C.D. Isbell, *Malachi* (Grand Rapids: Zondervan, 1980), 25.

Addressee
Malachi 1:1c

To Israel... The message of the final OT book is addressed to *Israel*. Since the fall of the northern kingdom of Israel in 722 BC this name was used for the entirety of the covenant people. The postexilic community was viewed as being comprised of former citizens of both Israel (northern kingdom) and Judah (southern kingdom).[292]

Agent
Malachi 1:1d

By the hand of Malachi indicates that Malachi is the instrument through whom God speaks to his people. Malachi means "my messenger."[293] While the name is unique in Scripture, it is still best to take it as a proper name for two reasons. First, the precedent of previous headings leads us to expect a proper name here. Second, if taken as a common noun + suffix this first person wording would be out of place with the third person language that introduces it. For a discussion of the name *Malachi* see introductory section.

Affirmation
Malachi 1:2-5

Malachi lays the foundation for all that he will say in the four vv following the heading. In this poetic unit[294] Malachi sets forth a proposition, and then offers the proof to sustain his proposition. This is the first of six rhetorical disputations in the book. The form characteristic of these disputations is

---

[292]Ezra refers to "Israel" 40x and Judah 15x; Nehemiah refers to "Israel" 21x and Judah 29x.
[293]The phrase is rendered "by the hand of his angel/messenger" in LXX.
[294]Recognized as poetic in BHS, but not in RSV, NRSV, or NIV.

Malachi: 1:1-5

this: 1) assertion; 2) questioning of the assertion; 3) response to the questioning; and 4) implications.

Proposition
Malachi 1:2a, b

A. Unchanging love of God (1:2a):

I love you, says Yahweh. The message begins with a grand assertion by Yahweh which can be translated either "I love you" (present perfect) or "I do love you" (perfect of certitude). In Hebrew the perfect can be used to express facts which were accomplished previously or conditions and attributes which were acquired previously, but of which the effects still remain in the present. Hence the language underscores the unchanging love of Yahweh for his people. This grand announcement presupposes widespread skepticism regarding Israel's status with the Lord.

Says Yahweh is the messenger formula. Some prefer to render it in past tense because the prophet is reminding the people of what he had heard from Yahweh in the recent past. The formula affirms that Malachi did not make up his message.

B. Ungrateful Attitude of the People (1:2b):

But you ask, In what way do you love us? Malachi verbalizes the doubts of the people in a question which he anticipates he will hear (or perhaps actually had heard) in response to the assertion of Yahweh's love. The emphasis is on the specific manner not the fact of Yahweh's love (Stuart). The present trials apparently had caused them to forget all the past mercies of the Lord.

Their doubt may have been rooted in several circumstances. They had returned from exile (as God had promised), and they had built their temple (as God had promised.) Yet the monarchy had not been reestablished. As yet there was no sign of the glorious priest-king predicted by Zechariah. They were not a great and victorious people. Gentiles were not coming to worship at Jerusalem. Prosperity had not returned. Enemies had not been crushed.

Proof
Malachi 1:2c-5

To refute the charge of the people, the prophet calls attention to the different fate of the twin brothers Esau and Jacob.

A. Argument from Past Circumstances (1:2c-3a):

1. Jacob had a twin brother (1:2c): **Was not Esau Jacob's brother? (oracle of Yahweh).** Malachi answered the question of the people with a question. The wording is often an idiomatic assertion of what was common knowledge. Some would render, "Esau is, of course, Jacob's brother." The oracular formula (n^e*'um Yahweh*) is even stronger than the previous messenger formula[295] in reminding the people that the words Malachi speaks come directly from God.

2. Yahweh's treatment of Jacob (1:2d): **Yet I loved Jacob...** Affirmations of divine love for the patriarchal ancestors of Israel are quite common in the OT (e.g., Dt 4:37; 10:15). Likewise, affirmations of love for Israel as a people appear frequently.[296] By *Esau* and *Jacob* Malachi means the nations which were descended from these men.

Loved (r. *'hb*) should not be interpreted psychologically and emotionally but politically and strategically. It was the word used to indicate political alliance in the ancient Near East (Cf. 1 Kgs 5:1; 1 Sam 18:1, 3). God had chosen or elected to use Jacob or Israel for his glorious purposes in this world as his special people. The choice was one of sovereign grace; it was undeserved. Esau was the eldest, the favorite son of his father. Yet Jacob was chosen. Jacob was not a righteous man in his youth, yet he was chosen. Yahweh had an alliance or covenant relationship with the nation descended from Jacob.

3. Yahweh's treatment of Esau (1:3a): **but Esau I hated.** *Esau* refers to the nation Edom (Gn 36:8) as it does in

---

[295]The messenger formula (*'āmar Yahweh*) and the oracular formula (n^e*'um Yahweh*) occur together elsewhere in a single v 14x (Jer 16:5; 23:2; 29:32; 30:3; 31:16, 17; 34:17; 35:13; 49:2; Hag 2:9; Zech 1:3, 4, 16; 8:6).
[296]Dt 7:6-8, 13; 23:5; Ps 47:4; Isa 43:4; Jer 31:3; Hos 11:1; 14:5; Mal 2:11.

Malachi: 1:1-5

at least seven other prophetic passages.[297] *Hated* (r. *snʾ*), like *loved*, was a technical term in the vocabulary of international relations to indicate enmity between nations. So the term here has a comparative force. Compared to his love for Jacob the divine attitude toward Esau was hatred.[298] Compared to the lot of the Esauites, the Jacobites were most blessed.

The choice of Jacob over Esau had nothing to do with eternal life. Edom was "the earliest, latest, closest, and most consistently hostile of all Israel's enemies" (Stuart). For this reason tiny Edom was the most frequently threatened nation by the prophets of Israel.[299] Yet Edomites are specifically included in messianic salvation (cf. Jer 49:11; Amos 9:12; Obad 19, 21). God simply is contrasting here the history of two nations, the one blessed, and the other unblessed.

B. Argument from Present Conditions (1:3b):

And I have turned his mountains into a wasteland and [given] his inheritance to the jackals of the wilderness. The evidence that God loved Esau less than Jacob could be observed in the condition of the nation Edom. *His mountains* connotes a region, not the mountains per se. *Wasteland* (*šᵉmāmāh*) is used 56x in OT. When used of lands the word refers to abandonment and loss of functionality.

His inheritance to the jackals of the wilderness reinforces and defines *wasteland*. The Edomites had been driven from their *inheritance* (land). While Edom lost population, the land was overrun by the *jackals*, representative of desert creatures (cf. Jer 49:33).

Malachi may be referring to the destruction of Edom by Nebuchadnezzar in the thirty-seventh year of his reign

---

[297] Edom is referenced 10x in ten of the prophetic books. Sometimes Edom is referred to by some geographical feature of that land such as Mount Esau (4x), Seir (1x), Mount Seir (4x).

[298] Cf. Lev 26:17; Dt 33:11. In contrast to *loved*, the opposite *hated* is sometimes used in the sense of "loved less." See Gn 29:31; Dt 21:15. This is not absolute hatred. The v is quoted in Rom 9:13. Perhaps in English the contrast is better expressed by accepted/rejected or approved/disapproved.

[299] Edom does not have the most vv; but it does have the widest distribution of vv among the prophets. From Isa 34 it is clear that sometimes Edom is used by the prophets to stand for all the nations that are hostile to Israel.

Postexilic Prophets

(Deane). On the other hand, the reference could be to the Nabataean invasion of Edom. This invasion caused the Edomites to migrate to the desert country of southern Judah. The exact date of this invasion is not known; it may have occurred during the lifetime of Malachi.

C. Argument from Future Prospects (1:4-5):

To spell out the future prospects of Edom, Malachi gives three quotes that may be summarized by the words expectation, declaration, reputation, and realization.

1. What Edom says (1:4a): **Edom may say, Though we have been crushed, we will rebuild the ruins.** Sometime prior to the writing of Malachi Edom had experienced a devastating blow from some quarter. *Crushed* (r. *ršš* in Pual) occurs only here and in Jer 5:17. Older Jewish commentators rendered the word "impoverished." Perhaps it means something like "beaten down."

Apparently some Edomites survived the incursion into their land that had dislodged them. These survivors, living in small communities on the fringes of their once proud land, were optimistic about their chances of rebuilding their nation. Edom's future prospects, however, were as bleak as its present condition. Like the modern Palestinian Arabs the dispossessed Edomites boasted that they would reclaim the land and rebuild their country.

2. What Yahweh says (1:4b): **Thus says Yahweh of Hosts: They may build, but I will throw them down.** The announcement of the divine intentions is underscored with the messenger formula used by prophets to remind the audience that they are passing on words received from heaven.

In contrast to the Judeans who were slowly rebuilding their homeland with Persian approval, the Edomites will never be able to make good on their boasts. This threat reflects the ancient futility curse of Deuteronomy (28:29-30; cf. Hos 9:12). Yahweh declared that every attempt to rebuild Edom will fail. God will *throw them down.* When God knocks a nation down, it stays down for the count!

Malachi: 1:1-5

The Edomites were successively beaten down by the Nabateans, the Macedonians, the Maccabees, the Romans and the Arabs.

3. What neighbors say (1:4c): **They will be called the border of wickedness, a people always under the wrath of Yahweh.** This line reflects the Deuteronomic dishonor curse (cf. Dt 28:37). Because of the desolation of their once proud country men will call Edom *the border of wickedness*, i.e., the wicked country. This conclusion will be based on the ongoing miserable condition of Edom's former territory. People will rightly conclude that Edom had been punished for some grave wickedness.

Always (*'ad 'ōlām*) indicates "on going," but not necessarily "forever" (NASB). The land of Edom will gain the reputation of being condemned by God in perpetuity. *Under the wrath* (r. *z'm*) can also mean "cursed." In the Hebrew there is assonance, whether intentional or accidental, that makes the words *a people always under the wrath of Yahweh* particularly memorable.

4. What Israel will say (1:5): **You will see it with your own eyes and say, Great is Yahweh--from beyond [with respect to] the borders of Israel!** Israel will observe from a distance, safe and secure in their own land. They will see the feeble attempts of displaced and subjugated Edomites to recover their land. The calamities that befall their brother nation are irrefutable proof to Israel of God's love and grace.

Those who currently doubt God's declaration of love will willingly or grudgingly confess openly his loving care for Israel, his mighty protection. Though Israel will have its share of setbacks, Edom's far more miserable circumstances demonstrate God's watch care over his people. They will acknowledge that Yahweh is not a hapless, helpless and hopeless local deity, but a mighty God whose might is displayed *beyond the borders of Israel*, i.e., throughout the world. *From beyond with respect* to is an attempt to translate *mē'al ligbhūl*.

275

Postexilic Prophets

PART ONE:
PRIESTS SIN AGAINST LOVE
Malachi 1:6-2:9

Having established how God had displayed his love for Israel, Malachi charged first the priests and then the people with slighting that love. In ch 1 the sins of the priests are considered. Malachi leveled several serious charges against the priests. They had polluted the altar, profaned the name, and perverted the covenant. For this the priests will experience punishment at the hands of their God.

Pollution of the Altar
Malachi 1:6-10

The most sacred duty which God delegated to priests under the law was their service at the altar of sacrifice. Here was where these priests helped sinful people find reconciliation with God. The ritual acts performed at that altar were rich in symbolism for Old Covenant worship. At the same time those rituals pointed forward to the perfect sacrifice of Christ. To officiate at that altar was a great honor and a solemn responsibility. Yet the postexilic priests polluted that altar both by their attitudes and by their actions.

Accusation and Denial
Malachi 1:6

The main body of the book begins with a double accusation against the priests and a double denial on the part of those same priests. The prophet accused these religious leaders of despising God's name and desecrating God's altar. The v is heavy with alliteration with the letter א, first letter of the Hebrew alphabet. This alliteration served to indicate that this is the first accusation against the priests. It also facilitated memorization.

Postexilic Prophets

A. Accusation Set Up (1:6a, b):

1. *Two observations (1:6a): **A son honors a father, and a servant his master.*** To set up the accusation Malachi states a proposition: God is deserving of honor. Certainly one can see the demonstration of honor of an inferior to a superior displayed, as a rule, in everyday life. A son honors a father, i.e., his own father. The imperfect verb form is frequently used to express actions that may be expected to occur time and again. Cf. the fifth commandment. A *servant* honors *his master* (lit., "masters"[300]). The plural may denote a king as in 1 Kgs 22:17; 2 Chr 18:16; Isa 19:4.

In the ancient world a son had no choice but to obey his father, and a *servant* (*'ebhed*) had no choice but to respect his master. Malachi is not appealing for an attitude adjustment on the part of the priests; he is condemning them for violating a fundamental principle of law and society.

2. *Two questions (1:6b): **If I am a father, where is the honor due me? If I am a master, where is the respect due me?*** The argument is *a fortiori* or, as it is called in rabbinic circles, *qal vachomer* (light/heavy). Clearly male authority in the ancient world is used to illustrate the authority of the deity in Israel.

Yahweh does not possess sexuality analogous to what we experience in this world. *Father* is a figurative way of indicating his authoritative role in respect to his people. God was the *father* of Israel by creation, election, preservation and watchful guardianship (Deane). The Israelites were called in the law the children of God (Dt 14:1). Yet God did not receive the honor due a father.

The second question charges that God did not receive the dread or *fear* (*môrā'*) which a servant should feel for his master or king.[301] *Master* is again plural. Perhaps it should be rendered "Lord." Yahweh is called "master" or "lord" almost 600x in the OT.

---

[300] The plural of this word compared to the singular appears in a thirty to one ratio in the OT. The masculine plural is the most common way of indicating abstraction in Hebrew.

[301] The term *fear* (*môrā'*) never denotes the loving fear of a child but dread, horror, or terror.

Malachi: 1:6-2:9

So in Malachi's day God was neither reverenced nor feared, just ignored.

B. Accusation (1:6c):
Says Yahweh of Hosts to you, O priests who despise my name. The messenger formula is used for the first of 4x in this unit (cf. 1:8, 9, 10) in its longer form (including *of Hosts*). The heavy emphasis on the authority behind the messenger may have been employed because Malachi felt a bit insecure addressing such harsh words to the religious leaders. Entrenched clergy in a religious society can be powerful adversaries. Malachi's only right to question the legal judgment and attitude of the priests was derived from his position as the messenger of Yahweh.

General disrespect for God charged in 1:6a-b was especially prevalent among the priests. Through Malachi Yahweh addressed these words to the priests *who despise my name*. The Hebrew participle denotes continuous manifestation of disrespect, a state of mind, a characteristic trait. The leaders of religion continuously mocked God and sneered at his name and will.

Yahweh's *name* (*šēm*) is that part of the divine nature that he has revealed to mankind through his word. His name includes his character, his identity, his significance, his presence, his power and his revelation of himself.

C. Denial (1:6d):
But you ask, How have we despised your name? Malachi depicted the priests pompously denying that they had despised God's name. They totally rejected the prophet's accusation.

Unholy Offerings
Malachi 1:7-8

A. Their Ungodly Attitude (1:7):
1. What they were doing (1:7a): **You are offering polluted bread upon my altar.** The fundamental principle of Mosaic sacrifice was that Yahweh got the best as his portion.

Postexilic Prophets

That principle was being flagrantly disregarded by the priests of Malachi's day. They were offering upon God's altar *polluted bread*. Any sacrificial substance whether animal or vegetable which was presented to God was call *bread* (*lechem*; cf. Nm 28:2).

Priestly offerings are called *polluted* ($m^e g\bar{o}$ '$\bar{a}l$)[302] because God rejected them as unqualified or unfit. They were not being offered in accordance with the ceremonial law (cf. Lv 22:18f). *My altar* emphasizes that the altar did not belong to the priests. They were not at liberty to do as they pleased there.

2. *What they were saying (1:7b):* **But you say, How have we polluted you?** The priests recognized the seriousness of the charge. They understood that to offer polluted offerings was tantamount to polluting God himself. So with bluff and bluster they asked: *How have we polluted you?*

3. *What they were thinking (1:7c):* **By saying that the Lord's table may be despised.** Most likely the priests were not expressing this opinion audibly, certainly not publicly. Their actions, however, spoke louder than their words. Instead of regarding the temple service as an undeserved honor, they regarded it as a contemptible, miserable job. The altar here is called a *table* because there the sacrifices were "eaten" by fire.

The motivation of the priests in offering such inferior sacrifices upon God's altar is unclear. Perhaps lowering the standards facilitated participation in temple rituals. This meant that priestly revenues were increased since priests derived their income from the sacrificial offerings. On the other hand, perhaps the standards among surround nations put pressure on the priests to not be so "legalistic." Then again perhaps there was some payoff to the priests from farmers who wanted to keep the choice animals for breeding stock. One thing is sure. The acceptance of the unfit animals was not due to ignorance.

---

[302] The term $m^e g\bar{o}$ '$\bar{a}l$ is a Pual participle. It refers to what is rejected as unqualified or unfit.

Malachi: 1:6-2:9

B. Their Unholy Offerings (1:8):
Malachi exposes the priestly audacity with two questions.

1. How they challenged God (1:8a): **When[303] you bring blind animals for sacrifice, is that not wrong? When you sacrifice crippled or diseased animals, is that not evil?** The priests (and perhaps the people as well) demonstrated their contempt for the altar of God by offering there unholy sacrifices. Blemished offerings were forbidden by the law; a sacrificial animal must be perfect (e.g., Lv 22:19-25). Yet these priests did not consider it *evil* to present blind, lame and sick animals as offerings to the Lord.

2. How God challenged the priests (1:8b): **Try offering them to your governor! Will he be pleased with you? Will he accept you? says Yahweh of Hosts.** Yahweh challenged the priests in two ways.

First, he challenged them with an audacious action. Let the priests offer the same animals to the governor of the land! In the Persian system a *governor* (*pechāh*) was the ruler of a district. He served under a satrap. The names of the Judean governors of this period are unknown except for Nehemiah.

Malachi's challenge suggests that the governor in Judah during this period was accustomed to accept offerings from those he governed. Since Nehemiah refused to burden the people with such offerings (cf. Neh 5:14-18), this v may indicate that Nehemiah was no longer governor. On the other hand, Malachi's challenge may be taken as hypothetical and general.

Second, Yahweh challenged the priests with sharp questions. The point of the two questions is that blemished offerings will not curry favor with an earthly ruler. On the contrary, a human superior would be insulted by such a present. Yet the priests thought that such animals were appropriate to present to the King of Kings as a sacrificial offering.

Accept you is lit. "lift up your faces," i.e., grant you a cordial reception or regard you with favor. This idiom can be

---

[303] The introductory *ki* might be rendered "even If" as in Prov 6:35; Pss 21:12; 37:24.

281

Postexilic Prophets

traced back to the priestly blessing of Nm 6:26, if not before (Cf. Job 13:10; 42:8).

Useless Intercession
Malachi 1:9

A. **Second Challenge** (1:9a):
Now entreat the face of God to be gracious to us. His voice oozing with sarcasm, Malachi urged the priests to *entreat the face of God.* The verb (r. *chlh*) in the Piel stem means literally "to soothe or make sweet the face of anyone." The idea is to mollify, or entreat the favor of someone. In the case of God, this is done through worship and sacrifice. The basic function of priests was to seek a favorable hearing for the needs of God's people. If they succeeded in their intercession, then Yahweh would *be gracious* to Israel.

B. **Challenge Reinforced with a Question** (1:9b):
While this is being done by your hand, will he accept any of your persons?--says Yahweh of Hosts. The expression *while this is being done by your hand* (lit., "from your hand this has been") is difficult.[304] The NASB renders "with such an offering on your part." The NIV is very similar. The idea seems to be that as long as they continue with their present sacrificial practices they need not expect any gracious response from the Lord. This is stated in the form of a question: *Will he accept any of your persons,* i.e., will he acknowledge you? Will he grant the favor to you? The implied answer, of course, is negative.

Undesirable Service
Malachi 1:10

In v 9 God will not answer priestly prayers. Here, he will not tolerate their worship.

---

[304]The clause is best taken as a circumstantial clause (GKC §156d). Others think this clause is parenthetical indicating that the custom of offering blemished animals originated with this group of priests. Still others interpret, "This depends on you," i.e., whether God shows favor or not.

Malachi: 1:6-2:9

A. Shocking Wish (1:10a):
Oh that there were even one among you who would shut the doors so that you would not light fires in vain on my altar! The divine dissatisfaction with temple ritual implicit in the questions of vv 7-9 is now made explicit. Verse 10 expresses a divine wish which in effect is also a threat. *Oh that there were even*[305] *one of you* is lit., "who also among you." One of them ought to shut (r. *sgr*) the temple doors. The reference is to the *doors* of the inner court where the great altar stood.

Light fires refers to the fire on the great altar where sacrifices were consumed. Rather than continue to insult God with their tainted sacrifices, it would be better, Malachi argued, to shut down the temple.[306] Sacrifices were no longer accomplishing their purpose. No sacrifices were better than improper sacrifices. The priests were lighting the altar fire *in vain* (*chinnām*), i.e., for nothing. The sacrifices were doing more harm than good. They angered God rather than pleased him.

B. Shocking Declaration (1:10b):
I have no pleasure in you, says Yahweh of Hosts, neither will I accept an offering at your hand. The reason God no longer desired temple worship is stated bluntly and personally: Worship acts are not acceptable unless the worshipers are acceptable to the Lord. By their attitude the priests had forfeited their right to be worship leaders. The term *offering* (*minchāh*) is the general term for all sacrificial offerings, animal and vegetable.

---

[305]Hebrew *gam* implies a thought wholly unexpected and shocking to the priests.
[306]The Essene community at Qumran used this v to justify their total avoidance of the temple.

Profanation of the Name
Malachi 1:11-14

The name of God—his character, reputation—was to be held in honor by all Israelites. One of the Ten Commandments prohibited taking God's name in vain (Ex 20:7). God's name can be profaned by actions and attitudes as well as words. The priests of Malachi's day were guilty of profaning the holy name in all three ways. Before he made this case against the priests, however, Malachi announces a day in which God's name will be honored worldwide.

Future Honor of God's Name
Malachi 1:11

A. **Worthy Attitudes** (1:11a):
For from the place where the sun rises even unto where it sets my name shall be great among the Gentiles. The polarity between the place where the sun rises and sets is a regional idiom expressing universality.[307] The Hebrew lacks a verb, and thus permits the translator to supply the appropriate tense. For this reason some insist that Malachi is describing a current situation.[308] More likely this is a prophecy of the conversion of the Gentiles in the days of Messiah.[309]

Among those Gentiles God's name will be *great*, i.e., treated with the utmost respect. In contrast to the indifferent attitude and blasphemous actions of the postexilic priests, Yahweh announces a future day when he is honored world-

---

[307]Stuart (*MPEEC*, 1306) cites examples from literature of the region dating back to the seventeenth century BC.

[308]The v has been taken to refer 1) to pagan sacrifices that Yahweh declares were in reality offered to him; 2) the faithful worship of Jews who at this time were widely scattered throughout the world; 3) the worship of proselytes. None of these views are convincing.

[309]Future Gentile worship of Yahweh is a hope expressed consistently in the biblical prophets: Isa 2:2-4; 11:10-12; 42:1-9; 45:1-3, 15, 22-23; Jer 3:17; Mic 4:1-2; Zeph 3:8-9; Hag 2:7; Zech 8:20-23; 14:16.

Malachi: 1:6-2:9

wide. The universal recognition of Yahweh's name is a theme often associated with the expectations of biblical writers.[310]

B. Worthy Offerings (1:11b):

In every place a burnt offering will be offered unto my name along with a pure offering... The worthy attitudes of the Gentiles will be demonstrated in worthy actions. The Hophal participle (used as a noun) *burnt offering* (*muqtār*) should not be limited to "incense" (NIV; NASB). Hebrew words derived from the r. *qtr* refer to offerings that were allowed to burn in their entirety rather than those that were eaten after cooking.[311] In so far as incense is involved, this term may symbolize prayer (cf. Rev 8:3-4).

The burnt offering will be accompanied by *a pure offering*, a reference to the pure worship offered by converted Gentiles to the Lord in the church. This replaced temple worship which ceased in AD 70. We then have messianic prophecy in Mosaic terminology. This future devotion by those considered unclean and unworthy further rebukes the priests of Malachi's day. It brands their actions as utterly reprehensible.

Under the Mosaic system any offering made apart from the temple was illegal and unclean. Yet this prophecy announces that all over the world such sacrifice will be offered by sincere worshipers. Furthermore, they will be accepted by a holy God. The implication is that the Mosaic system was to be replaced by a new worship system. In that day Gentiles were to be included among the people of God.

C. Emphatic Repetition (1:11c):

Because my name will be great among the Gentiles, says Yahweh of Hosts. For emphasis the prophet repeats his previous prediction.

---

[310]Isa 29:23; 48:11; 52:6; Jer 44:26; Amos 9:12; Acts 9:15; 15:17; Rom 9:17; Phil 2:10.
[311]Stuart, *MPEEC*, 1306.

Postexilic Prophets

Present Dishonor of God's Name
Malachi 1:12-14

Following the brief glance into the glorious future, Malachi returns to the inglorious present. The same name that will be treated with great reverence by Gentiles was currently being profaned, i.e., treated lightly or irreverently, by the priests.

A. Disdain for God's Altar (1:12a):
But you profane it by saying of the Lord's table, It can be defiled ... The language stresses that the priestly action was deliberate, not accidental. *Profane* (r. *chll*) is Piel participle, indicating on-going action. *It* refers to God's name, mentioned 3x in the previous v.

In the OT God's name can be profaned by any direct disobedience to God's commands (Lv 22:32), especially by offering up child sacrifice (Lv 18:21; 20:3), swearing falsely in God's name (Lv 19:12; Jer 34:16), stealing (Prov 30:9), or sexual misconduct (Amos 2:7). Priests could profane God's name by shaving head and beard (Lv 21:6) and by treating sacred offering with disrespect (Lv 22:2). Nationally Israel profaned God's name by being in a condition of servitude (Isa 48:11; Ezek 20:9; etc.).

Here it is the comments of the priests reflecting their attitude that profanes God's name. *The Lord's table* is the sacrificial altar (cf. v 7). *Can be defiled* indicates that the priests did not think that they had to be particularly circumspect regarding their actions while serving at God's altar.

The accusation is the same as in v 7. Malachi is making his point a second time by alternative wording. *Profane* is a synonym to the word translated *polluted* (r. *g'l*) in v 7. There Malachi represented these priests as denying that they had polluted God's table or altar. Their actions, however, indicated contempt for the entire sacrificial ritual. These actions constituted profanation of God's name.

Malachi: 1:6-2:9

B. Complaint about Compensation (1:12b):
And its fruit, (even) its food can be despised. Fruit/food refers to the sacrificial food prepared on the altar for consumption by priests and/or worshipers. Part of priestly compensation came from the offerings that were placed on the altar. Apparently the priests were complaining because God got the best part of the sacrificial animals while they were only getting the leftovers. In their view the high standards for sacrificial offerings set forth in the law did not need to be strictly enforced.

C. Complaint about Priestly Work (1:13a):
And you say, Behold, what a weariness it is! And you sniff contemptuously at it,[312] says Yahweh of Hosts. Malachi repeats the essential points that he made in v 8. The routine of sacrifice had become irksome to the priests. Slaying the animals, skinning them, gutting them and cutting them up were filthy, bloody jobs. The material reward was simply not adequate.[313] *Sniff contemptuously* (r. *npch* in Hiphil) means "to cause to breathe or blow."[314] The priests sniff *at it* (work of sacrifice) as one might sniff at spoiled food with putrid smell. To put it bluntly, the sacrificial ritual stunk!

D. Presentation of Unworthy Sacrifices (1:13b):
And you bring what is injured, lame or diseased when you bring the offering. Should I accept this at your hand?" says Yahweh. To that despised altar the priests brought *injured* (*gāzûl*), *lame* (*pissēach*) and *diseased* (*chōleh*) ani-

---

[312] Jewish tradition reads "sniffed at me," i.e., God. Possibly here is an intentional scribal alteration to remove the harshness from the passage.

[313] Another view is that the people were complaining about the sacrificial burden. What a heavy burden this lamb is! The donor thus pretends that it is a large healthy animal when in fact it is thin and lean (Kimchi). The Vulgate and LXX suggest that the people are complaining that they are doing the best they can do in view of their impoverished situation.

[314] Others take the Hiphil of *npch* to mean: "you cause it to blow" (but what?); or "you cause me (emending the text) to puff or get angry;" you caused me to breathe hard, i.e., get weary."

mals—animals not fit to be consumed even in non-religious meals.[315]

Some take the first of this triad to refer to animals stolen or obtained by fraud since the root *gzl* sometimes has the connotation of "ripped off" or seized illegally. The priests, however, could hardly be faulted for not knowing that a sacrificial animal had been stolen. Context demands that the word refer to the condition of the animal itself, not how it was obtained by the worshiper. More likely the sacrificial animal had been snatched from the jaws of a wild beast, hence was mutilated and unfit for sacrifice.

Rhetorically God asked: *Should I accept this at your hand?* The obvious answer is, No!

E. Cooperation with Hypocritical Worshipers (1:14a-d):
   1. *Threat (1:14a):* **Cursed...** Cursed (*'ārūr*) is covenant language. It is the crafty worshipers who are cursed, not all the people. As is sometimes the case the exact nature of the curse is not specified, thus making the threat all the more ominous.

   2. *Sinner (1:14b):* **is the deceiver...** Deceiver (*nōkhēl*) comes from a root which means "to be crafty, deceitful, and knavish." A modern equivalent is "cheater." The actions of the priests were encouraging people to cheat on commitments to God. People are not excused from their obligations because of the wickedness of the priests.

   3. *Commitment (1:14c):* **who has an acceptable male in his flock and vows to give it...** Mosaic Law provided for vows of various kinds ranging from the Nazirite vow (Nm 6:14) to vows of gratitude for what God had done or was petitioned to do. The vow might be taken informally in front of a priest, or privately. The commitment in the solemn promise to God was normally to bring a sacrificial animal to the Lord at some unspecified date. A vow sacrifice had to meet all the requirements of general sacrifice. The language suggests that the vow taker specified a particular animal that he intended to give.

---

[315]Ex 22:31; Lv 7:24; 17:15; 22:8; Ezek 4:14; 44:31.

Mosaic sacrificial law normally specified that male animals be offered. God graciously consented to accept the animals that were more expendable in the flock or herd so long as the male animal was without blemish. Female animals were permitted in certain voluntary offerings (Lv 3:1-6), and were required for guilt offerings in which the offender must feel the "pinch" of his infraction (e.g., Lv 4:28, 32).

4. *Cheating (1:14d):* **but then sacrifices a blemished animal to Adonay.** Perhaps influenced by the attitude of the priests, the worshipers were attempting to deceive or cheat God in their sacrificial offerings. They would never have considered such conduct had not the priestly inspectors lowered their standards. So laxity on the part of the priests actually encouraged the worst kind of behavior on the part of the worshipers.

The situation envisioned is that a worshiper had available what fully met the requirements of a vow that he had taken. Once the emergency was past, however, he cheated God by offering a less valuable blemished animal instead. Apparently the priests winked at this religious charade.

F. Failure to Reverence God (1:14e-g):

All of the failings of the priests could be traced to a fundamental theological error. Their concept of God did not remotely correspond to the truth. They did not recognize Yahweh's position, power or prestige.

1. His position (1:14e): **For I am a great king...** This is the third time that the greatness of Yahweh has been stressed in this ch (cf. vv 5, 11). The idea is not that Yahweh is just great when compared to other kings. In the context of the Persian Empire *great king* refers to an emperor to whom all other kings and peoples were subject.

The theme of the universal kingship of Yahweh is one that is common in the psalms (e.g., Pss 10:16; 47:2). Yahweh's sovereignty over the entire world is not negated by the fact that most people had never heard of this God.

2. His power (1:14f): **says Yahweh of Hosts...** The priests and people did not understand Yahweh's power. The title which appears for the eighth time in this ch emphasizes that he is commander of all hosts of earth and heaven. He is therefore "Almighty" (NIV). The abundant use of this title in the postexilic prophets is intended to bring encouragement to a discouraged and intimidated people.

3. His prestige (1:14g): ***and my name is to be reverenced among the nations.*** Malachi foresaw a day when Yahweh's name will be *reverenced* (*nōrā'*) among the Gentiles (cf. vv 5, 11). The theme that Yahweh ought to be feared among the nations is common in the psalms (e.g., Pss 9:20; 102:15).

Punishment of the Priests
Malachi 2:1-4

Priestly disdain, dishonor and disrespect demanded punishment. In terms of its origin that punishment is called here a "commandment." In terms of content that punishment is here called a "curse."

Threat of the Curse
Malachi 2:1-2

A. Ominous Address (2:1):
And now this commandment is for you, O priests. Because of their contemptuous attitude the priests merited punishment from the Lord. They were called upon multiple times daily to render decisions about various commandments in the Law of Moses. They were the experts in applying legal principles to specific situations. So these leaders who were accustomed to applying God's commandments to others will now have God apply a command to them. The threat or announcement of judgment is called a *commandment* (*mitsvāh*) because God ordained it and issued orders for its execution.

B. Conditions of the Curse (2:2a):
1. Heeding (2:2a): ***If you do not hearken, and if you do not lay it to heart...*** The priests would face the commandment of judgment if they did not *hearken* or hear God's warn-

Malachi: 1:6-2:9

ing. This involves responding to or obeying, not merely hearing.

For emphasis and explanation the phrase *lay it to heart* is added. The expression means something like "determine," "focus on," "get serious about." The repetition of the idea in different terms serves to emphasize the importance of this conditional clause.

2. Honoring (2:2b): **to give honor to my name, says Yahweh of Hosts...** the priests must give heed to the accusations and implied warnings of Malachi respecting honoring God's name. Only thereby can they avoid the "commandment"? *To give honor to my name* goes beyond merely using God's name appropriately. The expression sometimes has the connotation of "do what is right," "humble yourself before God," even "be honest" (cf. Josh 7:19). This honor was to manifest itself in due regard for the proper forms and rules of sacrifice.

C. **Nature of the Curse** (2:2c-e):

A *curse* is a pronouncement of divine punishment. Prophetic curses are based upon curses set forth in Mosaic Law (Lv 26; Dt 4; 28-32). The curse upon the priests is twofold.

1. *Persons cursed (2:2c):* **I will send the curse upon you.** Failure to conform to the requirements of Yahweh will bring down Yahweh's "curse" or wrath upon the offending priests. The language reflects the anger/rejection form of curse (e.g., Lv 26:17, 24). The *curse* ($m^e\text{'}ēr\bar{a}h$) is in effect collective. It does not refer to a single curse, but to a state in which all they experience is cursing or negative outcomes.

2. *Future blessings cursed (2:2d):* **and I will curse your blessings.** The second curse is called the futility curse (e.g., Lv 26:16, 20)—the frustration of one's plans and efforts. The curse will be sent, not only on the person of the priests, but upon their *blessings* as well. The reference could be to the blessing which they had received in being ordained to the priesthood. More likely, however, the reference is to the blessing that the priests pronounced over the people.

Those under God's curse can hardly pronounce divine blessings on others. Blessing was the business of priests. The priestly blessing promised God's presence and peace (cf. Nm 6:23-27) as well as material prosperity (Dt 28:3-6). Yahweh, however, is sovereign over blessings and curses. The priests' blessings were not magical formulas that guaranteed well-being. That greedy priests and worshipers should receive an economic blow is altogether appropriate.

3. *Present blessings (2:2e):* **Yes, I have cursed it already...** The curse or wrath of God already had begun to work in the ministries of the offending priests. The singular suffix *it* may refer to each individual blessing of the many just mentioned.[316] Turning a blessing into a curse was considered the ultimate punishment (Neh 13:1-2).

D. Reason for the Curse (2:2f):
Because you are not taking it to heart is lit., "setting upon heart." The idea is probably that they are being cursed for their failure to honor God in life and ministry. They were not devoted to the work of ministry. They performed their work in a haphazard and couldn't-care-less manner.

Result of the Curse
Malachi 2:3

The results of the curse on the priesthood are threefold: deprivation, dishonor, and destruction.

A. Deprivation (2:3a):
Behold, I am about to rebuke the seed... **Behold** introduces an announcement that is unexpected and shocking. The verb *rebuke* (r. *g'r*) suggests restraint or elimination. For example, when God rebukes crop pests, he restrains them (Mal 3:13). When he rebukes the sea he dries it up (Ps 106:9). The meaning seems to be that God will forbid the seed to sprout and grow and bear fruit because of the disobedient priests. Consequently these priests will be deprived of their dues from

---

[316] LXX (followed by KJV) has a plural suffix.

Malachi: 1:6-2:9

the people.[317] This clause is a specific example of the cursing of priestly blessings mentioned in the previous v.

B. Dishonor (2:3b):

I will spread dung upon on your faces, the dung of your feasts... The speaker is Yahweh. Dishonor is the second aspect of the curse upon the priests. The *dung* is undigested food and stomach juices in the sacrificial animal. Priests were to be the epitome of cleanliness, which was a symbol of the holiness of God. Faces smeared in dung would render the priests unclean and unfit for the discharge of their functions. Most take this clause to be figurative for the contempt for the priests in the eyes of the people.

The dung will be smeared upon the priests during the great festivals when they were the center of attention resplendent in their festival vestments. *Feasts* (*chaggim*) are the three annual pilgrim festivals (Passover, Pentecost, Tabernacles) when crowds were the largest, sacrifices most numerous, and consequently dung most voluminous. The priests could expect huge amounts of dung on their collective faces.

The fact that the text uses the second person possessive *your feasts* and not "my feasts" is significant. The contemptuous disobedience of the priests nullified the spiritual value of the feasts.

C. Destruction (2:3c):

You will be carried away unto it, i.e., unto the dung heap. According to the law the dung of the sacrificial animals was to be carried forth and burned outside the camp (Ex 29:14; Lv 4:12; 16:27). Once God has spread dung upon the priests he will never permit them to become ritually clean again. The priests will be treated as filth by the people. They will be swept out of office. In paraphrase God is saying, "I will throw you into the garbage dump."

---

[317] Orelli takes "seed" to refer to posterity, seeing here a reversal of such promises as Jer 33:18, 22. The ancient versions read "shoulder" for *seed*. God will take away from these priests the power of performing their official duties (Deane); or the shoulder might be the portion of the sacrificial animal allotted to priests (Lv 7:31-32).

Design of the Curse
Malachi 2:4

The curse against the priests is designed to accomplish two objectives.

A. **Negative Design** (2:4a):
Then you will know that I have sent you this commandment... When they begin to experience the effects of the curse, the priests will realize that *I have sent you this commandment.* They will recognize the source of their calamities and the reason for it. Reference to the *commandment* closes out the thought that was introduced in 2:1 (*this commandment is for you, O priests*).

B. **Positive Design** (2:4b):
So that my covenant with Levi may continue, says Yahweh of Hosts. The purging of the priesthood will fulfill the stipulations of the covenant with Levi. The purpose of covenant punishment was covenant renewal. Punishment is intended to lead to purging and purification. *May continue* (Qal infin. const. r. *hyh* + lamed) means "may continue to exist." The reference is to the selection of the tribe of Levi for the ministry of the sanctuary. The attitude and actions of the fifth century priests threatened the continuation of something very important—something that God was concerned to preserve. *My covenant with Levi* will be described in vv 5-7.

Language referring to a Levitical covenant appears previously in Jer 33:20-22 where the prophet declared that God will not arbitrarily abandon that covenant. Nehemiah, the contemporary of Malachi, speaks of "the covenant of the priesthood and of the Levites" (Neh 13:29). The reference appears to be to the entire body of stipulations that defined the priesthood of ancient Israel. The key passages establishing the Aaronic/Levitical priesthood are Ex 32:26-29; Nm 25:11-13; and Dt 33:26-29.

Malachi: 1:6-2:9

Priestly Covenant Perverted
Malachi 2:5-9

The covenant with (the tribe of) Levi introduced in v 4, is now further defined. That covenant involved certain privileges and responsibilities. Malachi first sets forth the ideal of that ancient covenant. He then points out how the priests of his day had shattered the ideal image of the priesthood.

Ideal of the Covenant
Malachi 2:5-7

A. **Provisions of the Covenant** (2:5):

1. *God's part (2:5a):* **My covenant was with him, a covenant of life and peace, and I gave them**[318] **to him [and] fear.** A covenant is an agreement between two parties. In the covenant with Levi God's part was to grant *life and peace.* Life (*chayyim*)[319] refers to long life, in this context, the permanence of the priesthood as stipulated in Nm 25:13. *Peace* (*šālōm*) embraces care, protection, favor and well-being. This too was part of the priestly covenant of Nm 25:12. This "peace" probably includes such things as the cities that were assigned to the priests, the portions of sacrificial offerings and tithes that were guaranteed to the priests. So by means of a covenant God established the priesthood and provided for its maintenance.

Along with the blessings of life and peace, God gave to Levi *fear* (*mōrā'*). In this term there is summarized the solemn responsibility of supervising worship, enforcing various provisions of God's holy law and making atonement for God's people (cf. Nm 25:13).[320] The structure of the Hebrew

---

[318]The plural suffix is not expressed in the Greek or Latin versions and is absent from many Hebrew MSS. Without the plural suffix the clause reads "I gave him fear."
[319]The masculine plural is the most common way in Hebrew of indicating abstract nouns.
[320]Others think that *fear* is a reference to reverence imparted by God to Levi and through him to the priesthood. Still another view is that God granted the blessings of life and peace so that Levi might fear. The very

295

sentence sets the covenant provision of *fear* apart from *life* and *peace* because it involves responsibility as well as privilege.

2. *Man's part (2:5b):* **and he feared me and before my name he was afraid.** Levi (referring to the tribe) responded on his part to the covenant in that *he feared me.* This verb is used in the OT to refer to worship and obedience. To *fear* God is to make his interests paramount. The verb connotes a bit more than the English reverence, for it suggests serious concern about the consequences of failing to carry out God-given responsibility.

Reinforcing the verb *feared*, Malachi adds: *and before my name he was afraid.* Again the emphasis is upon fear of the consequences of failing to fulfill God-given responsibility. Of course Malachi is speaking in generalities. There are specific examples of priests early-on who acted audaciously (Lv 10).

The proper response to God's gracious gifts is always reverence and humility. At Mount Sinai God stipulated that the tribe of Levi, led by Aaron, be set aside for priestly service. The family of Aaron occupied the priesthood; the remainder of the tribe had secondary sacerdotal responsibilities. Malachi is suggesting that those original priests took their responsibilities seriously and carried out their functions reverently.

B. Pattern Envisioned in the Covenant (2:6-7):

The priestly covenant envisioned a high standard. This standard was modeled for future generations of priests by Aaron and his sons in Moses' day. So in Malachi's day the descendants of Aaron were expected to exhibit six principal characteristics if they truly feared Yahweh.

1. Incorruptible in doctrine (2:6a): **The law of truth was in his mouth...** First, the priest was to be incorruptible in doctrine. The term *law* (*tôrāh*) embraces all forms of religious instruction. The priests were not to teach their own views, human theories or speculations. They were to teach only the infallible and unchangeable *truth* as revealed in the

---

thought of losing the high privilege of priesthood by disdain or carelessness was horrifying to Levi.

written word. *Law of truth* is equivalent to "true law." The phrase probably includes a truthful and accurate rendering of legal decisions as well as formal instruction.

   2. *Upright in speech (2:6b)*: **and iniquity was not found in his lips.** Second, the priest was to be unwavering in judgments. *Iniquity* (*'avlāh*) refers to injustice, whether in speech or deed, often with connotations of violence. *Found in his lips* again highlights the teaching function of priests. They were not to twist the law to fit their own fancies. Their legal decisions were to be made without prejudice. No unfair decisions or perverse judgments were to proceed from their mouth.

   3. *Devout in conduct (2:6c)*: **In peace and in uprightness he walked with me...** Third, the priest was to be devout in conduct. His life as well as his teaching was to be pure and good. He was to be a friend of God, walking in *peace* (*šālôm*, i.e., full harmony), i.e., perfectly, with him. *Uprightness* (*mîšōr*) lit., means "in levelness, in straightness." The term can embrace the ideas of righteousness and fairness; but in this context it probably means something like "consistently." A personal walk of godliness and fellowship is in view.[321] The expression *walked* (r. *hlk*) *with me* (God) recalls the commendations given to Enoch (Gn 5:22) and Noah (6:9).

   4. *Zealous in labors (2:6d)*: **and many they caused to turn from iniquity.** Fourth, priests were to be focused in labor. Their faithful word, walk and work caused many to turn from sin. *Iniquity* (*'āvōn*) or "crookedness" is used in the OT to refer to any sort of sin, iniquity or unrighteousness. It is a broad term that indicates something that is displeasing to God.

   5. *Profound in knowledge (2:7a)*: **For the lips of a priest ought to preserve knowledge, and from his mouth men should seek instruction...** Fifth, the priest was to be immersed in knowledge. The first two lines of v 7 are related synonymously emphasizing what a priest ought to do. The theme and even the language of v 6a are repeated. The proper

---

[321] Stuart (*MPEEC*, 1320) thinks *walked with* means "attend" or "serve," referring to ministerial function rather than personal life.

role of the priest as the teacher among God's people is being emphasized.

The duty of every priest was to study the law and to teach it faithfully. This includes the knowledge of correct ritual and ceremonial rules. The *knowledge,* however, is also the true knowledge of God that finds expression in a moral life and spiritual aspirations. The priest was the appointed interpreter of the law. The people should have confidence in their priest to teach the holy word accurately.

6. Honored in his office (2:7b): *for he is the messenger of Yahweh of Hosts.* Sixth, the priest was to be honored in his office. The term *messenger* (*malāch*) is used about 50x of that supernatural manifestation—theophany—of Yahweh who occupied the role of intermediary *par excellence.* This angel of Yahweh is often indistinguishable from Yahweh himself. In these passages the expression is generally translated *angel of Yahweh.* The expression is used 3x to designate a prophet (2 Chr 36:15-16; Isa 44:26; Hag 1:13). Malachi is saying that priests also were to have the high privilege and responsibility of being Yahweh's spokesmen. This passage establishes the importance of the priesthood and the great honor which devolved on those who filled that office. Unfortunately the priests of Malachi's day utterly failed in this responsibility, and thus relinquished all right to the honor associated with it.

Betrayal of Covenant Ideal
Malachi 2:8-9

This unit begins with a grammatical construction that signals a change in subject (from the original priests called *Levi*) and a contrast. The priests of Malachi's day had betrayed every standard of the covenant with the priesthood. Malachi's indictment against them contains six points.

A. Perverse in Life (2:8a):

But as for you, you have turned from the way... The idiom *turned from the way* sometimes indicates accidental or inadvertent deviation from a standard where the expectations

Malachi: 1:6-2:9

may not have been crystal clear. The context here, however, indicates that the priestly pattern was well established in law and in the conduct of godly priestly ancestors. The current crop of priests deliberately had chosen to go in a different direction. They were not just wrong; they were disobedient. *The way* refers to the way of holiness. Their lives were the opposite of exemplary.

B. Pernicious in Example (2:8b):

You have caused many to stumble in the law... By their example and teaching the priests had made the law a stumbling block, causing many to disregard and disobey it. They were *unfaithful to the people. Stumble* (r. *kšl*) is a metaphor for failure or disobedience, i.e., sin. This is the exact opposite of what the priests were required to do (Nm 6:27) and what godly ancestors had in fact done (v 6).

C. Unfaithful in Commitment (2:8c):

You have corrupted the covenant of Levi... The priests were covenant breakers. *The covenant with Levi* is the same as *my covenant with Levi* in v 4. In the ancient world an announcement of covenant violation set the stage for the Great King to execute a covenant curse upon the violator.

According to Ezra (2:36-58) 4,289 priests, 341 Levites, and 392 temple servants returned to Judea in 538 BC. There is no evidence to suggest that these priests were not faithful in fulfilling their duties. By the time Ezra (458 BC) and Nehemiah (445 BC) returned, however, there is evidence of serious decline within the priestly class. See Ezra 10:18-24; Neh 13:4-5.

This does not mean that there were no faithful priests in Malachi's time. Some priests worked faithfully on rebuilding Jerusalem's wall (Neh 3) and taught God's law (Neh 8-9). A number of religious leaders joined Nehemiah himself in signing an agreement to keep the covenant of God (Neh 10:1-13).[322] On the other hand, while Nehemiah was away in Susa

---

[322]Stuart (*MPEEC*, 1323) negatively interprets the priests entering into this covenant to keep the covenant, indicating that they had not been as faithful as they should have been in observing the priestly rules. This interpretation,

Postexilic Prophets

having his governorship renewed serious lapses are reported in the priestly family (Neh 13:4-6, 29). During the period of Nehemiah's absence Malachi arose to challenge the straying priests.

D. Contemptible in Reputation (2:9a):

So I have made you contemptible and humiliated before the people... So I ($v^e gam\ ^{a}n\hat{i}$) indicates that that Yahweh has responded to the conduct of the priests. The pronoun is emphatic as if to say, "You have chosen your path, now here is what I have done."

Judgment brings curse, which in this case is expressed in two adjectives. The priests had despised Yahweh, so he was causing them to be despised before the people. The verb *made* (r. *ntn* in perfect) is usually rendered "give." It could be rendered in English as a perfect of certitude ("I give/am giving = making) or as a prophetic perfect and rendered as a future ("I shall give = make) in English.

Contemptible (r. *bzh* Niph. participle) has the idea of despised, vile, worthless, and despicable. The term *humiliated* ($\check{s}^e ph\bar{a}l\hat{i}m$) has much the same idea. *Before the people* refers to those to whom the priests were intended to minister.

E. Negligent in Duty (2:9b):

According as you have not kept my ways... My ways refers to the priestly directives of the law. The priests had been unfaithful to their commission. Perhaps the priests who remained focused and faithful were tainted by association with those who took their responsibilities lightly. Thus the blanket condemnation is appropriate.

F. Prejudiced in Judgment (2:9c):

But have had respect of persons in the law. The priests had perverted judgment; they had shown partiality in the administration of the law. They were unfaithful to God's stan-

---

however, requires that Nehemiah himself had been unfaithful, for his name appeared at the top of the list of signatories. The most godly souls in the church are often the first to want to declare their rededication to the things of God.

dard. *Had respect* is lit., "lifting up faces." This idiom means to regard highly or, negatively as here, to show favoritism and partiality. The terms of God's law were to be administered without fear or favor.

Postexilic Prophets

PART TWO: PEOPLE SIN AGAINST LOVE 2:10-4:3

Sin of Intermarriage and Divorce
Malachi 2:10-16

Israelites were forbidden to marry those who were devotees of pagan gods (Ex 34:16; Dt 7:3). Yet religious intermarriage with unbelievers was a major problem in the postexilic community. A few years before the time of Malachi, Ezra had forced those who had married heathen women to divorce them (Ezra 10:3-5).

Unlawful Marriages
Malachi 2:10-12

The intermarriage problem had arisen again. Malachi points out three terrible truths about these unlawful marriages.

A. Intermarriage Defiled the Covenant (2:10):
Malachi asked three difficult questions that spell out the aggravations of intermarriage.

1. Question #1: common ancestry (2:10a): **Is there not one father to all of us?** The syntax ($h^a l\bar{o}$') is the same as in 1:2 in which the interrogative is in reality a bold declaration. The father of all Israel was not Abraham,[323] because he was the father of other peoples besides Israel. God was the father of Israel (cf. 1:6). He had created this special nation at Mount Sinai. The rhetorical question does not teach the doctrine of the universal fatherhood of God. Rather here the text is stressing the uniqueness of Israel as a nation. Yahweh was not only

---

[323] Abraham is called Israel's father in several passages. Isaiah (63:16), however, contrasts the notion of Abraham's fatherhood of Israel with that of Yahweh. In the light of Mal 1:6 this passage clearly refers to the spiritual rather than the biological father of the nation.

their father, he was their only father. The implication is that Israel owed Yahweh exclusive devotion. Malachi is laying the groundwork for his attack on religious syncretism.

Stuart[324] points out the appropriateness of referring to Yahweh as Israel's father in a marriage context. In the ancient world the father was the principal negotiator in arranging a marriage. The implication is that Yahweh is (or should be) in charge of their choices of marriage partners.

2. *Question #2: common purpose (2:10b)*: **Did not one God create us?** The second rhetorical question again stresses Yahweh's exclusive ownership of Israel. *Create* (r. *br'*) does not refer to the original creation as that would apply as well to all nations. Malachi is referring to the creative act by which God chose Israel as his own people. The use of creation vocabulary in reference to Israel is quite common in the OT.[325]

3. *Question #3: common brotherhood (2:10c)*: **Why do we deal treacherously each man with his brother to defile the covenant of our fathers?** *Deal treacherously* (r. *bgd*) means deliberately to fail to meet an obligation or expectation. In the OT the verb is used of disloyalty in personal or national obligations (e.g., Jer 3:20-21; 12:1), a specific example of which is marital unfaithfulness. Treacherous marital betrayal can be committed by a wife against her husband (Jer 3:20) or vice versa (Ex 21:8).

It follows that if Israel as a people has one father (Yahweh), then Israel is a holy family. Any sin that affects community life is a sin against a *brother*. In the third rhetorical question the prophet includes himself as a member of the sinful nation. The sin of the people, which Malachi has yet to identify, is a sin against brotherly love.

The yet-to-be-identified sin defiled (r. *chll*) *the covenant*. The same expression is found in Ps 89:34. The verb is used to refer to any actions that profaned, polluted, or tainted something that was holy. *Covenant of our fathers* refers to the Sinai covenant (cf. Jer 31:32; 34:12). The exodus generation accepted a covenant as the constitution of Israel on behalf of

---

[324]*MPEEC*, 1329.
[325]E.g., Dt 32:6; Ps 78; 121; 124; 135; 148; Isa 43:1, 7, 15.

Malachi: 2:10-4:3

all future generations. The sin, which Malachi is yet to identify, was a menace to the distinctive faith and very existence of Israel. God had often warned against marrying the daughters of unbelievers.[326]

B. Intermarriage Defiled the Nation (2:11):
1. Characterization of the sin (2:11a): ***Judah has broken faith, and an abomination has been done…*** *Judah* is used twice in the v. Here Judah is construed as feminine since it is used with a feminine verb, as is the case with Edom in 1:4. In its second use *Judah* is construed as masculine.[327] The mid-verse gender switch is probably intentional, signifying that the entire population is involved in covenant violation.

Has broken faith (r. *bgd*) is used of covenant violation. *Abomination* (*tō'ēbhāh*) indicates the seriousness of the infraction. This word is used to indicate something God will not under any circumstances tolerate.[328] An abomination automatically defiled the people (cf. Ex 34:15-16) or the sanctuary (Lv 20:2-3) or both.

2. Location of the sin (2:11b): ***in Israel and in Jerusalem.*** *Israel* is the covenant name, the honorable name of the twelve tribes of which the tribe of Judah was the major component. Here, however, the name is probably being used geographically. The abomination was being committed in God's land—the holy land. In *Jerusalem*, the site of the temple and capital of the nation, the abomination was evident.

3. Result of the sin (2:11c): ***Judah has profaned the sanctuary of Yahweh which he loves…*** *Judah* here is masculine—the bookend of a merism that embraces the entire population. *Profaned* (r. *chll*) is repeated from the previous v. *Sanctuary* (*qōdeš*) probably refers to the nation of Israel as in Lv 19:8, the only other passage where this precise terminology "profane the sanctuary of Yahweh" is used (cf. Ex 15:17; Isa 63:18). Holiness is a fundamental attribute of God. Be-

---

[326] Ex 34:16; Dt 7:3; Josh 23:12, 13. Ezra (chs 9-10) and Nehemiah (13:23-28) contended against it.
[327] In Hebrew *nations* can be construed as either masculine or feminine.
[328] Some of the abominations identified in OT are idolatry, child sacrifice, magical rites, incest, and temple prostitution.

cause Yahweh is holy, his people were to be holy (i.e., set apart from the world of sin) in all areas of their lives. Now, however, the holiness of the nation[329] had been violated.

Which he loves echoes 1:2 and reinforces the notion that God had chosen Israel. The presence of this parenthetical clause supports the interpretation of sanctuary = nation. The fact that God loved Israel so much aggravated the treachery of the national conduct.

4. *Identification of the sin (2:11d)*: **and has married the daughter of a foreign god.** At last Malachi names the particular sin that was an abomination in Israel. It involved marriage. The men of Israel were guilty of the sin of intermarriage with unbelievers. *Daughter of a foreign god (*'ēl*)* occurs only here in the OT; but the use of the term '*ēl* with the word foreign (*nēkhar*) is as old as Moses (Dt 32:12; Ps 81:9). *The daughter* of such a god is a woman who adhered to a foreign deity.[330] Such marriages always had been condemned because of the danger of seduction into idolatry.[331] The principle of holiness—separation from the world—had thus been violated.

Both Ezra (chs 9-10) and Nehemiah (13:6) battled the same sin in the postexilic community. It permeated all strata of society, including the officials and priesthood. Thus there was no enforcement of laws against the practice. Teaching that it was wrong was muted. So outrageous was this sin that the Book of Ezra closes with a list of those who had engaged in it.

C. Intermarriage has Terrible Consequences (2:12):

1. *It evokes divine judgment (2:12a)*: **May Yahweh cut off ... from the tents of Jacob...** The verb form invokes a terrible punishment upon those who profane the sanctuary of

---

[329]More commonly *qōdeš* refers to the temple. Others think the reference is to the marriage bond (Kimchi), or to holiness in the abstract as reflected in the holy nation.

[330]The idiom "daughter of," like its counterpart "son of," can mean one who identifies with, participates in, or represents something or someone. See Gn 6:2, 4, 27:46; 1 Sam 1:16; Isa 1:8; 22:4. Another interpretation: an alliance between Judah and a heathen nation.

[331]Ex 34:16; Lv 21:14; Nm 36:6; Dt 7:3; 13:6-9. In such prohibitions the Canaanites are mentioned as a synecdoche for all idolatrous nations.

Yahweh. *Cut off* (r. *krt*) is used throughout the OT in reference to a specific punishment, viz. removal from the community (e.g., Lv 17:10; 20:3-6). In the law the means by which the elimination is accomplished is ambiguous. Probably the removal could be by execution or excommunication as determined by the judges in particular cases. In some cases, as here, Yahweh himself does the cutting off. This probably refers to sudden or premature death.

Tents (*'oh°lîm*) is metonymy for the nation, the place where people live (e.g., Nm 24:5; Jer 30:18). *Jacob* is often parallel to *Israel*. The name refers to the nation as a whole, not some part thereof. Thus the punishment for those who engage in intermarriage with the heathen is loss of citizenship or expulsion from the people of God.

2. *It affects each participant (2:12b):* **the man**[332] **who does this awaker and answerer**. Some take this to mean that both the sinner and his kin will be exterminated. Probably, however, the reference is to the transgressor and his descendants. Both will be deprived of their position as members of the covenant nation.

Awaker and answerer is found only here in OT. This is probably a military phrase derived from the challenge of sentinels and the answer thereto.[333] In time the phrase came to signify totality,[334] e.g., all the inhabitants of a city. Here the idiom means "every single one." This v does not anticipate a complete extermination of the nation (Laetsch), but a judgment on each individual sinner.

3. *It will not be overlooked because of sacrifice (2:12c):* **and the one who offers an offering to Yahweh of hosts**. This clause has the sense "even if he offers an offering." Even if those guilty of intermarriage were faithful in temple worship,

---

[332] The Hebrew has a *lamed* on *'îš*. For this reason some translations take this as an indirect object or prepositional phrase (cf. NASB; NIV). It is best, however, to view *'îš* as a direct object. Lamed is regularly used in Aramaic, and occasionally in Hebrew, to introduce a direct object. See GKC §177n.

[333] Other suggestions as to the meaning of the Hebrew phrase: master & scholar; son and grandson; master and servant; stranger and kinsman.

[334] Hebrew has several word pairs that signify totality: root and branch (e.g., Mal 4:1); slave and free (e.g., 1 Kgs 14:10), head and tail (e.g., Isa 9:14), coming and going (e.g., 2 Sam 3:25), good and evil (e.g., Gn 3:5).

they will still be *cut off* by Yahweh. Propitiatory offerings will not placate the Lord. One cannot hope to find forgiveness for sins deliberately committed without genuine repentance and cessation of the offensive act.[335]

This statement was far more shocking to Malachi's audience than to us. It is a direct slam against pagan theology which viewed sacrifice as a means of controlling the gods. In return for sacrificial "food" the gods were obligated to do as the worshiper petitioned. Biblical sacrifice, however, expressed gratitude and symbolized repentance. Without a radical change in direction the person who had deliberately transgressed God's law could not find pardon through participation in religious exercises.

Unlawful Divorce
Malachi 2:13-16

Marriage was instituted by God; it is to be governed by his law. In Malachi's day the people had forgotten the fundamental purpose of marriage. They also were disobeying the divine principles which govern that institution. Malachi charged them with unlawful divorces as well as unlawful marriages.

Divorce under the Law of Moses was permitted. If a husband found some indecency in his wife he was permitted to send her away so long as he provided her with a legal document declaring her to be a free woman. Remarriage following such a lawful divorce was permitted (Dt 24:1-4). Unlawful divorce involved the casting off of a wife for any reason other than indecent behavior. Unlawful divorce was another sin against the covenant that had become common in the postexilic community. The prophet makes four observations about the sin of unlawful divorce.

---

[335] Another interpretation: God will cut off the priest who attempts to offer an offering to atone for the sin of one who has intermarried.

Malachi: 2:10-4:3

A. Divorce Hurts People (2:13a):
Another thing you do: You cover the altar of Yahweh with tears, with weeping, and with sighing... Another thing (*šēnît*) is lit., "a second [thing]." The term is often used by the prophets to introduce additional revelation (e.g., Jer 1:13). Malachi introduces a second charge of sin against the marriage covenant.[336] The *tears, weeping* and *sighing* probably come from the wives who had been cast out in favor of the younger pagan women.[337] They took their agony and anger to the temple altar.[338]

B. Divorce Disrupts Worship (2:13b):
Inasmuch as there is no longer facing unto the offering nor taking with good will from your hand. Intermarriage with unbelievers had created a barrier—a barrier of tears—between the sinners and God. Yahweh no longer regarded with favor any of their offerings.

C. Divorce Violates a Covenant (2:14):
1. Denial of the charge (2:14a): **You ask, Why?** The men deny responsibility for the agonizing wailing at the altar. *Why* (*'al māh*) is lit. "on account of what?" It is a common interrogative in the OT. This is now the fourth time that Malachi's audience has disputed an affirmation by the prophet.

2. Marriage vows are sacred (2:14b): **Because Yahweh has witnessed between you and the wife of your youth...** *Because* (*'al kî*) occurs only 5x in OT as an introduction to an explanation. This construction is most appropriate here as a response to the interrogative *'al māh*. Since the guilty men denied responsibility for the agonizing wailing at the altar, Malachi sharpened his accusation. He explains why their offerings were no longer accepted.

---

[336] Others take this to mean *a second time*, i.e., you are repeating the same sin you committed in the days of Ezra.
[337] Another view is that Malachi is describing the emotional pagan worship style (cf. 1 Kgs 18:26-30) in which God will take no delight.
[338] NIV seems to take the weeping to be that of the perpetrators. They were weeping because they knew that their offerings were not being accepted.

Postexilic Prophets

The term *witnessed* (r. *'ûd* Hiphil) indicates a covenant context. Covenants had to be witnessed. Israelite covenants, either implicitly or explicitly, have *Yahweh* as the witness. In the covenant context the term "witness" means more than a passive observer or one who bears testimony in a court of law. A covenant witness was the third party to the covenant whose task it was to enforce the terms of the covenant upon the primaries.

Apparently God is a witness to marriage vows. Malachi viewed marriage as a legal contract between a man and a woman with Yahweh as the third party or covenant enforcer. Biblical law does not view cohabitation or extra-marital sex as equivalent to marriage. The covenant envisioned here is between responsible persons, not families in some pre-arranged childhood betrothal.[339] Families might work to negotiate the terms of the marriage contract; but the covenant itself was between the principals.

The expression *wife of your youth* (*'ēšet n^e'ûrêkhā*) is designed to evoke emotional recollections of happier days. Surely the passing of years should not weaken marital love but rather purify it, solidify it and deepen it.[340]

3. *Violation of marriage vows is treacherous (2:14c):* ***against whom you have dealt treacherously...*** The hardened sinners suppressed the memories of youthful joy and the solemn vows of marital commitment. They *dealt treacherously*[341] against their Jewish wives. The one who initiates an unlawful divorce is a traitor! Only for the cause of fornication may a believer lawfully initiate divorce proceedings. All other grounds are unlawful. The language indicates the seriousness of divorce. In the ancient world women were virtually destitute after divorce, especially if they had no male

---

[339] Stuart, (*MPEEC*, 1338) assumes that marriages in Bible times were arranged even before children were born. With the exception of slave girls that were destined to marry within a master's family, there does not appear to be evidence of such a practice in Israel. Where marriages are arranged in the OT the parties, though in some cases young by western standards, where nonetheless viewed as "adult."

[340] Theo. Laetsch, *Bible Commentary: The Minor Prophets* (St. Louis: Concordia, 1956), 527.

[341] The LXX renders "whom you have deserted."

children to care for them. Casting off such a faithful spouse to satisfy the lust of the flesh is therefore considered by God a treacherous act.

4. *Violation of marriage vows is injurious (2:14d):* **even though she is your companion, your covenant wife.** Malachi already has used one phrase (*wife of your youth*) to underscore the heinous nature of the casting aside of Jewish wives. Now he adds two more descriptive phrases to describe the wife that has been cast aside.

First, the wife that has been cast aside is a faithful partner of many years. The former wife was *your companion* (*chabhērāh*). This noun comes from a root meaning "to bind, join or unite." The masculine and feminine nouns derived from this root indicate a companion in the sense of a friend or partner. This is clearly the language of equality. Although the surrounding culture treated women as inferior to men—and this idea leaks into Israel from time to time—the biblical ideal is that husband and wife are co-laborers in the vocation of home-building. God joined together man and wife in a union which was to be severed only by death. Godly men were to cleave to their wives in love and affection (Gn 2:24).

Second, the castoff wife was a covenant wife, or "wife of your covenant." *Covenant* refers, not to the Sinai covenant, but to the marriage covenant established in Eden. The previous phrase introduced a practical—perhaps even romantic—consideration. This phrase views the situation legally. Simply put, the men had no right to divorce their wives because they were bound by solemn, legal covenant to them.[342] Vows of fidelity had been exchanged before God and men. Now those marriage covenants had been set asunder because of lust.

---

[342] Another interpretation: the divorced wife belonged to the covenant between God and Israel, i.e., was of Jewish faith as opposed to the daughter of a strange god.

Postexilic Prophets

D. Divorce Frustrates Marriage Design (2:15):

This v is the most controversial and difficult v in the book (Laetsch; Packard).[343] The only clause in the v that is indisputable as to meaning is the last one that once again forbids divorcing the wife of one's youth. Most likely the preceding ambiguous clauses offer some argument as to why such divorce is monstrous. What better way to reinforce a prohibition of divorcing a wife of youth on no grounds other than lust for another than to contrast that practice with the original intent of marriage.

| TRANSLATIONS OF MALACHI 2:15 ||||
KJV	ASV	RSV	NASB
"And did not he make one? Yet had he the residue of the spirit..."	"And did he not make one, although he had the residue of the spirit? And wherefore one? He sought a godly seed."	"Has not the one God made us and sustained us for the spirit of life? And what does he desire? Godly offspring."	"But not one has done so who has a remnant of the Spirit. And what did that one do while he was seeking a godly offspring?"

1. Original marriage a unity (2:15a): **And did he not make one?** The literal rendering of the first three Hebrew words is "and no/not one he made." Some support for reading these three words as a question comes from ancient versions.[344] The reference seems to be the original marriage. Jesus may have been referring to this v in Mt 19:4. The first rhetorical question calls attention to the fact that in the beginning God created only one pair and made them one flesh.[345]

---

[343] An excellent study: Gordon P. Hugenberger, *Marriage as a Covenant; Biblical Law and Ethics as Developed from Malachi.* Grand Rapids: 1994.

[344] Reading $h^a l\bar{o}$' for $v^e l\bar{o}$' follows Targum Jonathan, the Syriac and the Vulgate.

[345] Traditional Jewish interpreters offer this interpretation: The people are trying to justify divorcing their wives. "The one" is Abraham. He "divorced" Hagar. Yes, but he had a godly spirit; he was seeking godly seed. The RSV offers yet another interpretation: "Has not the one God made us and sustained us for the spirit of life?" The NASB renders the first clause as a statement: "But not one has done so who has a remnant of the Spirit."

Alternatively, the meaning could be that God only made one woman for Adam, thus setting a pattern for life-long monogamous marriage.

2. *Original marriage monogamous (2:15b):* **although he had the residue of the Spirit...** This translation represents three Hebrew words that literally translated say "and a remnant of spirit to him." Again the words are ambiguous; but the reference seems to be to God who has an abundance of the life-giving spirit or creative power. The point is that God could have made several wives for Adam. Marriage is monogamous by divine appointment.

3. *Original marriage had lofty aims (2:15c):* **And wherefore one? Because he was seeking godly seed.** And wherefore one (*ûmāh hā'echād*) is literally, "what the one?" Paraphrased the words may mean, "What was the reason he created but one pair?"

The answer to the second rhetorical question is this: *He was seeking godly seed* ($m^ebhaqqēš\ zera'\ ^elōhîm$), lit., "seeking (ms part.) a godly seed." To make sense of this cryptic statement we must supply a subject. The idea seems to be that marriage was designed by God to perpetuate a godly seed (offspring) on earth. Ultimately that godly seed included Messiah (cf. Gn 3:15). So there was a messianic intention in the structure of marriage.

4. *Original marriage calls for introspection (2:15d):* **So guard yourselves in your spirit and against the wife of your youth let not a man act treacherously.** Based on the implications of his two rhetorical questions Malachi sets forth a stern warning. *Guard yourselves in your spirit*, i.e., your spiritual life, your faith in and love for God. Persistent disobedience in the matter of divorce can cause one to lose what spiritual life he has. The warning is made even stronger by being addressed in the second person to the guilty parties. On *wife of your youth*, see previous v. *Let not a man act treacherously* (r. *bgd*) is imperfect 3ms used as a jussive,[346] making the general warning of the previous verb very personal.

This seems to mean that no truly spiritual man would ever have divorced his covenant wife.

[346]GKC §107o.

313

Postexilic Prophets

E. Unlawful Divorce Angers God (2:16):
Again this v is very cryptic. Scholars have defended a wide-range of interpretations.

1. God hates the sin (2:16a): **For I hate divorce, says Yahweh God of Israel.** *For* introduces the reason for the admonition of the previous v. There is no equivalent to the first person pronoun in the Hebrew text. The three Hebrew words (*kî sānē' šallach*) literally translated are "for hating putting away." The popular English translations (NIV, NASB, NRSV) are justified in inserting the first person pronoun, for no other rendering of the three Hebrew words really makes any sense.[347]

Hate (*sānē'*) is a participle, indicating continuous action. There is irony in the use of this term by the Lord, for it is the same term used to describe a wife who has fallen into disfavor (Dt 21:15; 22:13; 24:3). Thus a worshiper who has divorced a wife who has fallen into disfavor has himself fallen into disfavor with the Lord.

Divorce literally is "sending away." God hates divorce because it was not a part of his original plan and because it involves all the difficulties cited by Malachi in the preceding vv.

Says Yahweh is the first of two messenger formulas in the v. The controversial nature of the sentiments expressed requires this forceful statement of authority.[348]

2. God hates the results of this sin (2:16b): **and him that covers his garment with violence, says Yahweh of Hosts.** The four Hebrew words preceding the messenger formula are again difficult to interpret. The presence of the second messenger formula in the v suggests that Malachi is

---

[347] The first person singular pronoun is justified because 1) Yahweh is the speaker; 2) *hate* (*sānē'*) is a participle requiring some subject in this context; and 3) the infinitive absolute *šallach* is difficult to connect to the participle otherwise.

[348] The presence of the two messenger formulas in the v supports the view that two independent statements are being made, not one conditional statement ("if one hates and divorces, then...") which some commentators prefer.

Malachi: 2:10-4:3

again saying something that is designed to be controversial, hence in need of undergirding authority.

The proposed translation follows NASB.[349] Literally the words read: "and he has covered violence/crime/wrong upon/over his garment." God hates divorce for what it does to women and children.

The man who treacherously divorces his covenant wife *covers his garment with violence*. Clearly this is an idiom of the postexilic era; but it is otherwise unattested. The idea seems to be that divorce is like a filthy splotch on a man's garment, on his reputation, his life. One commentator has suggested that in modern terms it means something like airing dirty linen in public.[350] In a similar vein Stuart suggests the idea of "crime on the clothes."[351] Whatever the precise meaning of the idiom, the men who engaged in aversion divorce incurred obvious and inescapable guilt. *Violence* (*chāmās*) is a strong word indicating crime, even serious crime. Such is the way that God's message characterizes frivolous divorce.

F. Final Warning (2:16c):

So guard yourselves in your spirit and don't ever commit treachery. This is an abbreviation of the warning from v 15. *Guard yourselves* again is Niphal imperfect 2mp. *In your spirit* refers to the inner attitude. *Spirit* is singular, suggesting that there was a collective attitude in the community that needed correcting. *Don't ever* (*lō'*) is stronger than *do not* (*'al*) used in the previous v. The latter term often indicates temporary prohibition; the term used here indicates permanent prohibition—Ten Commandments type prohibition. The verb *commit treachery* in the previous v was 3ms used as a jussive—"let him not commit treachery." Here the verb is 2mp, indicating a community-wide prohibition.

---

[349] The NIV treats the clause freely, adding a verb and re-pointing the existing verb as an infinitive absolute: "and I hate a man's covering himself with violence as well as with his garment."

[350] B. Glazier-McDonald, *Malachi: The Divine Messenger*. Atlanta: Scholars, 1987), 112.

[351] Stuart, *MPEEC*, 1343.

Sin of Doubt and Skepticism
Malachi 2:17-3:6

Malachi addressed a complaint of the people which he saw as an evidence of doubt. He answered that skepticism with a dramatic announcement of the coming of Messiah.

Complaint of the People
Malachi 2:17

A. Their Skepticism Wearies God (2:17a):
You have wearied Yahweh with your words. Skepticism wearies God. The Hebrew perfect tense describes the act in its completion. It is sobering to contemplate that our emotional outbursts and ill-advised, unfounded and unjustified questioning of God's workings are a source of irritation to the Creator. He gets tired of hearing our constant gripes.

B. Their Skepticism is Disputed (2:17b):
But you say, How have we wearied him? Again the people demanded proof of the charge against them. In a sense Malachi already has answered their question. The problem is in their speech which reflects, of course, the attitude of their hearts. The skeptics, however, are unaware that their complaints affect God in the way indicated. They want to know exactly what they have been saying that wearies God. Complainers generally do not realize how negative and obnoxious their snide remarks and cynical questions really are—to man as well as to God.

C. Their Skepticism Focused on Divine Justice (2:17c, d):
1. Their emotional observation (2:17c): **When you say, Everyone who does evil is good in the eyes of Yahweh and he delights in them...** We should not conclude that Malachi is quoting something that he overheard (as in Ezek 18:2). More likely he is summarizing the attitude of the people which was being expressed verbally in a variety of ways.

Malachi: 2:10-4:3

Many in the postexilic community felt that the moral and religious climate had deteriorated seriously. In their view Yahweh was doing nothing about it. This non-intervention was interpreted to mean that Yahweh was not overly upset about what was going on. In fact, as these skeptics viewed the situation, God must have endorsed all the shenanigans that were being perpetrated in the community. Malachi captures the frustration and resignation of the people by framing this emotional outburst.

Who are the skeptical complainers? Certainly the pious in the community must have been frustrated by all the ugly things Malachi has documented in the preceding vv. The complainers, however, are probably the entire population. No one squeals more when victimized by crime than one who is himself a perpetrator of crime.

Here is the age-old complaint: the wicked prosper while the righteous are in low estate. The underlying assumption is that material prosperity always results from divine blessing and implies divine approval. God must delight in the wicked else they would not be so blessed. The skeptics accused God of favoring the wicked. Syllogistically, their argument looks like this:

> God only blesses those in whom he delights.
> The wicked are blessed.
> Therefore God delights in the wicked.

2. *Their logical demonstration (2:17d):* **or where is the God of judgment?** *Judgment* (*mišpāṭ*) can also mean "justice." The two concepts are closely related, for without accountability and punishment there can be no true justice. Viewing this question theologically, it is clear that those who were complaining were believers, not atheists. Furthermore, the complainers were theologically correct in associating justice with God (e.g., Dt 4:5-8; Ps 89:14). Yahweh is in fact the God of justice/judgment.

In essence the discouraged people were asking, "Where is God when things go haywire?" This complaint-question is the logical conclusion which the people had reached in view of

Postexilic Prophets

their observation in the first half of the v. Evil is either pleasing to God or there is no God of justice. Both believers[352] and skeptics through the ages have echoed similar arguments against the God who has revealed himself as absolutely just. Stated syllogistically,

> If God did not delight in the wicked, he would bring judgment upon them.
> God has brought no judgment upon the wicked.
> Therefore God must delight in the wicked.

Promise to the People
Malachi 3:1

The God of judgment was nearer than any of the skeptics imagined. Malachi stressed that the coming of God will be both certain and sudden.

A. **His Coming is Certain** (3:1a).

Behold, I am sending my messenger, who will clear the way before me. In this v God responds to the frustrations expressed in the preceding v. An announcement of supreme importance is introduced by the word *behold!* The term suggests something shocking, yet certain to happen. *I am sending* (*hinneh* + participle) suggests action in process or imminent. *My messenger* (*mal'ākhî*) is the personal name of the prophet who wrote this v. The term is often translated "angel"; but here an earthly messenger is intended. The same messenger is mentioned in 4:5. The NT identifies this messenger as John the Baptist.[353]

---

[352]Some of the believers who raised the question of God's justice are Moses (Dt 32:5, 16-18, 28); the psalmists (Pss 37; 49; 73), the prophet Habakkuk (1:2-4, 12-17), Paul (Rom 1:29-32; Peter (2 Pet 3:4); and John (Rev 6:9-10).

[353]See Mk 1:2; Mt 11:10; Lk 7:27; Cf. Isa 40:3. Others identify this messenger as an angel (Kimchi); Malachi himself (Abarbanel); Messiah b. Joseph who precede the coming of Messiah b. David (Ibn Ezra); the whole choir of divine messengers who are to prepare the way for the coming salvation (Hengstenberg).

The messenger will *clear the way*. The verb (r. *pnh* in Piel) means "to turn aside, turn away," thus "remove or clear." Behind the phrase is the practice of clearing a road of people or obstacles when the sovereign was traveling. In a metaphorical sense messengers have been sent ahead throughout history to settle important issues before the arrival of great leaders. *Before me* indicates that the Sovereign (i.e. Yahweh) is the speaker. John prepared the way for the coming of God by preaching repentance and removing sin which stood between God and his people. The first person singular pronoun clearly identifies Yahweh with Messiah.

B. His Coming is Sudden (3:1b):

The Lord whom you are seeking shall suddenly come to his temple... Following the work of the preparatory messenger (John the Baptist) *the Lord whom you are seeking shall suddenly come*. The skeptics had asked, "Where is the God of judgment?" (2:17); thus the one who is coming is God. The Hebrew expression *hā-'ādôn, the Lord*, appears 8x in the OT. In each of the seven other occurrences it is used alongside the proper name Yahweh (e.g., Ex 23:17; Isa 1:24; 3:1). Thus *the Lord* (Yahweh) is about to come, the God of judgment whom the skeptics were seeking.

Suddenly (*pit'ōm*) indicates that his coming will be unexpected. The announcement of his birth and the commencement of his ministry some thirty years after his birth were both unexpected. The sudden intervention of God in the affairs of this earth is a theme of both testaments.[354]

The Lord (Yahweh) will suddenly come *to his temple* (*hêkhāl*). That the Lord should come to his temple is another theme common to both testaments.[355] The Hebrews viewed the Jerusalem temple as Yahweh's palace. In Malachi's day that temple—the Second Temple—had already been built. To that very temple Jesus made his triumphal entry on Palm Sunday.

The change in persons from *me* to *his* should be noted. The Gospel writers quote this as if it were spoken by the Fa-

---

[354]Isa 29:5; 48:3; Jer 15:8; 18:22; Lk 12:39-40; 2 Pet 3:10.
[355]Ezek 43:4; Zech 6:12-15; Mt 21:12-16; Eph 2:21; Rev 7:15-17.

ther to the Son that is, they use the second person in the second instance. It would seem from this that the coming Messiah is one with the God who is speaking in v. 1. He who comes is the same one who authorized the temple to be built in the OT. Jesus was presented as an infant in the temple (Lk 2:22ff). He also visited the temple for teaching purposes (cf. Jn 2:13; 5:1ff; 7:14ff).[356]

C. He Comes with a Covenant (3:1c):

The messenger of the covenant, whom you desire, behold, he comes, says Yahweh of Hosts. The Lord who suddenly comes to his temple is further identified as *the messenger of the covenant*. This is the only place where this title is employed. Apparently this *messenger of the covenant* is the same as "the angel of Yahweh" who appears throughout the OT as a visible manifestation of God (cf. Heb 9:15). The *covenant* is the new covenant announced by Jesus and ratified by his shed blood.[357]

Some prefer to take *behold he comes* as the opening words of v 2. For this there is no grammatical objection.

Problem for the People
Malachi 3:2

A. Power of his Coming (3:2a):

But who can endure the day of his coming? Who can stand when he appears? The Jews expected Messiah to come to judge their enemies. They considered their enemies to be God's enemies. The Jews failed to realize that because they had violated terms of the covenant they had made themselves enemies of God subject to judgment. Malachi warned the skeptics that they will be the first to be judged. None of the ungodly would be able to stand under the burden of this judgment.

The day of his coming is the day of Yahweh's coming, elsewhere called "the day of Yahweh." The two questions

---

[356]Some take the temple to be his people in a figurative sense (Laetsch).
[357]Other views: the Old Covenant (Keil); both covenants (Packard). Jews provide a chair for Elijah at the covenant of circumcision.

asked in the first half of v 2 are synonymous. The answer to these questions is well-documented in prophetic literature. Those who can stand before the coming of Yahweh are those who have been faithful to the covenant.

B. Purpose of his Coming (3:2b, c):

The double question of v 2a is answered by a double illustration in v 2b. *For* (*kî*) introduces the reason the unfaithful will not be able to stand before the coming of Yahweh. Fire and lye are used to point out the judicial purpose of his coming. Fire and lye share these properties: they burn, cleanse, and separate.

1. Refiner illustration (3:2b): **For he will be like the fire of the refiner...** Early in Israelite history God revealed himself through or in fire (Ex 3; 19:18, etc.). It was quite natural for later prophets to depict fire as an agent in divine judgment. In the refining process metal ores were subjected to intense heat that melted the ore and facilitated the separation of the precious from the worthless slag. Such refining fires were probably not uncommon around Jerusalem in Malachi's day. The figure of fire as a tool of judgment burning away the wicked and refining the people of God is common in the OT.[358] Messiah is the great discriminator. At his coming he will sever good people from bad.

2. Fuller illustration (3:2c): **or like the lye of clothes-cleaners...** Lye (*bōrît*) is alkali, particularly vegetable alkali or potash, obtained by leaching the ashes of plants. Lye was used in the process of fulling—cleaning clothes by soaking them in water in which lye had been dissolved. The garments were then massaged by treading upon them. Like refining, this too was a separation process—separation of dirt from clothes.

Both the fire and the lye figures depict the same thing. Messiah will be the great separator removing what is impure and worthless from what is useful and valuable.

---

[358]Isa 29:6; 30:27-30; 66:15-71; Jer 15:14; Ezek 22:20-21; 36:5; Joel 1:19-20; 2:3; Nah 1:6; Zeph 1:14-17; Zech 13:9.

Postexilic Prophets

Result of his Coming
Malachi 3:3-5

A. In Respect to the Priests (3:3):

1. What he will do (3:3a): **He will sit as a refiner and purifier of silver...** *Sit* could refer to either ruling (e.g., 1 Sam 1:9) or judging (e.g., Ex 18:13) or both. The refining process mentioned in the previous v is carried a step further. Now the coming one himself is the refiner. *Silver* is what is being purified, in this case the priestly ministry which in Malachi's day had become so lackadaisical, indifferent and downright disobedient.

2. Where he will begin (3:3b): **he will purify the sons of Levi...** *Sons of Levi* is equivalent in meaning to the collective "Levi" used in 2:4, 8. The following v indicates that the messianic cleansing will produce a cleansed nation. That cleansing, however, begins with the priests. Perhaps the more subtle suggestion is that the nation that emerges from the cleansing process is a priestly nation.

Some think that the cleansing of the temple by Jesus is in view. Others mention the fact that the teaching of Christ was directed against the religious leaders of his day. Still others point to the conversion of many of the Levitical priests in Acts 6:7. Actually the Hebrew uses participles implying that the refining work will go on continually. Perhaps the fulfillment is in the continuous cleansing of the antitypical Levitical priesthood, the church of Jesus Christ (1 Pet 2:9; 1 Jn 1:9).

3. What he will achieve (3:3c): **and refine them like gold and silver.** The impurities removed, Yahweh's priestly people become as precious as gold and silver.

4. What he will have (3:3d): **Then they will become to Yahweh those who present an offering in righteousness.** Following cleansing Yahweh will have for himself a body of purified priests. These words do not mean that Messiah's coming will restore the old covenant sacrificial system to pristine purity. The point is that the day of Messiah ushers in true worship.

Malachi: 2:10-4:3

Offering in righteousness is ambiguous. It could refer to the status of the presenters, the manner in which they make the presentation, or to the rightness of the offerings themselves. The point is that the offerings of the purified priests will in every respect meet the requirements of the Lord. The sacrificial abuses identified in ch 2 will be removed.

B. In Respect to the Worshipers (3:4):
And the offerings of Judah and Jerusalem will be pleasant to Yahweh as in ancient days, as in former years. The sentence which began in v 3 continues in this v. *Judah and Jerusalem* (capital and country) indicates Malachi envisioned a cleansed nation, not just a cleansed segment within a nation. He in fact visualized a new Israel of God the establishment of which was to be the work of Messiah (Gal 6:16).

Malachi focuses on one manifestation of Messiah's sanctification of the new Israel, viz. sacrifice or worship. *Be pleasant* (r. *'rb*) is lit., "be a sweet savor." The image of Yahweh smelling the pleasant odor of the sacrifices is anthropomorphic. The meaning is that the offerings of the messianic age will be totally acceptable to the Lord. What delights God in offerings is not their quantity or cost. In the final analysis it is the character of the worshiper that renders an offering pleasant to the Lord. The one who presents the offering must do so with a humble, loving, obedient and grateful spirit (cf. Amos 5:21-27).

In the light of subsequent revelation it becomes clear that the offerings of the messianic age are not atonement sacrifices, for Christ's sacrificial death took care of the atonement issue (Heb 10:18). The offerings presented by the NT priesthood of believers are those of thanksgiving for the grace of God in Christ that made our acceptance by him possible (1 Pet 2:5; Heb 13:15-16).

As in ancient days (*kîmê 'ōlām*) refers to the past far back. Elsewhere this expression is used of the time of David (Amos 9:11) and of the earliest days when Israel occupied the rich pasture lands of Transjordan (Micah 7:14). Malachi is probably referring to the golden age of sacrifice—the days of Moses (cf. Isa 63:9, 11). *Former years* (*kᵉšānîm qadmōnîyōt*) occurs only here in the Bible. Its meaning is not in doubt because it is synonymous with *ancient days*.

The prophet does not necessarily expect that the Mosaic ritual will last forever and be maintained throughout the world. Rather he is using terms with which the Jews were conversant to express the worship of the new covenant. It is the church of the NT which Malachi here foresees. Every member of this church is a member of the purified priesthood (1 Pet 2:5, 9). Each is capable of offering up sweet savor sacrifices to God (Phil 4:18).

C. In Respect to the Wicked (3:5):

1. Judge (3:5a): ***So I will come near to you for judgment.*** The Lord (in the person of Messiah) will be the judge. *Come near* (r. *qrb*) is equivalent to *come* in 3:1. The verb connotes coming to or presenting oneself formally at a particular place. Ironically the root is commonly used in the context of sacrifice (cf. 1:8). One "draws near" to sacrifice.[359] Those Messiah cannot refine come under his judgment.

2. Prosecutor (3:5b): ***I will be a swift witness against...*** Messiah will be Prosecutor as well as Judge. *I will be a witness...against* (*hāyîthî 'ēd + b*) means to "testify against." This is legal jargon attested in a number of passages.[360]

Swift (*mᵉmahēr*) is a warning, not a promise. The word has a similar meaning to the adverb *suddenly* in 3:1. The threat is not that of verbal testimony before an impartial judge. It is the judgment itself that is God's final testimony of wrath against sin.

3. Accused (3:5c): ***sorcerers, adulterers and those who swear falsely, against those who oppress the pay of an hireling, widow and orphan, and those who turn aside aliens, and do not fear me, says Yahweh of Hosts.*** Six categories of sinners are named as falling under the judgment of the Almighty.

---

[359]To draw near *for judgment* (*lammišāt*) appears elsewhere in Isa 41:1 where both Yahweh and his adversaries approach one another.
[360]Nm 5:13; Dt 19:15-16; 31:26; Josh 24:22; 1 Sam 12:5; Prov 24:28; Micah 1:2.

Malachi: 2:10-4:3

First, Messiah-Judge comes against *sorcerers*. Sorcery (r. kšp) is described as an abomination before Yahweh (Dt 18:12). The practice has its roots in pagan religion (2 Kgs 9:22); but it was very popular in Israel (2 Chr 33:6; Jer 27:9). Mosaic Law made the practice a capital crime. (Ex 22:18). Sorcery pretended to provide a reliable guide to the future. For this reason it was a practice that was dangerous to the entire community. *Sorcerers* is the umbrella term that includes sub-specialties such as necromancy (consultation with the dead spirits), rhabdomancy (interpreting the pattern of sticks falling to the ground), and hepatoscopy (examination of distinctive marking on internal body organs, especially livers and kidneys). Sorcery is excluded from the New Jerusalem (Rev 21:8; 22:15).

Second, Messiah comes against *adulterers*. Adultery (r. n'p) was a violation of the Ten Commandments (Ex 20:14; Dt 5:18) and a capital crime in Israel (Dt 22:22). This was considered "the great sin" in many countries of the ancient Near East (cf. Gn 20:9; 39:9). In the OT adultery was heterosexual intercourse by a married person with someone other than one's spouse. The NT also treats adultery as a serious offense.[361]

Third, Messiah comes against perjurers. Oaths taken in the name of Yahweh were legal and even commendable (Dt 6:13; 10:20; 1 Sam 20:42); but swearing to a lie was a violation of the Ten Commandments (Ex 20:16), a serious crime (Lv 19:12; 20:3), even an abomination (Jer 7:9-12). Since the oath was taken in Yahweh's name, a lying oath was both a crime against community and a sin against God. Swearing falsely is a specific kind of lying done in a context designed to prevent lying (Stuart). The phrase can refer to those who give false testimony in a legal setting and to those who go back on business or personal commitments taken in the name of God or with God as witness. That swearing falsely was a problem in the postexilic community is also suggested by Zech 8:8:16-17 (cf. Zech 5:3).

---

[361] Mt 5:27-32; Rom 2:22; 1 Cor 6:9; Gal 5:19; Heb 13:4; James 2:11.

Postexilic Prophets

Fourth, Messiah comes against oppressors. *Those who oppress* (r. *'šq*) is a participle in construct, lit., "oppressors of." The root has a range of meanings including abuse, suppress, oppress, wrong, rob, cheat, and defraud. The participle in construct governs three victims.

Some were oppressors of *the pay of a hireling*. One might expect the text to make *hireling*, rather than *pay* the object of the oppression.[362] The phrase used here, however, is attested in Dt 15:18. Furthermore, withholding of wages was the most common form of cheating a hired laborer. A *hireling* (*sākhîr*) was a landless day laborer who lived hand-to-mouth. Mosaic labor laws were specific regarding payment to a working man. The hireling's wages were to be paid at sundown. To withhold those wages constituted oppression.

Widow (*'almānāh*) and *orphan* (*yātōm*) is a common singular word pair used collectively. The phrase seems to be a way of referring to the needy in general, not just to those who have lost husbands or parents.[363] Mistreating this powerless class was contrary to the nature of Yahweh (Dt 10:18) and a sure way to bring down upon the community the curse of Dt 27:19.

Fifth, Messiah comes against abusers. *Turn aside* (r. *nth* in Hiphil) has a legal flavor (Isa 29:21; Amos 5:12). The more complete formulation was "turn aside justice."[364] The expression means to deny someone his legal rights or to treat him unfairly. *Aliens* (*nēr*) is a singular used collectively. The term refers to those who reside in a land where they are not citizens, thus resident aliens. Such people were at the mercy of the citizens who controlled the legal machinery. Israel was commanded to treat aliens fairly since they too once had been aliens in Egypt (Ex 22:21; Dt 10:18-19). Taking advantage of aliens was thus a clear violation of covenant standards.

Sixth, Messiah comes against the impious—those who do not fear Yahweh. Failure to fear God is the most general of

---

[362]On the ability of the verb *'šq* to take both a personal and non-personal object in the same clause, see Mic 2:2.
[363]Ex 22:22; Dt 24:17, 19-20, 21; 26:12; Prov 13:21; 19:17; 22:9; Isa 1:17; 10:2; Jer 7:6; lam 5:3; Zech 7:10; Jam 1:27.
[364]Ex 23:6; Dt 16:19; 1 Sam 8:3; Prov 17:23; 18:5.

the charges in Malachi's list. It is a sin in its own right (Dt 4:10; 5:29). On the negative side fearing Yahweh means fearing the consequences of disobedience to him. The positive side of fearing Yahweh is humble obedience to his dictates. A lack of fear for God is sometimes equivalent to non-belief or simply ignoring him (Jer 5:22; 32:39). Perhaps Malachi intends this category to be inclusive of the previous five. By violating God's covenant in the ways mentioned in this v the postexilic community was demonstrating that they were not God-fearers.

Proof of his Coming
Malachi 3:6

A. General Principle (3:6a):
For I, Yahweh, do not change... The reason the Lord must come to purify the priests and punish the wicked is because Yahweh does not change. He cannot be satisfied with less than perfect holiness (cf. Lv 11:44f). Thus at some point he must initiate judgment against those who transgress his law.

B. Specific Example (3:6b):
Therefore you, O sons of Jacob, are not consumed. Yahweh's absolute justice does not negate his boundless love and compassion. Because of God's grace the persistent covenant breakers have not been *consumed* by his uncompromising holiness. The Jews are called *the sons of Jacob*[365] because they were so much like their ancestor. Like Jacob, the Jews of Malachi's day were guilty of deceit in respect to God and man. God had kept his word to Jacob [Israel] thus far. Therefore, his promises/warnings for the future may be trusted.

---

[365]The phrase *sons of Jacob* occurs 16x in OT. It sometimes refers to the patriarchs (e.g., 1 Kgs 18:31), and sometimes is just an alternative to the more common *sons of Israel* (e.g., Ps 22:23). There are other times when *Jacob* seems to be chosen over Israel to hint at sinfulness.

Sin of Dishonesty and Theft
Malachi 3:7-12

The attention of Malachi now shifts to another sin of the people. First he presents his indictment for the sin of dishonesty. Malachi then indicates the predicament which had befallen the people because of this sin. Then the prophet offers an inducement to bring the people out of this sin.

Indictment
Malachi 3:7-8

A. **General Charge** (3:7a, b):
The idea of change links this unit to the last v of the previous one. God does not change, but Israel does.

1. Their attitude (3:7a): ***From the time of your fathers you have turned away from my statutes.*** This v echoes Zech 1:4. The charge that the current recalcitrance of the nation reflects a longstanding condition in Israel is quite common in the prophets.[366] *My statutes* (*chūqqay*) refer to covenant stipulations. Disobedience was an ever recurring sin in Israel. Divine blessing under the old covenant economy was contingent upon obedience to God's law.

2. Their actions (3:7b): ***and have not kept them.*** The object of the verb (*them*) is understood rather expressed, a regular feature in Hebrew. To turn aside from God's statutes in attitude leads to disregard of the law in practice. Therefore the charge is leveled against them: you *have not kept them,* i.e., the statutes.

B. **General Appeal** (3:7c):
Return to me, and I will return to you. *Return* (r. *šûb*), used 3x in this v, is the verb most frequently used by the prophets to call for repentance. Every turning is at the same time a turning *from,* and a turning *to.* Malachi calls for a turning away from all the actions that he has previously indicted

---

[366]See for example Isa 65:7; Jer 2:5; 3:25; 9:14; 14:20; 23:27; Ezek 2;3; Hos 10:1-2, etc.

as being contrary to covenant behavior. They must repent of their lack of faith in God's love (1:2-5), their offensive worship (1:6-2:9), their abuse of covenant marriage standards (2:10-16), and their wearisome complaints and societal abuses (2:17-3:5).

In spite of the fact that they deserved to be rejected as covenant breakers, God graciously pleads with his people to return to him. The God who does not change is willing to forgive his people if they will change.

I will return to you implies that they have been abandoned by their Deity—one of the old covenant curses in Israel (Lv 26:28; Dt 31:17; 32:19). It also promises to the penitent a renewal of Yahweh's favor, presence and consequent assistance.

C. Initial Response (3:7d):

But you ask, How shall we return? The people's response to the gracious invitation of Yahweh indicates how thoroughly depraved they really were. The Hebrew is ambiguous, perhaps purposely so. The words could mean: "In what manner shall we return?" They probably mean, however: "In respect to what sin shall we return?" Their self-righteousness blinded them to their own need for repentance.

D. Specific Charge (3:8a):

Will a man rob God? Yet you rob me. The specific charge is couched in the form of a rhetorical question. The Israelites were robbing God. *Man* (*'ādām*) is human being as contrasted with God. The idea is not *a man* = anyone (NIV; NRSV; NASB). The idea is that the Israelites were doing what a human being should never think about doing. *Rob* (r. *qbʻ*) occurs only here and in Prov 22:23. Jewish tradition took the word to mean "to rob, to take by force."[367]

E. More Specific Response (3:8b):

But you ask, How have we robbed you? Again the people, smarting under the seriousness of the accusation, vehe-

---

[367] The idea of force is included in the word, i.e., to take forcibly (Cashdan). LXX renders: "shall a man heel, grasp the heel," i.e., deceive God.

mently deny the charge. They demanded proof of this indictment.

F. Specific Evidence (3:8c):
The tithe and the offering! Grammatically this two-word Hebrew phrase is a simple exclamation (as in NIV). There is no reason to add a preposition to introduce the phrase as in NASB. *The tithe* (*hamm^a'asēr*) was an annual contribution to the Levites of one tenth of the yield of the field (Nm 18:21). The offering (*terûmāh*) may be offerings in general (Ex 25:2) or the heave offering which was given to the priests (Nm 18:11).

They had robbed God by withholding from his ministers those gifts which were rightfully theirs. The unfaithfulness of the priestly family was no excuse for failing to comply with the law of tithing. God makes the charge against the Judeans, for it would be very difficult for any person to know whether or not the complete tithe was being brought to the temple.

The Mosaic concept is that all wealth (Ex 19:5), and tithes in particular belong to Yahweh (Lv 27:30). In covenant law tithes are brought to their rightful owner. To withhold the tithe in modern legal terminology is called conversion.[368] Tithing per se is not a stipulation of the new covenant; but financial contribution is (2 Cor 9:6-7). Paul agrees with Malachi that there is a connection between the generosity of the giver and the reward bestowed upon the worshiper.

Predicament
Malachi 3:9

A. Covenant Curse (3:9a):
With a curse you are being cursed... The disobedience of the people in respect to their tithes and offerings had brought a curse upon their land just as the unfaithfulness of the priests had brought a curse upon their ministry (cf. 1:14; 2:2). The *curse* (*m^e'ērāh*) probably took the form of drought,

---

[368]Conversion is unauthorized assumption and exercise of rights of ownership over personal property belonging to another (*Random House Dictionary of the English Language*, 1979).

Malachi: 2:10-4:3

poor crops and economic depression. *Being cursed* (r. *'rr*) is a Niphal participle, the only use of the Niphal of this verb in OT.

B. Continuing Aggravation (3:9b):
Yet me you are robbing... Not only does the curse come as a result of tithe robbery, the sin is contemporaneous with the punishment. Even while the curse was in progress and in evidence the people were continuing to rob God.[369] The Hebrew word order stresses the audacity of this theft by placing the first person objective pronoun in the emphatic position.

C. Universal Sin (3:9c):
The whole nation. Malachi tacks on to his observation this two-word Hebrew phrase which serves as an exclamation. Withholding tithes from Yahweh was not an isolated sin; it characterized the entire community of Judeans. This exclamation tends to bring Malachi's national indictment to a climax. Earlier worship cheaters (1:14) and impious priests (2:2) were threatened with divine curse. Now the entire nation is experiencing the threatened curse.

Inducement
3:10-12

As an inducement to repentance in respect to tithes and offerings, Malachi sets forth a correction, a challenge, a commitment, and a consequence.

A. Correction (3:10a, b):
1. Imperative (3:10a): **Bring the whole tithe into the storehouse...** The verb (r. *bō'* Hiphil) is imperative. *Storehouse* (*bēth hā'ōtsār*) refers to the various chambers in the temple complex where food and other valuables were stored. It seems that a chamber in the temple court was set aside for the collection of the tithe and heave offerings (cf. Neh 10:38;

---

[369] NIV understands the second clause to be giving the reason they were under the curse.

331

Postexilic Prophets

12:44; 13:5, 12). It is clear from the rest of this book that God expected all of his covenant stipulations to be obeyed. Tithing is set forth as a concrete benchmark of the degree to which the postexilic community was committed to fulfilling covenant obligations.

The Mosaic tithing laws are found in Lv 27:30-33; Nm 18:21-28; Dt 12:6-17; 14:22-28; 26:12-14. Tithing was a compulsory system, not an optional guideline for giving back to the Lord. These laws established the minimum expectation as ten per cent of one's income. Tithes were used to support the temple personnel, including priests, Levites, temple singers and servants. They also were used for supplies and temple maintenance.

2. *Explanation (3:10b): that there may be meat in my house...* Vav plus imperfect (jussive) introduces a result clause. *Meat (tereph)* commonly means "prey" or "carrion;" but sometimes, as here, simply means nourishment (cf. Ps 111:5; Prov 31:15). Probably the reference is to the food of the priests and Levites. Another possibility is that the *meat* refers to sacrificial animals.

B. Challenge (3:10c):

And prove me now herewith, says Yahweh of Hosts... *Prove (chnn)* has the connotation of "put to the test." *Now* is the particle *nā'*, an optional imperative marker (Stuart) which some commentators believe has a softening effect (e.g., "please"). Malachi challenges them to do their part and see for themselves if their fortunes would change. Yahweh subjects himself to testing,[370] but not the sort that is condemned elsewhere.[371]

---

[370]God challenged Moses regarding personal signs of assurance (Ex 4:1-9). He authorized Elijah to arrange for the contest on Mount Carmel (1 Kgs 18:22-39). Ahaz was invited to ask for a sign (Isa 7:10-17). The Psalmist invites Israelites to taste the goodness of the Lord (Ps 34:8).

[371]The demand that God "show off" to prove his presence is condemned in Dt 6:16. Cf. 1 Cor 10:9.

C. Commitment (3:10d-11):

The v which began with an imperative now concludes with conditional imperfects describing what will happen if the initial command is obeyed. Like most of the old covenant promises of abundance, this one is corporate not individual. This v does not provide a guarantee that the individual tither then or now will get rich. The Lord committed himself to respond to the faithful tithing of his people in five wonderful ways.

1. Abundant rain (3:10d): **and see if I will not open the windows of heaven...** *Windows of heaven* and like expressions are indications of abundance of rain (Gn 7:11-12). When the "windows" are shut, there is a lack of rain (1 Kgs 8:35-36). Such expressions are no more an indication of ancient cosmology than the modern expression "rain cats and dogs." In an agricultural economy abundant rain is requisite for all other blessings and the foretaste thereof. Abundant rainfall was one of the blessing that God promised Israel for covenant faithfulness (Dt 11:13-14). This promise of rain hints that Malachi spoke during a time of less than adequate rainfall.

2. Blessing (3:10e): **and empty for your benefit a blessing....** While this may be a second allusion to the drought-ending rain, the expression also may include other abundant blessings as well.

3. Superabundance (3:10f): **until there is no measure.**[372] God will continue to pour out his blessing beyond anyone's ability to measure. They will be blessed superabundantly. Literally the Hebrew (*'ad bᵉlî dāy*) reads: "up to not sufficiency."

4. Pest protection (3:11a): **And I will rebuke for your sake the devourer so that it will not destroy for your sake the fruit of the ground.** The Lord promised pest protection if the terms of his covenant were observed. *Rebuke* (r. *g'r*) is used in the same sense as in 2:3. *Devourer* (*'ōkhēl*) or "eater" is used only here. It is not one of the several words used in the OT for locusts. The reference is probably to crop pests in

---

[372]The LXX renders: "until it suffice"; The Syriac reads "until you say, It is enough."

Postexilic Prophets

general (NIV; NASB) rather than locusts (NRSV) in particular. The rebuke of Yahweh will remove or at least thwart insect pests and crop disease that if left unchecked would ruin the crop. *Fruit of the ground* is any crop. Nothing will be allowed to injure the crops. This promise is a reversal of the crop pest curses set forth in the Pentateuch upon those who violated Yahweh's covenant (Dt 28:38-40, 42).

5. *Crop maturity (3:11b):* **Neither shall the vine cast its fruit into the field on account of you, says Yahweh of Hosts.** The root *šchl* means "to become childless; to make barren, to suffer a miscarriage." Hence, it is used of premature production, or unripe, undeveloped fruit falling to the ground.[373] God would prevent such a waste of resources if his people kept the terms of the ancient covenant.

Abundant crops in prophetic literature are frequently a way of indicating the copious blessings of the new covenant age.[374] Under the old covenant God's people were never able to achieve such complete covenant compliance as to warrant the full measure of Yahweh's blessing. So the fulfillment of the copious crop promises awaited fulfillment in the new covenant age when the sinless Jesus perfectly complied with covenant terms. He thus earned for all who put their faith in him the unparalleled blessings announced in the NT.

D. Consequence (3:12):

The thoughts of v 11 are carried forward to a new level as Malachi continues to spell out the promise of blessing which results from obedience to covenant stipulations.

1. Subjective evaluation (3:12a): **And all the nations will call you blessed...** Gentiles will be impressed with what God does for his people. Sin ruins a land; righteousness blesses it. To call someone or some people blessed is to acknowledge and extol their condition as desirable. In the OT such blessing statements are almost always spoken by one who is in a less favored position upon one who has achieved a superior position. In this case the nations recognize that Is-

---

[373] Cashdan says the term means "to fail to ripen."
[374] Amos 9:13-15. See also the eschatological implications of the term "vine" in Mic 4:4; Hag 2:19; Zech 8:12.

rael has something that they do not have. To call Israel *blessed* is not just a polite compliment; it is an expression of envy.

The reason the nations call Israel *blessed* is because God will transform Israel. The Israel of Malachi's day occupied only a fraction of the territory once inhabited by Judah and Benjamin. Jerusalem had only recently been rebuilt. It was sparsely occupied. The geographical realities of the area are not such that most people regarded it as ideal. The future, however, holds out the prospects of a land admired by all.

As is the case in similar land transformation passages, Malachi is depicting the spiritual blessings of the messianic age. An ideal land with abundant water, lush vegetation, and unprecedented fertility is an OT type of the kingdom of Christ.

2. *Objective reality (3:12b):* **for you, you yourselves will be a delightful land, says Yahweh of Hosts.** Here the personal pronoun *you* is repeated for emphasis: Obedience was the key to blessing under the OT economy. The heaven-blessed people of God will become *a delightful land ('erets chēphets).*

There is no indication of those who will find the land delightful, whether God, Jews or Gentiles. In the last days—the Christian age—Israel will in fact be a delightful place to reside. In this case, as frequently in prophecies of the last days, the land is a reference to the kingdom of Christ—the church of Christ. The phrase connotes a fruitful and well-nourished land.

Sin of Disillusionment and Cynicism
Malachi 3:13-4:3

The last accusation against the people revolves around the words of certain cynics, the words of the faithful, and the words of God.

Words of the Sinners
Malachi 3:13-15

A. Charge by Yahweh (3:13a):
Your words have overruled me, says Yahweh. The speaker is Yahweh. The verb overruled (r. *chzq*) more frequently is rendered "to be hard, strong, or harsh."[375] This verb in combination with *'al* (against) and *dābhār* (word) is probably to be translated idiomatically, as Stuart has argued. The idiom occurs in 2 Sam 24:4//1 Chr 21:4 in reference to David overruling Joab. People overrule Yahweh when they verbally contradict what he declares to be true, think that they know better than God, or they choose to act in ways that are contrary to his stated will.

In this life God has granted to humankind free will in which people are permitted to agree or disagree with what the Creator has declared to be true. Of course such statements of contradiction are an affront to the God of absolute truth. In temporal judgment here and certainly at the final judgment people will be held accountable for such words.

B. Denial by Judeans (3:13b):
Yet you ask, What have we said against you? Again the hardened sinners found the charge shocking and absurd. The rhetorical question indicates that they were not aware of having said anything that could be construed as criticism of Yahweh. They understood the seriousness of the charge. To overrule God is to say what is *against* him, i.e., contrary to his will and nature. Such words are in effect lies that hinder the redemptive process (Hos 7:13).

C. Proof of the Charge (3:14):
Malachi charges the Judeans with possessing negative attitudes in regard to their relationship with the Lord. They saw no value in obedience and worship, "the twin pillars of true biblical religion" (Stuart).

---

[375]Cf. "you have said harsh things against me" (NIV); "your words have been arrogant against me" (NASB); "you have spoken harsh words against me" (NRSV).

Malachi: 2:10-4:3

1. *Negative toward serving God (3:14a):* **You have said, Serving God is useless,** i.e., serving God is unprofitable business. This terse verbless clause has the appearance of a slogan or proverb that may have been widespread in Malachi's day. Certainly if the words were not publicly expressed, the underlying sentiment was there. The Judeans thought that serving God demanded too much and returned too little! They saw no value in keeping the ordinances and ritual observations. *Useless* (*šāv'*) has the root sense of "emptiness" or "nothingness."

2. *Negative toward obedience (3:14b):* **and what profit is it if we have kept his charge.** *Profit* (*betsa'*) literally means "cut," i.e., share. *Kept* (r. *šmr*) is from the same root as the following noun, creating assonance in Hebrew pronunciation, perhaps emphasizing the disdain expressed in the entire clause. An attempt in English to capture this assonance might be "kept his keep." *His charge* (*mišmartō*) could be read as a collective, "his rules." The reference is to the specifications of the Mosaic covenant.

Apparently the Judeans were observing Yahweh's ordinances, especially the ritual observances. Perhaps they had only been pretending to observe the ordinances. Or perhaps they thought that only a superficial outward ritualism was enough to secure God's favor. Or perhaps (if some interval had elapsed between this and the last section) they had made some attempt at reformation and had not been immediately blessed and therefore had lapsed into their old distrust.

3. *Negative toward worship (3:14c):* **and if we have gone about like mourners before Yahweh of Hosts?** *Mourners* (*qᵉdōrannît*) refers to those who donned dark clothing or who made their clothing dark by throwing dust over themselves. Here the term probably includes the entire range of mourning rituals, such as fasting and wearing sackcloth. This was done *before Yahweh of Hosts*, i.e., in the context of worship. Worshiping God was somber, joyless business, as boring to them as a funeral ritual. Was this part of some ritual appeal to God for mercy? Was this a reaction to the anger of God expressed in one of Malachi's earlier messages? The words probably are an exaggeration intended to articulate

337

their disgust for all temple ritual. In essence the people were saying, "God doesn't listen to us no matter what sacrifices we make in our personal lives. It just doesn't matter. He doesn't care."

D. Further Proof of the Charge (3:15):

In this v Malachi describes three assertions of the Judeans which further describe their negative attitude toward serving Yahweh. All three assertions make the same point, viz. that there are no negative repercussions for not serving God.

1. Viewed the wicked blessed (3:15a): **And now we call the arrogant blessed.** Now (*'attāh*) suggests consequence. The assertion *we call the arrogant blessed* results from serving Yahweh with no identifiable blessing. The *arrogant* (*zēdîm*) in the OT are the self-willed, malicious, unprincipled, and turbulent; those who defied God by disregarding his precepts (e.g., Ps 19:13). The word comes from a root which means "to boil, cook, to boil over in anger, pride or cruelty." *We call blessed* is a Piel participle (*m^e'aššrîm*) plus the self-standing pronoun.

Whether this assertion grows out of jealousy or discouragement is difficult to say; but in either case it oozes resentment. The majority of Judeans regarded keeping up with all the intricacies of God's covenant as costly in terms of wealth, time and inconvenience. It just wasn't worth it!

2. Viewed the wicked as more prosperous (3:15b): **even the workers of wickedness prosper...** Even (*gam*) indicates that the skeptics are escalating their argument. The previous assertion has to do with *being*; this one involves *doing*. *Workers of wickedness* (*'ōsē riš'āh*) is parallel to "arrogant" in the previous assertion. *Prosper* (r. *hnb* Niphal) is lit., "have been built up." It is equivalent to "blessed" in the previous assertion.

This assertion builds on the first in that it affirms that doing evil is rewarded. The skeptics claimed that the wicked prospered in spite of their wickedness. They have wealth and families and leave a name behind them. Cf. Jer 12:16. This assertion is a blatant contradiction of the biblical perspective which finds classic expression in Ps 1.

Malachi: 2:10-4:3

3. *Viewed the wicked as unpunished (3:15c):* **even they try God and get by with it**. The second use of *even* (*gam*) in the v indicates that the skeptics mean to carry their argument to the ultimate extreme. The argument moves from *being* and *doing* to *provoking*. The wicked can even go so far as to challenge Yahweh himself—the worst affront imaginable—and come away unscathed. *Try* (r. *bchn*) is the same verb used in 3:10 where God invites the people to test him. Testing God upon invitation is obviously not sinful;[376] but the testing here is uninvited, thus presumptuous.

In the second assertion the wicked thumb their noses at God; in the third assertion they shake their fist at him. The wicked were saying or doing something with the intention of trying to provoke or force God to respond. Such provocation of God is regarded in the OT as the ultimate manifestation of rebellion.[377] *Get by with it* (r. *mlt* Niphal) is lit., "are delivered; escape." The text is silent as to exactly what some were doing or saying that was construed by their contemporaries as "trying" God.

Word of the Saints
Malachi 3:16

A. **How the Saints are Described** (3:16a, b):
1. *They feared God (3:16a):* **Then those who feared Yahweh…** Among the skeptics was a cadre of the faithful, like the seven thousand in Elijah's day who had not bowed the knee to Baal. The quality of godly fear is mentioned twice in the description for emphasis. The faithful few now speak up in response to the majority.

2. *They encouraged each other (3:16b):* **talked with each other.** The verb is Niphal used reflexively.[378] In the

---

[376] God also tests people to see if they will respond faithfully. See Gn 22:1; Ex 15:25; 20:20; Dt 8:2, 16; 13:3; Judg 3:1, 4; 2 Chr 32:31; Job 7:18; Pss 11:5; 26:2; Zech 13:9.
[377] Ex 17:2, 7; Nm 14:22; Dt 6:16; 33:18; Pss 78:18, 41, 56; 95:9; 106:14; Isa 7:12; Mt 4:7; 1 Cor 10:9; Heb 3:9.
[378] Contra Stuart who takes the verb as transitive (as in v 13) introducing a direct quote contradicting the majority opinion: "Yahweh has paid atten-

Postexilic Prophets

midst of national skepticism and unbelief the faithful were encouraging one another with their words. *Each other* is lit., "a man with his neighbor."

B. How the Saints were Honored (3:16c, d):
  1. *God heard their words (3:16c):* **and Yahweh listened and heard.** What the faithful said to each other is not recorded; but it was certainly well-pleasing to God. Perhaps they argued with the impious skeptics; perhaps they warned others against them. If they questioned the circumstances of life it was in full faith that God does only what is good.
  2. *God recorded their names (3:16d):* ***A scroll of remembrance was written before him...*** Scroll of remembrance (*sēpher zikkārōn*) is found only here in OT; but the concept of a list to memorialize contributors, workers or ancestors is common in the ancient Near East and in the Bible.

The verb (r. *ktb* Niphal) is passive, leaving the origin of the scroll unclear. Surely, however, it is Yahweh who produces the scroll of remembrance, not the faithful.[379] The recording of the names and/or words of the faithful is a concrete way of promising that Yahweh will not forget them.

The book represents God's providence and omniscience, his ever-wakeful care, his unfailing knowledge (3:16b).[380] It is similar to the "book of life" concept where those enrolled escape the forthcoming wrath of God.[381]

---

tion!" The *vav* on initial verb, however, seems to indicate a response to what was being said, not the words that the God-fearers were speaking.

[379] Contra Stuart who holds that the faithful compose "some sort of statement of their commitment to Yahweh—a document in which the signatories disassociate themselves from the skeptical majority. He cites Ezra 10 and Nehemiah 7 and 9-10 as examples of such memorial lists from the period.

[380] Cf. the Persian custom: Ezra 4:15; Esther 2:23; 6:1. The same practice was common in Israel and Judah. Cf. 1 Kgs 11:41; 14:29 etc. Names of public benefactors were inscribed therein. On God's book see: Ex 32:32; Ps 56:8; 69:28; 139:16; Ezek 13:9; Dan 7:10; Rev 13:8; 20:12-15.

[381] Ex 32:32-33; Ps 69:28; 139:16; Isa 4:3; 65:6; Ezek 13:9; Lk 10:20; Phil 4:3; Rev 13:8; 17:8; 20:12.

Malachi: 2:10-4:3

C. Further Identification of the Saints (3:16e):
For those who fear Yahweh and those who meditate on his name. In his book of remembrance Yahweh took note of *those who fear* (reverence) *Yahweh.* The God-fearers are those who *meditate*[382] *on his name.* The *name* of God is his self-revelation, his word. So the Lord assured believers, those who truly reverenced God and possessed God-consciousness, that they were not forgotten.

Words of God
Malachi 3:17-4:3

Yahweh responded to the words of faith spoken by the saints in Zion. He spoke of four coming days.

A. Glorious Day for the Righteous (3:17-18):
1. Righteous will be acknowledged by God (3:17a): **They will be mine, says Yahweh of Hosts.** A day will come when God publicly acknowledges his own possession. This assurance addresses one of the aforementioned criticisms of Yahweh, viz. that there was no advantage in serving him. *They will be mine* ($v^e h\bar{a}y\hat{u}$ $l\hat{\imath}$), lit., "they will be to me," is the regular Hebrew way of expressing possession. The messenger formula makes clear that Yahweh is the speaker.

2. Righteous will be treasured by God (3:17b): **in the day when I make up [my] special possession.** Yahweh now addresses another criticism of the skeptics, viz. that God never gets involved in the affairs of men whether for blessing or for judgment. A day of reckoning is coming. *The day* is the day of Yahweh—the day when he intervenes in a dramatic way in human affairs. That day brings judgment to the wicked and deliverance to the righteous. *When I make up* is a participle plus an emphatic first person pronoun. The participle suggests that Malachi anticipates a process lasting throughout the day—the period of time when Yahweh intervenes.

---

[382]NIV *honor his name* is based on the LXX, i.e., those who esteem, revere his name.

Postexilic Prophets

On that day the faithful will be a *special possession (segullāh)*, i.e., a possession exclusively belonging to Yahweh. The meaning of the noun itself justifies the insertion of the possessive pronoun *my*. At Sinai centuries before this term had been used for all Israel (Ex 19:5; cf. 1 Pet 2:9). Now it applied only to the faithful minority.

3. *Righteous spared by God (3:17c):* **I will spare them...** The twice-used *spare* (r. *chml* + prep. *'al*) is lit., "have pity upon." Those who are spared are the ones that make up the special possession of Yahweh in the previous line. While others are being punished the faithful will be spared in that day. In this v the wicked are threatened by implication.

4. *Righteous beloved by God (3:17d):* **just as a man spares his son who serves him.** Those who are spared from Yahweh's wrath are compared to a son who has faithfully served his father. The implication is that those who are the special possession of Yahweh in the previous line are his loyal family.

A child who serves his parents is doubly loved. He has the natural love of the parents plus the special love that has been earned through loyal service. The point is that Yahweh has not failed to notice the stubborn loyalty and steadfast service of some within the community. When the day of Yahweh comes these sons who have served Yahweh faithfully in spite of the prevailing attitude of skepticism will be rewarded.

5. *Righteous separated by God (3:18):* **And you will again discern between the righteous and the wicked, between those who serve God and those who do not.** *You will again* is lit., "you will return (r. *šûbh*)," a regular Hebrew idiom for repetition of an action. The pronoun refers to the skeptics that questioned the utility of serving God. *Discern* (r. *r'h*) is lit. "see." The idiom "see between x and y" means to "recognize a distinction between," hence *discern*.

In this case discrimination will be between *the righteous* and *the wicked*. The former are identified as *those who serve God*, worship him and submit to his authority. So God directly contradicts the criticism of the skeptics in v 5 that such a distinction is not evident.

Malachi: 2:10-4:3

In times past again and again they had abundant opportunity to observe, both in their national and individual lives, the different treatment of the saint and sinner. The day of final discrimination, however, was coming when all men will see virtue rewarded and vice punished. In that day all will have plain and convincing proof of God's moral government of the world.

B. Terrible Day for the Wicked (4:1):
For the wicked a terrible day was coming.

1. Unexpected day (4:1a): **For behold the day comes.** *For* (*kî*) indicates why the skeptics will again see that Yahweh discriminates between the righteous and the wicked. *Behold* (*hinnēh*) generally introduces a shocking or unexpected announcement. *The day* is the day of Yahweh's intervention. *Comes* (r. *bō'*) is a participle. The construction suggests imminence. The believer lives his life with the expectation that the day of Yahweh's intervention might occur at any moment.

2. Judgment day (4:1b): **burning like a furnace.** Fire is often associated with the day of judgment in both testaments. Fire is a symbol of the holiness of God which consumes all impurity. It also represents the punishment inflicted on the wicked. *Burning* (*bō'ēr*) is a participle that appears only here. It depicts the hottest fire, that of the refiner's furnace (cf. 3:2)—a large beehive-shaped metal structure vented in the roof. Wood was piled up in the furnace, ignited and fanned into a fire so intense that the flames shot through the roof vents (cf. Dan 3; Hos 7:7).

3. Destruction day (4:1c): **All the arrogant and every evildoer will be stubble, and the day that comes will burn them up, says Yahweh of Hosts. Not a root or a branch will be left to them.** These lines stress three points about the coming day of judgment.

First, the judgment will affect all of the wicked. On the *arrogant*, see on 3:15. The arrogant are further described lit., as "every doer of evil." The singular individualizes the class called "arrogant." The sense is "every last one." *Stubble* (*qaš*)

Postexilic Prophets

refers to the unusable remains of grain stocks pulverized in the threshing process. Stubble was highly combustible.

Second, the judgment will be total. In that burning day of judgment those that the skeptics regarded as happy and blessed in this world will be removed from the scene in a thorough and painful way.

Third, the totality of the judgment is stressed by means of a plant metaphor. *Root or branch* expresses totality. The arrogant will be destroyed from bottom to top. As far as this world is concerned, the wicked will be totally removed. The figure is of a tree given up to be burned so that nothing is left of it. John the Baptist used this same figure (Mt 3:10).[383]

C. Healing Day for the Godly (4:2):

1. Visitation for the benefit of the faithful (4:2a): **But for you who fear my name...** The faithful of 3:16 are now directly addressed in the second person. Those who continued to fear Yahweh's name, i.e., worship, honor and revere him, will experience a visitation of healing in that future day. Their fidelity in the face of prevailing skepticism will be rewarded. The theme of fearing God's name has previously appeared in 1:6, 11, 14; 2:2, 5; 3:16.

2. Visitation by a special person (4:2b): **the Sun of Righteousness will rise...** This appears to be a title for the Messiah,[384] the "messenger of the covenant" in 3:1. *Sun* conveys the thought of light and warmth. That Messiah will bring light is a major theme of messianic prophecy.[385] Zacharias called him "the Dayspring from on high" (Lk 1:78), an apparent reference to this passage.[386] The figure points to Jesus as light after darkness, warmth after cold, beauty after bleakness and joy after gloom. Christ is the source of light, life, beauty,

---

[383]This formula has also been found in Phoenician literature.

[384]Other views of *the sun of righteousness*: righteousness as a sun; or the sun which is righteousness (Jewish commentators; Hengstenberg; Keil).

[385]That Messiah will bring light is predicted in Nm 24:17; Isa 9:2; 42:6; 49:6.

[386]Zacharias' Dayspring from on high (Lk 1:78) is an apparent reference to this passage since this ch of Malachi already has been cited twice in Lk 1 (vv 17, 76). See also 2 Pet 1:19; Eph 5:14; Rev 21:23.

healing, and joy. This v stands in stark contrast to the usual gloom and darkness associated with day of Yahweh passages.

Righteousness points to a time when all is right with God. The idea of Messiah ushering in righteousness is already present in Dan 9:24. Malachi's imagery has antecedents in Ps 37:6 and Isa 58:8. The term *righteousness* has a wide range of meanings in OT. Probably here it has the connotation of salvation.

3. *Visitation that is restorative (4:2c):* **with healing in its wings.** *Healing* in OT can refer to forgiveness and salvation (Jer 17:14) and restoration to divine favor (Isa 53:5; Ps 6:2). *Wings* figuratively refer to the rays of the sun. The rays of that Sun radiate healing for broken hearts and perplexed minds. Messiah awakens the righteous to a new life as the sun in the spring awakens nature to a new life. The figure of the winged sun may have been suggested to the prophet by the winged solar disk of Egypt, Babylon, Assyria and Persia.[387] The language of this v has been immortalized in the Christmas carol, *Hark the Herald Angels Sing*—"Risen with healing in his wings."

4. *Visitation with a happy result (4:2d):* **And you will go out and leap like calves released from the stall.** That Sun rise will usher in a joyous new day for the faithful. *Calves released from the stall* is lit., "calves of stall."[388] The picture is of an animal, penned up for some time, expressing joyous abandon when first released (cf. Jer 50:11). In the stalls they have the best feeding (the word of God, the ordinances, etc.) so that they will be able to go forth with joy and vigor when the day of release comes (Laetsch). Paul may have had this verse in mind when he spoke about the "glorious liberty of the sons of God" (Rom 8:21).

D. Victorious Day (4:3):

1. *Declaration (4:3a):* **Then you will tread down the wicked...** Empowered by their Lord, in that day of liberty and light the faithful will *tread down* (r. *'ss*) *the wicked.* The verb

---

[387]See ANEP, figs. 351, 531, 532, 536.
[388]Stuart denies *marbēq* means "stall." He renders "well-fed calves." The essential point of the line is unchanged.

Postexilic Prophets

is used metaphorically. The picture here is of the treading of grapes in a winepress (cf. Rev 14:19-20).[389]

2. *Explanation (4:3b):* **they will be ashes under the soles of your feet...** This is not a call for the righteous to go on a holy crusade to exterminate the wicked. They are ashes. God already has taken care of them. The wicked will be reduced to ashes by the burning judgment of God. The figure is appropriate in view of the burning metaphors of 3:19.

The v is pivotal to the argument that God in the end annihilates the wicked. It is always dangerous, however, to establish theology by metaphor, especially when that metaphor taken literally contradicts plain biblical teaching. Besides, ashes do not always indicate annihilation because people who were very much alive could refer to themselves as dust and ashes (Gn 18:27; Job 30:19). The basic idea here is that the oppressed will be victorious over oppressors.

3. *Timeframe (4:3c):* **in the day when I act, says Yahweh of Hosts.** *Day* is another reference to the day of Yahweh—the day when Yahweh makes his move into the arena of history. God is currently preparing that day when the righteous will be rewarded and the wicked will be vanquished.[390]

The v which concludes the optimistic description of Yahweh's day is itself concluded by a messenger formula to underscore the certainty of the promises set forth.

---

[389] The verb root is a hapax. It means "to press or tread" as the grapes in the winepress. The nominal form of this verb refers to the newly pressed wine. Cf. Rev 14:19-20.

[390] The root *'sh* is used here absolutely, i.e., "to act, do successfully" (Laetsch).

Concluding Words
Malachi 4:4-6

The prophecy of Malachi concludes with an exhortation and a warning.

Exhortation
Malachi 4:4[391]

In succinct fashion Malachi repeats what he has been emphasizing throughout the book. The best way to prepare for the day of Yahweh is to give heed to God's law. Malachi sets his seal of approval on the Pentateuch. This is a fitting climax to the entire OT. Six things in particular they need to remember if they are to be prepared for the coming day.

A. Remember the Law (4:4a):
Remember the law... Remember (r. *zkr*) is not calling for merely cognitive activity; it calls for integration of the law of God in every area of life. The problem was not that God's law had been lost to memory; it simply had been ignored. In short, *remember* calls Israel to give heed to, pay attention to, or be mindful of God's law. *Law* (*tōrāh*) refers to the instruction that is part of God's covenant with Israel.

B. Remember the Lawgiver (4:4b):
Of my servant Moses... Mention of Moses emphasizes that Malachi is not calling for adherence to some innovative law. Newness cannot be used as the excuse for disobedience of the people. The law that Malachi called upon his contemporaries to observe had been around for about a millennium. Note the honorable title given to Moses.

---

[391] LXX places this v at the end of the book probably because they considered the original ending (v 6) as too harsh.

Postexilic Prophets

C. Remember the Authority of the Law (4:4c):

Which I commanded him... The law that Malachi championed did not merely have behind it the prestige of the great lawgiver Moses. The Law of Moses came by divine command. Thus it was binding upon Israel until the God who gave it rescinded it. *Commanded him* clearly does not mean that the law originally was intended for Moses personally. Yahweh commanded him to implement that law in Israel.

D. Remember the Wonder of the Law (4:4d):

At Horeb... The name means "wilderness/wasteland." It emphasizes the barrenness of the range of mountains where God saw fit to bestow upon Israel his law. The particular peak where Yahweh entered into a covenant with his people was Sinai. The mention here of the place where the law was given served the dual purpose of 1) reminding the readers of the awful wonders that accompanied the giving of that law; and 2) underscoring the divine origin of that law.

E. Remember the Scope of the Law (4:4e):

For all Israel. For (*'al*) with a double accusative (*statutes and ordinances*) is paralleled only by 1 Chr 22:13. Nonetheless, the meaning is clear. *All Israel* sometimes refers to representatives of Israel or the Israelite soldiers (e.g., Josh 7:24-25). Here, however, the phrase is inclusive of everyone in the nation whether or not they personally participated in formal covenant ceremonies at Sinai (cf. Dt 29:14-15). The law was designed to set Israel apart from all other nations.

F. Remember every Detail of the Law (4:4f):

Even statutes and ordinances... This common hendiadys consists of two synonyms. The entire Law of Moses—legal, moral and ceremonial enactments—is frequently characterized as *statutes and ordinances* (e.g., Dt 4:8, 44-45).[392]

---

[392]Laetsch thinks the term *mišpāṭîm* (*ordinances*) refers to the decisions of judges that had been accepted as common law.

348

Malachi 4:4-6

Announcement
Malachi 4:5-6

A. Focus of the Announcement (4:5a):
Behold! I will send you Elijah the prophet... Hebrew uses *behold* (*hinnēh*) to introduce what is unexpected, perhaps even shocking. The speaker is clearly Yahweh. *I will send* (pronoun[393] + participle) could be rendered "I am sending" or "I am about to send." *Elijah* (*'ēliyyāh*) is the shortened form of the name of the great prophet which usually appears in 2 Kgs as *'ēliyyāhū*. In the previous v Moses was mentioned. Moses and Elijah were regarded as the quintessential models of fidelity to God's word.

The traditional Jewish view is that the prediction refers to Elijah the Tishbite. Jews set a cup for Elijah at Passover and a chair for him at circumcisions. Traditional Catholic exegesis supports this view.[394] The NT, however, seems clearly to indicate that John the Baptist is intended (Mt 11:14; Lk 7:27). John came in the spirit and power of Elijah (Lk 1:17).[395]

B. Chronology of the Announcement (4:5b):
Before the great and the fearful day of Yahweh comes. *Elijah the prophet* will sound the final warning to national Israel. He will come before a judgment day. *Great and fearful* is a common adjectival combo used often of Yahweh himself (e.g., Dt 7:21), Yahweh's deeds (e.g., Dt 10:21) or Yahweh's name (e.g., Ps 99:3).[396] It is used elsewhere of the day of Yahweh only in Joel 2:31.

---

[393] Malachi uses *'ānōkhî* for the only time in the book. He has used the shorter form of the pronoun (*'anî*) elsewhere in the book. This is exactly the same situation that exists in the Book of Ezekiel, and the reverse of the occurrences of this pronoun in the Book of Amos.

[394] The literal Elijah view is supported by LXX which adds "the Tishbite." Supporters appeal to Jn 1:21, Mt 17:10 and Ecclesiasticus 48:10. This was the view of many church fathers.

[395] The analogical Elijah view is also supported by the words of Zacharias (Mk 1:2-8) and the words of John himself (Mt 3:1-12). See also Mt 17:11-13; Mk 9:11 and Mk 1:2-8.

[396] The combo is also used of the wilderness of Sinai (e.g., Dt 1:19) and of the deeds of Moses (Dt 34:12).

Postexilic Prophets

Some think the reference is to the final judgment. According to this view when John prepared the Jews for the first advent, the forerunner was preparing them for Messiah's second advent as well. More likely is the view that *the great and fearful day of Yahweh* refers to the destruction of Jerusalem in AD 70. This event figures prominently in OT prophecy as well as in the teaching of Jesus.[397]

Advanced warning is designed to elicit repentance so that people can be spared from the judgment calamity. The key note of the preaching of John the Baptist was "repent, for the kingdom of heaven is at hand." John also warned of a judgment about to be poured out on national Israel.

Elijah the Tishbite is a good prototype of John since he fearlessly proclaimed the need for repentance in his day (2 Kgs 18:37). Like Elijah, John was a voice crying in the wilderness. Since most of Jesus' early disciples had previously been followers of John it must be said that the Baptist succeeded in his mission.

Concluding Warning
Malachi 4:6

A. Need for Conversion (4:6a):

He will turn the heart of fathers as well as sons, and the heart of sons as well as their fathers... Elijah (John the Baptist) engages in a ministry of restoration and revival. Turn (r. *šûbh* in Hiphil) regularly means "to restore" or "to bring back." The biblical *heart* (*lēbh*) refers to a person's emotions, intellect and will. *To turn the heart* is a metaphor for conversion. It means to move a person to repentance.

Fathers as well as[398] *sons* is lit., "fathers upon (*'al*) sons." Standard English translations ("turn the hearts of the children to their parents" NIV; NASB) convey the idea of family restoration. Elijah (John the Baptist) did not labor to bridge the gap between generations, although this may well have been

---

[397]Joel 2:31; Dan 9:26-27; 12:1; Mt 24:1-28; Lk 21:1-21.

[398]That the preposition *'al* can have the meaning "as well as" is established by Gn 28:9; Dt 19:9; Jer 4:20.

Malachi 4:4-6

the practical result of his preaching. He labored to get everyone to "repent for the kingdom of heaven is at hand." So *fathers* and *sons* (i.e., parents and children) constitute a merism that means "everybody" (cf. Jer 13:14; Mt 10:21). To state the matter differently, Elijah (John) will lead in a mighty revival among the Jews. Thus did the angel interpret this passage in the announcement of John's birth (cf. Lk 1:16-17).

B. Impending Catastrophe (4:6b):
Lest I come and strike the land with utter destruction. Malachi closes with warning about covenant punishment. Here again as in 3:1 the one who is coming is Yahweh. Since John's coming preceded the appearance of Jesus, both this and the previous passage imply that Jesus is Yahweh.

Lest I come does not imply that Yahweh (Christ) will choose not to come if "Elijah" succeeds in bringing about repentance. Context suggests the meaning is "lest in coming I strike." He is coming with or without their repentance; but the way in which his coming will affect people depends upon their response to "Elijah."

The warning is of the *destruction* (*chērem*) of the land (cf. Lv 26:32-35, 43; Dt 28:51). Just as the Canaanites were devoted to destruction by the armies of Joshua, so the land of Judea will be subject to total destruction by the Romans.

A warning of covenant punishment always holds open a window of opportunity to find salvation. Those who listened to John followed Jesus. In following Jesus they escaped the tragedy of the Roman war which devastated Judea in AD 66-70. At that time the land of Judea was smitten with *utter destruction*, i.e., the ban. Christians heeded the warning of Jesus to flee Jerusalem when they saw the abomination of desolation—the Roman armies—approaching the city (cf. Mt 24:15).

Thus the last prophet of the Twelve announces the coming of the last prophet under the old covenant (cf. Mt 11:12-13). Some four centuries after Malachi the Elijah of prophecy arose to warn of impending judgment and to point his auditors to Christ.

Postexilic Prophets

Bibliography

Baldwin, Joyce G. *Haggai, Zechariah, Malachi*. The Tyndale Old Testament Commentaries. InterVarsity, 1972.

Barker, Kenneth. "Zechariah," in *Daniel-Minor Prophets*, Expositor's Bible Commentary ed. Frank Gaebelein. Grand Rapids: Zondervan, 1985.

Barnes, W. Emery. *Haggai and Zechariah*. The Cambridge Bible for Schools and Colleges. Cambridge: University Press, 1917.

Baron, David. *The Visions & Prophecies of Zechariah*. 2nd ed. London: Morgan & Scott, 1919.

Bruce, F.F. *New Testament Development of Old Testament Themes*. Grand Rapids: Eerdmans, 1969.

Cashdan, Eli. *The Twelve Prophets*. Soncino Books of the Bible. London: Soncino, 1961.

Chisholm, Jr., Robert. *Interpreting the Minor Prophets*. Grand Rapids: Zondervan, 1990.

Coggins, R.J. *Haggai, Zechariah, Malachi*. Old Testament Guides. Sheffield, England: JSOT Press, 1987.

Curtis, A.H. *The Vision and Mission of Jesus,* Edinburgh: T. & T. Clark, 1954.

Deane, W.J. "Haggai" in *The Pulpit Commentary*; New Edition. New York: Funk & Wagnalls, 1909.

Delaughter, Thomas J. *Malachi: Messenger of Divine Love*. New Orleans: Insight Press, 1976.

Dods, Marcus. *The Post-Exilian Prophets*. The Cambridge Bible for Schools and Colleges. Cambridge: University Press, 1956 reprint.

Dorsey, David. *The Literary Structure of the Old Testament*. Grand Rapids: Baker, 1999.

Dumbrell, William. *The Faith of Israel: Its Expression in the Books of the Old Testament*. Grand Rapids: Baker, 1988.

Gill, Clinton R. *Minor Prophets: Micah, Nahum, Habakkuk, Zephaniah, Haggai, Zechariah, and Malachi*. Joplin, MO: College Press, 1971.

Postexilic Prophets

Glazier-McDonald, B. *Malachi: The Divine Messenger*. Atlanta: Scholars, 1987.

Hanson, P. *The Dawn of Apocalyptic*. Philadelphia: Fortress, 1975.

Horton R.F. and S.R. Driver, *The Minor Prophets* in "New Century Bible." Edinburgh: T.C. and E.J. Jack, 1906.

Hugenberger, G.B. *Marriage as Covenant; A Study of Biblical Law and Ethics Governing Marriage Developed from the Perspective of Malachi*. VTSup 52. Leiden: Brill, 1994.

Isbell, Charles D. *Malachi*. Grand Rapids: Zondervan, 1980.

Kaiser, Jr. Walter C. *Malachi; God's Unchanging Love*. Grand Rapids: Baker, 1984.

Laetsch, Theo. *Bible Commentary: The Minor Prophets*. St. Louis: Concordia, 1956.

Logsdon, S. Franklin. *Malachi, or Will a Man Rob God?* Chicago: Moody, 1961.

MacFadyen, D. *The Messenger of God*. London: Elliot Stock, 1910.

Morgan, G. Campbell. *"Wherein?"* New York: Revell, 1898.

MacFadyen, D. *The Messenger of God*. London: Elliot Stock, 1910.

Mason, R. *The Books of Haggai, Zechariah, and Malachi*. Cambridge New English Bible Commentary. Cambridge: Cambridge University Press, 1977.

McComiskey, T.E. "Zechariah" in *The Minor Prophets: An Exegetical and Expository Commentary*, ed. T.E. McComiskey; Grand Rapids: Baker, 1998.

Meyers, Carol and Eric Meyers, *Haggai, Zechariah 1-8*. Anchor Bible. New York: Doubleday, 1992.

_____. *Zechariah 9-14*. Anchor Bible. New York: Doubleday, 1993.

Mitchell, H.G. *A Critical and Exegetical Commentary on Haggai, Zechariah, Malachi, and Jonah*. International Critical Commentary. Edinburgh: Clark, 1912.

Motyer, Alec. "Haggai" in *The Minor Prophets; an Exegetical & Expository Commentary*. Grand Rapids: Baker, 1998.

Bibliography

Payne, J. Barton. *Encyclopedia of Biblical Prophecy*. New York: Harper & Row, 1973.

Perowne, T.T. *The Books of Haggai and Zechariah*. The Cambridge Bible for Schools and Colleges. Cambridge: University Press, 1908.

Peterson, David. *Haggai and Zechariah 1-9, a Commentary*. The Old Testament Library. Philadelphia: Westminster, 1987.

Smith, J.M.P. *A Critical and Exegetical Commentary on the Book of Malachi*. International Critical Commentary. Edinburgh: T. & T. Clark, 1971.

Smith, Ralph *Micah-Malachi*. Word Biblical Commentary; Waco: Word, 1984.

Stuart, D. "Malachi" in *An Exegetical & Expository Commentary—the Minor Prophets*, ed. Thomas McComiskey. Grand Rapid: Baker, 1998.

VanGemeren, William *Interpreting the Prophetic Word*. Grand Rapids: Zondervan, 1990.

Verhoff, Pieter A. *The Books of Haggai and Malachi*. The New International Commentary on the Old Testament. Grand Rapids: Eerdmans, 1987.

Wiseman, Donald. "Haggai" in *The New Bible Commentary*. 3d ed. Ed. Donald Guthrie and Alec Motyer. Grand Rapids: Eerdmans, 1970.

Wolf, Herbert M. *Haggai and Malachi; Rededication and Renewal*. Everyman's Bible Commentary. Chicago: Moody, 1976.

Wolff, Hans Walter. *Haggai, a Commentary*. Trans. Margaret Kohl. Minneapolis: Augsburg, 1988.

Wolff, Richard. *The Book of Haggai*. The Shield Bible Study Outlines. Grand Rapids: Baker, 1967.